CLEVER INTRODUCTIONS FOR CHAIRMEN

A Compilation of

Practical Speeches and Stories

by

LAWRENCE M. BRINGS, M. A.

Formerly, Director, Department of Speech, Teachers College, Aberdeen, S. D.; Instructor in Speech, the University of Minnesota; President, Northwestern College of Speech Arts; Professor of Speech, Luther Theological Seminary; Professor of Speech, Northwestern Theological Seminary.

PUBLISHERS

T. S. DENISON & COMPANY

MINNEAPOLIS

Copyright, 1954 by

T. S. DENISON & COMPANY

Printed in the U. S. A.
By The Brings Press

First edition November, 1954
Second edition January, 1955

❦

PREFACE

It has long been my desire to make available in book form concrete and definite aids to assist individuals in their preparation to assume the chairmanship of a meeting. I know from over thirty years of experience and observation as an instructor in speech that this specialized form of public appearance disturbs and frightens more people than almost any other type of public speaking. "If only there were some patterns to follow, I could handle the situation," has been a common remark.

To meet this demand for practical assistance, I have assembled a wide variety of material which has been contributed by many successful chairmen. Credit has been given to each contributor. Practically all these introductory speeches have been tested in actual use. Nevertheless I cannot vouch for the originality or newness of all the stories or anecdotes that are included in the speeches.

To enhance the value of this book, over two hundred different types of speakers have been classified and appropriate introductions provided for them. These are to be found in Section Two of the book. Shorter and more general material is listed in Section Three.

I do not recommend that users of this book follow these written introductions verbatim. To do so would eliminate the spontaneous adaptation to the specific situation and speaker that is so all-important. I must emphasize that these introductions are merely suggestive of a treatment to be followed. Secure all the necessary data about the speaker's background and work out your own style. Be sure that any stories you use are appropriate. However, I fully recognize that these guideposts will be of immeasurable help to the inexperienced chairman. The underlying formula will give him courage to face a task that he usually considers an ordeal.

Even the experienced chairman, I am sure, can profit by making a careful study of the many types of introductions contained in this book. Regardless of what evaluation he may give to this material, at least he must agree that the treatment is practical and down-to-earth.

Grateful acknowledgement is made to the many individuals who contributed their favorite stories and introductions to this collection. Without this cooperation, it would have been impossible for this book to be available for your use.

I am not naive enough to assume that this collection is so perfect as to meet the requirements of all chairmen. At least I have made an attempt to meet a need and I shall be satisfied if some users of this book agree with me. I shall appreciate your reactions and your constructive criticism.

—Lawrence M. Brings

Contents

SECTION ONE

The Chairman

SECTION TWO

Practical Introductions for Chairmen

SECTION THREE

Bright Bits for Chairmen

SECTION ONE

THE CHAIRMAN

THE ROLE OF THE CHAIRMAN

Much has been written concerning the place of the humorous story in public speaking, and volumes of stories have been compiled for use by the speaker on such occasions. It seems writers have neglected to suggest stories the master-of-ceremonies or chairman of a speech program might use, since each feels the urge or necessity to tell stories. Is telling stories the main business of the chairman? If so, to what extent? And also when, how, and why they should be told, if the chairman or master-of-ceremonies is to do a good job?

As a teacher of speech, and with some years of experience serving as a master-of-ceremonies, I have many calls, requesting good stories to use, from individuals who are to serve in that capacity. They have likewise been concerned about what to do to be an effective chairman. It is because of such requests that this chapter has been written.

It is not proposed that the master-of-ceremonies is to operate in the same identical way in any and every speech situation; nor is it expected that he is to be circumscribed by a set of rules so that the job becomes stereotyped. It does seem, however, that to be successful as a master-of-ceremonies, which is the "sine qua non" of a good speaking program, we must presuppose that the knowledge of certain worthwhile practices and principles is essential both in respect to the use of the story and the general conduct of the job.

These concern certain definite considerations for the chairman who wishes to improve his techniques. We have included specific suggestions about the use of the story, and suggested types of stories to use.

PURPOSE OF THE CHAIRMAN

In respect to the chairman, my son's favorite story, which, perhaps, he heard the late famous Joe Laurie, Jr., recount, concerns itself with the chairman on the occasion of a dinner who arose and began the introduction of the first speaker by saying:

"Ladies and gentlemen: I shall not take your time tonight by boring you with the telling of old stories or 'chestnuts,' but I shall be very happy to introduce speakers who will."

This little statement, by humorous indirection, embodies a rather important principle which must be observed if one would be a successful chairman. Fundamentally, the main business of a chairman is to direct, guide and control the speaking program. He administers it. Strictly speaking and yet not paradoxically, the chairman is not **a part** of the actual speaking program, but rather a thing **apart from** it. He guides it best by not making himself too prominent; by not projecting himself to a point where he is more important than the speaker or speakers. To serve a program well there are definite and specific things a chairman should know which embody the "do's and don'ts" of the job.

CHAIRMAN SHOULD NOT BE OBTRUSIVE

A speaking program is designed solely to give an audience an opportunity to hear the message of a speaker. If a chairman loses sight of his relation in this definite scheme and obviously projects himself, the tail wags the dog and, consequently, the true purpose of the program is denied or seriously affected. The chairman functions best if he is not obtrusive.

If there is only one speaker on a program, he will suffer immeasurably, if the chairman, by what he says or through his general demeanor, occupies too important a place. The chairman should not steal the spotlight from the speaker. He should not try to dominate the scene. If there are two or three speakers the harm increases two-fold or three-fold, as the bad chairman's proclivities for stealing the show increase in proportion to the number of speakers for whom he is responsible; each speaker suffers individually and in turn. The chairman is expected to set the stage and create the proper mood, but he is not expected to be a show in himself. Any over-attempt to be funny is a sure indication that the chairman has a wrong conception of his job. And here it seems appropriate to make a few suggestions about the use of the humorous story.

THE USE OF STORIES

Most laymen, who are not experienced in serving as a chairman, assume that in order to be effective, they must be funny; and to be funny they must tell many humorous stories. To them, this is their principal responsibility as a chairman.

It is not to be assumed that the chairman should refrain completely from using a story. The important question he must ask himself in respect to its use is: what is the motive for using the story or stories? Is it to satisfy a personal desire to be funny? Therein lies the danger. To be funny as an end in itself cannot but serve to detract from the purpose of the program. To make the story serve a purpose beyond the intrinsic worth of a whole program is fundamentally bad technique. Shakespeare wisely admonishes all those who seek to be funny for their own sake, when he says ". . . let those who play your clowns speak no more than is set down for them," for it shows ". . . a most pitiable ambition in the fool who uses it."

Finally, it may be said the humorous story has its place if certain definite criteria are observed.

If a story is not irrelevant to the speeches or program generally, and may appropriately aid the introductions, it has value.

If, however, it affects the mood or even tenor of the program by not being in harmony with it, it should not be used, no matter how well it may be rated as a story.

If it unduly prolongs the length of the program and digresses from the main purpose of the occasion, it should not be used. Even though it may be a proved laugh-getter, it may not be appropriate.

If it has any stigma of the personal, and may embarrass a speaker about to be introduced, it should not be used.

The over-all, complete and final test for its use is: is it apropos?

POOR STORIES

Mark Twain's observation about cigars may, wholly or in part, apply to stories, when he says, "A good cigar should be lighted once, a bad one never." A good story can stand being retold, but not to the same audience. Perhaps, the safest guide in respect to a bad story is, never tell it; certainly, never retell it; as it cannot always be determined in advance if a story is bad. A story may be poor for several reasons—it is weak in appeal, simply no good; or it may not be appropriate; or it has not been well told.

There is usually little doubt as to the effectiveness or appeal of a story. The teller definitely knows by the audience response whether his story is well received. If it is not, he can readily sense it. The chairman can readily sense if the story is not appropriate, or if it is not well told. He should profit by experience.

KNOW THE STORY

Above all else, when a story is used it should be well told. Nothing is worse than to have an audience listen to a story that is poorly told, because the one who recounts it is not sufficiently familiar with it and garbles the details. So, to those who tell stories, **be sure you know the whole story. Know the beginning so you get started well. Know how it develops to the climax and punch line and how to end it. When you reach the end, stop.** Nothing has a worse effect on the telling of a story than to be indefinite about the ending or to add an anti-climax. Know the punch line!

OTHER POINTERS FOR THE STORY-TELLER

In respect to telling a story well, there are other admonitions or suggestions, which it may be well to point out here as particular knowledge for the chairman. They are equally important for the speaker.

1. Don't stretch the story out or make it too long. Even if the point of the story is well told, it will not redeem stretching it out by unnecessary verbiage, as the lis-

teners' interest will be lost by the time you get to the point of the story.

2. Don't give the point of the story before you actually begin to tell it. Many a novice completely kills the interest in a good anecdote by announcing the story in a phrase which reveals pretty much its whole idea, such as: "Now I would like to tell you the story . . .," or, "This reminds me of the story of the Bishop who explained to the French chorus girl the meaning of the golden wedding anniversary, and she thought it meant a man can live with a woman fifty years before he marries her."

No, a good story-teller launches into his story without thunder, as a good mystery story writer builds up suspense and saves the solution for the end.

3. Don't tell a story at the wrong place or on the wrong occasion. A story which may be told to certain individuals or a few friends in a confidential way may fall flat or be resented in a formal audience. Many stories are considered by most audiences to be risque to the point of the indecent, but too often the people who tell them don't seem to know that. Some individuals are not safe before an audience, when it comes to telling stories. They just don't know the social psychology of audiences. The guiding principle, as, in part, has been previously pointed out, is "Is the story appropriate to the occasion?"

One of the best known contemporary story-tellers has summed it up this way: "The man who can toss off a funny story in the right spot is a wit; the oaf who is telling them indiscriminately all the time is a nitwit."

COLLECTING STORIES

Before a chairman or a speaker can tell stories, he must, of course, have collected a good supply. There are certain worthwhile practices and methods which can be cultivated to advantage, if a person is to develop a supply of appropriate stories.

WRITE THE STORY DOWN

Invariably among people the remark is heard, "I never can remember a story." This is not surprising when no effort is made to try and remember one. Too often, when hearing a story, a person trusts it to his memory, and he finds when he wants to tell it, it has fled completely. Psychology has established the fact that we forget one half of all we hear within ten minutes, and an amazing per cent of the remaining half within a week. We think we can remember; but the memory is treacherous. To remember things we must hog-tie them. To remember stories we must write them down. It may not always be possible to write a story down at the time we hear it told, but it should be written down at the first and earliest opportunity. It is not necessary, in order to remember a story, to write it down verbatim. Get the main ideas and above all get the punch line absolutely straight. Then at a later time rewrite it and complete the details of the narrative in your own words. Don't worry if it varies slightly from the original version. If it reads well and flows into the climax or punch line, which must be correct, the chances are a good story will have been added to your collection.

THE USE OF NOTES

Writing the story down, when it is first heard, as an aid to remembering it, carries no compulsion to read it from notes when telling it. As previously suggested in these comments, know the story so well that you can tell it from memory. This is the only way it will be told effectively and be well received.

The late Bishop Charles Brent, Senior Chaplain of the American Expeditionary Forces, World War I, explained to me one time why he preferred to speak or preach without the benefit of notes. He said he did very little preaching when he was with the doughboys in France and when he spoke he preferred to speak informally and "off the cuff." When he returned to the states he was, one Sunday morning, the preacher in the formal church atmosphere of the Cathedral of St. John The Divine, in New York City, and he elected to preach with notes. After the service, an American doughboy came up to him to renew an acquaintanceship made overseas. Quite unabashed the soldier said, "I heard you a number of times in France, Bishop, and I liked your talks better there. You spoke without notes then." And then he added smiling, "You know, Bishop, if you can't remember what you've got to say, how do you expect us to?"

RESEARCH IS NECESSARY

It is almost axiomatic that the best stories are still of the "hand to mouth" variety, or transmitted orally. Good stories may often appear singly in magazines or in newspapers, but it seems a collection or anthology of consistently good stories is yet to be printed. After stories are written down in good legible form, it is well to arrange them topically in a file, which once started will develop an interest in being built up.

I am reminded of a story which seems especially appropriate. It came from the keen mind of the late Nicholas Murray Butler, President Dwight Eisenhower's actual predecessor, as president of Columbia University.

Dr. Butler and one of his eminent professors, Brander Matthews, a reasonable keen wit himself, were having a conversation and Professor Matthews was giving his ideas as to plagiarism from an article of his own on that subject.

"In the case of the first man to use an anecdote," he said, "there is originality; in the case of the second there is plagiarism; with the third, it is lack of originality; and with the fourth it's drawing from a common stock."

"Yes," broke in President Butler, "and in the case of the fifth, it is research."

And here, Dr. Butler, not discounting the humor of the situation, could have been making a point in all seriousness for the potential story-teller. He must cultivate every source possible if he is to develop a collection of stories, which, literally amounts to research.

KNOW THE SPEAKER

Now, back to the chairman. Most important of his duties, he should know or get acquainted with every speaker on the program and, preferably, know something about them. He will be better able to do the job if he knows the speakers in advance of the speaking occasion and has a friendly and good-will attitude toward them. If the right man is chosen for the job it is almost axiomatic that he will serve better if he knows something about the speakers. Besides getting acquainted with the speakers, the chairman should manifest his interest in them, and in a friendly, deft manner learn whatever he can about their background which may be useful to him in making the introductions. This has an important bearing on the next point.

NEVER EMBARRASS THE SPEAKER

It is the chairman's job to make it easy for the speaker and to make him feel at ease before and at the time he speaks. The chairman should say nothing when he introduces a speaker which may embarrass him. If the speaker, before he speaks, can sense this good-will of the chairman, it will in many cases be of immeasurable aid to him. Too often, a chairman, in a desire to be funny, engages in anecdotes about the speaker, which verge on the personal, are irrelevant, and certainly not in good taste. As a result, the speaker may be ill at ease and the quality of his speaking may be affected.

It is not wise to use too much embellishment in these remarks. The sugary type of introduction is not appreciated by the experienced speaker; he wishes to make his own impression. Particularly, it is well to avoid praising his skill as a speaker. It too often makes the audience consciously critical of his speech techniques, when it should be intent upon his message.

Some chairmen inadvertently say things when introducing a speaker not intended to cause embarrassment but very often do, and more often cause a laugh to be directed at the chairman himself, thereby aiding the speaker.

And here is a classical example to illustrate the point. It is one of those stories which may well be used by an alert chairman. It is about the younger Joe Chamberlain, famous British statesman, whose speaking ability in Parliament brought the praise of the great Gladstone.

Mr. Chamberlain was the speaker and guest of honor at a dinner in an important English city. The lord-mayor presided and at the end of the dinner coffee was being served and the guests were informally chatting and visiting with each other. The lord-mayor leaned over and touched Chamberlain, saying, "Shall we let the people enjoy themselves a little longer, or had we better have your speech now?"

DON'T HAVE TOO MUCH TO SAY

Aside from indulging in some levity to create a good mood and to put the audience and speakers at ease, the chairman needs only to reveal the speaker's name, possibly a few facts about him, his qualifications as a speaker, and the subject on which he is to speak. If he presents these in a clear and interesting manner, without garbling any of the details, he is rendering the program a valuable service. The important thing he must remember is to be brief; the chairman is not making the speech. He must not give his own views on the subject. He can emphasize the importance of the speaker's subject, if necessary, and how it applies to the audience. He must not talk about himself, indulge in anecdotes about himself, or refer to his experiences as a speaker.

DON'T USE THE HACKNEYED OR TRITE EXPRESSIONS

A speaker who uses the cliché, "Unaccustomed as I am to public speaking," should be boiled in oil. The chairman who, when introducing speakers, employs such trite expressions as "We have with us tonight," or "It gives me great pleasure to introduce to you," deserves similar treatment. He should avoid the trite and over-used expression in the introduction.

And here it is well to point out, don't constantly address the audience as "Ladies and gentlemen." On formal occasions it may be all right, but this form becomes tiresome. Use your imagination and ingenuity.

When the speaker has finished, some expression of appreciation for his effort should be made and a brief allusion to the valuable and impressive parts of his speech. The use of a pause, to serve as a transition before introducing the next speaker is essential.

An example of the chairman overdoing, when introducing a speaker, is found in the recent situation when a prominent woman speaker had to sit and wait until the chairman engaged in a long harangue about her accomplishments and personality which was not especially appropriate. As she finally arose to speak she amusingly remarked, "After all the glowing remarks by the chairman, I could hardly wait to hear myself."

Some speakers are not as courteous and subtle when they have to wait on a long-winded toastmaster. Perhaps a little on the facetious side is this story which is a good illustration.

The chairman insisted on making a speech. Then he thought it necessary to introduce two or three prominent citizens and each of these indulged in extended remarks without purpose. Finally, with the audience tired and the hour late, the speaker who had been engaged for the principal address was introduced. The chairman took it upon himself to make a long-winded introduction, and concluded by saying, "We will now have the address of the distinguished gentleman."

The speaker arose and said: "My address is 1170 Delaware Avenue. Good night."

CHAIRMEN WHO LACK TERMINAL FACILITIES

Too many speakers and chairmen often spoil an otherwise acceptable speech by not being able to bring their speech or remarks to a close. They lack what has been referred to as a sense or need of terminal facility in speech-making.

Lew Sarett, the poet and an unusual speech teacher at Northwestern University, offers a sage bit of counsel to speakers in his book, "Basic Principles of Speech," in respect to ending a speech. Interestingly enough, the idea was suggested to him by Paul Whiteman, who in proposing techniques for conducting an orchestra said, ". . . when you quit, quit all over." Sarett admonishes the speaker thus: ". . . every speech when it quits should quit all over." And this is sound advice for the chairman.

Aristotle, the Greek scholar, proposed that a speech, among other things, to be a complete organism or an artistic whole must have a head, body and feet; or a beginning, middle and end. A chairman's remarks should be so planned, and so delivered.

This important principle also applies to the telling of a story. As previously stated, know the beginning; how to develop it; and, most important, know the ending. When you get there, end it. Don't try to embellish it with added remarks. When you quit, quit all over.

A chairman can very often indicate to the audience that he has a full awareness of the importance of the time element in respect to his remarks by the use of the anecdote or story about speakers or speeches which are dull because they are too long.

A movie executive famous for long after-dinner speeches suddenly became noted for his brevity. When asked about his reformation he replied: "It was a remark I overheard during a pause in one of my speeches. One man said to another, 'What follows this speaker?' And the other fellow replied, 'Wednesday.'"

NEVER APOLOGIZE

The chairman, as likewise a speaker, should always remember the mere fact he is asked to participate in a program is in itself an indication that the committee, and the audience in turn, have confidence in his ability and expect him to do the job. He should rise to the occasion and attempt to meet the challenge. With other things being reasonably equal, the chairman has confidence in his ability by virtue of some experience, has adequate background and has made the necessary plans for the occasion, he should assume the right attitude toward the job. If he then has any misgivings he should apply the psychology so aptly proposed by Shakespeare in **Hamlet,** "Assume a virtue if you have it not." He should never apologize. It is not good form. If he is any good the audience will find it out; if he is no good, the audience will find that out, without being told.

If a chairman feels a necessity to say something about any feeling of humility he may have, or even a slight inadequateness (which should never be made known to the audience), he had better do it in a spirit of levity, to take the edge off the effect that apologizing has.

In place of the vicious apology for making a speech or being the chairman, too often indulged in by speakers and chairmen, who by so doing, immediately depreciate their own value, it is suggested that a good story be used at the outset.

FINAL SUGGESTIONS

The chairman or master-of-ceremonies must be the master of the situation. He must know the people and the purpose of the occasion. It is not advisable to entrust the job to a stranger.

He should acquaint himself with the program; know who is going to speak or who is going to entertain. He should know each speaker's subject and the name of each entertainer's number or contribution. He should conceive and understand the function of each part of the program and its relation to the whole.

He should know how to speak little and yet say much. But he should prepare his opening and later remarks, even though it is expected he may have to modify these according to the trend or turn of events.

He should refrain from telling too many funny stories, even though he may be expected to be humorous and make apt introductions.

He should consult each speaker or member of the program. One of them may want you to include certain things in the introduction.

He should prepare a time schedule. He should know how long the program or meeting should last and apportion to each person his allotted time. He should, before the meeting, tell each of them how much time is at his disposal.

He must be on time and see that members of the program are likewise. He must start the meeting on time and then keep things moving on schedule as nearly as possible.

He must strive to be alert, alive, and resourceful. If he can, with other things being equal, possess wit and humor, he will make an exceptional chairman.

It is recognized, therefore, that he has autocratic power. He has the first and the last word. With it, he must possess tact.

He must, as a final admonition, never overdo; for overdoing has a tendency to "steal the thunder" of the other or main speakers.

A Hollywood writer in discussing "Echoes of the 1949 Academy Awards" brings something pertinent to our ideas:

"Robert Montgomery was the best master-of-ceremonies we've ever had. He must get credit for his excellent management and pace of the program. He was witty, right to the point, and didn't try to give a performance for himself. I vote for him as the master-of-ceremonies next year."

In his line on "The Toastmaster," James Metcalfe, with

some misgivings, admirably expresses what may be the bad chairman's fate. The poetry is not very good, but the ideas are.

"The Toastmaster"

He is the banquet boss whose job
Is not an easy one,
Because he has to guide the course,
Of business and of fun;
He introduces speakers in
A pleasant sort of way,
And gives a little hint or two
Of what they are to say.
He calls attention to the guests,
And tells a joke or two,
And he must have the parting word,
When all the rest are through.
Sometimes this kind of creature knows
Precisely when to pause,
And how to hold the audience
And draw the most applause;
But sometimes he is not so hot,
Or does not know the score;
And by his smart or clumsy style
Turns out to be a bore.

Considering the high importance of the position of chairman, an authority in a former day once said, "To be a good chairman, is to be greater than a King." The thought may suggest exaggeration, but it carries the idea that a good chairman is rare indeed.   —V. Spencer Goodreds

IT IS NOW MY PLEASURE . . .

The forgotten man of public life has been before you a long time—and you may have been glad to forget him.

He isn't Franklin D. Roosevelt's man at the bottom of the economic pyramid; neither is he William Graham Sumner's man delving away in patient industry. He is, rather, the man who introduces the speaker at — well, wherever you hear speakers.

The introducer is peculiarly a Western Hemisphere institution since in a good many other places on earth the speaker introduces himself and speaks for himself. But in the United States the fellow who brings on the speaker is the true forgotten man: unwept, unhonored, unsung—and frequently unprepared!

Sometimes he is a human parenthesis, bracketing the speaker with effusions. Sometimes he is a moralist, extracting meaning from the speech—and running the meeting overtime.

If he says too much, he's windy. If he says too little, he doesn't do Speaker Klotz full justice. If he comments on Klotz' topic, he's stealing the speech; if he makes no comment, he's stupid.

All of which is by way of saying that the introducer needs some preparation for his function. Usually it begins when the president says, "Say, Horace, how about sitting at the head table today and introducing the speaker? Name's Klotz. Come on and meet him."

So, Horace must then spend his lunch grilling Mr. Klotz and missing the meal—not necessarily a deprivation—or he must pick up the information between bites.

If Horace is not quite up to par this particular day, the introduction is apt to come out like this:

"Uh . . . Bill asked me to do this just a few minutes ago . . . uh. . . . Our speaker today is, er, Mr. Augustine Sebastian

Klotz. He is, uh, the, uh, third assistant to the third active vice-president . . . uh . . . of the Third National Bank. His topic is, uh, how to be 'Happy Though Poor.' It is, uh, my pleasure to introduce, uh, Mr. Klotz."

Everyone knows it's been no pleasure as Horace sits down. So does Mr. Klotz. This is known as the "wet blanket introduction."

It does not have to be. Any reasonably alert individual can introduce someone even if called upon at virtually the last minute. It's simple. Here are a few rules which will help to smooth the way:

1. Know the speaker's name. Usually the program will supply it; discover how to pronounce it as well. The speaker can help.

2. Take the time necessary to prepare an introduction, if possible. This may mean consulting some biographical references, but Joe Miller's joke book should be avoided.

3. Make your introduction long enough to convey some idea of the speaker's important attainments and professional standing. But make it short enough to avoid giving the audience fidgets.

4. Don't be effusive. Let the facts speak for themselves.

5. Don't be a human parenthesis. It's not necessary to agree or disagree from the speaker's table with Mr. Klotz' remarks; neither is it usual to be "inspired" by his message.

In other words, make your audience feel that you really are "happy" to introduce Klotz. At the end, make him feel your "thanks" are sincere.

And let it go at that. Otherwise you will join the ranks of the forgotten men. And, perhaps, it will be a good thing.

—L. L. Walker, Jr., Rotarian, Harrisburg, Houston, Tex.

THE FUNCTION OF THE CHAIRMAN

The toastmaster or chairman must keep in mind that his function in introducing a speaker is to bring together the audience and the speaker on a high level of good will. He must create within the audience the feeling that the speaker has something to say and that it is worth listening to. If the speaker is comparatively unknown to the audience or the chairman, he then should stress the subject which is to be discussed and presented and create within the audience a desire to hear the speaker because of the timeliness of the subject to be presented. If the subject is of secondary importance but the speaker is famous then the interest is created and heightened by letting the audience know how wise was their judgment in coming to hear the gentleman who is to make a contribution to their intellectual and spiritual life.

The chairman should avoid such commonly used phrases as "The speaker needs no introduction." However, he can give a turn to a commonly used phrase so that it makes a unique introduction of the speaker. For example, he can say of the well-known guest that he needs an introduction because his outlook on life is so wide and his grasp of knowledge so great that he is a constantly changing personality and he is never the same, even in his greatness, from day to day—he does need an introduction but it is one that can only be given by himself in his own address.

Seldom are long introductions wise. The only occasion for a long introduction is if the chairman needs to get the audience under control because of ill feeling present towards the speaker. Good-natured banter between the speaker and the toastmaster is usually in order unless both are strangers to the audience. It is the responsibility of the chairman to turn over to the speaker an audience that is ready to listen and believes that the speaker is going to give them something worth listening to. From then on the speaker is on his own.

The chairman should keep in mind the background of the

meeting and its purpose. If it is of a serious nature, he ought not to spend his time in light-hearted remarks.

Also of importance is quiet and order at the time the speaker rises to the platform. At a service club a gift was presented to one of the men present just before I got up to speak. It was apparent that the attention of the group was on the gift (for the package had not been opened before I was introduced) so that it was difficult for me to get attention. I, therefore, suggested we pause for a moment so that all might share in the delight of the gift by having the recipient show it to the audience, for he was proceeding to open the package during my first few remarks.

Kitchen noises, rattle of dishes, people coming and going, are all disturbing. The chairman must keep all these factors in mind. A splendid address is frequently spoiled by the lack of consideration for these important details. A good chairman can make an ordinary meeting a delightful memory. He can send the speaker away after the meeting feeling he has given an acceptable address and the audience satisfied that it was worthwhile attending the meeting.   —Dr. E. S. Hjortland

AXIOMS FOR THE CHAIRMAN

1. The chairman should not be the whole show. I have attended banquets where he was, and other banquets where he only thought he was. In either case, I would have been ahead of the game to the extent of a banquet ticket, a taxicab fare, and a pleasant evening, if I had stayed at home.

2. The chairman should allow the speaker a little of the time set apart for the speaking.

3. The chairman should under no circumstances deliver the speaker's speech in introducing him.

4. The chairman should not tell every known story in introducing the speaker. Leave a few for him to tell. Sometimes a

speaker's entire remarks are going to remind him of a story as a climax. Think what a chairman has done to a speaker when he has hogged not only the speaker's story, but his climax!

5. The chairman should not, after the speaker has concluded his speech, express his approval by making the speech over again, or trying to improve on it.

6. The chairman should try to make the speaker feel at home. There are moments when even the most calloused speaker wishes he were.

7. The chairman should always have in his repertoire the phrase, "We have with us tonight." This not only relieves the apprehension of the audience, but also allows the chairman to "say an undisputed thing in such a solemn way."

8. The words: "needs no introduction" can also be used with effect. Do not, however, follow with a biographical sketch, or excerpts from the Blue Book or Who's Who.

9. The chairman's introduction of a speaker should not, as a rule, be longer than the speech of the speaker.

10. The chairman's introduction, on the other hand, should not be so brief as to be brutal. To be introduced as I was once: "The next speaker is Mr. Williams, who will now talk to us" is nothing short of criminal, and incites thoughts of murder and revenge. In such cases, a chairman is unnecessary, and a printed list, or an illuminated sign, such as announces a vaudeville performance, is a big improvement.

11. The chairman should be empowered by law to kill a speaker who talks over an hour. Forty-five minutes should be the limit, and there **are** men who can say something in twenty minutes. Without arbitrarily fixing any given time, the real art in speech making is in knowing when to sit down. The average banquet is neither an endurance test, nor a Chinese drama.

12. The chairman must please everybody and offend nobody.

13. The chairman should have at least a speaking acquaintance with the speaker. Nothing is more embarrassing for all concerned than to have a chairman frame up a glowing speech of welcome to "our well-known friend, whose smiling face I now gaze into with feelings of fondest regard," and launch this at a totally innocent but amazed guest at the speaker's table, until someone pulls the chairman's coat-tails and informs him that the man he is trying to introduce is seated over here on the other side.

14. The chairman must keep sober. A faithful observance of this prerogative should entitle the chairman to a Carnegie medal for heroism and self-sacrifice.

—Arthur L. Kaser

CONFUSED CHAIRMAN

When President Syngman Rhee of Korea addressed a joint session of Congress on July 28, 1954, he was introduced by Speaker Joe Martin. It appeared that Mr. Martin had a little trouble explaining to Congress who President Rhee is.

When he began he said: "We are about to hear the president of India." Then he quickly corrected himself and said: "The president of Indiana." Martin hit it right the third time —"president of the republic of Korea."

No doubt Mr. Martin was confused, but this experience indicates how important it is for a chairman to get advance information about the speaker, his topic, and his background.

—Lawrence M. Brings

SECTION TWO

SECTION TWO

PRACTICAL INTRODUCTIONS
FOR CHAIRMEN

In the following pages there are assembled complete introductions for a large variety of speakers. These speeches have been contributed to this book by experienced chairmen who have used them in actual situations. For obvious reasons, the real names of the speakers have been eliminated.

As is stated in the preface, it will be advisable for you to adapt these introductions to specific knowledge you have about the speaker and his subject.

INTRODUCING A BUSINESSMAN

Tonight, ladies and gentlemen, our speaker is a man who has had more than his share of success in the business world. He is one of its leaders and we are proud of that. But much of his success is due to the typists and stenographers that he has employed. They are the people who should be given their credit for his progress.

One of his secrets in this story is that he never hires a pretty stenographer. He always hires one that is stupid. There is a method behind this system. He knows that he will find it easy to fire a stupid person while he might have a little trouble firing one that adds to the scenery around the office.

He had one encounter that was a little hard to explain. That was when his wife wanted to kiss him over the phone and he told the secretary to take the message and relay it to him. He hired one girl who assured him that she was the latest thing in typists. He found out what she meant on the very next day. She didn't come to work until noon and that was as late as anyone could get. There was one girl who just had to be fired. When he started dictating he never got beyond the word "dear." She thought it was a proposal.

I, ladies and gentlemen, also have a proposal. I propose to present to you a man we all know and respect, Mr. —————.

—Louis J. Huber

INTRODUCING A CHAIRMAN OF THE DAY

Your chairman today is Lewis L. Crosby who is appearing for the fourth consecutive year as head man in our 4-H talent show. He is executive vice-president of Cargill Carriers, Inc., when not busy with other outside activities.

This Cargill Carriers we speak of is only a part of Cargill, Inc., which is a tremendous world-wide grain company. They operate all over the world in grains, corn, soy beans, vegetable oils, etc. Their home office is at Wayzata on the shores of Lake Minnetonka. It looks more like a home than an office and includes such niceties as a swimming pool to keep the vice-presidents and their secretaries in good shape. It would appear that as far as shapes go it does more for the secretaries than it does for the Vp's.

It takes about 5,000 people to keep this vast enterprise rolling. Crop predictions, weather conditions, and state and federal regulations make it very complicated.

This business never stands still and so they organized Cargill Carriers to keep it moving and put Lew in charge of all this movement. The products move in steamships, barges, trains and trucks. Now while it is a very large company, Lew will deliver personally grass seed if you buy five pounds or more and will also deliver fertilizer, but you have to buy at least a hundred pounds of this and they will not break packages. For this special service, Lew recently traded in his faithful Studebaker and picked up a Cadillac. This only goes to prove that even with large companies business is where you find it.

New concerns as large as Cargill are bound to have some problems. One day at lunch Mr. MacMillan, who is the really Mr. Big at Cargill's, said he would like some oatmeal. So all the officers present decided they would do something about it. Each went out and signalled the traders to buy oats. They did. Lew got into the spirit of the thing and began hauling oats until all the grain elevators, all the grain bins, and all the bathtubs were overflowing with oats. It was quite a sight. I am reminded of General Custer's last words when the Indians attacked his valiant band of cavalry men in South Dakota: "That's a hell of a lot of Indians." Likewise, this was a hell of a lot of oats.

I believe that horses eat more oats than business executives and about this time someone in Washington, who owned a horse, needed a couple of oats for it. He sent Junior down to the store, but no oats. He tried another store, but no oats. He got sore and started an investigation. He learned that Cargill not only had all the oats there was, but owned all the futures for years to come.

Words were exchanged through counsel; the story leaked out to the newspapers and it was quite a tight situation for a few days. However, after it was explained how innocently the whole thing started, the government decided to forgive, but not to forget for some six months. So to this day, no one at Cargill can stand the taste of oatmeal. And it may still apply to corn fritters.

Well, Lew is really a grand fellow with practically no criminal tendencies, a gracious loser at golf and gin rummy, who is always hopeful that next time he will be more lucky. Your chairman, Lew Crosby.   —Evald C. Banks, President
Minneapolis Rotary Club

AN APT INTRODUCTION

In a speech course conducted by Elizabeth Ferguson von Hesse, the Speech of Introduction was employed as a class project. This excellent, brief introduction of John Dewey, the educator, was given by one of the members:

"All good things come in threes, we are told. During the past fifty years, the world has produced three great Americans with the same name, each of whom has excelled in his chosen field: a great admiral, a great district attorney, a great philosopher. Ladies and gentlemen—the great philosopher, John Dewey."

Elizabeth Ferguson von Hesse—**So To Speak,**
J. B. Lippincott Co., New York

INTRODUCING A CHAIRMAN OF THE DAY

Our chairman to day is Earl Winget, Jr. Earl is a product of Minneapolis and is the president of a company that was started in a very modest way by his mother who started making sun bonnets. They found out shortly, through research, that women have only one head while they have two of most everything else, so they quickly doubled their business by switching to other products that would appeal to milady.

The field of ladies' clothes is a very fascinating one. Style, materials, and ideas make a constantly changing theme. A wrong guess and you soon have ulcers. It is such a broad field that companies in it usually limit themselves to certain aspects. It is uplifting to note the outstanding job some companies do in brassieres. Others go the other way in an effort to control the field by making foundation garments to re-arrange and constrict the female form.

Now most of this improving on nature is done to please mere men and we should be flattered at the trouble they go to for us. The Kickernick Company, after carefully surveying the possibilities, decided to limit its operations. They specialize in slips, gowns, petticoats, negligee, nighties and panties. This, to me, does not appear to be a very limited field, for it practically covers the gamut of human emotions.

But whether their clothes be purchased for their practicality or for their allure, they have stayed in the lead in their field, and for Earl and all his associates in the Kickernick family we are happy for the joy they bring to mankind in general.

Your chairman, Earl Winget.

—Evald C. Banks, President,
Minneapolis Rotary Club

A FIRST CLASS MAN

The following introduction was made at a meeting of the Radio and Television Council at which I introduced Commissioner Robert E. Lee of the Federal Communications Commission:

"Ladies and gentlemen, may I welcome you to the annual open meeting of the Radio and Television Council. I have often been told that on occasions of this kind there are at least two kinds of speakers, those who have something to say, and those who have to say something. Our distinguished guest today is clearly among the former, your chairman among the latter. I was also told shortly before this meeting convened that I was invited to act as chairman for a meeting of the Council later in the spring because, as your president put it, I had 'the basic qualifications.' I have just discovered that your president is a firm believer in the tradition which holds that the primary function of a chairman or master of ceremonies upon an occasion of this kind is to be so infernally dull that all other speakers will sound brilliant by comparison. In that respect I am fully qualified, but the distinguished career and national reputation of our guest makes that precaution quite unnecessary.

Our guest is the most recent appointee of the President of the United States to one of the most important appointive offices in our land. As Federal Communications Commissioner he has an opportunity to influence the pattern of the development of the enormously powerful and influential mass media of this nation.

When the program for the annual open meeting of this Council was being discussed early in the spring, it was proposed that we might invite three speakers to present three different aspects of the communications problem. A number of us, however, felt that three second-class men would be no substitution for one first-class man, and it is, therefore, my pleasure, ladies and gentlemen, to present a first-class man: Commissioner Robert E. Lee, of the Federal Communications Commission!" —Dr. E. W. Ziebarth,
Dean of the Summer Session, University of Minnesota

INTRODUCING A JUDGE

Judge (name) will speak to us in a few minutes, and I think you will have a clearer insight into the way the wheels of justice operate. Due to political machines and crooked politics there are many places where the wheels of justice turn backwards. Scales are often over the eyes of Justice instead of in her hands. It is often easier for a camel to go through the eye of a needle than for a rich man to enter jail.

A judge said to a prisoner, "How many times have you been up before me?" Said the prisoner, "I don't know. I thought you were keeping score."

The judge said to the next man brought before him, "I'm fining you five dollars for breaking that window." The prisoner handed the judge a ten-dollar bill. "I don't have any change," said the judge. "Just go out and break another window."

A judge said to a colored man, "How do you plead?" The prisoner said, "I pleads guilty, suh, and waives de hearing." "What do you mean, you waive the hearing?" "I means, I don't wanna hear no mo' about it."

A judge was about to pronounce sentence on an old-timer. "I'm going to sentence you to ten years in the penitentiary. Have you anything to offer before sentence is pronounced?" "Yes, your Honor," said the prisoner. "Could you arrange it so I'd get my old number back? That way I wouldn't have trouble getting my mail."

A judge said to a prisoner, "I'm going to send you to the penitentiary. It may be the making of you. You can learn about any kind of trade there. When you get out you'll be all set to earn an honest living from the education you received in the penitentiary." "I don't think it'll work," said the prisoner. "I want to learn to be a sailor." There is one thing I could never understand. They lock up the jury and let the defendants out.

Ladies and gentlemen, His Honor, Judge (name).

—Arthur L. Kaser

ADDITIONAL MATERIAL

Foreman of the jury, after a long and unsuccessful debate with one obdurate juryman: "Well, bailiff, bring us eleven dinners and a bale of hay!"

After having paid a stiff fine and costs, a certain gentleman of Tuscaloosa directed some rather indelicate language at the justice, and then ran.

An officer captured him and brought him before the justice, who then fined him ten dollars more.

"Had you been more chaste and refined in your language," said the justice, "you would not have been chased and refined."

A pompous judge said to a little girl in the witness box: "Was your father under the influence of alcohol when your mother struck him with the poker?"

"No, sir," answered the little girl, "he was under the kitchen table."

"Did you present your bill to the defendant?" an Italian plaintiff was asked by the judge.

"I deed, sir," replied he.

"Then what did he say?"

"He tola me to go to de devil."

"Then what did you do?"

"Den, of course, I coma to you."

Ranted a lawyer: "Shall this man come into this court with unblushing footsteps, with the cloak of hypocrisy in his mouth, and take fifteen cows out of my client's pocket with impunity?"

There was no reply.   —George A. Posner

INTRODUCING A RED CROSS WORKER

The avocation of a Red Cross worker is a most commendable one. It requires many hours of strenuous training, and many hours of a person's time, helping those who are in distress. The women of America who have volunteered for this outstanding work are to be congratulated for their unselfish interest in the misfortune of others. In this category permit me to refer to Mrs. Amelia Watkins, a member of our local Red Cross chapter, and next speaker on the program this evening. Many are the stories Mrs. Watkins can tell about experiences in the disaster areas—the flood areas, the fire-stricken areas, and how the Red Cross, through first aid saves many lives.

In this respect Mrs. Watkins has had many an unusual experience. I'm thinking of one in particular: It happened in the early days of Mrs. Watkins' training for Red Cross work, and when she had just completed the course on resuscitation—an adjunct that is very valuable in saving lives. Now resuscitation, as you all know, is an art that requires bouncing on the victim, who is usually stretched out face down in a prostrate condition, pin him down with your knees and wallop him on the back until the breath that is knocked out of him returns. Well, on this particular evening, when Mrs. Watkins was returning home, she saw a man stretched out, face down, on the street.

Taking advantage of this opportunity to put into practice a lesson that she had learned that afternoon, she quickly stopped her car and rushed over to the man. Pouncing on his back and holding him securely with her knees, she began to administer the pile-driver technique of resuscitation.

"He's coming to," she said to herself as the man moved. So she banged away some more. Momentarily, the fellow lifted up his head, which he turned to see Mrs. Watkins astride his back, squeezing the air in and out of his lungs. The astonished man then said: "Quit tickling me, lady, can't you see I'm holding a light for that guy working down in the manhole?"

Ladies and gentlemen, Mrs. Amelia Watkins.

—Hugh Lincoln

INTRODUCING A PROFESSOR

I have the great privilege of presenting to you this evening a marvelous speaker. He is Professor—No, I'm going to be a meany. I'm not going to tell you who he is yet. But, ladies and gentlemen, he is a wonderful person with a most pleasing personality. He has more degrees than a Hotentot's thermometer. He has spent many years in the leading universities at home and abroad, but finally escaped and now is a fugitive from the brain gang.

You, no doubt, have heard it said many times that most professors are very absent-minded. Our professor is so absent-minded that he doesn't remember whether he is absent-minded or not. He has done research for years, consisting principally of hunting for his spectacles.

We have it from many sources that our professor is extremely absent-minded. For instance, not long ago he discovered himself standing on the City Hall steps holding a piece of rope. He was puzzled. He didn't know whether he had found a piece of rope or had lost a dog.

And another time he went to the barber shop for a haircut. He got into the chair with his hat on. The barber said, "Sir, if you really want a haircut you'll have to remove your hat." "Oh," apologized the professor, "I'm sorry. I didn't know there were ladies present." It's getting so when he leaves home his wife always says, "Wait, dear. Are you sure you've forgotten everything?"

But, I believe, the best one on our professor friend is when he went into a drugstore and asked for some prepared monacetic acidester of salicyllic acid. The druggist asked, "Do you mean aspirin?" "Yes," said our friend. "I can never think of that name." Come to think of it, I'm getting absent-minded. I can't think of any more to say. Perhaps it's just as well. So, ladies and gentlemen, allow me to introduce to you, Professor (name.)   —Arthur L. Kaser.

INTRODUCING A BABY FOOD EXECUTIVE

When I was informed by the committee that I was to introduce an executive of a baby food concern, I said to myself, "What the devil is baby food?" Then I figured that I had better find out something about this concoction that kids are lapping up by the tank car full every day of the week. So I went down to the hospital and called upon Miss Henrietta Spoon, the official dietitian of the establishment.

"Miss Spoon," I said, "I have to introduce a fellow by the name of Clark Adams who sells baby foods, and I want to pick up a little inside information about the stuff."

"Well," said Miss Spoon, "you have come to the right place at the right time. I am just at this moment predigesting a potion for Old Man Withers up in room 602. He has a ten percent stomach. The other ninety percent disappeared."

"You are doing what?" I exclaimed.

"I am predigesting Mr. Wither's food—doing what his stomach should be able to do—if he had one."

"Well," I said perplexedly, "what has Old Man Wither's stomach got to do with baby food?"

"The principle is the same," explained Miss Spoon as she stirred up a pot filled with an undescribable mixture.

"I can't see any connection," I said in astonishment. "When I was a kid I lived on Carnation milk, potatoes and sand."

"That's the trouble with you," she said. "If you would have dug a little deeper in the sand and nibbled on some limestone, your shoulders wouldn't be stooped. With these new baby foods modern kids are spared that extra work."

"Do you mean to say that these baby foods are sprinkled with limestone and that sort of stuff?" I asked.

"They certainly are," she replied. And then Miss Spoon looked at me with a professional air and added, "I can see by that left eye of yours, which is exactly one-thousandth of an inch lower than your right eye, that your baby-day diet was decidedly lacking in pablum-digilatum. And heavens! Look at your left ear. The lobe is hanging there like a dead leaf on a tree. That indicates no baby-day carrot-spinachtalitus. It is evident that you were brought up on a diet of potatoes and sand."

"It's too late to correct that now," I said. "But I still want to know something about baby food—those little cans with 57 varieties."

"Oh, mercy! Those little cans!" exclaimed Miss Spoon. "That's the answer. Everything a baby needs is in one of those little cans predigested just like Mr. Withers' meal."

"Do you mean to say, Miss Spoon, that everything a baby needs is in one of those little cans?"

"Everything," she said.

"Well then, why the 57 varieties?" I asked. "One with a spinach label. One with a squash label. One with an apricot label."

"That's just a variety of labels," said Miss Spoon. "The contents are the same."

"Miss Spoon!" I exclaimed. "Do you want me to get the impression that you are putting one over on the kid by showing him a can with a picture of spinach on it which isn't spinach at all, but some sort of tutti-frutti mixture?"

"What does a six-months-old kid know about spinach?" she replied.

"Well, I haven't learned very much about baby foods," said I.

"You have learned this much, Mr. Brown, that you would have been a much better-looking man had you been raised on baby foods. You are full of defects, and I have only seen a few of them. There are most likely many more disguised by your clothing. Well, I must be getting up with Mr. Withers' supper."

"I hope Old Man Withers enjoys it," I said as I left the hospital.

That is all I was able to find out about baby foods, so now I am going to present to you a man who is an expert on the subject. Ladies and gentlemen, Mr. Clark Adams.

—Sylvester McGovern

INTRODUCING A LABOR LEADER

The next speaker on our program this evening is a labor leader—a man who has championed the cause of the working man for a good many years. I know that you are all anxious to hear Jake Greene. But before he speaks, I have a few things that I want to say about Jake Greene.

Jake was called into the services during the last war, and reached the point of his induction along with a group of other young men of various professions. Some were Harvard graduates, some were bankers, some were clerks, some were lawyers, some were a little of everything. Jake was the only labor leader in that segment of the army. The first day at the barracks was pretty tough on the new recruits—a five-mile hike before a breakfast of bread, molasses and black coffee.

After breakfast the rookies sprawled about on the ground, panting and easing their worn-out limbs. After a few minutes rest, Sergeant Patrick O'Brien issued a command of "Attention!" This immediately brought the rookies to their feet.

"Men!" yelled O'Brien. "I'm looking for some brainy men to do clerical work for this outfit. All of you college guys, bankers, lawyers and the likes of that, step forward!"

Everyone stepped forward but Jake Greene. O'Brien walked over to him and eyed him up from tip to toe. Then he called out at Jake: "And what were you doing in civilian life?"

"I was a labor . . ." said Jake. But before he could say the word "leader," the sergeant interrupted: "Laborer! Well, I'll be - - - - - -! One guy in a hundred who says he worked for a livin'!"

O'Brien turned to the group of intellectuals that had stepped forward and yelled out in stentorian tones: "Men! Get them boxes and them spiked sticks. I want this whole parade ground policed by sundown!"

The sergeant then stepped over to Jake and said: "Greene, you go back to the barracks and take a nap!"

Ladies and gentlemen, Jake Greene.

—Sylvester McGovern

INTRODUCING A "SEE AMERICA FIRST" SPEAKER

Thousands of tourists visit foreign countries every year. A large number of these same tourists have seen only a small portion of these United States. And where in the world is there a more versatile land of beauty?

There is one outstanding authority on American sight-seeing, and we are referring to no other than Mr. (name), who will speak to you this evening. His motto is, "See America first. It's wonderful." Beautiful mountains that rise so high they interfere with the passing of the moon. Beautiful lakes where the water comes right up to the shore. Roads that run clear across the country and never come back. There are large cities where the bright lights are never dimmed. There are the little villages that go to sleep window by window.

Few foreigners realize the great expanse of this country. Neither can an American until he starts hitch-hiking. I did some hitch-hiking when I was young, so I know. The fact is, I got bowlegged hitch-hiking on oil trucks. One time in Nebraska I asked a man how far it was to the next town, Stonebroke. He said it was about ten miles, and that I could walk it in an hour if I'd run. I asked the man which road I should take, and he said it didn't make much difference. Whichever road I'd take, I'd be sorry I didn't take the other one.

I asked him if he knew the mayor of that town. He said he did. "Where can I get hold of him?" I asked. He said, "That's hard to say, he's so ticklish." As I started away he called me back. "About going to Stonebroke—I believe if I were you I'd go back about a mile and take the first right hand road. Come to think of it, you'd better take the first left hand road. No, wait, stranger. If I were you trying to get to Stonebroke, I wouldn't start from here at all." And so it goes.

Oh, yes, the Grand Canyon. Beautiful! Gorgeous! Stupendous! And to think it was made by just one man—a Scotchman who owned a ranch. One day he lost a golf ball in a gopher hole. Ladies and gentlemen, it is with pleasure I introduce our traveler and lecturer, Mr. (name.)   —Richard Drummond

INTRODUCING A MINISTER

I have just been reading where times are improving, and I have proof to prove it. Ministers are reporting that buttons received in the collection are of better quality and have a more qualified ring. Also that there are more good souls and less poor heels attending church. It may be that because there are so many motoring fatalities on Sundays that people go to church for safety's sake.

Churches have tried about everything else to get some people to attend. Maybe this will work. Parents insist their children go every Sunday. The parents go when they feel like it. Little David attended Sunday School every Sunday and usually stayed for church as well. One day he asked his mother, "Mommy, could I be a preacher when I grow up?" "Why, of course," said mother. "Why do you ask?" "Well," said David, "I suppose I'll be going to church all my life, anyway, and it's a lot harder to sit still than to stand up and holler."

I asked the little boy living next door to me why he didn't come to our church. He said he couldn't. He belonged to another abomination. I asked him if he said his prayers every night and he said he did. I asked him if he said them every morning. "No, sir," he answered. "I'm not afraid in the morning."

Then he told me he had learned a new song in church about a bear named Gladly, and it was cross-eyed. I think he was referring to the song, "Gladly, the Cross I'd Bear." I was amused at his answers and asked him one more question. "What do you suppose the land of milk and honey is?" And he said, "Sticky."

A new minister asked one of his congregation how she liked his first sermon. She said, "Very good, sir. So instructive. We really didn't know what sin was till you came here." A minister asked an acquaintance what church he belonged to. "None," was the reply. "Well, what church do you go to when you do go?" "Well, if you must know, the church I stay away from most of the time when I don't go is the one across the street." But enough of this. I believe Reverend **(name)** is ready to deliver his message. Friends, the Reverend **(name)** of **(name of church.)**   —Arthur L. Kaser

---

INTRODUCING A CATHOLIC PRIEST

Father John Clancey is one of Northville's most beloved citizens and it is always a pleasure to introduce him as a speaker, as then we are certain to hear a witty speech. But before bringing Father Clancey to the speaker's table, I am going to tell you about a misfortune he met up with last summer.

One day as Father Clancey was checking up around the parish house, he discovered six umbrellas hidden away in a closet. The umbrellas were badly in need of repair. "This is a terrible waste of money," said Father Clancey. "I must take them down town and have them repaired." Which he did.

A week later he returned to town to take home his six umbrellas. As he boarded the bus in front of the church, it was raining pitchforks, so Father Clancey turned up his coat collar to avoid the rain. This, incidentally, hid his identity as a clergyman. At the corner of Fourth and Main Father got to his feet, preparing to leave the bus, and no doubt thinking of his six umbrellas, absent-mindedly reached out and grabbed an umbrella belonging to a lady who was sitting beside him.

"Stop the robber!" yelled the lady, snatching back her umbrella from Father's hand.

Embarrassed beyond description, Father Clancey went directly to the repair shop where he obtained his six umbrellas. Later that afternoon he again boarded a bus for his return trip home. It was still raining pitchforks, and Father's coat collar was still turned up. As he took his seat in the rear of the bus, he was shocked to see the very same woman of his morning's adventure sitting across the aisle. It is needless to say that she was glaring at him in a most uncomplimentary manner. The woman looked down at the six umbrellas, and then said scornfully: "Well! You had a big day!"

—Walter S. Bacon

INTRODUCING A CHAMBER OF COMMERCE OFFICIAL

As a member of our Chamber of Commerce Joe Wilson has been doing a marvelous job. Once, last and always Joe is for our own home town and state, and through his efforts the fame of our community has gone far and wide. In Joe's opinion, and of course in ours, no community in the world can boast of so many things as we have right here in Northwood.

It seems to be the practice of chamber of commerce men to try and outdo one another. The California boys are continually leveling attacks at Florida, and vice versa. When it rains in California, it's a flood in the minds of Florida chamber of commerce people; and when it's a comfortable 85 degrees in Florida, it's a scorching heat wave, according to the boys on the west coast. And so on.

Last year Joe took a trip down to Texas, where he met a delegation of the local chamber of commerce, who took him on a tour to see the wonders of that great state.

"Just look at those grapefruit!" exclaimed Joe, as he was being escorted through the grove.

"Those lemons are awfully small this year," replied the Texan, who was watching Joe's examination of the grapefruit.

And so it went until the party crossed the Rio Grande river bed, through which a small stream of water was trickling. Before one of the Texas boosters could utter a word of praise, Joe asked, as he looked down at the parched river bed: "Has someone's radiator been leaking?"

Ladies and gentlemen, Joe Wilson.

—Horton Smith

ADDITIONAL MATERIAL

Will S. Brown of a Florida Chamber of Commerce made a visit to the State of California for the purpose of getting some first-hand information on some of the seemingly exaggerated tales that had been emanating from that region.

As Brown was being escorted through some of the growing fields by a local member of a California Chamber of Commerce, he picked up a melon. Looking at it carefully through his glasses he said to the California man, "Is this the biggest apple you can raise in this state?"

The California man watched Will Brown roll the melon back and forth between his hands for a moment, and then quickly commanded: "Quit fingering that grape!"

—Walter S. Bacon

INTRODUCING AN OPTIMIST

We have a speaker this evening who spends a good deal of time looking on the bright side of everything. Why, he's so optimistic he'd go looking for an apartment with a slide trombone under one arm and two kids and a dog under the other. He's so optimistic he still thinks the time will come when there will be no more wisecrack definitions of an optimist.

Did you know that a pessimist remembers the lily belongs to the onion family, while the optimist knows that the onion belongs to the lily family? And remember, too, that every cloud has a silver lining, and even an old suit of clothes has its shiny side.

Our office boy doesn't know whether he's an optimist or a pessimist. He says he's eaten three cakes of yeast and hasn't gotten a raise yet. But I think the top-notcher optimist is the man, who, instead of feeling sorry he can not pay his bills, is glad that he is not one of his creditors.

I said to my young nephew, "Aren't you ashamed to be at the bottom in a class of twenty boys?" "Oh," he said, "that's not so bad. Suppose there were fifty boys." All in all, optimism is a cheerful frame of mind that enables a teakettle to sing when it's in hot water up to its nose. If I keep on babbling you optimists will become pessimists. To prevent that I'm going to introduce our optimistic speaker, Mr. **(name.)**

—Arthur L. Kaser

INTRODUCING A NEWSPAPER EDITOR

As you may already know, our speaker this evening is a newspaper editor, and a well-known one at that. I might even add that he is a great editor. A great editor, by the way, is the one who tells the truth so plainly that many subscribers indignantly stop the paper, and then borrow it from the neighbors every day and keep it for a couple of hours.

Radio, television, nor anything else, will ever push the newspapers out of business. Newspapers have been in existence since time immoral. That doesn't sound just right. At one time I was a reporter on our home town paper. I pried into the crevices of old mother earth for the subscribers' amusement. In other words, I dug up the dirt.

I remember one time an irate man stamped into our editor's office and thundered, "Look here, you! You published an announcement of my death. I'm not dead, and your announcement must be retracted." "We never retract," said our editor, "but we'll compromise. We'll put you in the birth column tomorrow and give you a fresh start."

Editors have to be quick on the trigger. A frantic woman called our editor. "Oh, Mr. Editor, what'll I do? My baby has just chewed up your evening paper and swallowed it." "Don't worry," soothed the editor. "Just feed him a Literary Digest."

Editors know that there is never anything absolutely new to print. It's just the same old things happening to different people. I think the biggest mistake our editor ever made was during the paper shortage some years ago. There was more news than available paper to print it on. The editor placed a notice on the front page as follows: "Due to the paper shortage we cannot print all the local news. The release of several patients from the hospital, and birth of eleven babies will have to be postponed a few days."

Yes, my friends, newspaper work is a funny thing. I remember one time my boss sent me out to cover a murder. When I got to the scene of the crime a policeman stopped me. "You can't come in here," he said. "But," I said, "I've been sent here to do the murder." He said, "You're late, Mister. The murder's been done." To make all the headlines on the newspapers makes all the head lines on the editor's brow. Now, ladies and gentlemen, let us hear from a man who carries the woes of the world on his back, Mr. (name) editor of (name.)

—Arthur L. Kaser

INTRODUCING A COLLEGE PRESIDENT

We really should feel honored this evening to have as our speaker Dr. (name), president of (name) College. To our way of thinking, the job of college president is one of the hardest jobs imaginable. Anyone who has gone to college with serious intentions of learning knows what I mean. Most college presidents are convinced that the reason the modern student doesn't burn the midnight oil as he used to is because he doesn't get in soon enough.

College, in a way, is just like a washing machine. You get out of it just what you put in—but you'd never recognize it. The president is responsible for the entire faculty, and the greatest college faculty is the ability of going without sleep. For example, a college professor is a man who is paid to study sleeping conditions among students.

If all the college boys in class were placed end to end they would be more comfortable. But it is not all to the bad. In any college or university there are a number of aggressive, clean-cut young men who are diligently working their dads through college. And it costs from eight to ten thousand dollars for a college education. That's a lot of money to invest and only get a quarter back.

Which brings to mind the fact that the greatness of the modern college is largely measured by the size of its stadium. Some boys in college are so smart their letters home send their parents to the dictionary. Others are so smart their letters home send their parents to the bank. Ladies and gentlemen, it is my great pleasure to present Dr. (name.)

—Arthur L. Kaser

INTRODUCING A TELEPHONE EXECUTIVE

Telephones are wonderful. How in the world could we get along nowadays without them? Where would business be without telephones? Sometimes we wonder where it is with them. And it won't be long before there will be a combination of television and telephone so you can see to whom you are talking. It will be fun to see the party you are bawling out, but it might not be very safe. You can't always see how big a man is when he's seated at the phone.

I met an old friend the other day and remarked, "Well, Jim, I see you have a new car." He said, "Yes, I went into a garage to use the phone and didn't want to come out without buying something."

Yes, telephones are wonderful instruments. They connect you with so many strangers. I overheard this conversation on the phone yesterday—quote: "Hello! This is Mrs. Gladstone. Will you send me some nice cutlets right away? Oh, you haven't any? Well, then, a couple of nice pork chops? You don't have them either? Well—let me see. How about a small sirloin steak? You haven't any steak? For land's sake! Say! Aren't you Goober, the butcher? What? You're the florist? Oh, well, send me a dozen white lilies. My husband must be starved to death by now."

An Englishman once told me that he thought their custom of answering the phone was much better than the custom in the United States. I asked him why. "Well," he said, "in the United States you just say 'hello.' In England you say, 'Are you there?' Then, of course, if you are not there, there is no use going on with the conversation." Has anyone here ever talked on a phone in China? When you ring the exchange in China you will get something like this: "What number does the honorable son of the moon and stars desire?" Then you say, "Hohi, two-three." Then from the exchange: "Will the honorable person graciously forgive the inadequacy of the insignificant service and permit this humbled slave of the wire to inform him that the never-to-be sufficiency censured line is busy."

One time I called Hellespont 1234 in California. The exchange girl said the line was busy but she could give me Hellespont 2468 or Sunspot 3677. They were very interesting numbers. So I took a chance and called one of the numbers. When a rough voice answered from the other end of the line, I asked, "What number is this?" The voice said, "You ought to know. You called it." A few minutes later my phone rang. It was the same exchange girl. She said, "I just happened to run across a couple of right numbers. Could you use them?"

I just found out how to classify telephone girls. Theirs is not a business nor a profession. It's a calling.

Friends, we have with us an executive of the telephone company whom I feel certain has some things very interesting to tell you. Ladies and gentlemen, Mr. (name.)

—Arthur L. Kaser

INTRODUCING AN ACTOR

Friends, we have at the head table this evening, a man who is quite well known. He needs no introduction. So why should I give him one? For this reason: To tell you a few little known facts about him.

You know that he is an actor. Do you know when he actually does his best acting? On pay day. He acts just like he earned the money they pay him.

Right now I feel like part of a sandwich. Like a piece of bread, to be exact. Mr. (seated two seats away in the direction of the speaker) must feel like the other piece of bread. We have ham between us.

Our speaker will always remember his first part. It was a walk-on role. He walked on but he had to run off. He went from that to vaudeville where he was the star in an animal act. He stopped that when the other animals wanted him to be like them. They insisted that he also get fleas.

Enough of this nonsense. I give you the man who is a credit to his profession. He never acts down, he always acts up. Mr. —————.

—Louis J. Huber

INTRODUCING A HARDWARE DEALER

Tonight I have the pleasure of introducing to this very fine audience a stalwart member of our business community—one who deals in the every day necessities of life. I speak, of course, of Howard Smith, proprietor of one of the best hardware stores here in Midville.

As you folks all know, a hardware store is a very versatile institution. You can get almost any kind of an article at a hardware store, from a shingle nail to a dish pan, or if you want to go farther, from a lawn mower to an egg beater. If you need paint, you go down to Howard's store. When some kid smashes your cellar window, you take it to Howard's where it is promptly repaired. Speaking of repairing windows recalls an incident when Howard was forced to fix his own window.

About two years ago, Mr. Stephen O'Brogan, a handy man about town—handy with tools and handy with the bottle, was passing Howard's store on a windy day, carrying a plank across his shoulder. Suddenly, following a quick gust of wind, there was a resounding crash and a tinkle of glass descending on the sidewalk. This attracted Howard, who was in the back of his store wrapping up some putty, to rush forward, where he witnessed a most devastating sight—his front plate glass window shattered to smithereens.

When Howard spied O'Brogan through the huge gap where the glass had vanished, he made one leap in O'Brogan's direction, but not quickly enough, as O'Brogan, apparently sensing the oncoming leap in Howard's eyes, leaped first, and consequently was one leap ahead of Howard as they raced down Main street. During the chase Howard kept shouting, "Stop, you bounder!" . . . which attracted others to join in.

By the time the aggregation had passed the second street intersection, nearly half the town was in on the hunt. But O'Brogan was still in the lead, with Howard leading the rest of the pursuers. By the time O'Brogan had leaped through three red lights, he began to lose steam and his pace slackened, which permitted Howard to collar him in front of Joe Smith's shoe store.

Shaking O'Brogan by the neck, much to the glee of the other chasing citizens, who figured they had participated in catching a dangerous man, Howard said in a panting voice, "What do you mean by breaking my window and then running away like a criminal?"

O'Brogan looked Howard in the eye and between puffs exclaimed, "Sure and I did, but didn't ye see me a runnin' home to get the money to pay ye?"

Ladies and gentlemen, Mr. Howard Smith.

—Roger Hart

INTRODUCING A FAT MAN

I have the honor tonight of introducing to you the biggest man in Summittville, Mr. Henry Brown. Henry is such a good-natured fellow that he laughs with us when we talk about his weight. He got used to being kidded many years ago, so now he joins in the fun and enjoys the ribbing.

When Henry was in college he was the butt of many a joke, and some of them were quite annoying. One day while attending his Latin class, Henry was asked by the professor to stand up and translate a passage from Cicero. Henry failed miserably, stumbling on the first sentence; after which he abruptly sat down to the amusement of the class. The professor left his platform and walked down to Henry's chair. Then eyeing Henry up and down like a cattle buyer might be estimating the weight of a beef cow, the professor looked over his glasses and said: "Mr. Smith, you are better fed than taught."

Henry pondered over that remark for a few seconds and then spoke up: "That's correct, professor. You teach me— I feed myself."

Ladies and gentlemen, Mr. Henry Brown.

—Horton Smith

INTRODUCING A BOY SCOUT EXECUTIVE

Well, boys, I'm surely happy to see so many of you here this evening. Yes, sir! A wonderful organization. This gathering takes me back to when I was a scout.

I started out as a dub—I mean cubscout. We tried to do things differently than most patrols. We saved up soap coupons and sent them in and the company sent us an elephant—by mail. Don't ever send an elephant by mail. The postage is terrific.

And another thing; it's very difficult for the mail man to get an elephant into a mail box, especially if they are not male elephants. But our elephant came in pretty handy on our hikes. We would just put all our equipment in the elephant's trunk, and we'd travel light. But it didn't always work. Every time we came to a river or a small stream the elephant would fill its trunk with water and ruin our stuff.

When I was a scout I learned a lot of things. Do you know one of the things I could do? I could take two sticks and rub them together, and do you know what I would get? You're wrong. I got blisters on my hands.

But I did learn to do a good deed every day. I remember one day I saw an old lady on the corner. The traffic was bad, so I took her arm and guided her across the street. A little later I saw her back on the same corner again, so I took her arm and led her across the street again. And what do you know? A little later there she was right back there again. So I took her arm, but she jerked away and said, "Young man, you stop pushing me across the street. You've made me miss two buses."

I remember one especially good deed that I did. There was only enough castor oil for one of us to take, so I let my little brother have it. He didn't appreciate my good deed at all. I had a grandmother I loved a lot. She lived in the country. I was always thinking of good deeds to make her happy. During school vacation I would visit her and make her happy. And then when I went home she'd be happy again.

So now, boys, I'm going to ask a man who knows all about Boy Scouts to tell you some interesting and instructive things about the Scouts. Here he is, **(name.)**   —Arthur L. Kaser

---

INTRODUCING A BANK CASHIER OR TELLER

Perhaps one of the greatest ambitions of a young lad as he is growing to manhood is to become a banker. In this connection Bill Brown was no exception and as is known to all of us here in Brownsville, Bill fulfilled his ambition.

At an early age in life Bill took over in the teller's cage, piling up coins, pealing off fifty-dollar bills, accepting deposits, making change and doing the hundred and one things required of a teller in a bank.

About the time Bill was moving into the field of banking, Mr. Goldberg, fresh from the old country, was moving into the mercantile business. One day Bill noticed a series of checks written by Mr. Goldberg, which showed an overdraw on the merchant's account of $93. Bill, considerate banker that he was, called up Mr. Goldberg and informed him of the overdraft.

"Mr. Goldberg," said Bill over the telephone, "I want to inform you that as of the first of June, your checking account is overdrawn to the amount of $93."

"Is that so?" said Mr. Goldberg, who then paused for a few seconds, collected his thoughts and said to Bill: "Mister Brown, will you do me one favor?"

"Yes," said Bill. "What is it?"

"Will you please look at my balance on the first day of May?"

"Certainly," said Bill, who then went to the books, looked up the account and returned to the telephone. "Mr. Goldberg," he said, "on the first of May you had a balance of $142.50."

"See," said Mr. Goldberg. "And did I call you up?"

Ladies and gentlemen, Mr. Bill Brown.

—Fuller Marlow

INTRODUCING A FLORIST

John Wayne, our next speaker, is associated with an aggressive business, the retail florist. During the past twenty-five years the florist has hatched up more schemes to sell flowers than any other type of business we know. He started the slogan, "Say it with Flowers," which has brought millions of dollars into the florist's cash register. Then he instituted the lily pot on Easter, until, if a fellow is seen walking home on Easter Saturday without a lily under his arm, he is looked upon by his neighbors as a barbarian. A carnation in the lapel on Mother's day followed suit, which was quickly substituted by a thistle for Father's day.

One day John Wayne said to his wife, "Our industry has created nothing new for babies, and look at all of the babies that are bouncing into this world. We should think up something that would give these little fellows a rousing welcome when they arrive on terra firma. They had a pretty rough time getting in."

"Why don't we start a new custom," said Mrs. Wayne, "and educate these bewildered fathers, who now do nothing during the time of these blessed events but stand around the waiting room, moaning and groaning, and smoking cigarette after cigarette?"

"Why not greet the new baby with a rose—a big full-bloom American beauty?" suggested John.

"Mercy, no," said Mrs. Wayne. "Have you forgotten, John, that there is already a peg on the florist's agenda for a rose—the beautiful full-grown lady in silk and satin with hair like a raven, who accepts the tossed rose from her serenader as a message of passionate love? We can't have that for babies. That would be decidedly inappropriate."

"How about a bachelor button?" suggested John.

"Gracious, no!" exclaimed Mrs. Wayne. "A bachelor button! It would be a catastrophe to permit a new father to stand at the door of a delivery room with a bachelor button in his hand."

"Unless, perhaps," said John, "the new father has at this point become filled up with married life and wants to give his new son some early advice."

"John!" yelled Mrs. Wayne.

"Well, we'll give up that idea," said John, adding, "How about some baby roses?"

"That's it!" exclaimed Mrs. Wayne, "little, tiny, fragrant baby roses, symbolic of the pink little velvety skin that is tucked in that rose-colored blanket."

So the custom was adopted. And now if a pot of baby roses is not on hand to greet the first wail of the new-born babe, the babe is considered by hospital attaches as being a waif.

Speaking of roses recalls an incident that happened at John's florist shop some time last year. Andy Perkins was one of John's best customers, and Andy was in love with a beautiful young lady by the name of Alice. Upon the night before Alice's twenty-fourth birthday, Andy called to pay his respects. "Alice," he said, "I am going to give you a bouquet of beautiful roses for your birthday tomorrow—one rose for every year of your life." Then Andy went down to John's florist shop and left the order.

"Why, look at this," said John to Mrs. Wayne. "It's an order for two dozen roses for Andy Perkins. Andy's one of our best customers. I'll just throw in another dozen for Andy gratis."

To this day Andy doesn't know why Alice isn't speaking to him anymore.

Ladies and gentlemen, Mr. John Wayne.

—Sylvester McGovern

INTRODUCING A CERTIFIED PUBLIC ACCOUNTANT

Tonight we have with us one of Scottville's most promising young business men, John Scott, who specializes in the field of certified public accounting. Certified public accounting is a profession that requires great skill and accuracy as well as a high degree of integrity.

But like most self-employed businesses it is a hard road to hoe for a young beginner, and in this respect John Scott was no exception. After completing a long course in training and passing examination after examination, John opened up his offices in the Jones Block. That, of course, was several years ago, and before John enjoyed the extensive clientele that he now serves.

The office was thoroughly appointed with the latest in furniture. The telephone was on the desk and John's name emblazoned upon the door. Everything was in order for the customers, only there were no customers. As John was sitting at his desk pondering over that vital point of his business, he heard footsteps approaching, and soon a hand grasped the door knob.

"Aha," said John, "a customer is coming to see me. I had better give some impression of activity around this place." So he picked up the telephone, placed it to his ear and said: "Oh, that's you, Mr. Jones. No, I haven't had time to complete the annual report for you. When will I have it? Oh, perhaps the last of the month. I'm just swamped. I've been so busy preparing a financial statement for United Glass and Jar that I have had to more or less side-track your report. United, you know, is floating a billion-dollar bond issue."

At that point John hung up just as the man approached the desk.

"What can I do for you, my good fellow?" asked John.

"I'm from the telephone company," the man replied. "I came to connect your telephone."

Ladies and gentlemen, Mr. John Scott.

—Hillery Williams

INTRODUCING A HIGH GOVERNMENT OFFICIAL

It is a profound pleasure to introduce to you this evening the honorable John S. Waters, our attorney general. The responsibilities placed upon a man in such a high office are ponderous, and heavy is the burden that a man like John S. Waters carries upon his back. However, there are times when the drudgeries of holding office are alleviated with some little incident that seems to brighten up the dark clouds with a good laugh.

A few years ago General Waters arrived at the Union depot preparatory to leaving the city on a very important trip. As he hurried up to the ticket window to purchase his ticket, he suddenly realized that he had left his wallet at home and was completely out of cash. It was just a few minutes before train time and expediency was required at the moment.

"I'm the attorney general," he said to the clerk. "I left my cash at home and I must catch the Empire Builder. Will you take my check?"

"I've heard that stuff before," said the clerk. "We just had a guy here saying he was the governor and two other guys who claimed they were senators. Stand aside and let the cash customers get their tickets."

In desperation the General ran outside the depot to a newsstand on the corner. "Jimmy," said the General. "You know who I am, don't you?"

"Sure thing," said Jimmy the newsboy. "You're the attorney general."

"That's right, Jimmy, and I've got to catch that Empire Builder and I'm out of cash. Can you cash a check for twenty-five dollars?"

"Sure thing," said Jimmy, "I know how it is with you big guys when you go out on a tear and run out of dough."

Ladies and gentlemen, the honorable John S. Waters.

—Hillery Williams

INTRODUCING A CITY FIREMAN

The job of a city fireman is a dangerous one and requires plenty of courage at vital moments. True, there are relaxing moments, too, when a city fireman does nothing but work cross-word puzzles or watch television. We will hear more about that when we call John Swanson to the speaker's table. During his career as a city fireman, John has been confronted with many unique and exciting experiences. Among these this one might be cited here:

Precisely at the hour of two in the morning, the alarm sounded at John's firehouse. John jumped out of bed, slid down the pole, stepped into his boots and was off, siren sounding and waking up the whole neighborhood. When the truck arrived at the scene of the fire, pandemonium was everywhere. The air was filled with the horrified screams of persons trapped in the upper windows of a building, and immediate action was required, should the lives of those persons be saved.

While the ladders were being moved into position, John noticed a plump old lady in an old-fashioned night gown, waving frantically from one of the upper windows. Simultaneously, his eye was attracted by what appeared to be in the light of the roaring blaze a beautiful young woman in pea-green pajamas, also waving frantically from another window.

"You take her," said John to a fellow fireman.

"Which one?" asked the other fireman.

"The one in the old-fashioned night gown," John replied, and then added, "I'll take the other one."

Then John brushed his way through a group of firemen and ran up the ladder with breathless speed. Grabbing the beautiful girl in his outstretched hands, he carried her down to the safety of the street.

When John placed the lovely young creature on her feet, she said to him: "I am deeply grateful. You are a hero!"

"Thank you," John replied. "I had to knock down four other guys to get to you first."

Ladies and gentlemen, John Swanson.

—Horton Smith

INTRODUCING A POLITICIAN

We are right next door to Mexico, yet we have nothing like their bull ring. That is, unless we count the one the political candidates throw their hats into. I don't know which ring has the most bull in. The difference is that in Mexico you can see it. Up here you hear it.

I believe that you are aware that we are to have a political speaker on our stage this evening. I'm sorry it's just a stage and not a ring. This speaker is a bigger and stronger man than I am so right now I want it to be fully understood that anything I say is no reflection upon him.

Having said this I feel safe in saying that the political bee that buzzes in many a bonnet is a hum-bug. To be fair, however, I will say that politics isn't easy. If you think that politics is easy just try standing on a fence while keeping one ear on the ground.

And it's getting tougher. Nowadays a candidate has to pass his hat around before he tosses it in the ring. However, many claim to be called but only a few do not choose. A successful politician is one who keeps on his toes all the time but who never gets on the other fellow's.

We have long suspected that many a politician who claims that he hears his country calling is a ventriloquist. And, too, politics makes strange bedfellows, but they soon get accustomed to the same bunk. One last snip at the politicians. The political bee buzzes loudest around the candidates for office, but it's usually the public that gets stung! And now a politician who is not in the foregoing category, Mr. (name.)

—Arthur L. Kaser

———————

Bob Hope said, "A politician is merely a person who borrows your pot to cook your goose in. He works his gums before election and gums the works after election."

"The guy will shake your hand before election and you afterwards. His greatest asset is his lie-ability, and his chief product is soft soap, which is 99% lye." —George A. Posner

INTRODUCING A DENTIST

The career of a dentist is an interesting one. There are no dull moments in that profession, as Dr. Walter Dixon will no doubt say when he comes to the speaker's table. What goes on inside those little offices, with only the doctor, the nurse, and the patient to witness the happenings, is not often printed on page one of our newspapers.

On a Saturday morning last summer Dr. Dixon was filling a cavity in little Johnny Smith's tooth. While the doctor was gathering his implements prior to attacking the tooth, the boy sat tensely in the chair, holding his mother's hand. When the precise moment arrived to explore the cavern of Johnny's mouth, Dr. Dixon led off the invasion with his finger and the customary command of, "Open wide!" Sensing that some unknown intruder, quite unlike a popsickle, was trespassing where only lollipops and popsickles were permitted before, Johnny clamped down his jaws, firmly catching the intruder between the first and second knuckle. This brought a cry of "Ouch," from the astonished lips of Dr. Dixon. With a look of triumph Johnny turned to his mother and said, "I thought you said that he was painless!"

Upon another occasion a young lady patient said apprehensively to Dr. Dixon, "Doctor, you've pulled the wrong tooth!"

"Be calm," replied the doctor, "I'll get to it."

One day a very nervous man called at Dr. Dixon's office. The man stood beside the dentist chair, awaiting for the order to sit down. This procedure took some time, as Dr. Dixon was busy sterilizing some instruments and arranging numerous knives and other weapons on the little glass tray that overhangs the chair. As Doc was fumbling with the business end of the drill, attaching a rougher and tougher disc to the stem, he heard a whimper and then a sharp cry. Turning to the man, Doc said, "What's the matter, Pete? Not yet in the dental chair and already you're sobbing. Does it hurt that much?"

The man looked up at Dr. Dixon, tears streaming down his face which was suffused with anguish and moaned: "It's not my tooth. It's my bunion! You're stepping on it!"

Ladies and gentlemen, Dr. Walter Dixon.

—Paul C. Winthrop

INTRODUCING A LAWYER

Ladies and gentlemen, you have a treat in store for you tonight. You are going to hear a talk by a lawyer, a man who has something to say and who knows how to say it. Now, you all know how lawyers talk. Usually if they can use twenty words where one would answer the purpose, they'll use the twenty.

I said to a lawyer once: "I believe we're going to get some rain. What do you think?" He frowned, pursed his lips, looked up at the sky, sniffed the air, scratched his chin, and reflected a couple of minutes—then he cleared his throat and said—"Hmm. After giving the matter considerable thought and studying the evidence—that is, the condition of the atmosphere, the color of the sky, and various other natural phenomena, I would be inclined at the moment to answer in the negative—that is, provided that other circumstances do not arise which might possibly—and I say that advisedly—which might possibly cause me to alter or revise my previous opinion and compel me to give an affirmative answer—of course, unless there is a radical change which might force me to adhere to my original contention, in which case I will stand on my constitutional rights and state that you might be right and you might be wrong, but I don't think so."

Now, the gentleman you are about to hear is a lawyer—one of the best—but he has promised me that instead of using twenty words in the place of one, he will use only ten words in the place of one. Ladies and gentlemen, may I present a most distinguished member of the legal profession? Mr. ——— ———.

—Earl Jay Gilbert

INTRODUCING A PHYSICIAN

Difficult is the life of a doctor—up at all hours of the night, administering to the sick, mending the wounded and listening to the complaints of women who are everlastingly discovering something the matter with them. In addition to these troublesome assignments, the doctor is obliged, occasionally, to get out of some tight spots with a patient, as Dr. Walter Cox, our community's eminent physician, would tell you when I call upon him to speak in just a few moments.

About six months ago a patient called at Doctor Cox's office and asserted that he was suffering from insomnia of such a degree that he was awake the whole night through, and that only in the dawning hours of the morning, when he should be getting up, did he fall asleep. Dr. Cox, after a complete examination, said: "My good fellow, run along home, and don't take any food before you go to bed tonight. Follow my instructions and you will sleep like a kitten."

Yesterday the same man appeared at the doctor's office. After Doctor Cox had stripped off the fellow's shirt, thumped his chest and looked down his throat, he said, "What's the matter with you?"

"My insomnia is so bad, I can't even sleep in the waking hours of the morning," exclaimed the patient.

"Umhum!" sighed Doctor Cox, taking a peep in the fellow's eyeball. "You do have wide-awake eyes," the doctor continued. "I see no wearing on the lids. It looks like they hadn't been closed for six months."

"You said it," said the patient.

"Well, well," remarked Doctor Cox, "I'll tell you what you do, my boy. Run along home now, and then just before you go to bed, eat a great big steak. That'll fix you up. You'll sleep like a kitten."

"But, Doctor," said the patient. "When I was here six months ago, you told me not to eat a thing before going to bed."

"I did, did I?" said Doctor Cox.

"You certainly did," answered the patient.

Doctor Cox thought the matter over for a moment, and then slapping the patient on the back said, "Young fellow, that was six months ago. Science has made tremendous headway in the past six months. Next patient!"

Ladies and gentlemen, Dr. Walter Cox.

—Stephen Keller

INTRODUCING A BEAUTY EXPERT

Girls, this is for you. A talk by one of our most prominent beauty experts is on the slate for today. By the way, did you know that there is a big race on between the Government and you girls? Which spends the most money, the Government for gun powder or you girls on face powder? In other words, some powder goes off with a bang; some powder goes on with a puff.

I, for one, consider the American women the most beautiful in the world. However, there are some old-timers who contend that women paint what they used to be. Historians say that women used cosmetics in the Middle Ages. Women still use cosmetics in the middle ages. It used to be that lipstick and flypaper were much alike—they would catch the careless creatures that paused to investigate.

Now the cosmetic engineers are feverishly working on waterproof cosmetics. Until then women can do nothing but laugh, because laugh and the world laughs with you, cry and you streak your rouge. Every cosmetic dealer knows that woman's face is his fortune. I had an aunt who smeared mud all over her face to make her beautiful. Then she wouldn't take the mud off. She discovered she looked better with it on.

Tell me, pretty maiden, what makes your cheeks so red?

'Cause.

'Cause why?

'Cause-metics.

Ladies and gentlemen—or should I leave out the gentlemen? Ladies, I take pleasure in presenting our beautiful guest, (name).

—Arthur L. Kaser

INTRODUCING A CATHOLIC PRIEST

Ladies and gentlemen, tonight we're going to have the pleasure of hearing a man of the cloth—a Catholic priest, who has an interesting and important message to deliver. You know, sometimes we encounter a man who impresses us with his sincerity, his humility, his devout faith, his belief in the ultimate goodness of humanity—a man who can find some good in every human being, regardless of errors and mistakes that human beings can make. That is the kind of man you are going to hear tonight—the type of man who gives us renewed faith and courage in ourselves, at times when we most need it.

Recently I was having a friendly conversation with a priest —and somehow or other I usually feel a little embarrassed when I'm talking to a priest. It's probably because I stand in a little awe of these men who forsake all the pleasures of earthly existence in order to minister to the spiritual welfare of the rest of us. Maybe it's because my spiritual welfare needs taking care of. I realize that applies only to me—not to any one of you.

However, this priest told me a story which I enjoyed and I'm going to pass it on to you. It seems a Protestant minister died and went to Heaven. St. Peter gave the minister a little house and a Ford car. Shortly after this a Catholic priest died and went to Heaven. St. Peter gave the priest a bigger house and a Buick. The minister said to St. Peter: "Look here— don't I rate as much as the priest? Why should he get a bigger house than mine and a Buick, while I've only got a Ford?" St. Peter said: "In his life he made many sacrifices for his religion. He went without many of the ordinary pleasures of life which you had, and I feel that he's entitled to a little more up here because of that." A rabbi died and went to Heaven. St. Peter gave the rabbi a beautiful mansion with a swimming pool and two Cadillacs. The minister and the priest went to St. Peter and asked what caused the favoritism. St. Peter looked around, lowered his voice, and said: "Sh—! He's one of the boss' relatives!"

Now, if there's a moral to this story I suppose it's that it pays to have influence in high places, in this world or the next. Speaking of influence, while the good Father who is going to address us cannot guarantee how much influence he has upstairs, I know that he'll use what influence he possesses to do what he can for all of us. Ladies and gentlemen, the Reverend Father . . . . . Thank you.

—Earl Jay Gilbert

INTRODUCING A SHOE MERCHANT

There is probably no man of business who is a better connoisseur of a lady's ankle than a shoe merchant. In that respect, Gene Richter, our next speaker, is no exception. Perhaps half of the ladies in town visit Gene's shoe store for fittings in the latest of milady's footwear; and perhaps, the other half go to Joe Dudley's shoe store across the street.

One afternoon Gene was looking out of the window of his store, when he noticed a very beautiful and vivacious young lady walking hastily across the street. As Gene was following her movements with an eagle eye, the girl suddenly slipped and fell to the pavement. Gene, gallant man that he is, rushed out of the door and assisted the prostrate young woman to her feet. When he discovered that she couldn't stand, he carefully picked her up, placing one arm under her armpits and the other under the bend of her knees. It was while Gene was holding the girl in this position that his eyes scrutinized her ankles, one of which was swollen from the fall, but the other still had its natural and graceful contour.

"I don't believe that I have fitted you," Gene said with a professional air, his eyes still focused on the girl's good ankle.

"No, you haven't," answered the young lady. "I was just on my way to Mr. Dudley's for a pair of new pumps. Would you mind carrying me over there?"

Ladies and gentlemen, Mr. Gene Richter.

—Anthony C. Gregory

INTRODUCING A BAND OR ORCHESTRA LEADER

It is my pleasure this evening to present to you one of the finest band leaders in this section of the country. You have all heard his music, which I am sure has been delightful to your ears. Many of you have danced to the lilting tunes played by his famous band; and most of you have listened to his charming voice over the radio and television waves. But how many of you have heard him make a speech? If you haven't, you are going to hear him tonight.

But first permit me to say a few kind words about Terry Martin. It is a sad thing, but there are musicians who are stingy, cranky and unaccommodating. When you ask that kind of a musician to play a tune that you like, he usually gives you a blank stare, just as much as to say, "Who does that guy think he is, asking me to limber up my horn on some tune just because he fell in love with a girl in a canoe the year the tune was written?"

And then again when you ask another musician to play "Silver Threads Are Appearing," he says, "Pipe down, we got Bebop on the schedule for the next six numbers." When Tony Trombardo comes to town, you say to yourself, "Well, this fellow ought to play a few of my favorites." So you go up to Mr. Trombardo (You call him Mister because he is a little older) and say, "Mr. Trombardo, how about a little Dixieland?" "Dixieland!" shouts Mr. Trombardo, "that stuff doesn't flow, it's stuck to the molasses barrels down in New Orleans." Then Mr. Trombardo adds, snearing-like: "I just bought a new horn and I don't want to desecrate it with that kind of trash!" So you give up and listen to the ten top tunes reported last month by "Jukebox Digest."

But as I was saying, Terry Martin is different. He's the most accommodating person in the music business. Ask him to play any old tune and you'll get it; and you'll get it with a smile. Why, just last week Terry and his band were holding a jam session in the Blackstone Apartments. It was two-thirty in the morning and all other tenants in the apartment building work days, so they sleep nights. At that jam session the music was sweet but sort of crescendo tinged with a little fortissimo, which disturbed the caretaker who knocked on the apartment door and said to Terry as he opened it: "Do you fellows know there's a sick lady upstairs?"

"No," said Terry, placing his instrument in playing position. "How does it go?"

Ladies and gentlemen, Mr. Terry Martin.

—Sylvester McGovern

INTRODUCING A SMALL TOWN NEWSPAPER PUBLISHER

There is probably no more all-around man than a newspaper publisher in a small town. He writes his news stories and sets them in type. He sells his advertising and subscriptions and collects for them himself—if he can. If he can't, he will take the amount of the bill out in kind.

We are fortunate in having with us at this time Mr. John Jackson, publisher of the Times. John has recorded every birth, every death and every auction sale in this community for the past twenty-five years, as well as every circus and carnival that ever hit this town.

Speaking of a carnival, I am reminded that a few years ago when one of those carnivals was going full blast here in Centerville, I happened to stroll down to the seat of the jollity to absorb some of that shrieking colliope music that is always associated with a carnival. When I was in proximity with the merry-go-round, a lady, who evidently was a stranger here, called out to me and said: "Who's that man astride the giraffe? He's been riding the merry-go-round all day long."

By that time the contrivance had circled, and the giraffe was on the other side of the circle. Then when the giraffe appeared again, I saw a man sitting in the animal's saddle, his legs dangling from the stirrups and his hands hanging on to the giraffe's neck. "Why, that man," I said to the lady, "is John Jackson, publisher of the Times. He's taking an advertising bill out in trade."

Ladies and gentlemen, Mr. John Jackson.

—Rome Roberts

INTRODUCING AN ENGINEER

It is quite significant that the complexion of gatherings of this nature have undergone drastic changes during the past few years. As an habitual attendant at banquets and dinners, this change to me has been very pronounced. Tonight we are going to hear from an engineer, Mr. James Fulton. There was a time, not too far in the past, when it would have been difficult for Mr. Fulton to get up to this head table, as previously the only qualifications required were a good appetite and the ability to tell a funny story. In those good old days a comic would stand up and munch a left-over olive that had escaped the waiter's eye, and a gentle twitter would sweep across the room before the comic had said a word. Then when he threw the olive stone on the floor and said: "Have you heard the story about the traveling salesman down in Memphis who .," a roar swept across the room like a cyclone, and everyone slapped each other's legs in glee. And after the story was told, the guests tore up the table cloth in paroxysms of jocularity.

Today we have switched to the engineer as an after-dinner speaker. An engineer gets up and says: "Do you gentlemen know that there are twenty millions of tons of concrete in the Golden State Bridge, and that forty millions of tons and a fraction thereof of steel wire are meshed in that vast amount of concrete?" Immediately you think of Bugs Horan meshed in a barrel of concrete on the bottom of the Hudson River. Then you begin getting statistical yourself. You wonder how many years will have to pass before that barrel of concrete will burst open and Bugs Horan will bubble to the surface. While you are trying to figure this Bugs Horan thing out, you cock an ear and you hear a fresh stream of astronomical figures about the Alaska Spillway flowing from the speaker's lips. Not having any thought association with the Alaskan Spillway, you reach out for a stalk of celery, and while munching you contemplate on the yardage of celery consumed here this evening. Could it be ten yards, fifty yards or a hundred yards?

Not being an engineer, you have no way of knowing.

Recently I was talking about this serious situation with a professor of history. When I told the professor that some sort of a movement should be started that would put a stop to this engineering invasion of banquets, he said, "Think nothing of it. The world moves in cycles, and we're in for just such a statistical cycle now. Why, the same thing took place way back in King Tut's time."

"King Tut's time!" I exclaimed.

"Yes, King Tut's time," he repeated. "In the early days of King Tut's reign," continued the professor, "feasting of all descriptions was a nightly affair. At those sumptuous repasts dancing girls and jesters were the only persons permitted near the speaker's table. An engineer was unheard of, until one day along came a fellow with a slide-rule and a book of logarithms who thought up a pyramid. King Tut was so impressed with the pyramid that he issued an edict banning all jesters, jokesters and story-tellers from banquets and substituting engineers instead. From then on if an Egyptian dared tell a funny story to more than two persons he would be cleft asunder with the biggest cleaver in the Empire. That edict of King Tut's brought forth the greatest engineering dynasty of ancient times. Those early Egyptians were so imbued with figures and statistics that every schoolboy in King Tut's empire could recite the number of grains of sand used to construct a pyramid and the number of camels required to haul it.

"That was a sad affair," I said.

"Very sad, indeed," the professor answered, pulling on his beard.

"How long will this present statistical cycle of ours last?" I asked of the professor.

"I don't know," he answered. "There are so many different kinds of engineers now and they are pretty well entrenched. It might take another ice age to wipe them out."

"It looks bad," I said.

"Very bad, indeed," the professor replied, adding, "Do you know these engineers are branching out?"

"I knew that they had branched out, but I didn't know they were still branching," I said.

"They're still branching," affirmed the professor. "Why, there's an engineer down in New York who is working on a gadget to replace humorous after-dinner speakers like yourself."

"He is, is he?" I asked.

"He certainly is," said the professor, "and he hasn't slept for three months, so intensified is he on perfecting his device."

"That's the trouble with those engineers," I said. "They never sleep. What kind of a device is it?"

"Well, from what I can learn from the information that has come my way," said the professor, stroking his beard, "it's some sort of an electronic contraption that sends out waves that tickle the nervous system of the recipient, making him laugh. This engineer claims that once his machine is perfected all chairs at the speaker's table will be vacant, with the exception of just one, and that will be occupied by an engineer who will operate the device. When a small laugh is needed the engineer will push gently upon a button and the waves will go out, effecting a slight giggle on the part of all present. When a real roar is required, the engineer will give one long sustained push on the button. Then pandemonium will break loose, stirring up what is often referred to as belly-laughs."

"That sounds like bad news in the wind," I said.

"Very bad, indeed," the professor replied. "The inventor claims the entire procedure of a banquet will be revolutionized. Sad faces will immediately be livened up upon arrival at the banquet hall. The engineer will cautiously watch the door, and when he sees a couple of sourpusses approaching, he will give them a few jolts so that they will enter the hall laughing like hyenas. Then the engineer will look around the room for any grouches who are grumbling about the price of the dinner. There will be no waiting until after the dessert for laughs. The laughs will commence immediately upon serving the soup and will continue until the last spoonful of ice cream has disappeared."

"This looks like the end of Berle and Godfrey," I said.

"It's their end," affirmed the professor. "And it will be the end of your avocation, too. My good fellow, you had better look for a new one," the professor added and then turned and walked briskly down the street, swinging his cane.

I am going to take the professor's advice right now. I am going to give you an engineer. Ladies and gentlemen, I give you Mr. James Fulton of the American Society of Engineers. Mr. Fulton.

—Sylvester McGovern

INTRODUCING A FATHER'S DAY SPEAKER

It has become a good American custom to set aside days on which to honor persons, and weeks to devote to certain activities. Thus we have Fire-Prevention Week; Be Kind to Animals Week; Pay Your Debts Week; Children's Day, and Mother's Day.

And, after a while, they got around to having Father's Day. It seemed that Father was about to become the forgotten man, but once the idea of Father's Day was suggested, it took hold, and really went over with a bang. The idea was commercialized, of course, and now we are advised to "buy Father a new shirt, a new tie, a pair of socks," and many other kinds of haberdashery he may not care for. "Father needs a fountain pen; he ought to have an easy chair; a book and a pipe; fishing tackle, golf clubs"—and I suppose the next thing will be a motor boat.

And how has Father taken this? Oh, in his stride, as he usually does, but I think deep down in his heart he has been quite pleased that there has been a day set aside for him known as Father's Day. We are honoring Father tonight, and as we do so, we also honor his priceless companion—his son. Now we are going to hear a tribute to Father from ————.

—Helen Ramsey

INTRODUCING A PROFESSOR

Ladies and gentlemen, tonight we are going to hear from a man who has many accomplishments in the field of education. Not only does he know things but he also knows how to express his knowledge, and that's a gift in itself—the ability to express your thoughts, clearly and concisely, to teach, to impart your knowledge to others. Sometimes I think teaching is the least appreciated of the professions.

That reminds me—I had a teacher once. You may not believe it, but I did. He was not only a professor of English, but he had a deep grasp of the sciences and arts. He could explain the Einstein theory of relativity so clearly that he left you more confused than ever. Of course nobody knew what he was talking about but you had to admire and respect his knowledge of the subject. And when it came to art and culture—he was a whiz! He could tell you who painted Michael Angelo's pictures—who wrote Longfellow's poems—you know, high class stuff. Everybody gave him credit for having more brains than anybody else on the faculty and to prove it, he never, if he could help it, used a word that was less than four syllables long.

Well, one day his ten-year-old daughter brought another ten-year-old home with her and introduced her. She said, "This is my father. He is the smartest man in the world. He knows everything." "Gee!" said the other little girl. "Can you write good English?" "Certainly," said the professor. "Have you got time to show me?" asked the child. "All the time in the world," he said. "Give me a sentence that is phrased in correct grammatical English and I'll write it for you." "Okay," said the child. "Here goes. 'There are three too's (two's, to's, too's) in the English language'."

The professor put on his glasses, took out his pen, got a sheet of paper and started to write. Then he took off his glasses, put down his pen, and said, "You children run along and play. I'm a very busy man."

Later that night, after deep meditation and much mental research, he composed and wrote a treatise entitled "There ain't no such thing," in which he proved, incontrovertably, that the female race is a very disturbing and distracting influence, and should be nullified by due course of law. For years he's been trying to sell this treatise to the trustees of Harvard University for use as a textbook for general study. Last reports indicate he has encountered dubious success.

Now while the learned gentleman who is going to address you tonight might not be able to write "There are three too's in the English language," it's pretty hard to stump him on anything else, particularly on the subject of —————. My friends, I am happy to have the opportunity to present to you our distinguished guest, Professor —————.

—Earl Jay Gilbert

INTRODUCING A SPEAKER AT A SUNDAY SCHOOL BANQUET

The world is full of men and women who recognize the need of something to be done; conditions to be improved; ideals to be furthered; people to be helped.

The first question they ask is: "What can I do?" If they are at all analytical, they will ask: "Why should I do it?" and then, "Where is **my** field of activity and when can I give this help?"

Because there have been many sincere people who have asked themselves these questions, the present-day Sunday School has been evolved. The world, we are told, moves forward on the feet of little children. Perhaps this thought occurred to Robert Raikes when he saw small boys and girls playing noisily and even fighting in the streets of an English city one Sunday morning many years ago. Just how this great leader of the Sunday School movement went about the process of organization makes an interesting and inspiring story. I have asked ————— to tell us something about Robert Raikes and the first Sunday School.

—Helen Ramsey

INTRODUCING A BANKER

Friends, we all are interested in money and tonight we are going to hear a man speak who knows a lot about the subject. All I know about money is that once I got a quick glance at some as it passed through my hands on a triple play—from my boss, to me, to the Internal Revenue Department.

Which reminds me—I got a card once from a bank asking me to "Be Thrifty! Save your money! We'll invest it for you! Look at the men who started with a few dollars and now have millions!" I looked, but I didn't even see anybody who had one million.

Anyhow, I thought it was a bright idea, so I started to save —I scrimped—I scraped—I went without Cadillac cars—I stopped smoking two-dollar cigars—I gave up champagne and caviar for breakfast—and at the end of the first year I had ONE HUNDRED AND TEN DOLLARS saved up.

So I went into a food store and got a pound of coffee and three lamb chops. I paid the guy with a personal check for $8.00. The check bounced. I phoned the cashier of my bank and I said, "Look here. I just cashed a check for $8.00 and it came back marked 'Insufficient Funds.' What's the matter with you people? I've got a hundred and ten dollars in your bank!" The cashier said, "Listen, friend, just because your check for $8.00 came back marked 'Insufficient Funds'—that doesn't necessarily mean **you** got insufficient funds—it could also mean the **bank's** got insufficient funds!" Of course, that happened back in the days before bank deposits were guaranteed by the Federal Government.

Since then I've learned to love bankers. I'm seriously considering starting a "Be Nice to Bankers" week. Always be nice to bankers. You never know when you'll need a friend. Oh, did I tell you it's a banker who's going to speak tonight?

By the way, if any of you are figuring on making a little touch, don't ask him tonight. He doesn't carry it with him. Besides, I saw him first. My friends, I take great pleasure in presenting to you, Mr. ———— ———— of the ———————— Bank.

—Earl Jay Gilbert

INTRODUCING A DOCTOR

There are many humorous happenings in a doctor's career as well as many serious ones. The doctor who will speak here this evening related to me some of the laughable things that has occurred to him. For example. A man came into his office and asked for an examination. After going over the man thoroughly the doctor said, "I can find nothing wrong with you of any consequence. It seems to be all in your mind. I would say, offhand, it is due to drinking too much." The patient shook his head understandingly, and said, "Maybe I'd better come back when you're sober."

One night this same doctor was detained at the hospital. Tiptoeing through the children's ward he saw an open box of chocolates near one of the beds, and helped himself to one piece. The next day as he entered the ward a small boy's voice rang out, "There he is, Mom! There's the doctor who swiped my candy!"

Not long ago as a patient was leaving the doctor's office the doctor said, "Just do as I say and you will be another man." "Fine," said the patient. "Just send the bill to the other man." The doctor told another patient that he was going to give him some castor oil but he would mix it with orange juice so he wouldn't taste it. "Good," said the patient. "I don't like orange juice."

A patient called the doctor by phone. "Doc, I took that cough medicine prescription to the drugstore and had it filled, but I'm not going to take it." "Why not?" asked the doctor. "Because," said the patient, "it's marked on the bottle for adults. I got a sore throat. I never had the adults in my life." And then there was the girl from Georgia who asked the doctor that if she had her tonsils removed would she lose her Southern accent.

Ladies and gentlemen, permit me to introduce our speaker, Dr. (name).   —Arthur L. Kaser

INTRODUCING AN INSURANCE SALESMAN

Just about everybody carries insurance, and it's a good thing. Insurance gives one a feeling of security. Did you ever read a policy all the way through? It's interesting. Beautiful words and phrases, but no plot.

There is a family not far from where I live that is somewhat lax about insurance. There are nine in the family but only the father carries any insurance. It isn't quite fair to the others for he is the only one that dares go swimming. All professional dancers have their legs insured. This, however, is nothing but pin money.

A Mrs. Winters, whose husband passed away last month, told me that she is going to take out some insurance on herself because her late husband had such good luck with his.

There are all kinds of insurance, life, accident, wind, flood, fire—Yeah, fire. I was told by an insurance man that many fires are caused by friction—rubbing a ten-thousand-dollar insurance policy on a seven-thousand-dollar house.

Insurance policies are more or less difficult to understand. Some people cannot understand them at all. Take for instance, the Finleys down in Missouri. Mr. Finley took out some life insurance on himself. I think it was two thousand dollars. Premiums were paid promptly for several years, and then suddenly stopped. The company sent a number of delinquent notices, and finally received a letter which read: "We have been sorry account we can't pay no more to you account Mr. Finley died last November. Mrs. Finley."

I know one man who made an appointment with nine insurance salesmen. He wanted to insure his cat. That sounds foolish. I don't know whether to believe it or not, as I don't know much about insurance. However, we have with us this evening a man who does know insurance from A to Z, Mr. (name.)
                                                      —Arthur L. Kaser

INTRODUCING A SPEAKER ON NURSE'S TRAINING

Our country is urgently in need of more and more trained nurses. There is hardly a hospital of major size in the United States that could not use more nurses. And where can one find a more honorable and humanitarian profession?

We should feel gratified to have with us this evening one of these girls who is giving all her spare time recruiting girls for nurse's training. Many amusing stories are told of beginning nurses as well as those who have been in the profession a long time. A young nurse who had just begun her training approached the doctor with "Doctor, about that local anesthetic you wanted. I couldn't find a local one but I found one made in Rochester."

Not long ago a nurse's suggestion box was placed in a midwest hospital, and the nurses were requested to drop in any idea they might have that would better the routine and prove beneficial to the patients. One nurse suggested sleeping pills of various colors for the patients so their dreams would be in Technicolor.

A nurse friend of mine who works in the local hospital told me about two soldier patients confined there. They wanted to play cards but had no playing cards. One of the boys called the nurse. "What are those cards in that box?" She explained that they were filing cards that listed the condition of the patient's progress, of his case history and so on. "Good," said the youth. "Give us fifty-two of them. We'll use 'em for playing cards." The boys started a poker game. When the pot got pretty full it was time for a show-down. The first youth spread out his cards. "There," he said. "Full house. Three appendectomies and two oxygen tents." "Got you beat," said the other lad. "Five transfusions." Ladies and gentlemen, especially the ladies, it is my pleasure to present to you a wonderful nurse, Miss or Mrs. (name).   —Arthur L. Kaser

INTRODUCING A PROFESSOR

I have the honor of introducing a man of letters—a professor, if you please. Education is a fine thing. And so broadening. It makes it possible for you to worry about things all over the world.

Looking back, I have warm memories of my early school days. **(Cast a fleeting look backward toward the seat of your pants).** I can't sit on those memories.

The educators of my time thought the best Board of Education was a shingle. To them a boy was like a canoe—he behaved better when paddled from the rear. As for their idea of encouragement, they believed a pat on the back did a lot of good—if given often enough, hard enough, and low enough.

Yes, their motto was the well-known "spare the rod and spoil the child." In that case, I was the most unspoiled kid in school!

Anyway, I felt that way. I made so many visits to the woodshed they were thinking of creosoting me. What good would that have done, the way they kept whaling the creosote out of me! I don't know exactly what kind of end they had in view—but they sure kept it in view!

I'd ask, sometimes, on my trips to the woodshed: "Is this trip necessary?" They'd answer: "Yes, it's to impress what's right, on your mind." I'd say: "You have a strange idea of the location of my mind." . . . I got it in the end.

Well, maybe I wasn't a very bright student. I did spend two whole terms in one class. You know, I was telling someone of that remarkable record—two whole terms in the same class. He answered: "Pardon me, but that wasn't so very unusual. A lot of people have spent two whole terms in one class." I answered: "The terms of Coolidge and Hoover?"

I was in the same class so long they took me to be the teacher.

On promotion day I came home, and my dad who was an actor—yes, he was in the theatre—would ask: "Well, son, tell me, were you duly promoted?"

I'd reply cautiously: "Well, Dad, I'll tell you. It's this way —I was so good they're holding me over for another 26 weeks."

Oh, they tried everything with me. They'd sit me with the girls. But just when I got old enough to appreciate that, they quit it.

Looks like all I ever got out of grade school was myself. And I was almost grayed, too, when I got out.

It still looks to me they taught things the hard way in those days. Nowadays, it seems, a youth picks up his arithmetic from the dial phone. Or the football field . . . Gained two yards on second down; makes four, with six to go in two more downs. And Anatomy he gets from the rumble seat— but I won't go into that. . . . Call it Research . . . Experiment Lab . . . I don't know.

Ask a kid these days to show you how high he can count. You get: "One-two-three-four-five-six-seven-eight-nine-ten-Jack, Queen, King."

My father wanted me to have the opportunities he never had. So he sent me to Wellesley.

They told me there: "This school is for girls."

I said: "That's fine. So am I!"

Anyway, I couldn't pass the physical, or something. So I ended up by going to a college that had no girls at all . . . It was called Not-a-Dame—or something.

College, dear old college! Someone has defined it as "a four-year loaf requiring a great deal of dough as well as plenty of crust." Then you're supposed to be college bred.

Don't get me wrong. An education can be of much use to a man. In lots of ways. For one thing, you learn to use big words, don't you? That certainly can be helpful—besides confusing the other fellow, which is always a lot of fun.

I jokingly rebuked my negro janitor, Julius, one day for his fondness of using big words.

Said I: "How come you're so fond of using big words, Julius?"

"Well," said he. "A friend ob mine once saved his life by using a big word."

"Come now, Julius," said I. "How could that be?"

"It's a fac', suh. This fella called me a prevaricator. Ef he had called me a liar, I'd have gone fo' him at once; but by de time Ah looked it up in de dictionary to see whut it meant, he wuz blocks away."

Yes, education is a splendid thing, don't forget that. Take arithmetic, for instance. Through education we learn that two twos are four, that four fours are eight; that eight eights are— and then there's geography.

Hm! Ever know of a talk about professors going this far without any story about an absent-minded one? It's incredible! Unheard of! And so, before you faint, and just before I introduce our estimable guest, which I'll do in a moment, here's one about a Hollywood professor named Glickkatz.

This fellow had taken home a briefcase full of examination papers to correct and grade, and worked far into the night with them in the privacy of his den. Then, eyes blood-shot, and head woozy with the hours-long concentration of his thought, he stumbled into his bedroom, and absently began removing his trousers. When, what does he see, there in his big luxurious double bed, but a pretty female reading a book and calmly smoking a cigaret.

"Miss," said he, sternly. "I've had a very hard day, and I'm in no mood for any nonsense. If this is a joke, then it isn't funny. And, er, if you have anything else in mind—I'll have you know I'm a respectable man, as well as very tired. So will you have the goodness, Miss, to get into your things, and get out of this bed, out of this room, out of this house; best of all, out of this neighborhood? And give me the chance to get my night's sleep, alone!"

So she answered: "Are you through? Then may I tell you it isn't 'Miss,' but Mrs. And I **like** this neighborhood; and I **like** this house; and I **like** this bed; and I'm going to remain in it all night, with YOU—because I'm your wife—of three days—you silly, absent-minded jerk!" . . . . I'll introduce our professor, ——————   —George A. Posner

INTRODUCING A PSYCHIATRIST

Do you sometimes feel that you are not all there? Do you have a sneaking feeling that you are off the beam? Or are you positive that you are plain crazy? Do not worry. Try this simple test. If you think you are crazy, then you are not. But if you think everyone else is crazy, then you are.

We are going to hear from a well-known psychiatrist in just a moment. I had occasion not long ago to call on a man living on the outskirts of town. I had heard that sometimes he did some queer things. When I entered the house I was nearly tipped backwards by a terrible stench. He saw my look of amazement and said, "It's them goats I keep in the living room." "My land," I said, "Why don't you open the doors and windows?" "What?" he almost shrieked, "and let all my pigeons out?"

A few years ago I was a member of a committee visiting a mental institution. Two adjacent wards house two cases of delusions of grandeur. As we passed the first one the inmate said to us proudly, "I am the king of the South Pole." I said to him, "What makes you think you are the king of the South Pole?" He said, "God told me." The patient in the other ward said, "I did not."

A psychiatrist in the building told us of an amusing thing that happened. A patient was getting ready to leave the institution after five years there. He had his best clothes laid out and was preparing to shave. As he raised his razor a nurse passed down the hall and called pleasantly, "Good luck, Charlie." As Charlie turned to answer her his razor accidentally cut the string that supported the mirror and it dropped to the floor. The patient, turning around, was now gazing at the bare wall. "What do you know!" he murmured. "Just my luck. Here I am ready to leave after five years and I cut my head off." Ladies and gentlemen, Dr. (name).

—Arthur L. Kaser

ADDITIONAL MATERIAL

There was an actor who came into the office of a psychiatrist and said: "My worries are financial. Now tell me what's the first thing I'm to do."

The psychiatrist said: "First thing you do is pay me $500 in advance."

"$500!" screamed the actor. "How is that going to solve anyone's financial troubles?"

"It will mine and my landlord's," returned the psychiatrist. It's all also a matter of a point of view, eh?

An old maid, well over 50, was telling a psychiatrist of the strange dream which kept recurring to her.

"Nearly every night, lately, there is a big strapping man in my dreams who comes out after me suddenly from the dark shadows. It makes me jump like a startled deer, and I run and run as fast as I can until I escape."

"Yes?" said the psychiatrist.

"What I want to find out is, what can you do to slow down my reflexes, so he can catch me? I'm tired of escaping."

Dean Martin and Jerry Lewis were talking of psychiatry, and the influence of the mind on the body.

Said Jerry: "Gosh, one night I had a vivid dream—that some one had shot me. When I awoke I screamed! In the mirror I saw there was a big hole in my head!"

"Gosh," said Dean, "go on! What happened?"

"But you know," continued Jerry, "it went away when I closed my mouth!"

"Come, now, come," said the psychiatrist to his tearful patient. "You must cheer up. Be happy!"

"Be happy, he tells me yet," she answered. "Twelve children I've borne that husband of mine, and—and—he doesn't love me. What have I to be happy about, I ask you?"

Said the psychiatrist: "Imagine if he did love you."

There are different ways of looking at things, eh?

—George A. Posner

INTRODUCING A WRITER

Ladies and gentlemen, it is my distinct pleasure to introduce our speaker of the evening. I do this with a certain amount of reserve because of his ability in his own field. As a writer he has a better use of words than I. Therefore, I am forced to choose my syllables with great care lest he detect something wrong in them.

Our speaker, ladies and gentlemen, started life as a baby. Even then his writing ability was pronounced. He couldn't pronounce it but his mother could. She did it by slapping his fingers when he wrote on the walls with a crayon.

His writing in grade school was also outstanding. So much so, ladies and gentlemen, that even he couldn't read it. Not because of its depth but because of poor penmanship. He never had much success with his writing until he wrote a bad check. That got his name on the front page and he continued to soar upward.

As a writer he is a keen observer. He had never seen the Atlantic Ocean but he knew there was water in it. He arrived at this conclusion because he knew an ocean steamer needed water. Just that kind of thinking is needed in his field. His work has appeared under many covers. The cover of night, the cover of the trash can. It is said that the paper on which his writing appears is better for wrapping articles than any other kind. So buy some of his work; you might want to wrap something someday.

He knows we're just doing this to be annoying. He also knows that we admire his work and that we admire him. And so will you when you hear his words this evening. May I present Mr. —————?   —Louis J. Huber

INTRODUCING A TOP SALESMAN

We have with us this evening a top salesman. I do not mean by that that he sells tops just because he spins around the country a lot. He is not here this evening to sell anything but good advice and information. He is here to speak on salesmanship and what it means to business.

I do not vouch for this but I am told that this particular salesman is so good he can sell shoes to a footstool. He started out by being a house to house salesman, and bases his early success on his opening line when the lady of the house opened the door. He would say, "Is your mother in, little girl?"

Traveling salesmen are different. You can always spot a traveling salesman by the bags—under his eyes. Then there is the independent salesman who takes orders from no one. My brother was a live-wire salesman. He sold live wires. About the only orders he ever got were from his wife when he left home in the mornings. But the high-pressure salesman! Wow! The person who can withstand the high-pressure salesman really illustrates the power over patter.

Getting orders from some people is like pulling teeth. You have to give them a lot of gas. A department store hired my nephew. He had no sales experience, but he was capable. A middle-aged lady came into the store and asked to see some tablecloths. He quickly laid some out on the counter. She didn't like any of them. He laid out some others. They didn't suit her either. This was repeated a number of times without making a sale. Finally he told her that a new shipment had just arrived, the latest in design. He spread out a mediocre cloth. She looked at it a moment and said she could see nothing new about it. Then my nephew explained. "My dear lady, if you will look closely you will see that the edge of the cloth runs right around the border, and the center is in the middle." She bought two. Ladies and gentlemen, allow me to introduce our top salesman, Mr. (name.)

—Arthur L. Kaser

INTRODUCING A SPEAKER ON SOCIAL REFORM

As I entered the hall this evening a bright-faced young boy handed me this slip of paper and I'm going to hand the contents on to you. It says: The baby ear of corn said to the mama ear of corn, "Mommy, I want to ask you something." Mama ear of corn said, "Go ahead, Junior, I'm all ears." Her voice was husky. "Mommy," said little Junior corn, "where did I come from?" Mama said, "A stalk brought you." Junior corn was satisfied and went to sleep in his little corn crib. Popcorn should have heard it, but he was in the army. He was a kernel. Cute, wasn't it?

We are going to hear a talk this evening on social reform and I will introduce a very able speaker in a few minutes. The fundamentals of social reform may be found in every village, town or city if the searcher for the truth is observing, and to be observing is the duty of every loyal citizen. Observation should be taught in every school from the kindergarten on up through oo-la-la cum laude. A few days ago I had the pleasure of visiting the second grade in the school near my home to observe how my small nephew Omar was getting along.

While there the school superintendent dropped in. He asked the teacher if she stressed the importance of observation. "Oh, yes," said the teacher. "Then," said the superintendent, "I'd like to test the class. Now, children, I want you to close your eyes and sit very still and listen carefully." Then he made a slow "Tsh! tsh!" sound with his tongue against his teeth. "Now, children, what did you hear?" Quick as a flash little Omar piped up, "Heard you kissin' teacher." So you see, my friends, what an important thing observation is, especially when we are interested in social reform. Personally, I don't see any connection between kissing the teacher and social reform. And, now ladies and gentlemen, our speaker (name of speaker.)   —Arthur L. Kaser

INTRODUCING A BANKER

My friends, before we proceed with tonight's business, I have a question to ask you. If there is anybody here tonight who doesn't like money, will he please stand up? Don't all get up at once. We'll overload the bus for the crazy house. I'm glad to see there are no silly people here tonight.

(If one person rises, use the following line)

One man here who doesn't like money. I'd like to have your autographed picture to send to Bob Ripley.

The reason I asked is that we're going to hear a man tonight who handles money by the ton. Yes, my friends, he's a banker. One of those guys who has nothing to do but count money. He's really got a tough job. He has to swim in dough from ten o'clock in the morning until three in the afternoon—with only an hour and a half off for lunch.

Did you ever see one of those signs in front of a bank? "We loan money. Any amount. Welcome." So you get a bushel basket and go in. You stand around for an hour or so and finally get in to see the head man. He gives you a very stern look, like a motor cop who has just caught you speeding. He says, "Sit down." He's sitting in a big leather chair with soft cushions. He points out a little wooden chair with a hard bottom. You sit down. He brushes a pile of thousand-dollar bills off his desk into a waste basket and says to his stenographer, "Put this change in the petty cashbox."

Then he says to you, "Well?" You say, "I'd like to borrow about five hundred dollars, if you can spare it." He takes it big. He looks at you as if he couldn't believe his ears. He says, "You want to borrow what?" You clear your throat and lower your voice. You say, "Three hundred." He shakes his head sadly and says—"Quit clowning, fellow."

Then he says to his secretary, "Phone the chauffeur who drives my new handmade Cadillac and tell him to put about ten more gallons of Chanel No. 5 in the gas tank." You begin to fidget in your chair and finally you whisper "Two hundred." He takes two aspirins. Then he looks at you again. He shudders. Then he looks at you out of those big, sympathetic eyes and says, tenderly: "Hmmm. If you can stand an F.B.I. investigation, and have a steady job, and can give us plenty of negotiable collateral, we might be able to loan you ten bucks—provided you can furnish us with six co-signers who are solvent. I'll take the matter up with the Board of Directors when they return from their semi-annual two months' vacation in Florida." Then as you go out you hear him tell his secretary, "Tell the boys not to take in any more money today. I'm four days behind counting it up now."

Seriously, we all know that banks perform many necessary functions. A successful bank means a successful community. We couldn't get along without bankers—and they couldn't get along without us. So it's a good thing for the people of a community and their bankers to get together once in a while—which is why we're here tonight. Ladies and gentlemen, it gives me a great deal of pleasure to present to you a man who is an outstanding success in his chosen career—the banking profession. Mr. ———— ———— of the ———— ———— Bank.

—Earl Jay Gilbert

ADDITIONAL MATERIAL

Bankers do have occasional weird experiences. A banker told me of a farmer who had lost his farm several years previously and finally had accumulated enough money to buy another farm. The banker drew up the necessary papers and said, "Here, Mr. Jones, this is your deed. You keep that and I'll keep this mortgage." "Oh, no you don't!" cried Jones. "That's how I lost my other farm. The last time I kept the deed and you kept the mortgage and it finished up with you owning the farm. This time you keep the deed and I'll keep the mortgage!" Jones probably figured that he'd wind up owning the bank!

—Earl Jay Gilbert

INTRODUCING A FOOTBALL COACH

Well, folks, football is upon us. It happens every year as sure as November follows October. It just seems to get under one's epidermis, and there is no known cure for it. Why does the world stop when football steps in? Twenty-two men running hither and thither with a pigskin full of emptiness. There was more in that pigskin when the pig wore it. I've often wondered what held the pig together after somebody took the skin off.

We have invited the popular football coach from (name of school) to speak to us this evening, and we feel gratified that he agreed to come.

I'll never forget the good old days when I played on the school team. I can still hear the cheering fans in the stadium, those on one side wanting to see eleven men killed, and those on the other side wanting to see eleven men killed.

When I was just a little kid mother reprimanded me for playing with mud pies, but Dad said to let me go. I might grow up to be a great halfback on rainy Saturdays. When I grew older I knew the nationality of every man on the All-American team. Being on the school team didn't seem to hold me back any in my studies. I remember when the teacher asked me, "What does two halves make?" I said two halves make a whole—and the fullback goes through.

I'll never forget my first game. In the first half I was left—out. In the second half I was back—way back. After the game I passed a couple of girls. I heard one girl say, "He's a quarter back on the team." The other girl said, "Heh! He's not even a nickel back on the bottle." Then I started to shave, for I'd gotten my first down—on my chin. My greatest thrill was when I ran eighty-nine yards, but I couldn't catch the man with the ball. In the next quarter I was taken out and hospitalized because of a wrenched spine. I twisted myself trying to go around my own end. Now, friends, a man who knows a lot more about football than I do, Coach (name).

—Arthur L. Kaser

INTRODUCING A FARMER OR AGRICULTURAL EXPERT

The good old days! The good old days! Remember the good old days when the people in the rural districts had so much money they could buy a gold brick once in awhile? You could rent a bicycle for all day for fifty cents and didn't have to spend anything for gas. You could lean it against a hitching post without putting a nickel in the parking meter. Yes, those were the real days for the farmers.

But now, according to agricultural geography, a farm is a neglected body of land entirely surrounded by prosperity. The reason? The farms have given this country most of its great men. Now look what a fix the farms are in. Oh, sure, the farmer is raising lots of stuff, including howls at some of the Government controls. About the only thing the farmers aren't raising enough of is farmhands.

A great many farmers, however, are solving their farm problems by moving to the cities. The farmers know that their crops will be helped by the rains, but not by the reins of Government. We know of one very successful farmer. He made a lot of money. He sold his farm for an airfield. I have an uncle who converted his farm into a dog ranch. All his dogs are branded K-9. But look at the reputation he got letting his farm go to the dogs.

When I was a lad I worked on a farm during vacation. It's not easy. You go to sleep with the chickens, get up with the roosters, work like a horse, eat like a pig—Oh yes, early to bed, early to rise makes a man a farmer. If a few more city slickers would work on a farm for awhile they might learn something.

> Mule in a barnyard, lazy and sick.
> Boy with a nail in the end of a stick.
> Boy jabs mule, mule gives a lurch—
> Services Monday at the M. E. Church.

Right now, ladies and gentlemen, I want you to meet our friend, the farm expert, Mr. (name.)   —Arthur L. Kaser

INTRODUCING AN EDUCATOR

What is education? Education is the backbone of progress; the keystone of a better life; the road that leads to a better understanding between nations and peoples. We may have intelligence without education, but education is invariably necessary to put intelligence to practical purposes.

The tree of learning has many branches. For instance, one branch may be mathematics. How would we arrive at a practical solution of any mathematical problem without arithmetic? Through education we learn that twice two is four; that twice twenty-six is fifty-two, that three hundred thirty-two divided by eleven is—is—

And then there is geography. Good old geography. When we were young we learned that the shape of the world was round. Now from the newscasters we learn that the world is in an awful shape. From our geography we learn that up is north and down is south, and that a menagerie lion runs around the middle.

And history. Fascinating! How Rome burned while Nero fiddled around. How our brave men defied the English king by dumping a shipload of tea overboard and how the English soldiers all drowned drinking up Boston Harbor.

Yes, education is so wonderful. Not long ago I asked my little nephew if he could tell me of five things that contained milk, and he intelligently said, "Butter, cheese and three cows." And this education runs right up from the kindergarten through our colleges and universities. Many men never mention the fact that they went to college because their school had such a rotten football team. There are also many four-letter men who would like to forget their college days because their four letters were d-u-m-b.

There is one drawback about college. By the time some college boys succeed in accumulating the horsehide, the pigskin, the coonskin and finally the sheepskin, poor dad feels like he's been skinned for all of them. And now, ladies and gentlemen, may I present that renowned educator, Professor (name.)

—Arthur L. Kaser.

INTRODUCING AN EXPERT FISHERMAN

Well, men, I would say that we are pretty fortunate. You are going to hear some interesting things as well as some valuable advice on fishing by a man who has gained quite a reputation as an expert fisherman. You know, there are two kinds of fishermen; those who fish for sport, and those who catch something.

I've gone fishing a good many times in my life, but somehow or other the fish go on vacation the same time that I do. I may be wrong but I have a hunch that maybe fish go home and lie about the size of the bait they stole.

The only time that I really caught a good mess of fish was in the winter. I cut a hole in the ice and held my wrist watch over the hole. When the fish came up to see what time it was I'd hit them with a club. Now from the ridiculous to the sublime. Friends, Mr. (name).   —Arthur L. Kaser

---

INTRODUCING A COMMUNITY SINGING EXPERT

As you know, we are here this evening to promote some kind of community singing. We have engaged a speaker who has had much experience in organizing such groups. Singing is enjoyed by all nationalities. Singing is as old as the world itself.

I'm continually breaking into song. My wife says if I'd ever get the key I wouldn't have to break in. She asked me why I could never learn to carry a tune. I told her I could carry a tune. She said if that was so, why didn't I carry it out and bury it? I love to sing in the bathtub, but she objects to me singing long songs there. She says it takes too much soap.

I have a sister-in-law who was quite a singer. Whenever she would sing in public her voice would fill the auditorium. In fact, a lot of people would usually leave to make room for it. We tried to get her husband to sing with her. He refused at first but we egged him on. We never did find out who egged him off. Now I'll step aside so you may have the pleasure of hearing (speaker).   —Arthur L. Kaser

INTRODUCING A BUSINESS MAN (HEAD OF THE FIRM)

Ladies and gentlemen, I consider it a very fine accomplishment on the part of our arrangements committee to have been able to secure such an outstanding business man as our speaker tonight. Mr. C. Harold Reed has brought fame and prosperity to Blufftown. The product that he manufactures right here in our good little city is known across the nation as one of the finest of its kind on the market. Every time that item is sold, all of us in Blufftown share in the profits, thanks to the substantial local payroll Mr. C. Harold Reed maintains.

But Mr. Reed's job has not been an easy one. He has had to make many sacrifices. He has had to endure many a hardship. Yes, and he has had to put up with some embarrassing situations. In this respect, Mr. Reed never has flinched from any assignment, as is indicated by this incident:

A few years ago, Mr. Reed's sales manager, Jacob Jackson, came to him and remarked: "Mr. Reed, that man Schwartz who covers the middle west is the most insulting person we have in our entire organization."

"What has he done?" asked Mr. Reed.

"What has he done!" said Jackson. "Why, just today I received a letter from him that burned me to a frazzle. He had the audacity to tell me to duck my dome in a barrel of water."

"He did, did he?" said Mr. Reed.

"Yes, he did! But that's not all," the sales manager added. "He told you to take a jump for yourself."

Mr. Reed pondered the information for a few seconds and quickly he said to Jackson, "How are this fellow Schwartz's sales?"

"It's a funny thing," said Jackson. "This dunce is selling more stuff than any dozen men we have in our organization."

Reflecting for a moment, Mr. Reed looked at Jackson and said: "Perhaps I do need a little more exercise. And you, Jackson, I am sure that we can afford to buy you a barrel."

Ladies and gentlemen, Mr. C. Harold Reed.

—Paul C. Winthrop

INTRODUCING A FILLING STATION MANAGER

The American gas station is a product of this century. It was born with the automobile, and with it was born a new type of business man, of which our esteemed guest speaker tonight is a member. John Patterson has filled up more automobiles, greased more cars and directed more people to the rest room, than any other man in this county. He has been held up six times. He has taken a hundred bum checks. He has wiped more bugs off of windshields than the river valley marshes produce in a generation.

In spite of all this John is a happy man. That is, he was a happy man, until one night last week, when a questionable character drove into his station in a Buick Roadmaster, just as John was closing for the night.

"Fill 'er up," said the character.

"I can't," John replied. "We're closed for the night."

"Did you hear what I said?" exclaimed the character. "Fill her up!"

John was quite taken back by this wise guy in the sleek Buick with Chicago license plates, and he was determined to teach the smart alec a lesson. So John went into the station, picked up his revolver and an empty oil can. Throwing the can into the air, John shot it full of holes before it dropped to the concrete driveway.

The character immediately got out of the Buick, reached into one pocket and extracted an apple, and then he reached into the other pocket and drew out a razor. Tossing the apple into the air, the character peeled it clean before it struck the ground.

Then the character walked up to John and said, ". . . and wipe the windshield."

Ladies and gentlemen, Mr. John Patterson.

—Anton C. Wade

INTRODUCING A RESTAURANT OR CAFE MANAGER

The problems of a restaurant manager are complex. People are everlastingly grumbling about the food. When they are not grumbling about the food, they are grumbling about the service. It's just one thing after another, as may be learned when we hear from Gus Antropolis, the proprietor of one of Smithville's finest eating places.

People love to dine at Gus's. They like his nice big steaks, his fried chicken and his juicy apple pie. But they expect too much of Gus. They rush in, grab a table and then demand instantaneous service. Little do they know what is going on back in Gus's kitchen.

One day during the war, when the rush at Gus's was tremendous, I dropped in for lunch. After a long delay, I finally was able to get a waiter to take my order after which I sat back and relaxed, anticipating the tasty preparations that would soon be placed before me. I waited a half an hour, and no lunch. I waited a full hour, and no lunch. My beckonings to the various waiters were fruitless. In desperation I let out a shrill whistle that attracted a waiter, who came running. I could see immediately that this waiter was not mine. "Where's my waiter and where's my lunch?" I said to the waiter.

The waiter looked around and mumbled, "Ahem, table number 10." And then looking around again and pointing, he added, "There's your lunch on that serving table over by that post."

"That's a terrible place for my lunch," said I. "How did it get over there?"

"Your waiter brought it, sir," the man replied.

"Why didn't he bring it the rest of the way?" I asked.

"That's as far as he got, that post. He quit right there and went home," the man explained.

That is only one of Gus's problems. He has many more. A few weeks ago Gus asked one of his waiters to report to the office. Gus looked up at the waiter from his reclining position on the swivel chair and said sternly: "My good man, you have been working for Gus's for one week, and during that period you have smashed more dishes than the amount of your salary for the same period. What have you got to suggest that will correct this serious situation?"

The new waiter looked down at Gus in a customary professional pose, and remarked with the simplicity of a waiter quoting the price of a steak: "Increase my salary to meet the deficit."

Ladies and gentlemen, Mr. Gus Antropolis.

—Anton C. Wade

INTRODUCING A RADIO ACTOR

It is getting so we cannot say, "We have with us this evening an actor." We must be specific. We must state whether he is an actor on the stage, screen or television. The young man you will meet this evening climbed to success very quickly on radio. Speaking of radio, I remember the first one I owned a long time ago. I couldn't get a thing on it till I took it to the pawn shop. I remember that at the time a certain judge ruled that a radio was a musical instrument. Mine was a plain case of contempt of court. I had to use earphones. Then I got a radio with a loud speaker and I used the earphones so I couldn't hear the neighbors' radios. I had a parakeet at the time but I had to get rid of the bird. All it learned was static.

Here I am babbling about radio when I should be leading up to the introduction of a radio actor. In one way, a radio actor is lucky. He can reach millions of people, and they can't reach him. Some of the first radio actors got their experience on the air by falling out of balloons, which was quite a comedown for them to start with. Our entertainer this evening told me the first hit he ever did on radio was to announce that the ten minutes silence on the radio was not due to a technical breakdown, but was sent to the listeners by courtesy of Hush Noiseless Typewriters. But here he is, ladies and gentlemen, that star of many years duration on the radio, that ether wave favorite, (name.)

—Arthur L. Kaser

INTRODUCING A FLOOR COVERING DEALER

Perhaps one of the most exasperating businesses is that of selling floor coverings. Will Patterson, our next speaker, can vouch for that, as Will has been selling floor coverings for years.

It's the fussiness of the woman buyer, Will will tell you, that drives a man wild. One day last week Mrs. Willoughby, a lady of fashion, came into Will's store and said that she would like to look at some linoleum patterns.

"I have some lovely ones here," said Will. "Just look at that dragon design. That is one of the smartest creations of the creator's art. It was all the vogue at the Palace of Versailles in Paris last year."

"Goodness, gracious no!" said Mrs. Willoughby. "He positively would not like that."

"Well, here is something else," said Will, picking out a sample that portrayed a bee chasing a rose. "This magnificent design was adopted by King Gustav of Sweden. It gives a springtime touch to a room in the gloomiest days of the winter. Cheery, isn't it?" Will added.

"Heavens, no! If I brought that home there would be nothing but fluttering around the house," replied Mrs. Willoughby.

Then Will took off his coat and began to pile sample after sample of linoleum in front of Mrs. Willoughby.

"Ah, here's what I have been trying to find for you," exclaimed Will enthusiastically. "It's positively a sensation! What a fabulous reproduction of the cherry in cluster! Please notice, Mrs. Willoughby, how those tempting dark-red colors are inlaid in the pattern!"

Mrs. Willoughby threw up her hands in absolute disgust. "Good heavens, Mr. Patterson, if I should order that pattern, he would get a paroxysm of uncontrollable pecking. I don't believe that you have anything that he would like."

With that final remark Mrs. Willoughby began her exit from the store. However, before she had reached the door, Will Patterson called out after her. "Oh, Mrs. Willoughby, perhaps it would be advisable to bring your husband down here. Then he could make a satisfactory selection."

"My husband!" exclaimed Mrs. Willoughby, shaking with laughter.

"Why, Mrs. Willoughby! It can't be that . . . !"

"Yes, it can," said Mrs. Willoughby. "It's for the cage of my little dovey, Pettie, my pet parakeet."

Ladies and gentlemen, Mr. Will Patterson.

—Anthony C. Gregory

INTRODUCING A PARENT AT A GRADUATION BANQUET

Graduates, parents, teachers and guests: We are met to honor the graduates of the year. They have reached the place where the road turns; they are facing a wider highway of life down which they move toward their various goals and achievements.

There is one word which appropriately describes the mental attitude of all graduates; it is Expectation. What a pleasing picture is the throng of young men and women from the schools of every town and city! All are on tiptoe to receive the gifts of life, and in return, to offer to life their talents.

Toward this end, parents have given their cooperation and support; teachers have laid a firm foundation of knowledge; the graduates themselves have contributed their expectation which is hope and faith combined.

Around the table we have gathered a cross section of American life. We shall hear first hand the ideas that have created this occasion.

I have the honor of introducing one of the parents of our graduates, who will tell us of the cooperation needed to produce a graduate.

—Helen Ramsey

INTRODUCING A DETECTIVE OR POLICEMAN

It is a great pleasure to welcome this evening a prominent member of our police department, Captain Joseph Murphy, for it is not often that our organization has an opportunity to get some of the inside information about what is going on underground in our town.

Some time ago Captain Murphy was in charge of the morals squad, and in this connection considerable credit should be given to the captain for cleaning up this town. Woe be unto the gambler or the vice resort operator, once Captain Murphy got on the trail. When the word traveled swiftly through the grapevine that Captain Murphy and his squad were after them, the hoodlums made a quick exit, and departed to our neighboring city Baldwinville, where the police department does not measure up to the standards of our efficient force.

Some time ago a gambler with a national reputation came to town and opened up quarters over a pool hall, where it was said that poker games for big stakes were in progress every night. When that news reached the ears of Captain Murphy, he immediately got on the scent. That very night he walked into the gambling headquarters and caught four men red-handed, sitting at a poker table.

"Aha!" said the Captain to one man. "You're playing poker!"

"Not on your life!" answered the fellow. "I'm just sitting here."

"How about you?" the Captain asked of a second fellow.

"Me?" said the man. "I just dropped in for a short visit."

"And you!" yelled the Captain at a third fellow.

"Not me!" said the third fellow. "I came up to find out about tomorrow's weather. I'm going fishing in the morning."

The Captain walked over to the fourth fellow who quickly slipped a deck of cards into his pocket, but not quick enough to escape the eagle eye of Captain Murphy. The Captain grabbed the fourth man by the arm and exclaimed: "You've got the cards! You've been playing poker!"

The fourth gambler swapped glances with his three associates, and then looking Captain Murphy straight in the eye casually remarked:

"With who?"

Ladies and gentlemen, Captain Joseph Murphy.

—Stephen Keller

INTRODUCING A HIGHWAY PATROLMAN

A necessary adjunct to modern travel is the highway patrolman. Without him the transportation of the millions of automobiles on our highways would be an impossibility. He unsnarls our traffic, protects our lives and gives first aid when disaster strikes, which unfortunately is much too often.

Yes, the highway patrolman carries on his job with efficiency and expediency, and he is a mighty valuable man to have around when something happens to you on the open highway. Like every job, no matter how unpleasant at times, there is a humorous side.

One day last summer, Highway Patrolman Harry Black, our next speaker, was cruising down Highway number 10. Just at the point where Highway number 10 joins Highway number 6, there is a long curve, quite sharp. As Harry was rounding this curve, he saw a yellow car fly by. Then the car flew across the highway, vaulted the ditch, knocked down fifty yards of fence, careened back up on the highway, leaped across the ditch on the other side and abruptly came to rest against a telephone pole, shattering it to splinters.

Frantically, Harry ran over to the scene. The yellow convertible was in shambles, turned upside down. From under the wreckage a feminine blonde-head emerged. Then from the other end of the junk heap, a male black-head with a lip-stick carmined face appeared.

Said the blonde-head to the lip-stick carmined face: "Boy, that's what I'd call a kiss!"

Ladies and gentlemen, Highway Patrolman Harry Black.

—Paul C. Winthrop

INTRODUCING AN ARCHITECT

When I was told this evening that I was to introduce John Adams, the community's outstanding architect, I jumped with joy, for I have a little architectural scheme of my own that I want to talk to John about. I had planned on making a trip to his office, but now that he is here I will tell you all about it. In that way I will get not only John's opinion of my plan, but yours as well.

I first got the idea when my oldest son burned a hole in the carpeting with an electric iron. The iron hadn't worked for years, but it worked for Sonny. Then one day my nephews came over and together with my kids smashed the legs off of all the dining room chairs. That's when I got out my drawing board and began designing a house that would stand the pulverizing of the present-day younger generation. In my house all floors would be of air-inflated rubber, with exceptional resiliency, so that when the baby fell out of the high chair, he would immediately bounce back into it. The high chair would also be of rubber, fixed to one place on the floor. Dishes would be of cast iron, and cups and saucers of bronze, welded to the table.

Cabinets would be eight feet from the floor, and that would include the gas range, television set and all other devices having knobs and buttons. The walls would be papered in a design consisting of full hand prints, bordered with finger prints, with a red splash here and there, resembling the splattering of a tomato. The hallway would be constructed like an alley, a sort of an underpass speedway, leading from front door to back, through which tricycles, bicycles, railroad trains and doll buggies could shuttle back and forth. The kids' beds would be Air Force lifeboats, cemented in, and my bed would be a hammock, suspended six feet up. Oh, yes, there is one other thing. All television sets would be so equipped that when a cartoon or a western thriller comes on, it would immediately short circuit and shut the thing off.

That is an idea of my dream house. I am anxious to get a professional viewpoint on my plan from Mr. Adams. Ladies and gentlemen, Mr. John Adams, our community's outstanding architect. Mr. Adams.

—Sylvester McGovern

INTRODUCING A SPEAKER ON ANIMAL HUSBANDRY

We are honored by the presence this evening of a man who is fast gaining renown among the livestock men of the country. He is an expert in his line, and I am sure anyone interested in the raising of livestock will gain much by listening to him.

There was a time when I almost sold my home and car that I might invest in a farm where I could raise cows and sheep and pigs, but after talking to a real livestock man I realized what little I know on the subject.

For instance, this man asked me, "Do you know why Missouri stands at the head of mule raising?" And dumb me says, "Because the other end is too dangerous." No doubt such an answer was induced by the fact that when I was a young man I was kicked by a mule. Where was I kicked? Well, if my head had been in Boston, and my feet in California I would have been kicked in Omaha.

But I do like sheep. I think it is because my Uncle Steve owned the largest sheep ranch in the United States. He owned so many sheep he was known as the head sheepman. In fact, he was called a muttonhead. I remember one time he wanted to move a few thousand sheep across the ice of a small lake that was owned by a widow. She said, "No!" So he promised to marry her, and that's how he pulled the wool over her ice.

And cows. I had a great idea about cows but no dairy man would listen to me. My theory was, that if the cows slept on their backs the cream would be on top in the morning. When I was young I worked on a dairy farm during school vacation. The farmer had forty cows. Each cow would give five gallons of milk, and the farmer would sell ten gallons of milk from each cow. He was a milkman of the first water. Ladies and gentlemen, I take great pleasure in presenting Mr. (name).

—Arthur L. Kaser

INTRODUCING AN INTERIOR DECORATOR

It was the honeybees who first sang about their abode, the hive: "HOME SWEET HOME." Home is the place where you don't have to engage reservations in advance. The trouble is, the modern home today is supplied with everything except the family.

But what is home without the little woman to manage things? She's the one who knows just where the davenport would look best: in front of the picture window; across from the picture window; in the corner diagonally across from the picture window, or in the garage because it's worn out anyway.

But speaking of inferior—I mean interior decorating, have you noticed how many homes are being partly furnished with antiques? A number of factories are now turning out genuine antiques. Take for instance, period furniture. An electric chair is an example of period furniture because it ends a sentence.

A lady entered a furniture store and asked to see some really old furniture. The clerk said, "Now here is an old chair, Louis the 14th." The lady said, "Oh, that's too small. How about a Louis the 16th?"

A friend of mine asked me to visit them. He wanted me to see the three rooms they had furnished with soap coupons. I asked him if they were going to furnish the other three rooms the same way. He said they couldn't. The other three rooms were full of soap.

A few years ago my wife got a bright idea and bought an old-fashioned canopy bed, but we didn't keep it long. Everybody thought we had it because our roof leaked.

At another time I came home and was confronted by a new piece of furniture. I said to her, "What is that?" She said, "Hi, boy." And before I thought I said, "Hi, kid!"

Years ago an uncle of mine put in a one-way stairway. It would run down but not up. It was a winding stairs, but he lost the key and couldn't wind it, so it ran down. That winding stairs leads up to another story. They're building houses so small now the occupants have to use condensed milk.

The first house we lived in had defective bathroom faucets so the carpenters moved the hole in the roof so it was right over the bathtub. It was just right for showers. Ladies and gentlemen, our interior decorator, (name).

—Arthur L. Kaser

INTRODUCING AN ADVERTISING MANAGER

What is advertising? In a way, advertising is merely publicity which has been developed into a fine art. For instance, advertising can tactfully make you think you've longed all your life for something you never heard of before.

There are many ways to advertise. There are the newspapers. They get results. Just last week the Ajax Washboard Company advertised for a night watchman. That same night the office safe was robbed. Then there is the billboard advertising. Billboards! Billboards! Bill boards with us but never pays his board bill. Yes, billboards. Beyond the Alps lies Italy. Beyond the billboards lies America. If all the billboards in the United States were placed end to end they would reach just as far as they do now.

But there is going to be a change. If air traffic continues to increase the billboards will have to lie flat on the ground. Then the public will really look down on such advertising. And television. You are watching a thriller. The villain raises his dagger to murder the hero. The picture on the screen blacks out and you are confronted by a sideshow barker who tells you all the good points of Peabody's Peppersauce for poor pink people. The thriller comes back, but standing with raised dagger while Peabody's Peppersauce for poor pink people is being exploited becomes tiresome and the villain's arm becomes numb. He drops the dagger and sees the error of his ways and repents as the police arrive.

But let me turn this over to a man who really knows advertising in all its colors. Friends, I have the pleasant privilege of presenting our guest of the evening, Mr. (name).

—Arthur L. Kaser

INTRODUCING A BASEBALL PLAYER

It's not often that one has the opportunity to introduce a man from the sports world as prominent as Joe Brown. In that respect Joe needs no introduction, for his record is one to be envied by those who seek fame on the baseball diamond.

Yesterday, I called up the head coach at the High School and said, "Coach, I have to introduce Joe Brown tonight. What can you tell me about a baseball player?"

"A baseball player is always right," said the coach. "He never makes an error. He never strikes out. He is always safe at first, and he's never tagged out at home."

"What kind of a ridiculous statement do you call that?" I said.

"It's not ridiculous at all," the coach replied. "A baseball player never does those things. It's the umpire who says he does. All umpires are big liars!"

"That's kind of a broad statement also," I said.

"Not at all," said the coach. "If you want to prove it to your audience, tell them the story about the baseball player who died and went to heaven. (Of course, you can't say Joe Brown died and went to heaven, because we know Joe isn't dead, and we're not sure he's going to heaven.) But you can name any baseball player, for instance, Lou Gehrig."

"Well, go ahead with the story," I said.

"Okay," said the coach. "While Lou was up there with nothing but eternity on his hands, he rounded up a baseball team — all immortals of the diamond — Babe Ruth, Christy Mathewson and so on. While this team of immortals was working out in spring training, Satan heard about it, and radioed up and challenged Lou to a game. When Satan began to brag about some of the greats he had in his dominions, Lou said, 'Satan, my team will trim the pants off of any outfit you can round up down there.'"

" 'Oh, no you won't,' " Satan replied.

" 'You haven't got anything down there,' " said Lou.

" 'We haven't! Hmm, that's what you think!' "

" 'Who you got?' " asked Lou.

"Then Satan let out one of those diabolical laughs, the kind that shatters the universe, and said: 'We've got the umpires!' "

Ladies and gentlemen, Joe Brown.

—Howard C. Wilford

INTRODUCING A FOOD SPECIALIST

I am pleased to announce that later on this program we will have a very instructive talk by a very well-known food expert. I talked with this renowned food specialist this morning and learned many interesting things about our modern day edibles. Some of the specialist's remarks were not quite clear to a layman like myself. For instance, I was told that spaghetti is the best all-around food. But I wasn't told all around what. I was told to be very picky and choosey when buying meat. Some meat now in stores is so tough you can't even bend the gravy. I found this to be true a few days ago when I bought a four-pound roast. We had it for Sunday dinner. We tried to cut it, saw it, dynamite it. No soap. It brought to mind that old saying, "the bravest are the tenderest." If the bravest are the tenderest, the animal that provided that dinner was a coward. Have you noticed how many doctors now-a-days advise you to eat less meat? A doctor has a reason for telling you that. He's afraid that with meat prices as they are you won't have enough money left to pay him. And some other things I was told. Do you know that a garlic sandwich is nothing but two slices of bread traveling in bad company? And speaking of sandwiches, the first sandwich was said to have been made in the 17th century. Replicas of the original are exhibited in glass cases in most railway and bus stations. As I said before, I will introduce one of the best known food specialists of the present time. This authority has written many articles on food. Which is quite something in itself. Did you ever try to write anything on food? Especially with a sharp pencil on a mound of mashed potatoes. And just try writing on a tuna fish salad with a typewriter. Now on with the program. I'm happy to introduce . . .

—Arthur L. Kaser

INTRODUCING A BANKER

It isn't often that a chairman has the privilege to introduce to his audience such a well-known community leader as Paul C. Cotton. Mr. Cotton is known to many as the president of our local bank. He is known to many more for his untiring efforts in behalf of the numerous civic enterprises that have been so beneficial to all of us here in Pineville. When asked to head up this drive or accept the chairmanship of this movement or that, Mr. Cotton always promptly assented, and as a result of his abundant energy and spirit, as well as his sage advice and guidance, our community campaigns have been overwhelmingly successful.

However, a banker's life is not always a bed of roses. While it is sometimes said that a banker has you backed to the wall with a note, there are times when a banker has to take it—to speak in slang parlance—and like it.

A short time ago a man walked into Mr. Cotton's bank and said, "Mr. Cotton, I want to borrow the sum of five dollars."

"Five dollars!" exclaimed Mr. Cotton. "We don't make loans that small."

But the man persisted, and Mr. Cotton thought he could throw him off by emphasizing that some collateral would be required.

"Fine," said the man. "Here's $10,000 in government bonds. I have just saved the cost of a safety deposit box."

Upon another occasion a flippant office boy was hired by the bank. This fellow had a habit of coming to work in the mornings quite late. When the tardiness persisted and the lad kept showing up later and later each morning, Mr. Cotton called him to his desk for a lecture.

"Billy," said Mr. Cotton. "There is such a thing as banker's hours, which is sometimes misunderstood by the public. But we do put in a full day's work here, and I want you to reform. Beginning tomorrow morning you will report punctually at the appointed hour. Remember, Billy, it's the early bird that catches the worm."

Billy broke into a big grin and said: "But look what happens to the worm!"

Mr. Cotton pondered over the answer for a few seconds and then quite authoritatively said: "Billy, the worm had it coming. He was out all night and got caught on the way home."

Ladies and gentlemen, Mr. Paul C. Cotton.

—Rome Roberts

INTRODUCING AN AIRLINE STEWARDESS

We have with us this evening a young lady who is a stewardess on one of our big passenger planes. She is so in love with her job she wants to tell other girls how wonderful it is. She has been flying for quite awhile. In fact, she's been flying so long she can recognize most of the clouds between here and Walla Walla. Going from place to place now is so comfortable, and so fast. The last trip I made was from New York to Los Angeles. There was an elderly man sitting near me. At Chicago a red truck pulled alongside and delivered gas to our plane. We took off and again landed at Denver. Again a red truck pulled up alongside. I turned to the elderly man and remarked, "This plane is making good time." He said, "Yes, 'tis. And that red truck is doing pretty good, too."

I see where some of the passenger planes are being turned to stunt planes just to give the passengers a thrill. When the cook on these planes wants to toss a pancake he simply stands still and calls to the pilot to loop the loop. Most pilots' wives are always glad when their husbands are down and out.

I have a cousin who has a yen to fly to the moon because he realizes that he's no earthly good. I asked a veteran pilot the other day, "If all your engines went dead at ten thousand feet, how would you get down?" He said, "That has always worried me. I know three pilots that had that very thing happen. They just had to stay up there and starve to death." My friends, allow me to present Miss (name).

—Arthur L. Kaser

INTRODUCING A BABY SPECIALIST

Everybody loves babies—or should. And all parents want healthy babies. So, this evening, ladies and gentlemen, we are going to hear from a baby specialist on the proper feeding and care of the little rascals.

There are about three hundred babies born every minute in the United States. It is only fair to point out that the poor little things are given no choice in the matter. What is the first thing a new born baby does? It cries. They seem to sense that they have been brought into a place distraught with worry and anxiety. It's like arriving at one's destination only to find it on fire. All this amplifies the fact that babies must be healthy to face what is before them.

I think our baby specialist will agree that healthy babies are a delicate pink, but some in our neighborhood are robust yellers. It's only the babies that are born in a tornado or cyclone that really realize so quickly what life is like.

Some of the biggest problems facing the parents is to have babies get enough sleep. This is very true when the baby is eighteen years old. When our baby was just three weeks old I asked the doctor why it cried so much and he said, "If all your teeth were out, your hair off, and your legs so weak you couldn't stand on them, you'd cry, too."

Some people say that a baby reigns as king in a family. Not ours. It was the Prince of Wails. And was I glad when it learned to walk. Instead of me getting up and walking the floor with him at night I let him get up and do his own walking. That way I thought he would follow in his father's footsteps.

And speaking of children, a little girl hurried to school one morning to tell her first grade teacher the big news—they had a brand new baby at their house and she wanted the teacher to hurry right over and see it. "I will," said the teacher, "but I'll wait awhile until your mother feels better." "Oh," said the excited little girl, "you don't have to be afraid. It isn't catching." I know you are anxiously waiting to hear our baby specialist, so here (she or he) is. (Name of speaker.)

—Arthur L. Kaser

INTRODUCING AN ORCHESTRA LEADER

I am happy to announce that (name of guest), the well-known orchestra leader, has consented to say a few words to you this evening. I believe that most of you at some time or another have heard Mr. (name)'s band.

Mr. (leader) jokingly told me that the first time his present orchestra played in public an elderly man approached him and asked, "Does your orchestra ever play anything by request?" "Oh, yes," said our guest. "Good," said the old man. "Tell them to play pinochle."

Mr. (leader) also told me that his drummer used to be a grocery boy. The reason he gave this youth the job of drummer in his band was because the young man was so honest he gave full weight to every pound.

Once when (leader) was directing his orchestra a lady stepped up to him and asked, "What is that book you keep looking at?" The band leader said, "That's the score." The lady wanted to know who was winning.

There used to be a banjo player in this orchestra but he quit. He was getting three dollars an hour but he wanted four. Personally, I think three dollars an hour for playing the banjo is pretty easy pickings.

When our friend first applied for a job directing an orchestra he was asked, "Are you sure you are qualified to direct an orchestra?" Mr. (leader) quickly answered, "Absolutely. I've had two nervous breakdowns. I was shell-shocked in the last war, and I live in an apartment above a family with eleven noisy kids." And now, ladies and gentlemen, here is that same orchestra leader, Mr. (name).

—Arthur L. Kaser

INTRODUCING A TAX CONSULTANT

'Tis said that there are two things for sure—death and taxes. When you finish one you are through with the other. A tax consultant and a tax collector are two different men. The tax consultant tells you how to get rid of your money. The tax collector is the one that gets it. It is always well to listen and heed the tax consultant.

He's a man of wisdom when it comes to tax.
He's studied hard and he knows the facts.
Heed him not or be an objector,
You'll have as a guest the tax collector.

The tax consultant tries to save you money. Once in awhile he succeeds. We have with us this evening just such a man. He is here to untangle some of the snarls in a tax blank. Some people call them blanketyblank blanks. A blank by any other name would smell just as bad. When you try filling out this blank without the assistance of an expert you shorten your life and learn to use naughty words.

To some of us a tax report is about as easy to understand as a Red peace proposal. For instance, here's a column and another column, and another—Therefore, "A" from Column One placed beneath Column "B" or "C" in Sub-Column Three, unless otherwise stated in red marginal letters, equals the combined total of Column "D" which is ignored if more than twice the amount is found in Column "E" before breakfast, or Column "F" after breakfast. What you don't put in the report is known as untold wealth. If you want to snitch a little bit do it with your eyes closed, then your conscience won't bother you so much. But the tax collector will.

From all this you will see how fortunate you are to have advice from an expert on this puzzling thing. Without this advice you might have to proceed as follows: First you list your dependents—Wife. Then wife's mama. Wife's mama's husband. Wife's mama's husband's brother. Wife's mama's husband's brother's wife. Wife's mama's husband's brother's wife's family. This is the gross income, especially when their income is three or four o'clock in the morning. Now divide this by the daily amount of food you have to pay for to stuff this gang.

If you have anything left it is called net, and this goes to the Government, too. In other words, you should drop dead. There is only one way to get out of paying income tax. Be a nudist. The Government can't pin anything on them. Ladies and gentlemen, take my advice and take the advice of our tax consultant, Mr. (name.)

—Arthur L. Kaser

INTRODUCING A GARDENING EXPERT

Spring, spring, beautiful spring. What a temptation to toss the seed catalogue out the window and reach for a road map! Spring is so near—only a few cold-wave lengths away. It is the time for enthusiasm. We know of one person who is enthused. That is our speaker of the evening, our gardening authority.

I've already ordered my flower seeds. The flowers will take two years to bloom so I ordered them from last year's catalogue. The flowers always look so big and wonderful in beautiful colors in those catalogues. The seed companies guarantee the flowers to look like those illustrations provided the seeds ever come up.

I believe in cleanliness in the garden as well as in the house. That is the reason I dig up my seeds every morning and wash the dirt off of them and then put them back into the ground.

I've had a lot of experience with flowers and vegetables. I was appointed one time to judge the scent of roses, but I couldn't accept the job, because I don't smell good.

Last year I planted thousands of flower seeds but the only thing that showed up was the neighbor's chickens. The best way to tell the flowers from the weeds is to watch the neighbor's chickens. They know. There is one objection to gardening. By the time your back gets used to it your enthusiasm is gone. Now let's listen to the man who can give us expert advice on gardening, Mr. (name).

—Arthur L. Kaser

INTRODUCING AN INVENTOR

Ladies and gentlemen, we are fortunate to have as our next speaker a man who is outstanding among that talented fraternity who have helped to make life easier and pleasanter for all of us—the inventors.

When we think of what existence was like before the discovery of electricity, the radio, television, the telephone, the sewing machine, the washing machine, the steam engine, the ice-making refrigerator, to mention only a few of the many wonders these men of gifted imagination have created for us, then we can begin to realize how much we owe these geniuses.

I purposely avoided mentioning the cellophane that is used to wrap up packages, because I still haven't been able to decide whether it was worth all the trouble it took to invent it.

However, here is a simple thing (Takes out a lighter with no flint in it)—a lighter. Think of all the trouble it saves when you want to light a cigar or cigarette—no searching for matches—just a little press of your thumb—(Presses the lighter, but no light) just one little press— (Presses again, no light— presses several times with no results) well, anyway (Returns the lighter to his pocket) it's a great invention when it works. We all have tough days.

Anyway, I was about to say that I have a friend who has been working on an invention that should be a God-send to humanity. It's an idea to prevent automobile accidents. He has just discovered the solution after many years of research and experimentation. Like so many inventions, his idea is simple. We'll take two cars going sixty miles an hour—they are about to crash into each other (Illustrates with hands)—just as they are about to collide—one car suddenly rises up into the air—jumps over the other car—lands on the other side— and each car continues on its way—no collision, no accident. See what I mean by simple? He has his invention practically perfected—except for one little detail. He hasn't quite figured out how to make one car jump over the other.

He's sitting in his laboratory, quietly biting his finger nails, waiting for the idea to come to him. Now my friend's idea isn't patented yet, but I know the gentleman who is going to address you in a moment is a man of proved integrity and honor. I'm sure he won't grab my friend's idea and work it out himself. But if he should, I'd like to ask him to remember where he got the thought. Ladies and gentlemen, our speaker, Mr. —————————. Thank you.   —Earl Jay Gilbert

INTRODUCING A TEACHER

The task of teaching ABC's in these modern times is not an easy one, as I am sure that Mr. William Odgen, our next speaker, will tell you. There was a time when writing, reading and arithmetic was taught to the tune of the hickory stick; and there was a time when only about two kids in a classroom were problem children. Today the whole class consists of problem children, and there is no hickory stick available.

Mr. Odgen, like every other teacher, has a room full of these problem kids. One of his kids in particular was getting too smart for his breeches. One day last week, Mr. Odgen said to this kid: "Johnny, recite the first paragraph in the Declaration of Independence."

Johnny looked up at Mr. Odgen and said, "I don't know it."

"What!" said Mr. Odgen, "You don't know the first paragraph in the Declaration of Independence?"

"Naw, I don't know it," Johnny repeated.

"Didn't you study it last night?" Mr. Odgen asked.

"Naw," replied Johnny. "I was watchin' television."

"Well, Johnny," said Mr. Odgen, "you should be ashamed of yourself. When Abraham Lincoln was your age, he was an authority on the Declaration of Independence and the Constitution as well."

Johnny appeared to be thinking, and then he looked up from his desk and mumbled: "When Abe Lincoln was your age, he was president of the United States."

Ladies and gentlemen, Mr. William Odgen.
                              —Howard C. Wilford

INTRODUCING A TRAFFIC OFFICER

Traffic is becoming more dense year by year. However, traffic is only as dense as the drivers. The job of a traffic cop is not an easy one. The fact that a traffic cop whistles at his work is no sign that he is happy. And the one he whistles at may not be happy either. When a traffic officer loses all patience and bawls you out, be nonchalant—light a bomb.

A traffic officer is a large, forceful person of few words, but often. Just try going the wrong way on a one-way street and you'll find yourself at the wrong end of a one-way argument with a cop. And women drivers should remember when a traffic officer whistles at you and waves he is not necessarily flirting. He just wants to make a date with you—to appear in court.

We have with us this evening Officer (name) of the traffic department who will give us valuable advice on how to prevent accidents. Remember the slogan: the life you save may be your own.

I happened to overhear a conversation between a traffic officer and a speeder. Said the cop, "Okay now. What's your alibi for going sixty miles an hour in a thirty-mile zone?" Said the speeder, "I just heard that my wife's church was giving a rummage sale and I was hurrying home to save my other pair of pants."

A traffic officer arrested a driver whose car was zig-zagging down the street. The officer told the judge about the car weaving from one side of the street to the other. The judge asked the officer if the steering apparatus was loose. "No," said the cop, "the driver was tight."

Another driver who had over-imbibed drove his car into town with the front grill and one fender bashed badly. A policeman stopped him and asked, "What did you hit?" The driver said he hit a cow. The cop asked him what kind of a cow. The driver said, "Ain't sure. Had four legs and . . ." "No, no," said the officer, trying to be patient. "Was it a Jersey cow?" The driver thought a moment. "Couldn't tell, offisher. Didn't see its license plate." We will now hear from the man in the street, Officer (name).   —Arthur L. Kaser

---

INTRODUCING A TOP SALESMAN

(Can also be used for the executive who objects to his employees saying, "I think that . . ." To which the executive's reply is "You think? Don't you know?")

Gentlemen, Bill Brown is a positive man. He never deals in negatives or uncertainties. That's why Bill's sales are soaring in this organization. Nothing upsets Bill more than the use of the phrase, "I think it is so or I think it is that." Bill wants to know, "Is it or isn't it?"

To illustrate this point permit me to recall an incident that happened to Bill a short time ago in the lobby of the Ritz Hotel. At that time Bill made a visit to the Ritz lobby to meet an important client. He threw his twenty-dollar homburg hat on the seat of a sofa and walked over to the desk to announce that he was waiting for the arrival of an important person. When he returned to the sofa he found that it was more than half occupied by an elderly lady of extensive girth; and Bill's hat was nowhere in view.

Petulantly slouching down on what remained of the seating capacity of the sofa, Bill looked sheepishly at the elderly lady; and the elderly lady looked sheepishly back at Bill. After a few moments of exchanging such glances, the good lady reached down behind the folds of her black dress, which draped an elphantine posterior, and produced what remained of Bill's hat.

Handing the battered homburg to Bill, she said in a most apologetic voice, "Young man, I think I sat on your hat!"

Bill took the squashed and crumbled headpiece from the lady's outstretched hand and looking at it remorsefully exclaimed:

"You **think** you sat on my hat! You know darn well you sat on my hat!"   —Sylvester H. McGovern

INTRODUCING A MINISTER

A young theologian had made up his mind that when he became ordained he would revolutionize the standards of sermons from the pulpit. The older preachers of the gospel, he claimed, were as outmoded as a mustache cup. When it became his turn to take the pulpit, he would show those old fellows something different in the way of pulpit oratory. He would set his congregation on fire; he would carry them to the loftiest pinnacles of thought. He would become a Cicero who with words could make Caesar tremble.

Throughout the years of his study he emulated Demosthenes of antiquity and went down to the lakeshore where he filled his mouth with pebbles and orated above the din of the waves. His views on pepping-up sermons from the pulpit were, of course, well-known to his professors; and his reputation followed him to his first assigned church where he became assistant to the very distinguished and scholarly Reverend Peter Williams, our next speaker this evening. (Now don't get curious, this happened in another city. The young pastor is unknown to this audience.) Well, anyway the young minister was not bashful in informing Reverend Williams that from now on there was going to be something new in the way of sermons in the parish, and that the change would take place on the next Sunday, when the young man would give his first sermon.

The Sunday of the inaugural arrived with a packed congregation, as it was announced that a pastor of great eloquence would appear. When the time arrived for the young minister to mount the rostrum, an air of expectancy rippled through the church. Five hundred eyes followed the young man, sartorially perfect in his new cassock, as he walked hurriedly across the altar, shoulders erect, eyes full of confidence, and a general air of "there's nothing to it" suffused over his confident face. Reverend Williams, sitting on a chair in the corner of the altar, noted this cocksure manner of the young minister.

The young minister stood before the congregation, pulled up the left sleeve of his cassock; then he pulled up the right sleeve of his cassock. For a moment he fumbled with his book and gazed out at the audience as if seeking words in the ceiling. After a continuance of this procedure for a minute or so, there was heard an incomplete and obscure murmur of a sentence as if it were lingering from his lips. Then he left the pulpit without an audible utterance, walking in slow dejected strides, his head bowed and a bitter look of defeat all over his face.

As he took his seat adjoining that of Reverend Williams he was an utterly defeated man. His dreams of years had been shattered in a few split seconds. Reverend Williams, who was expecting just such a denouement, leaned over and whispered paternally in the young man's ear: "If you would have walked up like you walked down, you would have been able to walk down like you walked up."

Ladies and gentlemen, Reverend Peter Williams.

—Sylvester McGovern

INTRODUCING A PUBLIC LIBRARIAN

Mr. President, friends of the library, ladies and gentlemen. It gives me a great pleasure to be with you this evening and participate in this celebration. When we commemorate the founding of a library we are paying tribute to one of the oldest institutions in civilization. What could be more important and significant than the records of the history, the science, the literature and the arts of mankind?

When we stand in a library and view the vast array of books filled with the lore of centuries a feeling of awe comes over us. There they are, thousands of books, waiting for us to appropriate their knowledge. Ours for the taking.

Ours for the taking. A score of questions rise to our lips. Whence came the library idea? Who first thought of making records of men's lives, their accomplishments, their learning, their governments, their religions? How were they collected into libraries? Where were they first found? I shall ask Miss ——————— to answer some of these questions.

—Helen Ramsey

INTRODUCING A HUMORIST

It is not often that your chairman has the distinction of presenting to a gathering of this sort such an outstanding humorist as Mr. Cecil Mills. As you all know, Mr. Mills has a wide reputation for making people laugh, sometimes at the expense of other people. Earlier in the evening I met Mr. Mills out in the lobby and he said to me: "I am going to take a few cracks at the Germans tonight."

"Good gracious," I said. "You can't do that here in Pottsville. There are too many Germans in the audience."

"How about the Swedes?" Mr. Mills asked.

"Mercy no!" I cried out, waving my hands in despair.

"Well, that rules out that story," he said, adding quickly, "how about the Irish?"

"The Irish!" I shouted in amazement. "The last man who took a crack at the Irish in this town lies buried down by the mill pond."

Just at the precise moment Dennis McMann and Marty O'Toole passed through the lobby. "See the size of those fellows," I said, pointing.

"Sounds like a very plausible reason," said Mr. Mills.

"I'm just trying to protect you," I said.

"I appreciate it," said Mr. Mills, adding, "But I have to talk about somebody. I have one last resort, and that's the Japanese."

"That's fine," I said, greatly relieved. "There are no Japanese within two hundred miles of Pottsville."

(Pause for laughter)

So now, ladies and gentlemen, I present to you a man of wit. If there are any slips of the tongue, don't blame me. I warned him. Mr. Cecil Mills.

—Sylvester McGovern

INTRODUCING A SPEAKER AT A P. T. A. MEETING

Parents, teachers, and guests: A P.T.A. banquet may seem to be an unusual place to talk about gifts. Most of us associate gifts with something definite; something tangible that we can take home with us, to show to our friends and family.

And yet, all gifts are not of this variety. There are gifts in the abstract—contributions that come, not from the pocketbook, but from the heart and mind and the spirit.

There are many ways in which a P.T.A. can make contributions, other than contributions that are the result of money-raising projects. While ours is a comparatively new organization, it numbers millions of members. Naturally, a group of this size makes valuable gifts to the life of the community.

Our first talk will be given by a member who has had wide experience in the community, and is at the same time, conversant with the work of the P.T.A.   —Helen Ramsey

---

INTRODUCING A DOCTOR

Our principal speaker, ladies and gentlemen, is a man who is well known in his profession. Some things about him are not as well known by everyone. I know them. So, being known as a man who can't keep a secret, I'll tell them to you.

Not many of you know that our speaker is a nerve doctor. After he treats you he has the nerve to send you a bill. As a patient he got some of his own medicine one time. They gave him an anesthetic. He never came out of it.

He had a strange case the other day. He advised a patient to give up drinking coffee. The patient told him that he never drank it. So our doctor ordered him to refrain from smoking. The patient did not smoke. This was getting serious; there was nothing wrong with this patient. So the doctor handed him his bill. The patient is recovering but it will take time.

Doctors have a neat way of getting away from serious charges. Everyone knows that they are just practicing. Here is our guest who never practices because he knows his profession, Dr. ——————.   —Louis J. Huber

INTRODUCING A GOVERNOR

Friends, I'm really on a spot. I've been requested to introduce the head man of his state—the Governor. How do you go about introducing a man everybody knows?

I'm reminded of the story about a certain young lady who called at a veteran's hospital and asked to see Bill Jones, a patient. She was told that only relatives were permitted to visit patients. "Oh, that's all right," she said. "I'm his sister." So they sent her up to his room. She knocked on the door and it was opened by a dignified, matronly looking lady, who looked at her and said, "Yes?" "I want to see Bill," the young lady said. "I'm his sister." "Well," said the matron, "it's nice to meet you. Permit me to introduce myself. I'm his mother."

Anyhow, about the Governor. I could mention some of his splendid achievements—his never-ending efforts to benefit the people by making this a better and healthier and happier state to live and work in. But everybody is aware of his many accomplishments, so I'd just be repeating things you already know.

I'm really in awe of Governors. I've met several of them and found them to be men of dignity and charm—courteous and friendly—easy to talk to—but I never seem to know what to say to them. I don't know how to approach them. You know, you can go to your alderman and say: "Hey, Charley, would you mind doing me a little favor? I got a little traffic ticket here . . ." Or when you run across a Mayor you can say: "Hi, kid, where'd you pick that armload of blonde you were dancing with at the First ward ball last Saturday?" You know, a perfectly normal approach.

But with a Governor—you know a Governor is a big guy—you can't stop him on the street, like anybody else, and greet him in a normal way, and say: "Where've you been, Butch? Howdjuh get home that night?" You get kind of a feeling that maybe it isn't just the right thing to do. It sort of leaves you at a loss for something to say. And when it comes to introducing a Governor—well, all I can think of is to tell you something you all know. He's not only a credit to his state and the intelligence of you voters who put him there, but he's a regular guy and a real human being, and like most of us present, I'm proud to be one of his constituents. Ladies and gentlemen, the Honorable ——————, a great Governor of the great State of ——————. Thank you.

—Earl Jay Gilbert

INTRODUCING A SPEAKER AT A GOLDEN WEDDING ANNIVERSARY PARTY

As I sit here watching the friends who have reached the fiftieth milestone of their lives together, I am reminded of the words of Robert Browning:

Grow old along with me,
The best is yet to be.
The last of life for which the first was made.

I like to think, and I firmly believe, that the best is yet to be for the two friends we are honoring today. Surely, when two people have shared a half century of life together, they have little to fear in the years that are to follow. No, their matrimonial bark has passed safely over the rocky shoals of adjustment; they have ridden the rapids of difficult middle life, and now they are on calm seas in the golden sunset of their years.

This marriage took place not only fifty years ago, but in another era, we might say. While it seems a pastoral period in comparison with the hectic present, I imagine in those days long skirts seemed just as swift and exciting to the people who lived at that time. To me, those days had a quiet charm of restfulness; perhaps a young couple starting out then had a more harmonious outlook than couples face in this present restless age.

Whatever it is, our friends today have given us—by rounding out fifty years of successful married life—a fine example of what can be accomplished by mutual effort and esteem.

God bless you both for bringing us this inspiration.

May we have a few words from the groom? Mr. ——————.

—Helen Ramsey

INTRODUCING A PUBLIC - SPIRITED CITIZEN

And now, my friends, the man I would like to introduce at this time really needs no introduction. He is known far and wide. He often goes too far, and he is plenty wide. He is held in high esteem, is of high caliber, has high standards, high ideals. He is one of those "Hi, neighbor!" boys. As I said, he is of high caliber; his decisions are as quick as the crack of a pistol, whose advice is like a shot in the arm, and whose speeches go off with a bang. In other words, he's a big shot! The man of whom I speak comes from sturdy timber, dating back to 1620 when they settled in this country. In recent years very few of the descendants have settled for anything. His family tree is beyond reproach, but the fruit it bears doesn't amount to much. Three of his brothers ran for office. The other two ran for the border.

The man I would like to introduce is free with money, regardless of to whom it belongs. Easy come, easy grow — at twenty per cent interest. Mostly interest, as he hasn't any principle. Free with money? Ah, me! One year ago he spent six thousand dollars to have his family tree looked up. Six months ago he spent twelve thousand dollars to have it hushed up.

Yes, ladies and gentlemen, he is the type of man you could go to in time of distress; in time of dire need you could go to him for succor. In no time at all you could return happily to your home fully indoctrinated in the art of being a full-fledged sucker. So do not hesitate to approach him if you are caught in the web of difficult circumstances. For example, if you should ask him for an apple he will give you a seed so you can start an orchard. If one of your family is at death's door he will be the first to try and pull them through.

Yes, my dear friends, the man I would like to introduce at this time is fortunately out of town—by request of the judge—so, therefore, I take great pleasure in introducing to you . . . (Name of speaker, or well-liked citizen of the community.)

—Arthur L. Kaser.

INTRODUCING A SPEAKER ON THE Y. M. C. A.

Tonight we celebrate and commemorate the organization of the Young Men's Christian Association. We want to reminisce briefly about its origin and growth of accomplishment. Many of you know the early history of the organization; some of you may have known at one time of its struggles in the beginning; still others know none of these details, and have taken for granted this magnificent association that is now more than one hundred years old, and has a membership of more than a million and a half.

We may wonder why the "Y" has survived and grown to such proportions. Perhaps the reason may be tersely stated in the words used by General MacArthur at the formal surrender of the Japanese. Speaking of the successful peace, he said: "It must be of the spirit if we are to save the flesh."

This seems to me to be the test of any movement. Is it of the spirit? If any cause or aim is "of the spirit" it will further both the mentality and the physical body. Let us keep this in mind as we listen to the amazing story of the Y.M.C.A. It will be told by a man who believes in our work and supports it whole-heartedly. May I present Mr. —————, who will speak on "The Early Days."

—Helen Ramsey

INTRODUCING A PROTESTANT MINISTER

Ladies and gentlemen, tonight we are going to hear a few well-chosen words from a man who by character, by temperament, by training and disposition is well-fitted to his profession, a Minister of the Gospel. He has been, and is, spiritual advisor to many. He has offered consolation and solace to those who have been weary and distressed in mind and body

While I understand on fairly good authority that certain people start to fall asleep as soon as a minister opens his mouth, I don't believe we'll hear many snores tonight. You know, I'm particularly interested in church work—I like to carry the collection plate, although conditions have changed recently. We got a new minister a few weeks ago and after his second Sunday he called me in and said: "Brother, I certainly admire the way you juggle that plate. However, to test your dexterity I'm going to install a new system. It's what they call in show business the Shubert System. A plate in each hand." (ILLUSTRATE WITH HANDS HELD PALMS UP) Business hasn't been so good since then.

I don't know whether any of you recall, years ago, a young Hindu mystic who came to the United States and called himself the Second Messiah. He attracted a lot of attention and a lecture tour was arranged for him and a theatrical publicity man I knew named Leo was engaged to handle his tour. This publicity man sent several advance agents out to build up the tour of this self-styled second Messiah. One of the advance agents wrote back to his boss and said, "Dear Leo: Be nice to this guy. If he's on the level, we're sittin' pretty."

Which reminds me—a Texas family, who were very devout church-goers, decided to move to New Jersey. The night before they left, their little four-year-old son knelt down to say his prayers. After asking the customary blessings on all members of the family and friends, he finished by saying "Goodbye, dear God. We're moving to Jersey tomorrow."

Ladies and gentlemen, I realize that you're growing impatient to hear the speaker of the evening, a man who has a important message for you. And I might add that I am proud of the opportunity to introduce a man whose spiritual guidance we all need and respect, the Rev. Dr. ——————.

—Earl Jay Gilbert

INTRODUCING A MINISTER

Gentlemen, I could talk for an hour about the next speaker, so numerous are his good works in this community. I could tell you about his diligent efforts in preaching the word of God. I could tell you about his many charitable deeds, about his long record of public service to all of us here in Pineville. But a reiteration at this time is unnecessary, as his record stands like an open book to all of us in Pineville. We all know Reverend John Anderson. We all know him as a man of eloquence, but like every man, there is always something that we don't know—some little anecdote or happening that has been hushed up over the years. So tonight, I am going to let you in on a little secret in Reverend John Anderson's career.

It happened many, many years ago, when Reverend Anderson was a young man, and I might add, at that time a young speaker. The church was packed on that particular Sunday, and Reverend Anderson was filled with the fire of eloquence. He began his sermon in perfect form, but before long he hit a snag. Piling clause upon clause and phrase upon phrase, and when clause upon clause had been added to each other, one branching off in one direction, and another in that, he discovered that he was involved in a hopelessly entangled sentence, and that the starting point was quite out of sight. Reverend Anderson paused in his speech and for the moment he was frustrated. For a short time he hesitated, and then with a sudden impulse he said: "I don't exactly know where I went in, in beginning this sentence, and I don't in the least know where I'm coming out; but one thing I do know, I'm bound for the kingdom of Heaven."

Ladies and gentlemen, Reverend John Anderson.

—Sylvester McGovern

INTRODUCING A SPEAKER ON HEALTH AND ACCIDENT WEEK

It seems that the custom these past few years is to devote certain weeks for certain causes, things or hobbies. I wonder i that means that in time to come we will become a week nation Let's hope not. I also hope we will never have a whole week o fasting. Think of nothing to eat for a whole week. Wow! Tha is, when seven days would make one weak.

We have with us tonight a man who, in my personal opin ion, has a very bright and outstanding idea. He is campaignin; for the inauguration of what he calls Health and Acciden Week wherein a week each year would be set aside for every body to get healthy and have no accidents. It sounds like . wonderful idea. Why can't it be done? We have a week where in we are supposed to eat an awful lot of eggs. Then we hav butter and milk week where we are supposed to help use u; the surplus dairy products, and breathing week when we ar supposed to breathe more often. In this way we help natur balance the world's supply of hydrogen and oxygen.

This man believes we could become healthy enough in on week to stay healthy the other fifty-one weeks in the year. Alsc by avoiding accidents for a week we would form the habit an would have no accidents for the remainder of the year. Thin of all the money we would save. We would save on both docto bills and hospital bills. Using the old saying, an apple a da keeps the doctor away, two apples a day keeps two doctor away. In other words, the better it is the more doctors we kee away. The only thing is, if we instituted a health week man doctors would suffer from good health.

There is one thing in favor of this man's idea. The abolitio of fireworks. Many states are banning the manufacture, sale c use of fireworks. Only this morning a neighbor's little boy wa rummaging around in the attic and found an old bunch of fir crackers. Not knowing what they were he proceeded to swa low them. He was rushed to the hospital. A couple of hou later I called his father and inquired about the boy. The fath said the firecrackers must have been duds. He hadn't heard any bad reports.

Some people are not so fortunate. About a year ago Sam Snager's brother Adolph swallowed a frog. He croaked. I, a number of years ago, had a brother who was badly hurt by a swordfish. For two weeks it was a duel between life and death. I might class myself as one of the luckiest persons alive. I fell off the roof of our house and wasn't hurt one bit. I just kept bouncing and bouncing. I had on a pair of light spring pants.

I have a lot of faith in the man who is trying to put across this health and accident week and I believe that after he has explained his plan you, too, will become very enthusiastic about it. Ladies and gentlemen, I have the great pleasure of introducing Mr. (name,) who will speak on Health and Accident Week.
—Arthur L. Kaser

INTRODUCING A CONGRESSMAN

You've heard it said that two things are sure—death and taxes! But there is one thing about death—it doesn't get worse every time Congress meets. Congress tells you one thing one day and out the other. That doesn't sound just right, but who is?

If you ever get to Washington be sure and see Congress at work. Don't miss it if you can. We shouldn't talk about Congressmen like this. We vote them in and bawl them out. They run for office, and after they are in they run for cover.

As soon as an important issue comes up somebody wants to investigate something. What we need is more investigators to investigate the investigators. The last we heard some of these investigators were looking for bones in animal crackers. But congressmen are not alone. There are two groups that seldom know just what the people want. They are the congressmen and the people. If there are any congressmen present I hope they will accept this patter as all in fun. Ladies and gentlemen, our very popular representative, Congressman (name).
—Arthur L. Kaser

INTRODUCING A WORLD TRAVELER

The man whom we are about to hear has made it his purpose in life to visit all parts of the world. He has traveled through all of the countries of Europe, Asia, Africa and the polar regions. In fact, William C. Otis is a man of hemispheres. There is no place on the face of this earth where William C. Otis fears to tread; and it is known that he volunteered to make an expedition to one of the darker regions of the universe. It must be emphasized that during the past centuries millions have been told to go to this dismal place, but there is no record of any one who willingly made the trip. But one thing is certain, our next speaker made an attempt. Let me tell you about it.

It all happened in this city some years ago on a certain Sunday when Mr. Otis was attending church services. On that particular Sunday Mr. Otis was exceptionally tired. As the sermon was rather dull and the atmosphere of the church was filled with drowsiness, Mr. Otis fell asleep in his pew. Accustomed to sleeping in strange beds nightly, or in no bed at all as is the habit of world travelers, his sleep was profound. During the deepest moments of Mr. Otis' repose the minister asked all members of the congregation who wanted to go to Heaven to stand up. Every person in the church with the exception of Mr. Otis stood up. Mr. Otis, no doubt, at that time was dreaming that he was sailing down the Nile or some other such remote body of water. Then when the members of the congregation had re-taken their seats, the minister said: "All those who want to go to Hell, stand up." At the precise moment the minister said the words, "stand up," Mr. Otis' dream boat must have docked at some port, as he abruptly stood up, while every other parishioner remained seated. Looking about the church and noting that he and the minister were the only persons standing, Mr. Otis firmly but emphatically cried out: "Well, Reverend, it looks like we'll have to go it alone!"

Ladies and gentlemen, Mr. William C. Otis.

—Sylvester McGovern

INTRODUCING A SUCCESSFUL SALESMAN

One of the principal reasons the next speaker is an outstanding success on our sales staff is that he always bears in mind the purpose of his mission. When Jack Brown goes out on a call to see Mr. Jones of the John Jones Company, he sees Mr. Jones, not the office boy. Jack Jones knows why he is making the call and Jack Jones is never diverted or sidetracked. If he doesn't know, he asks, and he does what some of you fellows are sometimes afraid to do, he asks for the order. Jack's persistency in this respect reminds me of the persistency of little five-year-old Elaine.

Little five-year-old Elaine was a frequent visitor to hospitals, where her numerous aunts were continually bringing new little cousins into the world. On these occasions little Elaine would go to the hospital with her mother, chat childishly with her bed-ridden aunt for a half an hour or so, after which the new baby was carried into the room for the first showing.

One day little Elaine's uncle got an attack of appendicitis and was rushed to the hospital for an operation. A visit to the hospital was promptly followed by little Elaine and her mother. After the usual half hour had elapsed and little Elaine had occupied the time by jumping from one chair to another, pulling on the sheets of the bed and performing various other childish antics, she became restless. Something was decidedly missing on the visit, little Elaine was certain about that. She wasn't seeing what she came to see. She was sidetracked to some strange thing called appendicitis. But little Elaine spoke up.

Toddling over to the bed of her recuperating uncle, she whispered into his ear: "Where's the baby?"

(Pause for laughter)

Gentlemen, meet Jack Brown, the man who gets what he goes after—the man who is never sidetracked from the purpose of his sales visit, and gentlemen, the man who like little Elaine, always asks for an order.

—Sylvester McGovern

INTRODUCING A JUDGE

Ladies and gentlemen, tonight we are going to hear a man who never speaks unless he has something important to say. He spoke to me once and while he had only a few words to say, I have never forgotten them.

It seems that while I was taking a little stroll one day, a sudden gust of wind blew my hat off and carried it right out into the middle of the street. I chased after it and I was just about to grab it when all of a sudden a mean-looking dog about the size of a baby hippopotamus dashed in out of no-where and sat down and planted his front paws right on my hat. I stopped real quick. I wasn't afraid—I was just a little anxious.

The dog looked up at me and frowned. Then he lifted his upper lip. He had about two thousand teeth. They looked like they belonged on a man-eating alligator. Then he spoke. "Gr-r-r-ruff-ruff." I just stood there—you know, still hesitating —don't think I was frightened—I am a man who is unafraid of anything in the world—except my wife and her mother. Well, I've always known that a dog is man's best friend, so I smiled very politely and said, "Hello, best friend. Nice best friend. Good best friend." The dog said, "Gr-r-r-ruff! Gr-r-ruff!" Then I remembered what the animal trainers say. "Never let an animal think that you are afraid—stare him right in the eye and he'll back down."

So, I got down on my hands and knees. I was about ten feet away from him—and I looked at him very sternly—right in his eyes! Well, after a minute or so he looked a little embarrassed and dropped his eyes and hung his head and wagged his tail a little sheepishly. Well, I got up and straightened my shoulders. He got up and straightened his shoulders. I started over to get my hat. He suddenly decided to meet me halfway. He came in a hurry. I lost interest in the hat. It was an old one, anyway, and I figured it was time I got a new one. I withdrew a little rapidly and just as I reached the top of a nearby fence the dog made a flying leap. I limped into a drug store and got some iodine and soft bandages and then rushed right into the courthouse to make a complaint.

I said, "Judge, a dog just bit me." The Judge said, "Where did he bite you?" And when I told him he fined me fifteen dollars for contempt of court! Well, I've forgiven him long ago, and it's a genuine pleasure to introduce him tonight. But a word of warning first. If you ever get bitten by a dog—**don't tell him where!**

My friends, let me present to you that eminent and distinguished jurist, the Honorable Judge ——————.

—Earl Jay Gilbert

In court, a judge was bawling out the prisoner before pronouncing his verdict. Said he:

"Horse-whipping is too good for one of your kind. And it's the second time you've been up before me, too. The idea of a man your size beating a poor little woman like that!"

"But, your Honor, she kept irritating and irritating me all the time," said the prisoner.

"How does she irritate you?"

"Why, she keeps saying: 'Beat me! Just hit me once and I'll have you hauled up before that bald-headed old reprobate of a magistrate and see what he'll do to you'."

Judge (choking): "Discharged!"

A gentleman from Cucamonga was summoned as a witness in a case in Santa Ana. He had been cautioned that he must be very exact in his statements.

"Was the man a total stranger?" he was asked.

After duly pondering the question, he replied: "I'd say he was what I would call a partial stranger."

"Either you knew him or you did not," he was sternly advised. "There is no such thing as a partial stranger."

"Well," he answered, "I don't know how else to describe him. He was a one-legged man."   —George A. Posner

INTRODUCING AN ACCOUNTANT

Tonight I have the pleasure of introducing to you a man who is engaged in one of the most abused of professions—an accountant. An accountant is a man who keeps the books, balances the bank account, issues paychecks, but gets practically no paycheck himself. He used to be called a bookkeeper, until one day an industrialist called in an efficiency expert and said, "We've got to do something about these bookkeepers. They're belly-aching all of the time. But," added the industrialist abruptly, "we can't raise their pay!"

So the efficiency expert went to his office, traced a bookkeeper back to the stone age, consulted his slide rule, and then after two weeks of intensive study returned to the industrialist with a fifty-page report.

"What have you come up with?" snapped the industrialist.

The efficiency expert looked at Chart C and then glanced at Chart B, and said very methodically: "Our calculations reveal that in lieu of an increase in salary, a bookkeeper must be referred to in a term that sounds a little more dignified than is now indicated by the nomenclature in usage. This fifty-page report that I am now submitting to you developed the remarkable disclosure that a bookkeeper should be termed 'an accountant!'"

The industrialist rolled the word, "accountant," across his tongue several times, and then cried out: "Efficiency expert, you're a genius! Miss Smith, get out a memo!"

So a bookkeeper became an accountant with no increase in pay. But don't think for a moment that an accountant is not a valued man around a business institution. Several years ago, before John Adams, our next speaker, became connected with the very fine firm he now represents, he was associated with a concern that had great difficulty in showing a profit. In fact, the firm had lost money for five consecutive years. Each year John would work diligently at his books and then prepare the company's year-end financial statement, all of the time in red ink. Then on the sixth year a miracle happened, as John discovered after he had compiled the company's statement for the year. Rushing into the boss' office in great excitement, John shouted: "We're in the black! We're in the black!"

The boss threw both hands upward in supplication and cried out: "Bless the heavens! Bless the heavens!" Then the boss added quickly: "Get out six copies for the six vice-presidents at the bank!"

"We can't," said John. "We haven't any black ink!"

"Run out and buy some," said the boss, indignantly.

"We can't do that either," said John.

"You can't!" said the boss, perplexingly. "Why?"

"If we do," said John, "we'll be back in the red!"

Ladies and gentlemen, meet Mr. John Adams.

—Rome Roberts

INTRODUCING THE TOWN MAYOR

Tonight we are to be honored by the presence of our esteemed mayor. We all know how reluctant he is to make himself conspicuous, but he has something important to impart to you as citizens of this town. We are all proud of our community, and equally proud of our worthy mayor.

I think we are all aware that our town, though not the largest city or town in the world, is the cleanest, and most livable place in the U. S. In addition to this, my friends, our town is exceptionally rich. It is full of golden opportunities.

Fellow citizens, do you realize that our town is overrun with wealth? You cannot turn but what you see wealth and riches. Listen, my friends. You know, as well as I, that every blade of grass has a greenback. Every duck in the puddles has a bill. You never find a garbage can without a scent. Wealth everywhere. Every ditch has a bank. Our bakeries have all kinds of dough. Even our clouds have silver linings. We are so wealthy all our lawns get a rake-off.

My friends, you should feel grateful to live in a one-horse town even if the horse has sleeping sickness. And now the town mare—I mean mayor. Ladies and gentlemen, Mayor (name.)

—Arthur L. Kaser

INTRODUCING A WORLD TRAVELER

Travel talks are always interesting, and when accompanied by movies or colored stills, it gives one the thrill so precious to the fireside travelers. As soon as our narrator has his equipment in place we will enjoy a trip with him through (name locale where pictures were taken.)

They say that the sun never sets on the British flag. Heh! Neither does it ever set on the American tourist. I was reading recently that the one crop harvested green in Europe is the tourist crop. Among the 3,227 American tourists who arrived last week from Europe there were eighteen millionaires. The statistics didn't say how many millionaires there were before they made the trip. There are more tourists now than ever before because it is so much easier to see the world than it was only fifty years ago. You can even do it now on the installment plan. But just imagine falling down on the installments in the middle of Afghanistan. Compare the mode of travel today with that of a hundred years ago. Now we have luxury liners on the water and in the air. Practically all the hazards of ocean travel have been eliminated. Even the skippers can't marry passengers any more.

One of the most confusing things that meets the tourist is the difference in foreign money and ours. For instance, so many are puzzled about the franc. But to a great many American tourists the price of the franc doesn't worry them so long as there is no decline in the Latin quarter. In nearly all the hotels where there used to be signs reading: "Have you left anything?" the signs now read: "Have you anything left?"

I have selected a few bits of information, excerpts from a Government bulletin on travel. If anyone in the audience is contemplating a trip abroad these informative bits might be of great value to them. For instance, all the little rivers that flow into the River Nile are Juveniles. In this country we drink our coffee out of cups. In France they drink their wine out of doors. In Switzerland they take the census by counting the number of echoes and dividing that by the number of mountains. The reason that so many European guides have short index fingers is because they wore them off pointing out interesting places and sights.

For those of us who find it impossible to travel to far off lands we welcome the opportunity to hear these talks, and to see the pictures. There are many places we can visit on our television. We have many channels to tune in, but the best way to see the British Isles is to turn to the English Channel. I see that Mr. (name) is now ready to entertain us. (Introduces narrator.)

—Arthur L. Kaser

_____

INTRODUCING A MOVIE STAR

This evening, friends, we have with us a well-known movie star. She (or he) is one of the stars the movie producer loves to have on the payroll. And this particular star's producer is one individual who can truly thank his lucky stars. Also, this star's producer is noted for his kindness. In order not to show anything brutal on the screen, his movies end just as the couples are about to be married. I believe his company is the only one that screens a picture to take the trash out.

But now about movie stars. I really feel sorry for some of them, for they know not where their next husband is coming from. I read this morning where a movie actress just remarried her first husband. It must have been his turn again. The actress was noted for her long slender fingers. Her fingers got that way by the continual slipping on and off of wedding rings. Stories about movie people getting married should end with a comma instead of a period, for the period is usually too short.

One film star had a secretary who made a terrible mistake. She didn't keep the records straight and now the star has two more divorces than she's had weddings. The young son of a movie star said to the young son of another movie star, "How do you like your new father?" Said the second son of a movie star, "Oh, he's pretty nice." Said the first one, "Isn't he, though? We had him last year." And now, ladies and gentlemen, the famous (name of star).

—Richard Drummond

INTRODUCING A CREDIT MAN

The next speaker on the agenda is engaged in one of the most trying of professions, that of a credit man. By the very nature of his occupation he must assume the demeanor of a man with a rhinoceros hide, through which not even an atom bomb will penetrate. When the suave and patronizing salesman downstairs gets through selling Mrs. Smith half of the store, Mrs. Smith drops up to the credit department to give the necessary explanations to Bill Jones, our next speaker.

"How do you expect to pay for the purchase?" Bill asks Mrs. Smith, noting that Mrs. Smith has just bought the entire left wing of cloak and suits.

"I hadn't thought of that minor matter," said Mrs. Smith, getting red in the face.

Then Bill says, "There is another little minor matter that has been overlooked for about six months. It's only $600.00."

"Ho, hum," says Mrs. Smith. "That little oversight."

"I'll have to have a note endorsed by your father-in-law," says Bill, very firmly.

Then Mrs. Smith becomes very indignant and storms out of the office in a huff. So Bill cuts Mrs. Smith's order in half. "We'll let her have the chemise, but not the chenile," Bill says to a clerk. "Scratch out six pairs of pajamas; four pairs are enough for any woman. Eliminate the bra, that woman doesn't need 'em. We'll let her keep the aqua-blue suit, but not the pea-green in-between."

When the word got down to the sales department that Credit Man Brown had cut Mrs. Smith's order in half, the salesman said quite peevishly to a group of his associates: "That sourpuss of a pen pusher upstairs can kill off more business in a day than we guys can sell in a month."

So by that time everybody in the place is mad at Bill Brown, including the boss, who looks over the books one day and says: "Brown! What's the meaning of this $600 past due item of Mrs. Smiths'?"

"I'm working on it," said Bill.

"Well, work a little harder," says the boss, with a boss' customary grimace.

So Bill writes Mrs. Smith a letter and calls her attention to something that she had known for a long time. Does he get a check by return mail? I should say not. He gets a perfumed, monogramed letter from Mrs. Smith, who admits that she received Bill's letter, but who tells Bill that she has devised a new system for handling payment of her bills. Every month, she says, she places all invoices in a waste basket, and then at the end of the month she picks out just two, and pays them promptly.

Then Mrs. Smith had the audacity to tell Bill that if he sends any more letters like the last one, Bill's statement won't even get into the wastebasket.

Ladies and gentlemen, Mr. Bill Brown.

—James Bolden

_____

INTRODUCING A DENTIST

You and your family should visit the dentist at least once or twice each year. Then when the dentist and his wife return the visit feed them something soft. They may have bad teeth. However, don't expect a dentist to fill every engagement. He may have to fill a tooth instead.

The best dentists are ex-soldiers. They've learned the art of drilling. As a rule dentists don't make very congenial guests anyway. They're always looking down in the mouth, but will spare no pains to get at the root of something. Some people are bored to tears in the presence of a dentist. Many dentists are retired riveters who got too nervous to climb high buildings.

These are the same dentists who sing while they work to quiet their nerves. Their favorite song is "The Yanks are Coming." But I ask you, my friends, what would we do without dentists? Answer: We'd live on soup, which is a soup-perior food anyway. So take to heart this bit of advice: Be true to your teeth or they'll be false to you. And now, ladies and gentlemen, more sensible advice from our speaker, Dr. (name.)

—Arthur L. Kaser

INTRODUCING AN APPLIANCE DEALER

It is my privilege this evening to present to you as one of our speakers, Mr. John Peterson. Mr. Peterson is one of Cliffville's foremost citizens. Through the services offered to the people of our town, John's appliance store has played an important part in the development of this community. John came out of the gas age, flourished all through the electric age, and as we are approaching the atomic age, John is ready for that, too.

John sold the first electric washing machine in the county, thereby helping to put the washboard manufacturers out of business. He was a pioneer in selling electric refrigerators, which melted away our local ice plant. He flooded the town with radios, television sets and dishwashing machines. Now John aims to bankrupt our garbage pick-up service with that new disposal he sells. John not only wiped out the washer-woman with his electric gadgets, but he put an awful dent in some of our most prosperous laundries as well. I understand that the directors of the power and light plant are worried, for it has been reported that John is prepared to introduce some new atomic devices that'll put an abrupt stop to the dynamoes. When this news got around town, power and light stock dropped ten points.

But everything is not a bed of roses for John. He has his problems, for he deals primarily with women. One day last week a lady came into his store, and said to him: "Mr. Peterson, I want to look at a refrigerator." John promptly and courteously took the good lady over to his large display and very carefully pointed out the features in each model.

Turning to one gleaming white unit, John opened and closed the door of the box, saying to the lady, "Now it's lit. Now it's out."

"Will you repeat that?" asked the lady.

"Certainly," said John. "Now it's lit, now it's out."

The lady stooped down and looked at the door of the refrigerator, and watched John open and close the door, noting that a light inside the box was on when John opened the door.

"I can't quite get what you're driving at," said the lady.

"Now it's lit," said John, opening the door. "Now it's out," he added, closing the door.

The good lady stood up to John and said in a skeptical tone of voice: "How do you know?"

Ladies and gentlemen, Mr. John Peterson.

—Hugh Lincoln

INTRODUCING A DOG FANCIER

There are many, many kinds of dogs. They range from thimble size to those that weigh two pounds less than a horse. Many types of dogs originated in Europe. Even the hot dog came from Germany. Some dogs are a necessity, some are a luxury, and others keep knocking lids off of garbage cans.

I used to do a lot of hitch-hiking. I bought a dog to help me get rides. He was a pointer. As soon as I was married it ruined everything. My wife taught him it wasn't polite to point. Later when I became a newspaper photographer the dog was a great help. He was always snapping people.

Too many people take dogs for granted. But dogs need care and training, otherwise they are no better than children. There are too many people who do not understand dogs. A cousin of mine was visiting us and I asked him to take our dog out for air. He took him to the nearest filling station.

As I said, too many people do not understand dogs. I was that way at first. The first dog I owned ate a tape measure and died by inches. The second dog crawled under the bed and died by the foot. The third one chewed up a bolt of dress goods and died by the yard.

I bought my sister a lap dog, but when she tried to sit in its lap it bit her. It was a poodle, and every time she would give the poodle a bath it would go right out and get dirty. That poodle just loved to paddle in a puddle, and when a puddle poodles—uh—poodle pedals in a pud muddle—What I mean is, when a paddle poodles in a dirty mud pedal—muddles in a paddle—When—a—poodle—paddles— Ladies and gentlemen, do I sound dogmatic? And now, our speaker, the prominent dog fancier, Mr. (name).   —Arthur L. Kaser

INTRODUCING A SPEAKER TO DISCUSS THE PROBLEM CHILD

Some of you might think that we are not doing just exactly the right thing by placing our next speaker on the program. However, this speaker insists that even if she is middle-aged and unmarried she knows as much about the problem children as any of the mothers. Her defense is, she has no children to influence or prejudice her. She also insists that she was once a child herself. She did add, with a little sadness, that when the audience found that she was—er—well, a spinster, you might say, they would tilt their noses upward and snort. However, she doesn't mind a short snort, but a long snort might distort any sort of retort.

She says that being an old maid is like a row boat with only one oar. You can get across the river of life okay, but it's better to have two oars when you reach the troublesome rapids. I have known this lady for a long time and I can assure you she is sincere and conscientious in her work among children. For a good many years she has had the opportunity to study her younger brother. I can also assure you she had about the meanest kid brother that ever lived. He was in trouble so much that no matter what happened in their town of Toadville he was blamed for it. Even when he was a tiny baby they were pinning things on him. When he grew older his patient father wore out seven razor strops on the boy. And, believe me, that's a lot of razor strops to wear out on a little shaver. When he was twelve years old he graduated from the first grade because he was too big for the seats. In the second grade he had a special seat— a stool in the corner facing the walls. In the second grade there were two reading classes, one for the regular readers and the other for the backward readers. Of course, Bertram was in the class for backward readers. It seemed so utterly foolish. I knew every child in Toadville and never ran across one child that could read backward.

It appears that our speaker is a bit tardy. While waiting I might give one example why there are so many problem children. A lady who lives not very far from where I live was all-fired angry not long ago when she discovered that the teacher had whipped her darling little Waldo for smearing mucilage on the blackboard. This lady then sent a sizzling note to the teacher. The teacher showed me the note later. It read: "Miss Blank, I don't want to hear of you whacking Waldo again. He is a delicate child and not used to such treatment. We never hit him at home except in self-defense." May I offer just a wee bit of advice? My friends, if parents took as much care of their children as they do of their automobiles they'd run better and smoother, be easier to steer right, and wouldn't backfire when they least expect it. Ah, here she is. Ladies and gentlemen, allow me to present Miss (name) who will now speak on the problem child. —Arthur L. Kaser

INTRODUCING A CONGRESSMAN

It is a profound pleasure to bring to you this evening the eminent and distinguished congressman from our district, the Honorable Benjamin T. Smith. Congressman Smith has served this district long and faithfully. His convictions have always been firm; his decisions in the best interests of the people. Congressman Smith has never been a fence-straddler. He has faced every issue with courage, and certainly his frankness should be emulated by all who seek high office. Many of you have heard him speak, and you all know that he walks right up to an issue and meets it face to face.

His courage and frankness are probably best demonstrated by an event that took place in the northern part of our state during the last election. It was towards the close of the campaign, and the hall was packed with citizens eager to hear how Congressman Smith stood on various issues. When it came time for questions from the audience, a farmer stood up and asked: "Congressman, are you for or against the Rural Rehabilitation Bill?"

"I am, sir!" exclaimed Congressman Smith.

"I thought you were," said the constituent, and he sat down.

Ladies and gentlemen, Congressman Benjamin T. Smith.

—Rome Roberts

INTRODUCING A BARBER

Ladies and gentlemen, my next honor is to introduce to you a barber—Mr. Jerry Barnes, one of our community's most prominent citizens. But before I invite Jerry to stand up before you, first I am going to tell you what I found out about a barber. So that my facts would be correct, I telephoned Professor Thornton at the college, and said, "Professor, I have to introduce a barber tonight, and I thought you could give me some information on the history of that profession."

"Well, well," said the professor, "You are talking about a very old institution, and a very versatile profession."

"Versatile, did you say?" I asked.

"Very versatile," replied the professor. "A barber at one time was a musician, a surgeon, a dentist and a fisherman, all combined into one."

"That's taking in a lot of territory," I said. "How about the musician angle?"

"Aha! You hit the nail right on the head, for the conjunction of the barber and the harp was one of the most important amalgamations in world history. But for that fortunate alliance, that ugly thing called a beard might still be bristling from the face of man."

"A beard!" I exclaimed.

"Yes," replied the professor, "a beard!"

"Well, how did this all happen?" I asked.

"It happened," said the professor, "in the third reign of Caesar the Great. You will remember, my good fellow, that a full-grown beard in those days of antiquity was an indication of manliness. In that period of world history, it looked as if the beard was to stay until the end of time. And it would have stayed, too," continued the professor, "if it hadn't been for Cicero, a great orator, who could also wield a razor and play a harp. One day Cicero said to his colleagues Plato, Quintilian and Maxmilius, 'See here, gentlemen, we've got to shave off

Caesar's beard.' All of the three leaders of the empire shouted out in unison: 'What! Shave off the beard of the mighty Caesar! He will slay us openly in the Public Forum!' 'Ah, my good friends,' replied Cicero, 'that is where you are mistaken. We will cut off his beard while he is under the influence of our words and music!' "

"So the learned men invited Caesar down to Cicero's house to hear a speech. When Caesar arrived Cicero placed the great man in a chair and then gave a stupendous oration about fishing which made the rafters tremble. Then Cicero picked up his harp and began to play and sing, accompanied by the strong voices of Plato, Quintilian and Maxmilius. When Caesar was properly under the influence of the music, Cicero got out his lather and razor and sliced off Caesar's beard."

"What did Caesar do when he came to?" I asked.

"At first he was furious," the professor replied. "But when he saw his image in the mirror, he danced with glee. 'What a handsome man!' he shouted and then rushed back to the Forum to issue an edict that all beards in the empire be shaved off immediately."

"Then Cicero was the first barber," I said.

"The very first," replied the professor, "and Cicero, Plato, Quintilian and Maxmilius comprised the first barber-shop quartet."

"Do you suppose that Cicero's oration was of any significance," I asked.

"Considerable," replied the professor. "It was firmly established that talking was a necessary adjunct to barbering."

"Then that was the first fish story told aside a barber chair," I said.

"Absolutely the first," said the professor.

"Many fish stories have been told since," I said.

"Millions of them," he replied, "and they're getting bigger every year," the professor concluded as he hung up.

Ladies and gentlemen, Mr. Jerry Barnes.

—Howard C. Wilford

INTRODUCING A DOCTOR SPEAKING ON OBESITY

As you are aware, ladies and gentlemen, Dr. (name) is with us this evening to offer some good advice for overweight people. I've always had a hunch that doctors who specialize in treating overweight patients live on the fat of the land. Some specialists refer to their ultra overweight as Hippo-chondriacs.

Personally, I like the overweights. They are usually so good natured. I think everybody loves a fat man until he sits down by them in a bus. Furthermore, I consider it very crude to refer to heavy people as fat. They are merely over-emphasized. If you are overweight, do not develop an inferiority complex. Doctors claim there are three million women overweight. These, of course, are round figures.

Some time ago I found my belts were becoming too tight. My doctor told me to stop eating bread. But I couldn't stop eating bread. It didn't leave me any way to pick up the gravy. The fact was, my shirts were getting so tight the buttons popped off. One day my wife fastened a button on with wire. "There," she said, "try and laugh that off."

An uncle of mine is so overweight he had the mumps for three weeks before he knew it. He tried all kinds of diets but he was just a poor loser. He just loves to play golf but he can't play. If he stands where he can see the ball, he can't hit it. If he stands where he can hit the ball, he can't see it. And now, friends, may I introduce Dr. (name)?

—Arthur L. Kaser

INTRODUCING A BEAUTICIAN

A beautician is something like a barber—only a beautician is a comparatively new species, being not much more than a generation in age, while a barber has a history back of him of at least twenty generations.

There was a time, not too long ago, when only a Mrs. Vanderbilt visited a beautician. The rest of the women stayed at home and waved their hair in the kitchen with a curling iron and newspaper wrappers, which unfortunately gave a very unsavory appearance to a lady's head at bedtime. Psychologists say that is one of the reasons so many men disappeared and never were heard from again.

One day someone got a bright idea. The fellow who got the bright idea was a barber. He got the idea from another fellow whose idea wasn't so bright. It seems that a fellow down in Scottsville, Missouri, took one look at his wife when her hair was curled in newspapers and went stark mad. So mad was this fellow that he grabbed a pair of lawn shears and bobbed her hair. It was a noisy operation, according to the neighbors who heard the screaming coming out of the kitchen.

Now the fellow who got the idea from the fellow whose idea wasn't so bright (the barber, I'm speaking about now) got mixed up in this deal by a mere stroke of luck. It seems that the neighbors, after being certain that the irate husband and his lawn clippers had vanished, ventured into the house to console the poor wife. The sight was horrifying. The kitchen was in shambles; bunches of hair matted the floor. It was an unprecedented international event—the shearing of a woman's crowning glory, her golden tresses.

"This woman needs medical attention," shouted one of the neighbors, and she proceeded to call Dr. Jenks. Now it appears that there was a close similarity between the telephone numbers of Dr. Jenks and the barber in question. As was to be expected the neighbor dialed the wrong number and got the barber on the phone.

"A woman's been sheared over here!" she cried into the mouthpiece. "Come right over! Hurry!" Now in all of the barber's thirty years at clipping heads and shaving chins never had he received such a strange request. For a moment he pondered on the word "sheared." That word was certainly closely related with his business. He was the only person around that part of Scottville who was a professional shearer, outside of Farmer Jones, who sheared sheep. Who would be calling old Jones in a hysterical voice like that? "They must mean me," he said, and rushed over to the given address.

"My, my!" said the barber. "I have never seen such an ugly clip of hair in all of my life." But the barber was a man of ingenuity. "Madam," he said professionally, "your hair has the appearance of a disarranged haystack. But cheer up," he added, taking a comb from his pocket and picking up the old-fashioned curling iron, "within a few moments I'll have it looking like a blooming rosebush." Then the barber went to work, nimbly twisting the lady's locks, and at the same time relating his favorite fishing experience.

That's where the barber got his bright idea from a man whose idea wasn't so bright. The next day every woman in Scottsville came to his shop for a bob. The senior girls from Scottsville college formed a queue down Main street. Before noon the bob had spread upstate. By sundown it had crossed the great divide, and within two days half the women in Brooklyn and San Francisco had bobbed their hair. Within a week the thing was universal.

Before introducing our speaker of the evening, Miss Harriet Kent, one of our outstanding beauticians, I want to issue one word of warning to the young fellows in this audience: "Don't flirt with the girl coming out of a beauty parlor. She might be your grandmother."

Ladies and gentlemen, Miss Kent.

—Hugh Lincoln

INTRODUCING A BUSINESSMAN

I asked a friend this morning, "How's business?" He said it was looking up. It had to. It was flat on its back. Tonight we are to hear from a successful businessman. He is going to give us some advice on how to have a going business. I bought some stock once in a going business, but I never found out where it went. It must be still going.

Some businessmen tell us that all business needs now is more confidence. Wouldn't it be a good idea for business to hire more confidence men? Seriously, though, it isn't easy to conduct a business. If you build a big business, you're a sinister influence. If you don't, you're just a darn failure.

So what can a businessman do? Some of them become discouraged and get Government office jobs in the Swivel Service. Perhaps our speaker can discourage discouragement among businessmen. Ladies and gentlemen, Mr. (name).

—Arthur L. Kaser

INTRODUCING A FINANCIER

The speaker of the evening, ladies and gentlemen, is one whom I am proud to present. His success is well known to all of us. The fact that he owns more than one dollar bill is also no secret. I am trying to tell you that he has a big bundle but I am also trying to tell you how he got some of it.

Thrift, that's the answer. There was the time when a friend came to him and asked for the secret of his success. Our speaker proceeded to tell the story. Before he got very far he turned out the light since there was more sense in talking in the dark. His listener didn't need to hear the remainder of the success story; he had just had a demonstration.

At one time in his life he was offered a job of cleaning out the bank. He turned it down because he didn't know if they were offering him a position as president or that of the janitor. He dropped a little money on Wall Street one time. It fell through a grating in the sidewalk and he had quite a time getting it back. Another friend asked him for a tip. Our speaker told him to get interested in something that would be sixty in the morning and ninety at noon. It turned out that he wasn't talking about the stock market, he was just quoting the local temperature of the day before.

But here, ladies and gentlemen, is the man we all admire. His money never went to his head. He still has it in his pocket. I give you Mr. —————.

—Louis J. Huber

INTRODUCING A PLUMBER

Tonight we are going to meet a man who deals in the necessities of life . . . a man who when needed, is needed badly . . . Henry Dawson, proprietor of Bluffville's best plumbing shop.

When I was told that Henry was to be our speaker, I hurried over to the public library to dig up some stuff on a plumber, where I found Miss Constance, just as she has been for the last fifty years, checking a list of overdue books.

"Miss Constance," I said, "I am going to introduce Henry Dawson at a dinner tomorrow. What do you know about a plumber?"

"I could tell you a lot of things about that plumber when he was growing up around here . . . about the time he tied the tin cans on the tail of Farmer Jones' cow . . . !"

"No, no, Miss Constance," I said. "I want to know about A plumber, not that plumber."

"Well," said Miss Constance, "A plumber is pretty much of an antique. Let me see," she added, "It is recorded here on page twenty-two in the 'Anthology of the Trades,' that a plumber came into being during the rule of Nero."

"How was that?" I asked.

"Well, it appears that Nero was about to draw some water one day for his bath, when he suddenly discovered that the wooden troughs had busted somewhere down the line, and there was no water. That made Nero furious. He promptly set aside his fiddle and called in his couriers.

" 'Fetch in that man, Plumb, from the mountains,' " Nero commanded.

"Who was Plumb?" I asked Miss Constance.

"Plumb," said Miss Constance, "was a fellow who discovered plumb. We call it lead. He was working in the mountains twenty leagues from Nero's palace."

"Did Plumb show up?" I asked Miss Constance.

"After about a week Plumb appeared and said to Nero: 'What is it, my Emperor?' "

" 'What is it!' " exclaimed Nero. " 'I haven't been able to take a bath for a week. My fingers are so dirty I can't reach high 'G' on my fiddle. I am now issuing an edict. I command you to replace that old wooden water trough with one of those Plumb pipes you are developing back in the mountains.' "

" 'It will be done,' " said Plumb, " 'but I have to go back and get my tools.' "

" 'What?' " said Nero, " 'You have to go back and get your tools?' "

" 'I never carry my tools on the first trip,' " said Plumb.

"Well," I said to Miss Constance, "Did Plumb fix Nero up?"

"He certainly did," Miss Constance replied. "That was the beginning of the plumbing business."

"I noticed that Plumb had to go back for his tools," I said.

"Yes," replied Miss Constance, "the practice of going back to the plumbing shop for tools was established right then and there."

"It has been going on ever since," I remarked.

"Yes, with one exception," she replied. "Sometime during Shakespeare's era, a plumber inaugurated a one-trip system. But it was a failure and the practice was promptly discontinued."

That, ladies and gentlemen, is the history of a plumber. Now to present Henry Dawson, a descendant of Plumb, the first man to forget his tools. Mr. Dawson.

—Adolph Hintz

ADDITIONAL MATERIAL

A few weeks ago Henry Dawson was holding a sale at his plumbing shop. Among other things that Henry was trying to dispose of were a number of sinks. Henry piled them up out on the sidewalk in front of his shop, and placed a sign alongside which read: "Cast Iron Sinks."

The village nitwit walked up the street, and as he passed

Henry's shop he noticed the sign. "Hm," he said, "Cast Iron Sinks." Then as he started lazily away, he turned around and looked once again at the sign, remarking, "Any darn fool knows that!"   —Adolph Hintz

---

INTRODUCING A SENATOR OR CONGRESSMAN

All of us here this evening are highly honored with the presence of Congressman Wilfred A. Barton, the man who represents this district in the House of Representatives. Congressman Barton has served the citizens of this district well, for which we all are grateful.

The job of a congressman is not an easy one. In addition to his duties on the floor of the house, where he must be vigilant at all times, he is deluged with all sorts of requests from people in his election district. Some of these requests are reasonable ones — many are impossibilities. Among the most numerous of the various types of requests asked the congressman, is the person seeking a government job.

Congressman Barton, of course, meets the job-seeker daily, and in every instance he does everything possible to help secure a position for the applicant that meets his qualifications. However, among his constituents there was a fellow after a job who was relentless in his approach. In fact, the fellow became the worst sort of a pest. Now it appeared that this fellow had little or no ability in any line of endeavor, and there was no opening into which Congressman Barton considered the fellow would fit. After a time the man became such an obstreperous visitor to the congressman's office, that one day Congressman Barton lost his temper and told the fellow off.

Then repenting for losing his temper, as all good people should do, the congressman called the job-seeker back, and in a pleasing tone of voice asked, "Have you read my last speech?"

The job-seeker sneered, and then in a contemptuous tone of voice replied: "I hope I have!"

Ladies and gentlemen, Congressman Wilfred A. Barton.
                                              —Kirk Kirsten

INTRODUCING A BASEBALL PLAYER

Very soon you are going to meet a young man you know and love. I am referring to no other than **(name of speaker)** of **(name of ball club).** Baseball is a truly American dish like chop suey and Italian spaghetti.

Ah, yes, the busiest little sphere of influence in this country is sewed up in a horsehide cover. How I loved to play ball in the vacant lot back of Jake's Grocery Store. The members of our team were a vacant lot, too. Our local sporting editor always printed our team's standing in the league upside down on account of local pride. We were in the cellar so much we looked like a row of canned vegetables.

But we did have one player, Limpy Loco, who was really hot. He played center field just back of Jake's trash burner. Limpy could catch anything from mumps to poison ivy. And fast! Boy, oh, boy! He could hit a home run and reach first base before the spectators heard the crack of the bat. When he'd round second base the second baseman usually insulted him, so Limpy would slap the third baseman in the catcher's mouth.

One time Grandma Jane went with me to watch us play. Our pitcher wasn't very good that day and the other team hit him all over the lot. Finally Grandma said, "That boy throwing that ball is mighty good. He hits the bat every time."

But big baseball is a great sport. Many grown men are now glad they learned decimal fractions when they were young. They can now figure baseball percentages. One time while visiting some friends in Boston we watched a ball game on television. Suddenly the announcer exclaimed excitedly, "He swang at the ball and missed." Over two thousand television sets in Boston burned out. Ladies and gentlemen, Mr. **(name.)**

—Arthur L. Kaser

INTRODUCING A LABOR LEADER

Tonight we are to have a talk by a prominent labor leader. There are many labor leaders, but only a few that are real leaders. In fact, one doesn't know where some of them will lead you. I am positive that our speaker will lead us in the right direction.

My father was one of the greatest labor leaders that ever lived. He was always leading me to some kind of labor. He claimed that work never hurt anybody. I agreed with him. Personally, I wasn't afraid of work. I could lie right down beside it and sleep peacefully.

One trouble today is that people do not put themselves into their work. When I first started working I dug sewer holes. I put myself right into the work, and I've been in the hole ever since.

People should consider their work important, no matter what it is, and take it seriously. There are too many workers who do not quit work when the whistle blows. They stopped an hour ahead of time and wait for the whistle. In other words, too many hands make light of work. More people get crooked trying to avoid hard work than become bent from too much of it.

If I look tired now it's because I dreamed last night I had a job. My cousin Foley is the one that doesn't like work. And all the time he says he loves work. I asked him the other day if he loved work why didn't he find some. He said love is blind. When Foley found out that I had this job, he said, "My, my, what some people won't do for money." I said to Foley, "Foley, if your wife set her foot down and made you look for work, what would you look for?" He said he'd look for another wife.

I told Foley I knew of a place where he could work for his meals. He said that wasn't enough because he was a light eater. I came right out and asked him why he wouldn't work. He said he was on strike. I said, "Strike? My land! Strike for what?" He said he didn't know, but he wouldn't go to work till he got it. And still he's the idol of the family. Been idle for twenty years. The job he's really waiting for is munitions sales-man in the next war. I've lost all patience with him. I told him yesterday that it's certainly no disgrace to work. He said he's been telling his wife that for years. He said if people would just leave him alone he'd carve a career for himself. He ought to; he's a good chiseler. Pardon me for dwelling so long on family affairs. Ladies and gentlemen, our speaker, Mr. **(name.)**

—Arthur L. Kaser

INTRODUCING A TRAVEL AGENT

Good evening, travel fans. I anticipated your desires, and here's hoping I didn't anticipate wrong. I have asked Mr. **(name)** of **(name of travel bureau or vacation resort)** to speak to you this evening on vacationing.

What is summer without vacations? What are vacations without a summer? But remember, the bigger the summer, the harder the fall. Personally, I think the most comforting place to spend a vacation is just inside your income.

To have a real vacation requires four weeks—two weeks to get poached, and two weeks to peel. Every time I go on a vacation I get a wonderful tan. It usually takes about five days. Sort of a Woolworth vacation—five and tan.

I see where the vacation hotels are now giving you the second cup of coffee free. The first cup remains the same price—$1.65. I wrote to a resort hotel last year for weekly rates. They wrote me that they hardly knew because nobody had ever stayed that long.

Last summer I stopped at a wayside motel on my way to vacationing in the north. I drew the proprietor's attention to the much-soiled roller towel in my room. "Don't you know," I asked, "that it's been against the law in this state for three years to have roller towels?" He said, "Mister, that towel was put up there before that law was passed." Now I'll be big-hearted and relinquish the floor to Mr. **(name.)**

—Arthur L. Kaser

INTRODUCING A GAME WARDEN

My early conception of a game warden comes from my boyhood days when the game warden was usually cartooned as a vicious old sleuth with whiskers, sneaking up on some youngster who was angling in some little stream. However, that conception is, of course, entirely false. We know that a game warden is a very valuable member of society, and that without him our natural resources would by this time have become badly depleted. The game warden is a conservationist. He helps protect our wild life so that posterity will also enjoy our great outdoors. Such a man is Harry Fields, our next speaker on this evening's program.

Harry's experiences are numerous and there are many tales he can tell about fur, fins and feathers. But there is one story about Harry that I will tell myself.

About a year ago, out of hunting season, Harry was working his way across the northwoods, making a routine check on the countryside. Suddenly a man appeared from the brush, attired in hunting clothes and carrying a rifle. Harry approached the man and greeted him with a cheery good morning.

"Good morning," said the hunter.

"Nice day for hunting," said Harry.

"Wonderful!" exclaimed the hunter. "But not as good as yesterday."

"How's that?" asked Harry.

"Well," said the man, "I shot the biggest buck you ever saw yesterday. Must have weighed 250 pounds. It was a whopper, and out of season, too. Ho, ho!"

"Ahem," said Harry to himself, "this is a good one." Then he said to the man, "Do you know to whom you are talking?"

"Can't say that I do," said the fellow.

"Do you know you're talking to the game warden in this area?"

For a few moments the man was taken aback, but suddenly

regained his wits. "And do you know who you are talking to?" he asked Harry.

"No, I don't" Harry replied.

"Well," said the hunter, "you're talking to the biggest liar in the state of Minnesota."

Ladies and gentlemen, Mr. Harry Fields.

—Horton Smith

INTRODUCING A DOCTOR

Gentlemen, Dr. Walter Peters, our next speaker, needs no introduction to this audience. We all know him well, and we probably know some things about the doctor that the doctor doesn't know we know. For instance:

Some time ago Doctor Peters' young son, Willie, invited a little friend over to his house to play. When the play became dull, as it usually does with children, the boys sought other diversions, one of which was exploring the house for interesting discoveries. After the youngsters had rummaged from room to room, the visiting playmate came upon a closet door, which he quickly opened. The young fellow stood before the open door, paralyzed with fear, his eyes terrified at what stood before him. For there standing in the closet was a skeleton.

"What's this?" said the visiting boy, horrified.

"That's a skeleton," answered Willie, adding, "The bones of a dead man."

"Gee!" exclaimed the visitor.

"Yah," said little Willie, "my dad's awfully proud of that skeleton."

"He is?" said the visiting youngster. "Why?"

Little Willie thought the matter over for a while and then he turned to his playmate and said: "He was my dad's first patient."

Ladies and gentlemen, Dr. Walter Peters.

—Horton Smith

INTRODUCING A PSYCHIATRIST

Ladies and gentlemen, I don't know how much experience any of you may have had with psychiatrists, but when anyone visits a psychiatrist the caller usually does the talking while the psychiatrist listens—and collects.

Tonight the procedure is going to be reversed. A psychiatrist is going to talk while we listen, but we do not collect, except in knowledge. This gentleman is a leader in his particular field and is a most interesting and entertaining speaker and we're very fortunate in having him here—not that any of us here needs the services of a psychiatrist.

Does anyone here know anything about the science of psychiatry? No? Then I can speak freely. A psychiatrist is a man (or woman) who studies diseases of the mind. He does this by psychoanalysis, which means a diagnosis of mental and nervous afflictions by analyzing the emotions and investigating the history of the patient, based on the theory that in many forms of neurosis and mental disorders certain factors persist unconsciously while rejected consciously.

Now that I've made that clear I'll continue. There are many types of mental ailments, including that aggravated form of imbecility which seems to possess those who disagree with our political beliefs. When you visit a psychiatrist he'll tell you to lie down on a couch. Then you start searching your subconscious for things to tell him, while he sits back in a big easy chair and reads the Saturday Evening Post. So after a few preliminaries from your childhood days, you finally break down and tell him you have a strange desire to kick your brother-in-law out of the house because he hasn't worked in three years and does nothing but sponge on you. Then the doctor explains that's because you got a severe spanking when you were seven years old because you playfully shot your school principal with a bean blower when she was stooping over picking sweet peas. He tells you not to let it get you down, because there is nothing wrong with you but a slight case of double paranoidism with involutional halitosis. Then you slip the man fifty dollars and leave, free from all your troubles—until you can dig up something else to worry about.

A clever race of people, these psychiatrists! And by the way, I've never seen one who didn't look well-fed and contented. Who wouldn't look that way, at fifty bucks per half-hour just for listening to people talk? Sounds like easy money but there are people I wouldn't want to listen to for double the amount.

In medicine, as we all know, there are specialists for almost everything—for the heart, the liver, the stomach, ingrown nails—almost every ailment you can think of. They are starting the same thing in psychiatry now. A fellow I know went to a modern psychiatrist and said: "Doc, I'm afraid there's something a little wrong with me. I like to play in hotel hallways." The psychiatrist said: "I'm sorry, but I specialize only in inverted schizophrenia with clusters. You'll have to go to someone who specializes in reverse senile compulsory hallucinations with delinquency traits."

Eventually he found the right brain specialist who told him to start talking. So my friends said: "Doctor, I like to play around the third floor hallway of the Blank Hotel." The doctor said: "Why?" So my friend said: "Well, there's a beautiful young blonde widow in the corner room, and every time she opens her door, for some unexplainable reason, I run up and down the hallway, and jump up in the air and click my heels together." "Hmm," said the psychiatrist. "Undoubtedly, because of some forgotten incident in your childhood, this female has some effect upon your syndrome which causes your peculiar reactions. Better give me her room number, so I can check on this." My friend said: "But what do you think about my condition?" The psychiatrist said, "Don't let it bother you. I can cure you in no time." "But Doctor," said my friend, "I don't want to be cured. I just came here to talk about it."

And that's me. I don't know anything about psychiatry. I just came here to talk about it—and to listen to someone who knows a lot about it and is really qualified to talk about it—a man who has accomplished a vast amount of good in the practice of his chosen profession. And I'd like to add—at the risk of embarrassing him—that he deserves a lot of credit not only for his outstanding professional success but also for his many personal attributes and human qualities. Ladies and gentlemen, Dr. ————.

—Earl Jay Gilbert.

ADDITIONAL MATERIAL

Then there was a haggard individual who came into a psychiatrist's office, and complained:

"Night after night, night after night, I get nightmares that I'm a castaway on an island in mid-ocean, with a bunch of movie stars like Marilyn Monroe, Betty Grable, Hedy Lamarr. I tell you, I can't stand it any more! Do something for me!"

Said the psychiatrist soothingly: "But Betty Grable, Marilyn Monroe, and all those beauties around you—what's so terrible about a dream like that? Why call them nightmares?"

"But," moaned the gent, "I'm always Jane Russell!"

This one, which they say happened in a psychiatrist's office, I won't vouch for.

But there was a woman who visited a psychiatrist and said: "I'd like some advice from you—it's not regarding me, but my husband. He thinks he's a chicken. What should I do?"

"Have him put away," said the psychiatrist.

"What? With eggs at 80 cents a dozen?"

—George A. Posner

INTRODUCING A BOOK PUBLISHER

I was over to a friend's house the other evening and saw not more than a dozen books on the shelf. I asked my friend if he didn't care for books? His reply was, "What's the use of going in for books? There's hardly a word in all the books that I can't find in my dictionary."

That doesn't coincide with what our speaker of the evening has to say. This speaker, by the way, is a well-known publisher of books. Do you recall what Bill Nye, the famous humorist, said about books? He said, "There should be a book in every home. To the illiterate the picture will be pleasing. The wise will revel in its wisdom, and the housekeeper will find that with it she may easily emphasize a statement or kill a cockroach."

I have a certain acquaintance whom I visit occasionally just to look over **my** library. He's a bookkeeper. If you want to have fun just stand in a public library and listen to some of the customers. I've done it. Try it. You'll hear things like this: "May I renew this book for another week? I'm reading it but I don't like the ending." "How did you like the beginning?" "Oh, I haven't come to that yet." "You must read backwards." "I'll be glad to. Who wrote it?" Here's another one. "Have you read 'Freckles'?" "No, mine are brown."

Our book critics say that most new books are forgotten within a year. Especially by those who borrow them. Here's a little tip for any energetic fellow who desires to launch into the book publishing business. If he wants to succeed he should get the censors to suppress his first four or five books. Now for the more serious side of publishing allow me to introduce a publisher who knows books from A to Z, Mr. (name.)

—Arthur L. Kaser

INTRODUCING A BUSINESSMAN (MERCHANT)

My friends, most of you are familiar with the phrase "a successful business man." The term conveys a lot. I've been asked to say a few words about our next speaker, who exemplifies that phrase—a successful businessman. You know him as one of those men whose enterprises and abilities have raised the standards of living in this country to the highest in the world. You know him for his reputation of integrity, of fair dealings in his contacts with his fellow men, both in his business dealings and his private life. You know him for his record of humanitarianism as well as his record of high ideals in his business career. You know he isn't alone in possessing those qualities, of course, but he's a splendid example.

You also know that he doesn't need me or anyone else to say a few kind words for him. You're all familiar with the fact that when a man enters into practically any line of business, he's up against the toughest competition in the world, and when he meets that competition successfully, he's really accomplished something.

I've often wondered what particular qualities and circumstances combine to make a man successful in any business field. Of course, advertising, both by word of mouth and public print, has a lot to do with it.

And speaking of advertising, I met recently a successful merchant named Jones from a small city who told me he didn't believe in advertising. I asked him how he got along without advertising and he said: "It's very simple. I just put up twenty big billboards and painted them a deep yellow. Then I had a sign painter print on them in big black letters: **"Shop at Jones! You Save Money Here Because We Do Not Advertise!"** He said: "Those signs made me a lot of money—but I wouldn't spend a nickel on advertising. It's a waste of money."

I still haven't got that one figured out. Reminds me of the story of the successful merchant who told me of how, as a boy, he worked twelve and fourteen hours a day, seven days a week, as delivery boy, porter, salesman and so forth at a salary of ten dollars a week. He said he saved his money and in three years he had enough to buy out his employer. Someone asked him how he managed to save enough out of ten dollars a week to buy the store in three years. "Well," he said, "I took the eighty dollars I had saved up, and with the four thousand Uncle Fred left me, I was able to swing the deal."

I asked a man who owns a small store what he thought about success. He said: "Brother, with all these high taxes we're hooked with, any man who can even stay in business today is a success!" Seriously, I believe that sometimes a man's good qualities bring good fortune, and when we look back over the career of the gentleman who is going to address us, it is easy to understand why a man such as he is, who practices fair dealing, is honest in his advertising, and who is content with a fair profit, is entitled to success.

Oh, by the way, I became curious about the phrase "businessman," so I looked it up, and I was really surprised at the variety of terms that the word "business" embraces. According to Webster, the definitions of business include, among other things—employment, trade, art, vocation, occupation, profession, something transacted or required to be done, affair, matter. That's only part of it, but that shows you what business means. And to give you an idea of what man means, let me present our next speaker, Mr. —————. Thank you.

—Earl Jay Gilbert

ADDITIONAL MATERIAL

The famed Hetty Green, the eccentric financial wizard, acquired immense wealth through huge stock manipulations and business deals. According to legend her reputation was one of extreme frugality. Her son wrote her from his school that he needed fifteen dollars. She replied, refusing to send him the money and giving him a stern lecture on thrift. Several days later she received a letter from him saying, "I have taken your advice. I just sold your letter to a collector for twenty dollars. Please write more often." In return she sent him a collect wire saying: "Will write every day, provided I get a fifty-fifty cut on the deal."   —Earl Jay Gilbert

INTRODUCING A NEWSPAPER EDITOR

Ladies and gentlemen, tonight we are going to have th privilege of listening to a man who has one of the softes jobs imaginable—a newspaper editor! Just think of having job where you get free passes to everything—theatres, priz fights, flower shows—everything! And all he does is to si in his air-cooled office all day long reading and smoking goo cigars and listening to the radio.

Once in awhile he suggests, in a kindly manner, that som of his help do something, like turning off the heat, or open ing the window, or going out to find some news, like wh got murdered, or where the fire is. The only time he eve makes a pretense of being busy is when he answers the phon every few minutes.

He is never lonesome because his office is usually crowde with people asking for some little favor, such as can he ge somebody's innocent son, Willie the Moocher, out of th sneezer where he was tossed when the police raided the poo room the night before, and please keep it out of the pape because little Willie is very sensitive and notoriety might in jure his inhibitions.

He calls the Chief of Police by his first name, asks th Mayor why he doesn't get a haircut, and at times he gets im polite and rude enough to ask a certain judge where he go the big chunk of dough he stashed away in his bank last Fal and why didn't the judge declare it in his income tax return And he gets paid a nice salary for all that!

Of course, he has the grace to blush and hang his hea when they hand him his pay envelope, but that's probabl caused by his natural timidity and modesty. In spite of th fact that his daily contacts cover almost every phase of huma existence and give him a knowledge of life and human natur that is equalled in very few other fields, he is apt to becom a trifle hard-boiled and cynical and slightly suspicious of any thing and everything.

As a minor example of the normal cynicism of an editor, a friend of mine recently told an editor he knew that a mutual acquaintance was about to be married. The editor said: "I'm glad to hear it, although I don't know why. He never did me any harm." I know most married men here will disagree with the implied thought behind that remark.

However, outside of the few things I have just mentioned concerning his labors, his duties are really very simple. Of course, he's responsible for every news item that appears in his paper, and he's got to scan each article before it's published to make sure it carries nothing than can invoke a suit for libel. Also, he's got to be a man of determination and forceful character, capable of making split-second decisions practically every minute of his working hours. And he's got to have a mind trained to distinguish immediately between the true and the false, what constitutes news and what doesn't. He's got to see that his paper publishes stories that are told quickly and concisely and are easily readable, and make sure that the stories are factual. He's got to be honest and truthful with his reading public, and must be able, at a moment's notice, to write vigorous, meaningful editorials about any subject under the sun.

He must stick to the editorial policies of his paper without being swayed by outside influences. He is constantly besieged by political propaganda experts, people seeking publicity and people striving to avoid publicity, and others, all looking for favors, all the way from squaring a traffic ticket to getting four free tickets to tomorrow's ball game.

Which reminds me of the very important citizen who stormed into an editor's office with a couple of traffic tickets and demanded that the editor immediately call upon the authorities to curb the activities of pedestrians. "Some of these pedestrians," said the man, "act as though they owned the streets." "Unfortunately that's true," sighed the weary editor. "And some of these motorists act as though they owned their cars."

Oh, I forgot to mention that in addition to the few chores I just spoke of, an editor must also please his employers, his reading public and the advertisers. See what I mean by a soft job?

My friends, all the requisites and requirements that an editor needs to hold down his job call for a man of outstanding abilities. Whatever qualities it takes to make a good editor, our guest tonight possesses them. I hope he'll forgive me for dwelling so much on his job, but I think these attributes deserve special attention, and I think he deserves special praise for his well-earned success in his career. Ladies and gentlemen, Mr. —————, editor of the —————. Thank you.

—Earl Jay Gilbert

INTRODUCING A TRAVELER

Tonight's speaker, friends, is a man who has done his share of seeing the world. He has been in a variety of places and has met with a variety of faces.

Little does he realize that we know what happened to him on his first ocean voyage. He won't admit it but he was the victim of mal de mar. This, in plain English, is seasickness.

They were at mid-ocean when he had his worst attack. He was too sick to live and too well to die. The captain stopped to offer condolences.

"Captain," our speaker said to him. "Do something for me. Get me to land, I'm at the end." The captain did a little sharp thinking. "Don't worry," he consoled. "We are near land. We're less than four miles from it." Our man sighed his relief. "Which direction, Captain?" The captain gave him a two-word answer. "Straight down," he told our hero.

Now let me present to you a man who has been going straight up ever since. Mr. —————.

—Louis J. Huber.

INTRODUCING A BANKER

There are ever so many people unfamiliar with the operation of banks that we have asked Mr. (name) of a local bank to enlighten you on some of the problems that confront you in such an institution.

I remember my grandfather. He had quite a bit of money which he kept hidden in the house. One day the president of the local bank asked Grandpa why he didn't put his money in his bank for safe keeping. Grandpa said, "Well, I'll tell you. I've noticed you in the bank and you always wore a hat like you might be going some place."

Many people think that all cashiers have hearts of gold—yellow and hard. I know of several high school graduates who would like to work in the bank because there is money in it. To some people a bank is a one-way affair. This is based on the theory that a banker can write a bad poem and be applauded, but let a poet write a bad check and see what happens to him.

I heard a conversation between a man and his wife and it went something like this: He said, "My dear, I just received a notice of being overdrawn." She said, "Well, can't you try another bank? Surely they can't all be overdrawn." He said, "You don't understand. **Our** bank account is overdrawn." She said, "Maybe all our checks aren't in yet." He was losing patience and produced a returned check, and said, "See that? The bank has returned this check." She said, "Oh, goody! What can we buy with it now?" She is the same woman who lost her checkbook. It didn't worry her a bit because she had signed all the checks and nobody else could use it. And now, ladies and gentlemen, some good sound advice from our banker friend, Mr. (name).   —Arthur L. Kaser

INTRODUCING A RECRUITING OFFICER

Sit tight, fellows. We have with us this evening a young man who is going to tell you why it is a good idea to join the army. He is Sergeant (name) from the recruiting office. You will hear from him in just a moment.

My friends, do you know what the Army and Navy are for? The Army and Navy are for—ever. I had a cousin in the army who spent most of his time in the guard house for going on too many furlongs. Yes, furlongs. He'd go too fur and stay too long.

He had a brother who was always boasting that he was a West Pointer, but he looked more like an Irish Setter. When he was in the last war, right in the thick of the battle he started running back to safety. His alibi was that he was backing up to get a good running start to charge. He finally got shot. Got a bullet in the chest. It would have gone through his heart but his heart was in his mouth.

He was on guard duty one night when the enemy opened up with mortars. He was alone but he formed a line—a beeline, that is, to the rear. He was awfully dumb in a lot of ways. One time the sergeant said to him, "In the midst of battle, why should you never lose your head?" My cousin thought for a long time and then said, "There would be no place to put the helmet."

One time his company was lined up for a bawling out. The lieutenant roared, "Not one man in this company will be given liberty this afternoon." My cousin piped out, "Give me liberty or give me death!" The lieutenant looked from one man to another. "Who said that?" My cousin piped again, "Patrick Henry." Friends, I want to introduce to you, Sergeant (name).

—Arthur L. Kaser

INTRODUCING A POET

And now, folks, let's take a dive into the realm of poetry, and the one person who is most capable in helping us make this dive is a young man whom I am about to introduce. I love poetry, but I do not always agree with the poets. Take for instance, this line, "I long for the wings of a dove!" Personally, I would much rather have a thigh from an old rooster cooked southern style. Poets, as a rule, are shy. Some people think it would be better if we were shy a lot of them. The young man who will shortly appear before you is exceptionally shy. He has asked me to read one of his poems as a tester. If you like it he will come out and recite more. If it doesn't go over, he will sneak out the back door. Allow me. It is called "WINTER."

Beauty's gone from vale and hill,
And in the air is an icy chill.
The trees are gaunt and nude because
There are no leaves where there used to was.

Flowers ailed and have passed away
And the green grass grows not green today.
Where once the haughty weeds did thrive,
You can't find a gosh-durn weed alive.

The cat meows at the kitchen door,
The shady nooks he seeks no more.
He shivers in the tangy air
For he has no winter underwear.

We, too, shiver through months so long
Awaiting for the bluebird's song.
We know not why a winter is
So we just sit 'round and friz and friz.

I think that poem calls for a good hand. Now our young poet (name.)
—Arthur L. Kaser

INTRODUCING A GOLFER

It is indeed a privilege to have as our principal speaker this evening a good golfer. At past gatherings we have heard from numerous golfers, but not all of them were good. So tonight we will hear from a good golfer.

Our next speaker, Bill Jones, started at an early age to master the art of golf. While other boys in his neighborhood were mowing lawns, raking up the yard and performing various other chores, Bill was practicing golf. A bunch of us went over to Bill's house one day to watch him practice on his home-made small course. "What's this?" I asked, watching Bill wiggle his knees and oscillate a little white ball with a metal club.

"This," said Bill, "is a game that was invented by a couple of Scotsmen. The general idea is to wallop this little white pill around a cow pasture and sink it into a tomato can."

"You got to have a lot of tools to play this game," I said, noticing some bludgeoned weapons sticking out of a gunny sack.

"And the right kind of clothes," added Bill. "You see," he continued, "these two Scotsmen who thought up this game were a couple of tailors. They invented the game for the purpose of selling pants, as there was a surplus of kilts in Scotland that year."

"What kind of pants?" I asked.

"Plus fours," said Bill. "These two tailors just took the Scotch kilt and added four inches to the knee."

"How did these Scotch tailors get the idea?" I asked.

"Well," said Bill, "it was a kind of a practical move. When one of these inventors of the game was out in the cow pasture inventing, he knelt down in his kilts and got his bare legs punctured with cow thistles. That made him sore and he rushed back to his factory and sewed four inches on to his kilts."

"That must have saved the game," said I. "No one would want to play a game where his knees got pierced with cow thistles."

"It saved the game for posterity," answered Bill, "but other inventors helped."

"Other inventors," I exclaimed. "Were other guys mixed up in this project beside these two Scotch tailors?"

"Yah, there was a Scotch hatter."

"A Scotch hatter?" I repeated.

"Yes," continued Bill, "this Scotch hatter had some sort of a design for a cap that had been covered with dust since the days of the Norse invasion. So this hatter went to the two tailors and said, 'See here, you fellows, you got a great invention, but it needs a little more inventing. If you accept my new plaid cap as a part of your plus four ensemble, I'll help you fellows invent.' "What can you invent that we haven't invented?" said the Scotch tailors. 'I can invent plenty,' answered the Scotch hatter. 'just let me get out in that cow pasture and observe you boys in action. I'll come up with an idea.' "

"So the Scotch hatter went out to the cow pasture the next day to watch the two Scotch tailors play the new game. 'What are you guys shooting at?' said the Scotch hatter to the Scotch tailors. 'We're shooting at that Angus cow over there,' replied the tailors. 'Which Angus cow?' yelled the hatter. 'I see twenty of them over there.' 'The one with the big backside,' answered the tailors. 'Sandy just parred, and I just birdied.' 'You did what?' asked the hatter. 'When we hit that Angus cow directly on either the right rump or the left rump, we par. When we hit that Angus cow in the center, we birdie. True as a bird, do you get that?' said the tailors. 'This game's all wrong,' said the hatter. 'You guys are shooting at the wrong cow. That Angus you birdied is now over in Mac-Tavish's pasture. You've got to be shooting at the same thing all of the time, if this game is ever going to amount to anything. And furthermore,' added the hatter, 'I'm telling you fellows right now that we got to improve the rules if my cap's going to be a part of this game.' 'Well, if you're so smart, you see what you can do about it,' said the tailors."

"So the Scotch hatter went back to his hattery and began to think. Now in that year there was a tremendous surplus of tomatoes in Scotland," continued Bill. "Tomato cans were everywhere. So the hatter got an idea. He took an empty tomato can and went out to the cow pasture, dug a hole in the ground and said to the two tailors, 'Now you guys aim at that sunken tomato can.' 'We can't see it,' said the two tailors. 'By George, you can't,' said the hatter. 'You got to do better than that,' said the tailors. But the hatter wasn't going to be outdone by the tailors, so he went home to think. The very next day the hatter went out to the cow pasture with a red geranium bush, which he planted inside the tomato can. 'There,' burred the hatter to the tailors, 'now **put** it in!' "

"Were there other inventors beside these three Scotch guys connected with this game?" I asked of Bill.

"Plenty of them," he answered. "There was one other who was very important. He was an Irishman."

"An Irishman!" I exclaimed. "How did he get mixed up in this game?"

"It was like this," said Bill. "There was an Irishman up in Ireland by the name of Michael O'Toole. He made potato-mashers and other tools, which you can tell by his name. Now, in that year there was a potato famine in Ireland. There wasn't a potato in sight. So one day O'Toole said to his wife, 'What am I to do with all of these potato-mashers?' 'Sell 'em to the Scotsmen,' answered his wife. 'They've got some sort of a game going on down there that uses weapons of all sorts and there ain't a better weapon to swing on the noggin of man or beast than an O'Toole potato-masher.' 'Nothing would please me better,' said O'Toole, 'than to go down to Scotland and trim some of the bark off those tight Scottish hides.' "

"So O'Toole went down to Scotland and looked up the tailors who were practicing in the cow pasture, trying to hit the geranium plant. The hatter was also playing, as he had taken up the game. 'See here,' said O'Toole to the tailors, 'I'm O'Toole and I make tools, as you can tell by my name. I've got the best tool made for driving that little pellet right through that flower.' With that the Irishman took a potato masher from his pocket and handed it to one of the tailors. 'Try this,' said O'Toole. One tailor took the potato masher (it doesn't matter which one), and taking deliberate aim, swung on the little white pellet which flittered through the red flower right into the tomato can. The second tailor tried, and he did likewise. Then the hatter took the potato-masher and emulated the two tailors. It was a tie for all three Scotchmen at the end of the first hole. 'It looks like this will fill the bill,' said both tailors and the hatter. 'What do you call it?' asked one of the tailors. 'A masher,' answered the Irishman. 'We can't use that name,' said one of the tailors, 'it sounds too much like an Irish uprising. We'll just call it a mashie for short.' "

"That's only a small part of the history of this great game," said Bill, as he chipped a neat little twenty-foot approach over his mother's wash basket.

As the years went by Bill continued to play golf. His score improved with the discarding of the plaid cap and the plus fours, until now he clips off eighteen holes in strokes equivalent to the dollars on my weekly paycheck; while I, starting much later at this great game than Bill, clip off eighteen holes in strokes equivalent to the dollars in my boss's paycheck. That's how I keep track of our score, by transposing my weekly salary with that of my boss. Ladies and gentlemen, meet Bill Brown, a great golfer and a great guy. Bill Brown.

—Sylvester McGovern

INTRODUCING A HOUSE-TO-HOUSE SALESMAN

Gentlemen: A house-to-house salesman is a man that requires special ingenuity, courage and resourcefulness, a man such as Elmer Olson, who is our next speaker. Elmer is a type of a fellow who never takes no for an answer. That is one of the reasons why he is such a success at selling from door to door.

Elmer is also a man with ideas. While the other fellow is sitting in his store hoping that someone might come in and buy a vacuum cleaner, Elmer is thinking up an idea about how to sell a vacuum cleaner, and then he goes out and does it.

Elmer has a bag full of tricks. When the lady of the house starts to slam the door, Elmer will agilely thrust his foot forward, and thereby impede any further closing movement of the door. But that is an old trick used by good house to house salesmen everywhere; something about as worn out as the "working your way through college stuff." But here's a new one that Elmer thought up by himself:

One day last week Elmer was more aggressive than usual. What he needed was sales, sales and more sales. "If I could just get a method that would insure a demonstration in every home, my sales would soar to the high heavens," Elmer said to himself. Elmer worked out a method, and set out to make the first test at the home of Mrs. Eliza Woods, who lived at the end of the lane near the woods. Elmer rang the bell and was greeted by Mrs. Woods in the customary front-door demeanor usually given to a stranger.

"Good afternoon, my good Mrs. Woods," said Elmer. "I am going to give you a demonstration in cleanliness that you haven't had since your grandmother scrubbed the kitchen floor down to the nails in the boards."

"You should talk about cleanliness, young man," said Mrs. Woods, noting that Elmer's right hand was full of mud. "If my hands were as dirty as yours," continued Mrs. Woods, "I certainly would scrub them before calling on a lady and talking about cleanliness."

"I am going to give you a demonstration," said Elmer.

"Oh, no you're not," answered Mrs. Woods.

"Yes, I am," said Elmer. "I am going to throw this mud right on that front room rug of yours, and then I am going to pick it all up in a jiffy with the marvelous new Cleanall vacuum cleaner."

"You're going to do what?" exclaimed Mrs. Woods. But before she could say more, Elmer tossed the mud on the front room rug and then started looking around for an outlet to connect his vacuum cleaner.

"What's all that racket going on in that house?" one passerby said to a companion. Both men halted for a moment, and one of the passersby said: "From what I can gather above the din of that yelling and screaming, there ain't no electricity in that house."

Ladies and gentlemen, Elmer Olson.

—Lester Hunt

INTRODUCING A FISHERMAN

At my side, ladies and gentlemen, sits the man who is going to speak to you tonight. You will notice that he rests quietly and contentedly. It reminds me of a fisherman, on the bank of a river, waiting for the fish to strike.

This, of course, is a sneaky way of slipping up on him and shouting to you that he is an ardent Izaak Walton. Don't fret, friends, it's just a long way of saying that he fishes.

Not always. There are times when he is teaching the worms how to swim. Like the time he fished in Massachusetts at Lake Chargog ga goggmon chaugg ag oggchaubunga-unamaug. This, in Indian language means: You fish on your side, we fish on our side, nobody fishes in the middle. When he couldn't pronounce the name of the lake he came here to us.

So here he is, ladies and gentlemen, with his "bassed" foot forward and with a "whale" of a lot of materials. You're a "sucker" if you don't listen as you'll be "herring" from him right now. Mr. ——————.   —Louis J. Huber

INTRODUCING A COLLECTION MANAGER

The vocation of a collection manager is one of the most unfortunate things that can befall a person in this life, for his job is that of procuring what everyone hates to give up—cash of the realm. People who ordinarily conduct themselves in the most courteous of manner spit in his face, throw him out of home and office and in general avoid him like a plague. He has been told to take a flying trip down to the Stygian realm more often than any other class of people we know. Even his polite letters are referred to as insults of the worst order. Such is the life of Oscar Johnson, our speaker this evening.

When one takes such beatings in the pursuit of his daily work, he by nature becomes exceedingly resourceful, and in this respect I am going to tell about one of Oscar's experiences, which emphasizes the resourcefulness of a collection man.

A fellow, let us call him John Jones although his name wasn't Jones, owed Oscar's firm $150.00 for a period of over four years. During that time Oscar chased Jones all over the state, trying to collect the account. But Jones was a wiley fellow and he eluded Oscar in the chase, always being a step or two ahead. Oscar wrote Jones all of the letters in the collection book, including one that starts with "The Jig is Up." . . . which made absolutely no dent whatsoever on Jones' immunized skin. The $150 was a goner. Even Oscar's boss admitted that.

Finally after four years of this kind of a chase, one day Oscar cornered Jones in a neighborhood tavern. And then Oscar went to work. First he used threats, then persuasiveness. Then he threatened violence, and abruptly switched his tactics, appealing to Jones' personal pride. After an hour of this kind of an attack, Jones broke down and wrote a check for the $150.00.

A miracle of miracles had happened. After four years of exhausting efforts, Oscar had collected the Jones account. Gleefully, Oscar rushed out of the tavern on a dead run to Jones' bank. Presenting the $150 check to the teller, Oscar said: "I want this check certified."

The teller took the check, looked at the books and said, "Can't do it. Not sufficient funds."

A pall of gloom befell Oscar. Defeat after such a near victory. It was heartbreaking. Oscar was on the point of leaving the bank, when he suddenly turned back and said to the teller: "How much can you certify?"

The teller again looked at his books and remarked tersely, "$100.00."

Oscar reached in his pocket and extracted five ten-dollar bills. Pushing the money through the teller's window, Oscar said in a business-like voice: "Deposit this fifty dollars to Jones' account and then certify this check."

Ladies and gentlemen, Oscar Johnson.

—Stephen Keller

INTRODUCING A RAILROAD EXECUTIVE

Tonight, ladies and gentlemen, our speaker is a man who is in the transportation business. Although he is not an engineer he has much to do with keeping the trains running on time. On time? What am I saying?

Even on this trip he had trouble with his own trains. He complained about it and the conductor told him to get off and walk. That's why he arrived before the train. While still on the train he almost got into trouble. He was leaning out the window when they passed a farmer's small berry patch. He got enough for a pie. He might have got more if they hadn't made the engineer stop drinking sloe gin.

They had a serious incident on one branch of his railroad. A man, tired of living, tried to commit suicide. He stretched himself across the rail. He heard the train! Then he starved to death waiting for it to arrive.

We know, friends, that you have not been railroaded into coming here tonight. You came because you wanted to hear our speaker and here he is, Mr. ——————.

—Louis J. Huber

INTRODUCING A HIGH SCHOOL PRINCIPAL

It is a distinct privilege this evening to introduce to you the principal of Arden Center High—Mr. William Greene.

When Mr. Greene is not down at the athletic field cheering for the team, he's back in his office giving advice to our young people, who love him dearly. When he's not in his office giving advice but still in the building, he's out in the hall, routing the loiterers into the various classrooms. When Mr. Greene is in his office and not giving out advice, he's taking it from some outraged parent. Such is the life of a high school principal.

Parents expect him to channel their offsprings into study preparations that will insure the lad of becoming the president of a billion dollar corporation. It is not unusual for a mother to anticipate from Mr. Greene a statement something like this: "Why, Mrs. Brown, I can tell by looking at Pettie's hands that a great career awaits him in the field of surgery—or could it be a concert pianist? Anyway, it's a toss-up which road he decides to travel. One appears to be as good as the other."

And then another mother hurries down to the school with Willie, anxiously waiting for Mr. Greene's analysis, which is certain to be something like this: Mr. Greene looks at Willie's pug nose with this exclamatory remark: "I have never seen such a profile! This lad will without a doubt become another Barrymore."

And along comes Mrs. Jones, dragging son Archie. Mrs. Jones is expecting a comment something like this from Mr. Greene: "My goodness, Mrs. Jones, this boy can't be anything but a judge. Look how his shoulders stoop. Already he has the appearance of having served a lifetime on the bench. After we fill him up with a little algebra and some chemistry, he'll be prepared to take up the gavel."

Yes, it is quite disappointing to many parents that their children grow up to become plumbers and carpenters and are thereby able to support the parents in their old age.

At the beginning of the fall semester, Mrs. Toten Penny-weather appeared at Mr. Greene's office to enroll Wilfred in the freshman class.

"What would you advise Wilfred to study?" asked Mrs. Pennyweather in a tone of voice that might be put to a $100,-000 a year New York psychologist.

Mr. Greene closely examined Wilfred, and was about to say, "a bricklayer," when he caught himself. Then Mr. Greene reflected that he himself should have taken up bricklaying many years ago.

That same year Mrs. T. Emerson Wright came in with her son, Chester. "What are Chester's plans?" said Mr. Greene, beating Mrs. T. Emerson Wright to the punch. "Will it be mechanical drawing, modelling or . . ." and then noticing Chester's size, he added, "football?"

"It will be Latin, Latin, Latin!" exclaimed Mrs. T. Emerson Wright.

"Latin!" said Mr. Greene, astounded. "Why, whenever we mention Latin around here, the students scatter like flies. Miss Warbler, our Latin teacher, has only two pupils in her class, and one of them is absent about half of the time."

"It will be Latin for Chester," Mrs. T. Emerson Wright repeated.

"Well, Mrs. Wright," said Mr. Greene, "do you know that Latin is a dead language?"

"That is very appropriate," said Mrs. Wright with an air of finality. "Chester plans on becoming an undertaker."

Ladies and gentlemen, Mr. William Greene.

—Dale Farnsworth

INTRODUCING A FISHERMAN

We have as our speaker this evening one of the world's outstanding anglers—a man who goes after the wiley fish with skill and agility unequalled in the annals of the Izaak Walton League. Nowhere in the written history of the outdoor man are there accomplishments equal to those of our own John Brown. John Brown is a natural-born fisherman. When he was two he plucked angleworms from the black earth and stored them away in a tomato can for future use. When he was three he fished a goldfish out of a bowl and threw it back just to prove that he could catch 'em. When he was ten he owned the best willow rod in the community, which resulted in catching some of the biggest sunfish that Willow river ever produced. As John grew, so did the fish. Today sizes of unusual proportions are reported, some confirmed, others not.

But let me tell you about one fishing expedition that John and I made last summer. I drove up to John's house at the crack of dawn. John was already up and waiting for me on the front porch, surrounded by enough paraphernalia to catch an entire school of salmon. It took us twenty minutes to get John's gear into the car—rod after rod of various types and definitions, hook after hook, reel after reel, and box of accessories after box of accessories. I never saw so much fishing equipment in one place outside of Peterson's sporting goods store.

When we arrived at Clear Lake, I said to John, "You don't plan on putting all of that junk in a boat, do you?"

"We'll fish from a rock," said John. "I know just the spot," he added, pointing to a big rock that lay along the shore with the waves of the lake splashing its side.

John opened one box, took out some sort of a newfangled spinner or whirler with a commercial name of "Nailembigger," looked at it and placed it back in the metal box. Then he opened another box and removed another gadget. After scrutinizing it for a moment he said, "That won't do either."

"Why?" I asked.

"Because with the present temperature of the water, these reflectors will throw light beams through the water at the rate of only three trillion beams a second. It is necessary to have a reflection rate of four trillion to get the big ones. I'm after the big ones," John added.

Curiously I asked, "How do you know the temperature of the water?"

"I took it," said John.

"I thought you were washing your hands."

Then John started to open box after box and remove gadget after gadget, until the shore-line was strewn with poles, feathers, hooks, reels, warblers and various other items of the fisherman's art.

I said, "John, why all of this fuss and bother? Why don't you just attach one of those Indian clubs with feathers on it and throw it in the water?"

John became indignant. "See here," he cried out, interrupting some calculations that he was making with a slide rule and a pencil and paper. "I'm a scientific fisherman." Then he walked over to another pile of instruments and selected a gadget that looked like a small torpedo with prongs. Looking up at the sun John said: "Unless it warms up, I'll never get four trillion beams of reflection with any of these gadgets. I'll have to amplify!"

"You'll have to do what?" I cried out in surprise.

"Amplify!" he answered. "Speed up the reflection by electric power." And then John walked over to the car and removed two batteries and a long line of cable.

"You see," he said, "there is an electric motor inside this 'Atomhooker'. I'll just string a power line from these batteries to the 'Atomhooker', which will be in addition to the regular fishing line, and I'll get twenty trillion."

"Good thunderation, man!" I called out. "What are you going to plant out there in that lake, a mine?"

"When I get twenty trillion in beam reflection, I will attract the biggest thing that ever swam the seven seas. In fact, I will fish all of the big ones out of this lake before you can snap your fingers three times."

"Do you mean to say," I asked, "that when that 'Atom-hooker' gets a spinning, all the big fish in the lake will immediately swim after it?"

"That's it precisely," answered Jack. "When I get through, there'll be nothing left for the late fishermen but the three-inch perch."

With that exclamation Jack tossed his equipment into the water, which effected a splash that resembled a deep-sea diver going into action.

"Hold that power line! I'll reel in!" Jack yelled. As he turned on the juice from the batteries, I grabbed the cable and began to take in the slack and Jack spun his reel with the efficiency of a housewife beating-up an egg.

Suddenly I heard a horrifying groan, and as I looked up at the rock I saw Jack standing there, his body doubled up like one who has had the wind knocked out of him. Jack's hand was frozen to the reel; and I noted that his line was as taut as a violin string.

"Come over and give me some help!" Jack cried out excitedly. "I got a big one! Too big to handle alone!" So I rushed to the top of the rock and grabbed Jack around his midsection with both arms. Bracing my feet in two holes in the rock and locking my head in the small of Jack's back, I hung on for dear life. Jack continued to groan and grunt, holding fast to the rod and reel.

"I can't budge 'em," Jack shouted.

"Oscillate 'em! Oscillate 'em!" I yelled, using the only technical fishing term that I could think of at the moment.

"You don't oscillate 'em with an 'Atomhooker'," Jack said between puffs. Then when he had regained a little breath he said, "Right now that fish is getting a severe beating. When contacted, the 'Atomhooker' switches from alternating current to direct current. When that happens it stops sending out reflection beams and starts shooting direct rays of some unknown terminology into the fish. It'll be stunned soon and we'll haul it in."

"I see no signs of it weakening," I said, noting Jack's flushed face and thinking about the terrific strain on my arms.

"This is the biggest one that I have ever seen," said Jack.

"How do you know? You haven't seen it," I said in a panting voice, as I was nearly played out, holding Jack from what would be a certain fall into the water.

"A good fisherman doesn't have to see, he knows," answered Jack. And then Jack said, "Take a look at the 'Tenseometer'," pointing over at a tree.

"'Tenseometer'! What in the devil is that?" I asked, as my eyes followed Jack's pointing hand to some kind of a contraption nailed upon a tree. It resembled one of those grip-testers found at amusement parks. I had overlooked that device in the maze of accoutrements. Then I looked at the thing again, and lo and behold, I noticed a line running from the gadget to Jack's pole.

"Shows thirty-five pounds, doesn't it?" said Jack.

"It sure does. We'd better land it. It'll set an all-time record for these parts," I said.

"Heave away," grunted Jack, straining on the rod and I straining on my rock-braced legs, my arms numb from hanging onto Jack's mid-section.

"Better get a couple of clubs ready," said Jack. "The 'Atomhooker' might not be able to knock this fellow completely out. We might have a fight on our hands on this rock."

"How can I get a couple of clubs?" I asked. "If I let go, you'll fall into the lake."

"Kick over those two short branches with your feet," said Jack. Then Jack got excited and cried out, "Be ready! The 'Atomhooker' must have stunned that whopper by this time."

I kicked over the branches of the tree, which appeared as suitable weapons for the attack. All of this time Jack was grunting and groaning and pulling and pulling, first on the pole and then on the reel. Then all of a sudden Jack's body lurched backwards, and there was a terrible splash in the water. "The clubs! The clubs!" yelled Jack. "Smack 'em the minute I land 'em on the rock!" Something on the end of Jack's line whirled through the air, swinging directly for the rock. When the object came to rest, both Jack and I smacked down our clubs furiously. When the din of battle had subsided, we found that we had conquered a battered and squashed little three-inch perch.

"It must have got away," said Jack mournfully.

"While Jack was dejectedly gathering his gear, I went over and examined the prongs on the 'Atomhooker'. On one of the prongs was a pierced piece of bark."

As our car twisted and turned over the snaky road that led back to the main highway, Jack said remorsefully, "That was a big one."

"Are you sure," I asked, "it wasn't a tree?"

Ladies and gentlemen, Mr. Jack Brown, the best fisherman in this neck of the woods.   —Sylvester McGovern

INTRODUCING AN ARTIST

Mr. Jack Meadows, the celebrated artist, honors this organization by his presence here this evening. Mr. Meadows, as you all know, has brought fame to this community by his untiring efforts in seeking out the outstanding subject for his creative genius.

Now there is nothing that disturbs an artist more than meeting up with people who have no appreciation for art. In this respect Mr. Meadows came in contact with just that sort of a man when he made a visit to Lake Cayuga last summer. One evening Mr. Meadows was standing on the shores of beautiful Lake Cayuga chatting with Antonio Brinnelli, originally from Italy, who operated a fruit stand in the village near the shore of the beautiful lake. Brinnelli was a decidedly practical man who dealt in the more prosaic things of life, such as bananas, apples and grapes; and he had little time to bother about scenic beauty.

As the men continued their talk on politics and other mundane things, a full moon rose out of the eastern sky and cast a brilliant glow upon the dark blue waters of the lake. Mr. Meadows had seen the Cayuga moon many times before; and he never ceased to wonder at the awe-inspiring spectacle.

Turning to Brinnelli, Mr. Meadows remarked: "I have heard from world travelers that the moon over Lake Cayuga is equally as picturesque as the moon over famous Lake Como in Italy."

Brinnelli wiped off his chin with a red bandana handkerchief, looked up at the moon and casually answered: "Why shouldn't it? It's the same old moon."

(Pause for laughter)

Ladies and gentlemen, it is my privilege to introduce to you, Mr. Jack Meadows.   —Sylvester McGovern

INTRODUCING A DENTIST

My friends, our next speaker is a dental surgeon. Now ordinarily even the thought of meeting a dentist is enough to make strong men turn pale and suddenly remember important engagements elsewhere, but I can assure you that you need feel no apprehension in meeting this skilled practitioner tonight.

He was thoroughly searched when he came in to make sure he didn't bring any of his tools with him. Anyway he wouldn't hurt you for the world.

I think now would be a good time for me to say a few words in defense of dentists. I particularly want to dispel the rumor that the tools they use are really medieval instruments of torture handed down from the Spanish Inquisition. That is not true; they are merely models of those ancient devices.

And when a dentist plunges an old fashioned ice-pick into your tender gums or starts grinding on a sore tooth with a jagged-edged circular saw he's just trying to be playful. He's human; he's got a right to have a little fun. It's just his way of releasing his inhibitions.

And you've got to give the average dentist credit for being honest and truthful. When he says: "This may hurt a little," you'll usually find out that he's right. Of course it may hurt you more than a little, and it doesn't hurt him, but that's beside the point. And when he hits a nerve and you jump three feet in the air and he smiles sweetly and says: "Hmm—a little sensitive, huh?" he's just being sympathetic and consoling. His kindly nature is peeking through.

I'm very fond of dentists. I like to meet them—in purely a social way. I met a dentist recently and he told me a funny story. The minute I started to laugh he leaned forward and peered in my mouth. "My goodness," he said, "been having much trouble with that molar?" I said, "No, it had never bothered me." "Strange," he said. "Strange. The last man

I saw with a molar like that had to go to the hospital and have his jaw operated on. Sure it doesn't bother you?" "No," I said, "I don't **think** it does." "Don't be discouraged," he said. "It will. Better have it looked at right away."

He took me in a corner and told me confidentially that my tooth looked very bad, and that a bad tooth could affect my nerves, my liver, my stomach, my heart and a number of other organs I had never even heard of. I got slightly uneasy and suddenly discovered that my tooth was aching a little, and then I began to feel little strange aches and pains all over my body. I kept thinking of what he had told me and the pains got worse.

I couldn't sleep that night. My tooth was really jumping by that time. So the next morning I found myself strapped in his chair with a dish towel pinned around my neck. He said I could smoke if I wanted to while he was getting ready. I used four matches before I got my cigarette lighted. I wasn't shaking from fear—I was just a trifle nervous.

By that time he had dragged out a lot of mean-looking tools, including a large size plumber's wrench, and put them on a little swinging shelf attached to the arm of the chair. Then he laid a tomahawk on the shelf. "What's that for?" I asked him. He said, "Oh—just in case." He stuck a long-handled mirror in my mouth and prowled around for a while and said, "Hmm." Then he took a nutpick and tapped my tooth. "Feel that?" he asked me. I said, "Uh." He tapped a little harder. I said, "Uh-uh-uh." The next time he grabbed a small crowbar and really hit my tooth. I yelled. "Just what I thought," he said. "It's got to come out."

He filled a horse syringe from a small bottle and jabbed the needle into my gums. I yelled again, a trifle louder. "It stings!" I told him. He looked at the syringe closely and said, "Oh, dear, I'm afraid I owe you an apology. I must have used iodine instead of novocaine! Excuse it, please. I'm a little nearsighted." I started to crawl out of the chair but he pushed me back and started to laugh heartily. "It's all right," he said. "It's novocaine—just a little joke of mine. Ha-ha-ha!" I sneaked in a weak ha-ha. You know—ha-ha. "Just lean back and relax," he said. I did. Ha-ha.

My mouth was beginning to feel like it was full of wet, stale, cold mush. He picked up the plumber's wrench and tried to keep my spirits up by telling me a very interesting and entertaining story about how he had once pulled a horse's tooth with those same pliers. Then he suddenly jabbed the nutpick in my gums and said, "Feel that?" I shook my head and he grabbed the wrench, forced my mouth open and got a strangle hold on my tooth, and started to wrestle with it. He kept muttering: "I'll whip this yet—can't fool around with me—I'll whip this son-of-a-gun yet!" After about fifteen minutes of this, finally—pop! Out it came.

He looked at the tooth and broke out in an amazed smile. "Well, what do you know!" he said. "I pulled the right tooth!" "Congratulations!" I said. "Thanks," he said. "You know, you're my first patient. I just graduated from a dental correspondence school day before yesterday." He suggested that I return the next day. "Maybe I can find another tooth that needs treatment," he said. "Uh-uh," I said. "From now on I do my own dental work."

Of course, ladies and gentlemen, that story is made up out of whole cloth. I've never heard of an actual correspondence course in dentistry. We all know that in modern dentistry, as practiced by the gentleman who is going to address us, there is no real cause for worry or apprehension. It is because of the skill and study and work of men like our speaker that pain is no longer associated with dental work. He rightly deserves his reputation of being a leader in his profession and we owe him a lot of thanks for his unending efforts to make painless dentistry a fact instead of a hope. My friends, Dr. ————.

—Earl Jay Gilbert

INTRODUCING A P.T.A. PRESIDENT

Did you ever stop to realize just what parents are? Parents are one of the hardships of a minor's life. What are teachers? Teachers are another of the hardships of a minor's life. Put them together and pity the kids. And for some reason, that the kids could never figure out, the P.T.A. was born.

Perhaps I am prejudiced. The only school I ever attended was the school of experience. When I graduated I enrolled in the Immoral College. It had no principal, and no class. However, I learned the three R's—Rah! Rah! Rah! But I found out later I should have gone to a regular school. You can browse around and pick up a living without an education, but even a jackass, to be of any use to the world, must be trained.

Schools have changed a lot in the past few years. Take the kids nowadays. They pick up geography through the windshield, arithmetic from a dial phone, and the alphabet from radio and television station breaks. If I were going to school today I would be in favor of the older women teaching. Younger girls now do most of the teaching, and if they are a bit flirtatious they make poor teachers. If they can't make their eyes behave, they can't make their pupils behave.

The modern kids spend too much time watching westerns on television. For instance, a teacher asked a small boy to spell straight. The boy spelled it correctly—S-t-r-a-i-g-h-t. The teacher said, "That is correct. Now use it in a sentence." The boy recited, "I'll take mine straight."

Sometimes a teacher can be real mean. A teacher announced to her class, "Children, there will be only a half-day of school this morning." The whole class let out a wild "Whoopee!" The teacher continued, "We'll have the other half this afternoon."

Ladies and gentlemen, I would like to present our speaker, the president of the P.T.A., **(name.)**

—Arthur L. Kaser

INTRODUCING A SPEAKER TO JUNIOR VOTERS

It is gratifying to see so many young people here this evening. It goes to prove that **all** the younger set is not ignoring its place on the ballot box. We are privileged to vote as we please, and everybody should take advantage of this privilege. It is the only way we can prevent crooked politics, and battle crooked politicians. There are too many politicians out to get the best votes money can buy.

For many politicians the keynote in a campaign is the first one in the scale: "Dough." A practical politician is a man who shakes your hand before election and your acquaintance afterward. Good political timber does not always come from Congressional blocs. It seems that about the only thing a man needs to become political timber is the ability to prank down.

I was waiting at the poles to vote at the last election when a man nudged me and whispered, "See those two men over there? I saw them stuffing the ballot box." I asked him, "When did you see that?" He whispered, "The third time I went in to vote." I told him those men were taxidermists. They'd stuff anything.

I read recently that the mayor of a midwest town was arrested for stealing the last election. But he was acquitted when he proved that he paid spot cash for it.

A few years ago I was in the South. I arrived in a small Mississippi town a few days after the town's election. I asked a man sitting on the hotel veranda how the election came out. He seemed glad to unburden his feelings. He exclaimed, "Crooked politics beat us. We were fixing to offer one dollar for votes, and then the other side came along and offered two dollars. It sure was a blow to reform."

Junior voters, and future politicians, I take great pleasure in introducing our speaker, **(name.)**

—Arthur L. Kaser

INTRODUCING A MILLINERY BUYER OR PROPRIETOR OF A LADIES HAT STORE

What the well-dressed lady will wear this fall astride her crowning tresses is one of the great concerns of womanhood, as no doubt you will learn when you hear from Miss Cynthia Sparks, our next speaker.

Whatever the styles are to be, you may be certain that they will be replicas of every conceivable object from a Roman Charioteer's helmet to an eagle's nest on the crest of a pine tree. In fact, anything that has been on the top of anything else has been used as a design for a lady's hat, from a mountain to a horse's saddle. It wouldn't be so bad if, when the designer had selected the object, say such as Don Quixote's shield, she would stop there. But, of course, many things must be added; for instance, a feather for every spear that came Don Quixote's way; or a swishing plume as a remembrance of the great warrior's horse.

The material utilized in decorating a lady's hat comes from many fields. Botany has been completely explored and every species put to use, with the result that it is not unusual to hear a woman's hat referred to as a "Nasturtium pot." Sometimes a designer will change moods and switch to symbols of manly combat in arms, and knives, swords, pitchforks and clubs will bristle forth atop milady's bonnet.

A woman's hat has become such a mess of nondescript things that sometimes even a woman becomes alarmed at the spectacle. A short time ago, a rather plump lady walked into Miss Spark's store and said: "Take out that pea-green one," pointing to a hat in the store window.

"The one with the grapes and the violets?"

The lady looked defiantly at Miss Sparks and then in an indignant tone of voice cried out: "Yes, take it out! Take it out of the window and keep it out! I'm getting sick and tired of looking at that horrid old thing every time I walk down this side of the street!"

Ladies and gentlemen, Miss Cynthia Sparks.

—Milton Hargrave

INTRODUCING A TOP SALESMAN

My friends, to me, one of the most comforting and sooth-
ing sounds in the world is the voice of a master salesman when
he really goes to work—and that's what we're going to hear
next. Our speaker is a top salesman—and folks, he's good.

He reminds me of a story. A man went into a delicatessen
store and asked for a bottle of ketchup. The storekeeper
looked through all his shelves, but there was nothing there but
salt—no ketchup. He said, "Maybe I got some in the basement." So he and his customer went downstairs and found
the basement filled with salt—bags of salt, barrels of salt, boxes
of salt, on all sides. The customer said, "My, you must sell a
lot of salt." The storekeeper shrugged and said, "No, I don't
sell so much salt, but the fellow that sold **me** this salt— could
he sell salt!"

I have it on pretty good authority that our speaker was
the man who sold that salt while he was taking a vacation
from his present job. You know, some people don't realize the
physical and mental effort that goes into a top salesman's or
sales manager's job. A friend of mine, a sales manager, who
was in the middle of a strenuous sales campaign, recently went
to a doctor and complained that he felt all in. He tired easily,
and found it difficult to concentrate. The doctor told him to
rest and take it easy and avoid any mental activity. My friend
said: "But I've got a lot of work to finish." "That's all right,"
said the doctor. "Go ahead with your sales campaign—just
avoid any brainwork."

On the other hand there are some salesmen who fully
realize what a sales manager's job entails and don't want the
responsibility of it. They just want to be salesmen and travel
around the country telling farmer's daughter jokes in Pullman
smokers and collect their pay checks. I'm interested in those
men. As a matter of fact, I'm compiling a sales-training manual for men who do not want to be top salesmen. I haven't
quite completed it, but I'll give you an idea of what it is.

In the first place, it is customary for any man desiring not to rise above a certain level as a salesman to try to find a job. That's usually the first step. Picking a prospective employer is easy. Just take the classified phone book, close your eyes and stab with your finger, and you've selected your possible employer. When you call on him, ignore his secretary or anyone else who might try to stop you, rush into his private office, clap him on the back, say "How's tricks, bud?", pick a cigar out of his pocket, ask him for a match, sit on his desk, mention that his closest competitors certainly put out a swell line of merchandise, tell him you've got a hot horse for him in the third at Jamaica, ask him how far can you go on the swindle sheet, try to touch him for a little advance on your possible commissions, and any other little thing you can think of that will convince him that you're alert and on the job.

Next, if he is drunk or weak-minded enough to give you a job, is my advice upon how to call on customers. I can't over-emphasize the importance of your first move. Always call upon a prospect just as he's going to lunch. He'll love you for it. It gives him a chance to stick around the office a while longer and build up an appetite. Make your opening remark brisk and snappy and to the point—something like: "You don't want to buy no automobile tires, do you?" That will impress him with your personality—and also keep you from feeling too humiliated if the guy doesn't want tires.

But if you should happen to be wrong, and he is interested in buying automobile tires, pretend that you've lost your price list and quote prices strictly from memory, like: "Oh, I guess they run about fourteen, sixteen, eighteen dollars—something like that, I think." That will really show him something about your ability. If he should ask you about the durability and quality of your tires, just shrug and tell him you don't know how they'll stand up under ordinary usage because the management burned up the results of tests they made recently.

Now if the customer should suddenly go nuts and insist on buying some tires from you, and start to get his checkbook out, you quickly excuse yourself and duck out in the hall so you can figure out your commission on the deal. Take your time about this. Then after you've got it all figured out, go back in his office. If he's changed his mind about buying, just laugh it off. If he's gone, ask his secretary how she'd like to take you out to lunch. That will make her remember you if you should ever go back.

Now, my friends, any man by following these few simple suggestions can realize his ambition of how not to become a top salesman. With very little effort he can learn how to successfully avoid eating regularly and will doubtless find greater comfort sleeping on a park bench than he would in a regular bed. Perhaps some of you may recognize the individual I am trying to reach with my little manual of helpful hints.

My friends, seriously we all know that salesmanship is selling ability. We all possess it to a greater or lesser degree. We all use it in our daily contacts, whether we sell ourselves to others, or sell some product. The kind of salesmanship that brings a man to the top is an art, a science, a profession. Any man who possesses it to the extent that our speaker does is not only an asset to his product but to his community as well.

We know that a top salesman must have personality, persistence, and enthusiasm among other qualities—which all go to make up the most important quality of all—the ability to persuade others to buy what he has to sell. Naturally, our speaker has all those qualifications, but he also possesses something else—the ability to inspire others to emulate him—which is one of the many good reasons why he has had such a deservedly successful career. My friends, it is my sincere pleasure to present to you, Mr. —————.   —Earl Jay Gilbert.

INTRODUCING AN INSURANCE SALESMAN

Most of you have heard from Pete White before. Individuals, such as Pete, like all good insurance men, get around, and he gets there when you least expect him—just as your wife is putting on the dinner, or just as you are about to leave the house on an important engagement. But tonight you are going to hear from him collectively.

Sometimes remarks are made about an insurance man that are never repeated in his presence. Nevertheless an insurance man is a mighty handy fellow to have around when disaster strikes. By all the laws of common sense, the insurance industry shouldn't need salesmen. People should just flock out and buy insurance. But, of course, they don't, so fellows like Pete have to work hard convincing others that coverage is needed.

One evening last summer Pete called upon Mr. Jacobi Withers, a punctilious gentleman over in the other end of town. Pete talked to Mr. Withers with machine-gun rapidity about the good qualities of the policy he was trying to sell. But for every good point that Pete brought up, Withers countered with an objection.

"My good fellow," said Withers. "I have been told by the Providential man that their company is pretty fast in paying a claim. How about that?"

"Well," said Pete, "Providential is fast. It's a good company."

"You durn right they're fast," said Withers. "According to that fellow, Providential pays a claim before the ink in the obituary column is dry."

"Hum," said Pete. "But we've got that beat."

"You got that beat?" asked Withers.

"Well," said Pete, "Our offices are on the fourth floor of the building. One of our clients has his offices on the tenth floor. One day the client fell out of the window. As he passed our floor we handed him the check."

Ladies and gentlemen, Mr. Pete White.

—Baxter Alton

INTRODUCING A CHEMIST

I have the distinction of bringing before this meeting a celebrated chemist, Lloyd R. Gammens. Mr. Gammens has made many a valuable contribution to that very valuable field of chemistry—a science that in a great measure is responsible for the tremendous forward strides we have taken in our mode of living.

The work of a chemist at the test tube, delving into the unknown, is the first step towards a new discovery that ultimately will bring salubrious benefits throughout the world. Yes, the science of chemistry is an exacting one—a science that requires many years of hard study, of hard work, and of untiring concentration. In that respect it might be advisable to review some of Mr. Gammens' early days when he was ploughing his way through college, hurdling obstacle after obstacle. He was a busy young man in those days, working at odd jobs to procure enough sustenance to supply his physical being with enough strength to absorb the cramming of the classroom.

One day Mr. Gammens hurried down to Dr. Ralph A. Brown's office, a noted specialist. The reception room was crowded with patients, pondering over their illnesses and eagerly awaiting the call into the doctor's private office, where the verdict, good or bad, would be given. One by one a nurse ushered each patient into a small waiting room.

Approaching Mr. Gammens, the nurse said very professionally, "Step right over into that private room, young man, and remove all of your clothes. When you hear a buzzer, walk through the door with the red light, and there you will come face to face with Dr. Brown."

Mr. Gammens followed the nurse's instructions and carefully took off his clothes. Standing thus in the little cubicle, trembling in every limb and fiber and embarrassed beyond words, Mr. Gammens anxiously awaited the impending buzzer. Momentarily it sounded—one long buzz—which was followed by a red light over a door. Mr. Gammens made for the door, leaped through it, where he was received by the eminent **Dr. Brown.**

Scrutinizing his patient through his bifocals, the doctor cleared his throat and said: "What's the matter with you, young man?"

"Nothing," said the young Mr. Gammens, "I'm working my way through college by taking subscriptions for the 'Saturday Evening Post.'"

Ladies and gentlemen, Mr. Lloyd Gammens.

—Walter Coleman

INTRODUCING A MEAT DEALER

The next speaker on your program is well acquainted with this audience. Many of you have been customers of his for years. You have all seen his smiling face back of the meat counter. But tonight you are going to see his smiling face on the speaker's platform. However, before I introduce our good friend, Harry Schmitz, I am going to tell you about an incident that happened at his store last year. I am going to give you my version of it first, before Henry stands up here and distorts it.

It was a lazy summer afternoon, Saturday to be exact, and most of Henry's customers had already purchased their week-end supply of meats and had by that time gone fishing. The only customer in the store was Mrs. Jones, who was examining a steak that Henry had just sliced off from a big piece of beef on the block. Suddenly a masked man entered and with a threatening gun in hand advanced towards Henry's counter.

At that moment Mrs. Jones let out a terrifying scream, and the hold-up man made a quick about-face and fled out of the store.

"Goodness," said Henry, regaining his breath. "Mrs. Jones, I want to thank you. You saved my cash, and probably saved my life when you screamed. How could you tell a bandit was coming in the store? Your back was to him."

"I knew nothing about a bandit," Mrs. Jones said. "I screamed when you mentioned the price of that steak."

Ladies and gentlemen, Mr. Henry Schmitz.

—Lester Olds

INTRODUCING A DRUGGIST

Gentlemen, it is a distinct pleasure to introduce to you our popular friend, John Adams, proprietor of Adam's Drugs, where you can get anything from a lollipop for the youngster to a hot water bottle for Grandma.

When I was told by the arrangements committee that John was to be our speaker, I concluded that I had better find out something about a druggist, so I made a call on Dr. Friedenleiter, dean of the school of pharmacy at the college.

"Dr. Friedenleiter," said I, "I am going to introduce a druggist tomorrow night."

"Introduce a druggist!" exclaimed the doctor. "Why, good heavens, I've been introducing them by the hundreds for the past twenty-five years. My boys can make the niftiest sandwiches and squirt the foamiest soda water in the entire drug field."

Then I said to the doctor, "When did this drug business transform from the blue vase, the pestle and mortar to the malted milk and the ham sandwich?"

"That's a sad story," Dr. Friedenleiter replied. "It all happened a number of years ago in a drug store in Scotterville, when the founder of this devastating reform hit upon an idea."

"What kind of an idea?" I asked.

"Well," said the doctor, "the worst part of it was the fellow who was one of my students—Schwartz was his name. The packers of ham-meats set up a monument in his honor, although he should have been hung at an early age. This fellow Schwartz was a great eater. All day he would eat sandwiches and drink coffee. Finally one day a fellow came into his store and said, 'Schwartz, I want to buy one of those ham sandwiches and a cup of coffee from you.' 'All right,' said Schwartz, and he sold it to him. The news that Schwartz was selling sandwiches and coffee spread like wildfire, and it wasn't long before Schwartz moved his headache powder department to the rear of the store and replaced it with a lunch counter."

Then Doctor Friedenleiter paused to light his pipe. "Then a short time later," the doctor continued, "as Schwartz was grinding up some pills with his pestle, a clerk accidentally lobbed a hunk of ice cream into the air, which landed in Schwartz's mortar. But Schwartz kept right on grinding away with his pestle, and that was the beginning of our milk shake."

"So that's how it was," I said to the doctor.

"Yes," said the doctor, "this thing has gone so far that now scholarships for the School of Pharmacy are based upon the recipient's ability to make a ham sandwich."

Then Dr. Freidenleiter pointed to his class and said: "See that class over there. They're concocting a new sandwich spread, which is a conglomeration of pickles, apples, vinegar and quinine. The quinine is the only ingredient having anything to do with pharmacy."

"Will they all get degrees?" I asked.

"All but that fellow over on the end," the doctor replied. "He's too slow with the knife. He makes a very sloppy sandwich."

Ladies and gentlemen, that's what I found out about a druggist. Now meet John Adams.

—Sylvester McGovern

ADDITIONAL MATERIAL

John Hanson, our next speaker, was extremely busy at his store one Saturday evening, when a young lady came in and asked John if it were possible to disguise the taste of castor oil. After making light of the question, John asked the young lady: "Would you like a nice chocolate soda? The chocolate is exceptionally good this week."

"I believe that I will," said the young lady, and John mixed up one, squirting the soda in a professional manner so that just a few bubbles of the delicious foam lingered over the top of the glass.

"My, that was a good soda," said the girl, wiping her lips. "Now tell me, Mr. Hanson, how do you disguise the taste of castor oil?"

"It's already been disguised," said John—"in that chocolate soda."

"Heavens!" said the girl. "I came to get it for my mother!"

Ladies and gentlemen, Mr. John Hanson.

—Scott Carlyle

Mrs. Peabody received an invitation from our local doctor to attend a dinner party. As the note was scribbled in the doctor's handwriting, Mrs. Peabody was unable to decipher it. She then handed it to Mr. Peabody, who examined it carefully. But he, too, was unable to make anything out of it.

"I'll tell you what to do," said Mr. Peabody to Mrs. Peabody. "Take it down to John Hanson, the druggist. He is the only person in this county who can read Dr. Blue's handwriting."

So Mrs. Peabody hurried down to John's store and gave him the note. "Just a few minutes, please," said John, as he picked up the note from Mrs. Peabody's hand. Then John retired to his private quarters at the back of the store.

In a few minutes John returned from the back room, handed Mrs. Peabody a small box and quietly said, "That will be a dollar and a quarter, please."

Ladies and gentlemen, Mr. John Hanson.

—Scott Carlyle

INTRODUCING A CORONER

The job of a coroner is a gruesome one, indeed. While going through the routine of his daily work, the coroner is confronted with the last days of the derelict and the last days of a person or persons whose lives have been snuffed out in some tragic event.

But yet, a coroner is a very important man in a community, as he is the first line of defense against foul play. Such is the life of Dr. Herbert Watters, our next speaker. Dr. Watters, in his capacity as coroner of this county, has been a faithful and tireless public servant. The citizens of this community owe him a debt of gratitude.

However, there are times when even a coroner gets a laugh out of his work—when humor seeps in amidst the gloomy atmosphere of death and violence. A short time ago Dr. Watters was called down to the colored district, where the death of an elderly colored man had been reported. There had been yelling and screaming in the neighborhood, which indicated that there might be an association of violence with the man's death.

Dr. Watters arrived promptly on the scene, entered the house and examined the dead man. There was no question but what the fellow had departed this world. Turning to a weeping rotund old lady who was sitting on a chair in the corner of the room, the doctor said sympathetically, "Was that man your husband?"

"Yas, suh," said the old lady. "He done be my husband."

"Had he been ailing?" the doctor further questioned.

"He done been sick two or three days," said the woman.

Then Dr. Watters asked quickly, "Did you have a doctor?"

The old lady wiped a tear from her eyes and looking up at the coroner quietly said, "There was no doctor. He died a natural death."

Ladies and gentlemen, Dr. Herbert Watters.

—Baxter Walker

INTRODUCING A REALTOR

Jack Hunt is one of the most popular realtors in Jefferson-ville, for Jack is a community-spirited individual. His untiring efforts in behalf of the expansion of this city are monumented in the numerous real estate developments with which this town has been blessed during the last decade.

Yes, Jack has left his mark upon Jeffersonville. But in order to attain such an accomplishment, Jack has had to work hard, persuading this person or that person to better his living conditions by buying a new home or a new lot—to move forward and keep step with progress. Jack is so aggressive that he is known in the trade as a super-duper salesman.

Jack's reputation as a super-duper salesman did not stop with those in the real estate business. It also traveled down to the lower stratas.

On a dark and stormy night last summer, two burglars planned an invasion of Jack's home, where they expected that some loot of considerable value would be waiting. It was learned that the names of those characters were Pat and Mike. Slowly and cautiously, Pat and Mike crept across Jack Hunt's lawn, hiding alternately behind a bush, behind a tree, and waiting now and then for a clap of thunder, when they would hurry forward towards a window through which they planned an entrance. As Pat carefully placed a jimmy under the win-dowsill, Mike looked around the grounds, which seemed to be familiar to him.

"Just a minute," said Mike to Pat who was working fever-ously on the jimmy.

"Why?" said Pat. "Do you hear someone comin'?"

"No one's comin', but hold the jimmy," exclaimed Mike in a whisper.

"What the devil's the matter with ye? Turning chicken?" said Pat.

"I'm not turnin' chicken," said Mike, "but there's somethin' familiar about this joint." Then as a flash of lightning outlined the house, Mike added, "I've been in here before and I'm not goin' in again."

"You're not goin' in again?" exclaimed Pat.

"Sure and I'm not goin' in again," Mike repeated. "This is Jack Hunt's dump, the real estate man."

"Why do we care whose dump it is?" said Pat.

"Sure and I do," said Mike. "The last time I was in here that guy Hunt collared me and sold me six suburban lots!"

Ladies and gentlemen, Jack Hunt.

—Larry O'Keefe

INTRODUCING A SPORTING GOODS MANAGER

Gentlemen, I was pleased to learn from your chairman of the arrangements committee that Bill Peters was going to appear on our program this evening. Bill is quite a fellow, and I consider it an honor to be able to stand here and say a few kind words about him.

Bill, as you all know, operates the Peters Sporting Goods Store on Main street. He has outfitted most of the golfers in this community, good and bad; and he has uniformed our baseball nines. When you need a handball glove, you go down and see Bill. But Bill is somewhat of an athlete himself. He specializes in golf; and Bill's golf contests are bitter ones, particularly when he's playing with his neighbor, Jack Jones.

A short time ago Bill and Jack were having a game at the country club. The score was even up at the seventeenth hole. Then Bill sliced one into the rough. Jack stood leisurely on the fairway, while Bill hurried over to recoup his ball.

After Bill's ball came soaring back on the fairway, he said enthusiastically to Jack, "I got out of there in two strokes. Not bad, eh, Jack?"

"Two strokes!" exclaimed Jack. "Why, I heard you beat the ground five times with your iron. Where do you get that stuff, two strokes?"

"Well," said Bill, "I was killing a snake."

Ladies and gentlemen, Bill Peters.

—Walter Coleman

INTRODUCING AN ARCHITECT

It is not often that one has the opportunity to introduce such a celebrated professional man as Harry Benson, the architect. Harry's creative mind has been responsible for many changes here in Swanville. Some of our finest buildings, many of our beautiful homes, our bridges and our parks—all were conceived at the point of that green Dietzgen 4h pencil that Harry always carries in his pocket.

Harry and his pencil are boon companions. They are never separated. While talking on the phone, he doodles with it. While waiting for lunch, he scribbles on the table cloth with it. In fact, that green Dietzgen 4h pencil is more necessary to Harry's existence than his—trousers.

Last summer Harry and his friend Jack Brown took a trip to Cuba to study Spanish architecture. As neither man spoke Spanish, they met with considerable difficulty in making known their wants as they traveled about Cuba. One day Jack Brown craved a glass of milk, since he hadn't had a glass of milk since he left the states. So Harry and Jack entered a restaurant, where Harry ordered coffee by pointing to an urn, but Jack was unable to transplant his thought to the Cuban waiter. After about fifteen minutes of waving arms, making gestures like milking a cow and eating grass, Jack gave up. The waiter just could not make out what he wanted.

"I'll show you how to make him understand," said Harry, producing his green Dietzgen 4h pencil. "I'll draw a picture for him."

Harry took a paper napkin and proceeded to caricature a cow, which when finished he handed to the waiter. The waiter took the sketch from Harry's outstretched hand, looked at it for a moment, and then suddenly rushed out the door, crossed the street and entered a bar.

Both men followed the waiter's movements, and then Jack turned to Harry and asked, "Is that fellow going to get a glass of milk in a bar?"

"He'll get it all right," said Harry, adding, "See what you can do with a pencil—a little sketch, the universal language."

After a delay of about ten minutes the waiter came prancing back across the street, rushed into the restaurant and threw two small paste-boards on Harry's table.

"What the devil is that?" Harry asked excitedly.

"That," said Jack, examining the paste-boards, "is the result of your universal language—two tickets to a bull fight."

Ladies and gentlemen, Mr. Harry Benson.

—Phil Jeffries

INTRODUCING AN IMPLEMENT DEALER

Gentlemen, Dave Owens has been attending to the needs of the farmers in this area for a long time. His machinery and equipment are a part of most of the farms in this community. But like every other businessman, Dave expects to get paid for what he sells.

A few years ago, several of the best farmers were behind in the payment of their accounts. Now it happened at that time a young fellow by the name of Ole Larson came back to town. Ole had been down to the city, and he said he had done some collection work. When Ole heard Dave remark that the farmers around here weren't paying as promptly as they should, Ole asked for the job of collecting the past due accounts.

So Dave gave Ole three delinquent accounts. In a few days Ole returned to Dave's store and reported on his progress.

"This fellow Bill Smith," said Ole, "Will pay in August. And this fellow, Joe Jones, will pay in September. And this fellow, Yon Yonson, is going to pay up in Yanuary."

"January," exclaimed Dave, "There's no cash crop coming in January. Are you sure he said January?"

"Well," said Ole, "this fellow Yon Yonson said it vould be a pretty cold day vehn he vould pay up, and I figure it vould be Yanuary."

Ladies and gentlemen, Dave Owens.

—Adolph Hintz

INTRODUCING A POLITICIAN

Ladies and gentlemen, I have a very pleasant task before me. I have been requested to introduce to you a man who has spent many years in the public service. He really needs no introduction because many of you know this man personally. Those of you who have never met him before are aware of his splendid reputation for service to us all—to the public he represents.

You know, I have often wondered why a man of integrity, of honor, and of sincerity stays in politics. He can accomplish many fine things for the people he represents—the greatest good for the greatest number—and he's admired, respected and looked up to. In doing these things sometimes he steps on somebody's toes. Then his enemies start to work on him; they call him a bum; he's slurred, slandered, insulted, criticized and picked on and blamed for all the ills in the world. Sometimes even the very people who he has benefitted forget the many good things he has done and yell for his scalp. We've all seen that happen.

So I did a little research work to find out why a man becomes a politician — where and how he gets the idea in the first place. Well, friends, I came up with this. It seems a couple had a twelve-year-old boy and they naturally wondered what he was going to be when he grew up—what occupation or profession he was going to adopt for his career.

So the old man said to his wife: "Look—here's how we'll find out. I'll put my wallet, a bottle of whisky and a glass, and a Bible on the table. We'll watch the boy when he comes in. If he drinks the whisky, he's going to be a drunkard. If he takes my wallet, he's going to be a bandit. If he starts to read the Bible, he's going to be a minister." Well, the boy came home and they watched through a crack in the door. The boy picked up the bottle of whisky, poured a big shot and drank it, then he took the money out of the old man's wallet and stuck it in his pocket. Then he picked up the Bible, stuck it under his arm and walked out. The old man said, "My God, he's going to be a politician!" But the boy fooled him. When he grew up he became a master of ceremonies, introducing politicians—and broke the old man's heart.

Ladies and gentlemen, permit me to present the Honorable ———————————. Thank you.   —Earl Jay Gilbert

INTRODUCING AN ADVERTISING EXECUTIVE

I consider it an honor to be able to stand before you and introduce such an exemplary member of the community as Harry Pierce. Harry is an advertising man—one of those fellows who deals in ideas or what is commonly referred to as intangibles.

About the middle of last March Harry was winding up an extensive trip with one last stop at Kansas City. When he arrived in that great mid-western city, he went directly to the Garden Gate Hotel, stepped up to the desk and registered. When he had completed that operation, he turned about to come face to face with a patronizing porter, who had been standing by waiting for the moment to offer his services.

"How many trunks you got goin' up to the sample room, Mr. Pierce?" asked the porter.

"Trunks to the sample room!" Harry exclaimed. "Why, I have no trunks."

"Oh, beg your pardon, suh. I thought you was one of those traveling salesmen," said the porter.

"I'm a traveling salesman," Harry retorted. "But I sell brains."

"You sells brains?" said the astonished porter.

"That's it!" said Harry. "Brains!"

"Glory be!" exclaimed the porter with a chuckle. "You is the first traveling man that's been here all year without his samples."

Ladies and gentlemen, Mr. Harry Pierce.
                                        —Charles Marvin

INTRODUCING A HOLLYWOOD ACTOR

I have the honor of presenting a gentleman from Hollywood—a motion picture actor.

A wonderful place, Hollywood; a truly remarkable city. A **different** kind of city, from all we hear about it.

There have been a number of things regarding Hollywood which have puzzled me, and probably others. Maybe our guest, in the course of the proceedings here, will have the graciousness of enlightening me, and you.

A motion picture celebrity, for instance, they say, is one who works all his life to become well known and then goes through the back streets wearing dark glasses so he won't be recognized!

They say they even wear those dark glasses in church. Are they afraid that maybe God will recognize them and ask them for their autograph? I don't know.

And when some heart throb of the feminine gender is interviewed, and asked what her great ambition in life is, it seems she almost invariably answers: "Oh, my tastes are really very simple. I'd like nothing better than to marry some good man, be a good housewife, and have four or five children."

But what happens? Later on we read that **Miss** Glamortorso now has two, or three, or four, or maybe five children. And **Miss** Glamortorso may also adopt three or four more. Because both **Miss** Glamortorso and **her husband,** Gregory Sock, are very fond of children. But has Miss Glamortorso changed her name to **Mrs.** anything? No! She still calls herself **Miss** Glamortorso. And no one thinks there is anything strange about it. A remarkable town, Hollywood. Where else but in Hollywood could this be?

Ah, Hollywood! Breathes there a man with soul so dead who hasn't dreamed, in his subconscious mind at least, of being an actor in the movies. Embracing Lana Turner one day, Betty Grable the next; Marilyn Monroe—. Imagine, and getting paid for doing it!

Yeah, for most of us the subconscious mind dreams of embracing Marilyn Monroe. But the conscious mind finally settles for Marjorie Main!

Okay, I can almost hear that! The women are going to say that on their part, they settled for Lon Chaney! Let 'em. Go ahead and say it, girls. We want to be fair.

A fabulous town. You either own a private swimming pool, or you can't keep your head above water.

Hollywood! What a town! The women stars wear all kinds of jewels, corsages, bunnies, dew-dads, and knick-knacks in front. But their backs? They're left entirely bare in those backless evening gowns. That's so they can knife each other without spoiling the dress.

Fabulous! Look at Sinatra. A fellow who gets a million dollars a year for making girls scream. You or I make 'em scream and we'd get thirty days. They say they shipped a Sinatra picture to Europe last week—and now they're starting to ship food packages to **us**!

It isn't all milk and honey in Hollywood. An actor said to me only the other day: "This life isn't all it's cracked up to be. One day you're kissing Lana Turner, Jane Russell, and Marie Wilson—and the next day you're a has-been."

"Yeah," said I, "but look where you has been!"

Yes, we understand they're having rather hard times in Hollywood these days. With all the cuts in salary, some wag has said they're signing their contracts with styptic pencils. They say that when parades pass down Hollywood Boulevard, the confetti thrown down from the buildings is made up mostly of actors' contracts.

They tell of one extra who went to a doctor. This doc gave him five pills and told him to take one after every meal. That was a week ago, and the extra still has four pills left.

They say the actors are complaining of sinus trouble—"they won't sign-us." They say things are so tough even the yes men are saying "maybe." And so on.

They say television did it. Well, I don't know. Television

is something they shouldn't worry about. It will **never** take the place of the movies. Can you neck in a television?

I've been kidding, of course. Don't worry about Hollywood. And don't sell Hollywood short. She'll survive. She'll survive the hard times, and she'll survive the wise-cracks—and the wise-crackers. She has had these crises before, and has always managed to survive them, to bounce right back with a wallop. Don't let us forget that.

Considering some of the pictures of the past year—truly marvelous productions, I think—we have a mighty healthy corpse. A useful as well as entertaining industry—we need it, and we are proud of it, and we hope it will long endure.

And now, without further ado I am proud to present our guest of the evening, a motion picture star right out of Hollywood. Ladies and gentlemen, Mr. —————.

—George A. Posner

ADDITIONAL MATERIAL

Speaking of Hollywood actors, I heard a little story about one, a character man. It seemed he had worked only three weeks of the last fifty-two. And one day he saw a former associate—big producer—coming out of the Brown Derby.

So he walked up to him, and said: "Oh, Sam, you dear fellow, how **are** you? Fine? That's **great**! Where are you going?"

"Oh, I'm going over to Hollywood Boulevard to see my tailor," answered the other cautiously.

"Hollywood Boulevard? That's **great,** just **great,** I'm going your way. I'll walk along with you."

And as they walked along the character actor—the one out of a job—seemed to suddenly have a bright idea, an inspiration. He said to the producer: "Say, Sam, I've had a rotten season. I need a new suit, and I have no money or credit anywhere. Slip me a twenty-dollar bill. Then, when you're paying your tailor, pretend you are twenty dollars short, and ask me to loan it to you. When the tailor sees I'm a friend of yours, and apparently have money to lend, he'll insist on making me a suit."

The producer laughingly agreed that the scheme was worth trying and handed the actor the $20 bill. When they reached the tailor shop he faithfully carried out his part of the program, turning to the actor for help.

"I find I'm $20 short. Loan it to me, will you?"

"I'm sorry, Sam," answered the actor. "I haven't got a cent with me."

A certain Scotch director whom I shan't name, took a movie company to Europe to make a picture.

One of the scenes called for a street brawl, and this director thought of a way of getting this inexpensively, as well as possibly getting more realism into it.

So he told one of his actors: "You see that man coming with his wife? You go up and insult her. The husband will get mad, and when he comes at you, then the camera man will start grinding!"

So the actor goes up to the man, and says: "Pardon me, is this your wife?"

"Yes," answers the man. "What about it?"

"I think she's the homeliest, most horrible thing I ever saw. How were you ever silly enough to marry her?" And the actor braced himself for the expected fight.

Instead, the man turned to his wife and said: "See? Didn't I tell you?"

During the worst of the financial crises in Hollywood, things got so bad that most of the major studios hired efficiency experts so that everything possible could be trimmed from overhead costs. These experts were empowered to recommend the firing of any personnel they considered could be dispensed with, or who weren't performing up to the required efficiency.

The very first morning, at a top studio, one of these experts wandered into an office, and saw a slothful-looking gent in a loud sports coat, slumping in an overstuffed office chair, with his feet up on the desk, cigaret drooping out of the corner of his mouth, and reading a book.

Immediately the efficiency expert shouted: "You, there! Get those feet off the desk, and get to work!"

The gent blinked, looked up, knocked the ashes off his cigaret, and then without a word, went on reading.

The efficiency expert purpled, and shouted: "Give me your name!"

The languid one looked up and said: "Oh, go jump off a cliff!"

And the efficiency expert, now livid, said: "I'll report you to Mr. Mammoth, the manager himself!"

"Oh, tell him to go sit on a tack!" was the smug one's response.

So the efficiency expert bustled into the chief's office and told the whole tale. "When I remonstrated with him, he told me to jump off a cliff, and when I said I would report him to you, he said 'tell him to go sit on a tack'," ended up the outraged disciple of economy. "He wouldn't tell me his name but he's at the big desk in room 100." And he described him.

From the description the manager recognized that the culprit was the producer of "The Robe" which had grossed about $10,000,000.00 to date (in a matter of about six months). He thought a minute, then answered sadly:

"Well, I've got a tack. Do you know of a good cliff?"

—George A. Posner

INTRODUCING A FORESTER

The science of forestry is a fascinating one, for it is associated with the great outdoors—the forests and the wilderness. It carries with it a spirit of adventure and romance, that of exploring the frontiers.

The science of forestry is also a practical science, as Dr. Jonathan Blake could tell you when I call him to the speaker's table in a few moments. It is a science that preserves our natural resources through the development and growth of our timberland. There is no doubt that, without the diligent efforts of our foresters, our lands would have long ago been depleted of that wonderful blessing of nature, the tree. But I am not going to get into the subject of forestry, as I know very little about it. I will leave that to Dr. Blake, whose reputation as a lecturer on forestry is renowned, as Dr. Blake is continually on a tour, speaking before celebrated audiences on this interesting subject.

Last summer Dr. Blake and an associate were traveling to Philadelphia, where the doctor was to address a meeting of the country's leading scientists. At Chicago the doctor and his friend got aboard the Pennsylvania Limited, where the doctor was assigned to berth number lower 12. Before the Pennsylvania Limited left the station, a midget who was on tour with the 101 Ranch circus, stopped in the cafeteria for a cup of coffee, which was followed by a second cup. After the midget had completed his second cup, he said to the waitress, "I shouldn't have done that. I won't sleep all night!" Then the midget hurried on board the Pennsylvania Limited and was tossed up into berth upper 12 by the porter.

The next morning as the doctor and his friend were making their toilets, the friend said to Dr. Blake, "Well, doctor, how did you sleep last night?"

"Very poorly," the doctor replied. "I could swear that someone was walking up and down in that upper berth all the blessed night."

Ladies and gentlemen, Dr. Blake.   —Walter Coleman

INTRODUCING A MUSIC DEALER

Tonight, ladies and gentlemen, I have the privilege of introducing to you our good friend John Brown of Brown Music, Inc. Most of the noise, outside of the fire engine siren, that we hear in Paynesville was conceived in John's store. A few weeks ago little Susie Smith, who lives next door to my house, rushed up to me and said joyously, "Mommy's taking me down to Brown's to buy a fiddle."

"Isn't that lovely?" I said to little Susie.

At that precise moment a horrifying shriek disturbed the atmosphere, which reminded me that the week before little Bobby Jones, my neighbor on the other side, said the same thing, only it was a trumpet instead of a fiddle. But a situation like this has some consolation. I merely stuff my ears with cotton, knowing that as long as the whines and the blasts keep coming from each side of my house, my flower bed is safe from trampling. In this respect, I have been tempted to go down to John Brown's and buy the kid across the alley a bass viol.

One day last summer Mrs. P. P. Merryweather and her little son Horace came down to John's store to report on little Horace's progress on the violin. It was a sort of an annual report, as three years before John launched little Horace on a musical career with the sale of a fiddle; and each year little Horace would give a performance by playing "My Old Kentucky Home" for John, who would inform Mrs. Merryweather on Horace's progress, if any. On the occasion that I am now speaking about—the third annual visit—Mrs. Merryweather sat at the piano and flitted her ringed-fingers across the keyboard, as Horace rosined up his bow. While these preliminary acts were being performed, a distinguished looking gentleman with a white mustache and string bow-tie stood by taking in the proceedings.

With considerable ceremony little Horace drew his bow across the strings and then promptly began to manufacture sounds that had some semblance to the tune, "My Old Kentucky Home." Mrs. Merryweather counted off the beats with repetitious nods of her head.

Just at the time when Horace slurred into that part of the song which referred to a weeping lady, the gentleman spectator burst into tears. When the song was completed with one last fade-away scratch, the man was still weeping.

It was apparent that John was deeply moved by such a mournful combination—Horace on the fiddle and the man shedding tears. In all of John's business years he never had witnessed such a touching scene. Out of curiosity he stepped over to the weeping man and said consolingly: "My good man, are you a Kentuckian?"

"No," replied the man between sobs, "I'm a musician."

Ladies and gentlemen, John Brown.   —Larry O'Keefe

INTRODUCING A CONFECTIONER

I was pleased to learn just before the meeting that I was going to introduce Joe Markos of the Palace of Sweets, for Joe is a witty fellow and perhaps he will tell us something about the "goings-on" in his establishment when the teen-agers gather there to chatter and sip ice cream soda.

But before Joe takes the stand, I am going to relate very briefly something that I heard about the Palace of Sweets. It appears that some time ago Joe hired a soda squirt whose intellect wasn't up to par. This young man who had a percentage brain seemed to get along all right, until one day a young customer with a lower fraction of brain matter than the soda squirt, came in and put in an order.

"What'll it be?" asked the soda squirt.

"Glass of plain soddy without no flavor," said the nitwit.

"Without what flavor?" said the half-baked soda squirt.

The nitwit thought that over for a minute and then rattled off, "Without no strawberry flavor."

"You can't have it," said the soda squirt. "We ain't got no strawberry flavor. You've gotta take it without no chocolate!"

Ladies and gentlemen, Mr. Joe Markos.

—Dale Irwin

INTRODUCING AN AIRLINE EXECUTIVE

I can think of nothing more fascinating than that of arranging air transportation for people to all corners of the earth. It must be wonderful to say to Mrs. Peabody: "Mrs. Peabody, you are scheduled for Flight 500, departing at 9 a.m. tomorrow. At midnight you will be in London. And remember lunch and dinner will be served aloft, Mrs. Peabody—a wonderful dinner, equal to anything at Savoy's."

That's Bob Brown's job, and he calls it work. Well, it is work in a sense, but very pleasant work. But, of course, an airline executive has other things to do. He has to think up new plans. He has to hatch plots to get new passengers, and he has to dream up ideas to overcome objections to flying. For instance: The pipe smoker or the cigar smoker is indignant because he is not permitted to smoke while in flight. So Bob says to him, "Mr. Hammerman, have you tried a Camel lately?"

"Of course, I haven't," replied Mr. Hammarman. "I'm a cigar smoker."

"Well," said Bob, "try a pack on your next flight. You'll be a confirmed Camel smoker by the time you reach New York."

Some time ago Bob took part in a scheme to entice women to fly. As an inducement the airlines offered to carry the wives of male passengers at half fare. When this liberal proposal was published in the newspapers, there were riots in the households of air travelers. Wives got the idea quickly, and the tormentation started the minute hubby arrived home from the office and continued way in to the night.

"Well!" said Mrs. Thornwinkle to Mr. Thornwinkle over the breakfast coffee. "Half fare for the wife. I'm going with you to the convention, Horace!"

Then Thornwinkle rushed down to the office, his convention plans shattered. When he arrived at the office, he sat back in his stuffed leather chair and said to C. Wilfred Appleboard, the vice-president: "C. Wilfred, Cynthia saw that special airline ad. She's going with us to the convention."

"Agatha saw it, too. She's going also," replied C. Wilfred. "What a time we'll have at the convention with Cynthia and Agatha along!" exclaimed Horace Thornwinkle, who then called in his secretary and said to her: "Get Chicago on the wire and cancel my reservations for the 'Follies Bon de Bon'."

However, some husbands were more fortunate. Their wives didn't see the airline advertisement. This was disclosed as a result of one of Bob Brown's ingenious efforts to build up good-will. As a part of this good-will campaign Bob wrote a letter to Mrs. F. Nelson Schwartz, praising Mrs. Schwartz for her courage to take to the air, and then after several other compliments, he concluded his letter with a request for a short expression on how Mrs. Schwartz enjoyed her recent airplane trip to New York.

Within a few days Bob received a pithy reply from Mrs. Schwartz, written on perfumed paper, which read: "What airplane trip?"

Ladies and gentlemen, Mr. Robert Brown.

—Dale Farnsworth

INTRODUCING A SPEAKER ON BOY SCOUTS

I am glad for the honor of being chairman for this program. It is a privilege to give a tribute to the Boy Scouts; it's really something new to **give** anything to the Boy Scouts, for as a general thing, it is they who do the giving. Giving—not getting—has long been an ideal of Scouting. It is a part of the Boy Scout plan.

Ralph Waldo Emerson once said: "The only gift is a portion of thyself," and we all know that the Boy Scout has been giving a portion of himself for as long as Scouting has existed. He gives to his family, to his friends, to his community, to his country, to other Scouts and to other people everywhere. Now I am going to ask Mr. —————, long interested in this fine work, to tell us in more detail what it means that the Boy Scout is on the giving and not the receiving end of life.

—Helen Ramsey

INTRODUCING A JEWELER

Ladies and gentlemen, tonight we have for our main speaker Mr. Sam Jones, proprietor of the Jones Jewelry, one of Pine Oakes' most popular stores. The business in which Mr. Jones is engaged deals with the happiness of people—with the milestones of life, birthdays, weddings and anniversaries. In this respect Sam has had a close association with the important things that have happened here in Pine Oakes during the past two decades.

Along with the many beautiful things stocked in Sam's store is the precious stone, which has been considered as a symbol of permanent beauty since the days of antiquity. Down through the centuries people have plundered, robbed and even committed murder for the possession of a precious stone. And the same thing is going on today.

Last fall Sam made a journey up to the northern part of our state, where he took in a county fair, watching the horse races in the afternoon and the fireworks in the evening. Between times he strolled around the grounds, mingling with people who were doing the same as he. While walking leisurely down to the Pike, where a number of side-shows were in progress, a tough-looking character with a hard face stepped up to Sam and said: "Are you Sam Jones, the jeweler from Pine Oakes?"

"I certainly am," said Sam.

"Well," said the character whispering behind a cupped mouth, "Don't talk out loud, but I've got a business proposition for you."

"You got a business proposition?" asked Sam curiously.

"You bet I've got a business proposition," repeated the character. "I want to sell you a stone—a big diamond—fifty carats."

"What!" exclaimed Sam, "Fifty carats! Hand it over and let me examine it," Sam added.

"I can't do it," said the character, "but I can get it for you. Name me a price."

"Now look here!" said Sam. "You say that you want to sell

me a diamond, and then you say you haven't got it! What kind of talk do you call that?"

The character then grabbed Sam by the lapel of his coat and putting his mouth close to Sam's ear whispered while pointing, "See that fat fellow standing over there by the House of Freaks. It's in his tie."

Ladies and gentlemen, Mr. Sam Jones.

—Baxter Walker

_____

ADDITIONAL MATERIAL

Before introducing Sam Jones, Pine Oakes' popular jeweler, I want to tell a little anecdote about Sam. Two years ago the village dead-beat, Jed Hopkins, bought a five-dollar ring at Sam's store, and as was to be expected he has not up to this time made payment. Every time Jed walked past Sam's place, Sam would rush out and corner him, but without results.

Last week Sam caught Jed for the fiftieth time, grabbed him by the arm and said rather irritably: "Now look here, Jed, I am going to ask you for the last time—for the last time, get that, for that five dollars you owe me!"

Jed spat out a chaw of tobacco, looked up at Sam through his bleary eyes and said: "Sam, then that's the end of that silly question."

Ladies and gentlemen, Mr. Sam Jones.

—Baxter Walker

_____

INTRODUCING A SPEAKER SMALL IN STATURE

The next speaker on our program this evening is a very small man. By that I mean, of course, small in physical size. The first time I heard him on the speaker's platform, I was reminded of James Boswell, the famous Scot author, who made the following remark in reference to a speaker of small physical stature:

"I saw what seemed a mere shrimp mount upon the table; but as I listened he grew and grew until the shrimp became a whale."   —Sylvester H. McGovern

INTRODUCING A CLOTHING MERCHANT

Gentlemen: Harry Burns, our next speaker, is an authority on men's fashions. If you want to know something about what the best dressed man is going to wear this season, talk to Harry. He'll tell you. Harry has been in the clothing business since the days of the pegged trousers and the high button shoes; and throughout his career as a clothing merchant he has seen the pegged trousers discarded for the tight trousers, which was later discarded for something a little wider. Harry has successfully met every expansion and every contraction in the men's clothing business.

Some authorities give Harry credit for hatching up a scheme that disguised the paunch of the fat male, and in that respect middle-aged men the world over are singing Harry's praise.

It appears that one of Harry's customers—we might call him Lester Jester—was a man of considerable girth. So mammoth was Jester's midsection that Harry was obliged to send to the factory for the fat man's pants, as nothing of Jester's proportions was carried in stock at Harry's store. Upon one occasion, when Jester had ordered a beautiful salt and pepper pair of woolens, a tailor at the factory inadvertently added six inches to the waistline.

It was an exceedingly disappointed Jester who stood before the store mirror, his ponderous midsection completely sacked-in, in the tent-like folds of cloth. It was while Jester was standing thus, scrutinizing himself in the mirror, that the ponderous garment slipped over his global contour and dropped in a heap to the floor, exposing Jester's bare legs and barber-pole shorts. Unfortunately, at this precise moment Mrs. Cynthia Gossip entered the store to purchase a handkerchief for a nephew back east. It was Cynthia's scream that attracted Harry's attention to Jester's predicament, which called for immediate action. Rushing over to Jester, Harry, with the assistance of a clerk, tried to usher the fat man back to the dressing room, but

Jester's ankles were so hobbled by the clinging cloth that he was unable to effect any locomotion whatsoever.

It was then that Harry, acting quickly with the help of the clerk, hoisted the flapping woolens upward, thereby obscuring the hairy legs, barber-pole shorts and fluttering shirt tail that had scared Miss Cynthia Gossip out of her wits.

Harry's next act was an ingenious one. With deft hands and fingers that moved like lightning, he pinned four tucks around the waistline of the embarrassed Jester, which held the trousers snuggly in place. After the excitement had subsided and composure had been regained by all, Harry discovered that he had created a miracle. Jester's inverted ski-slide had completely disappeared—camouflaged by the four pleats that Harry had pinned in the waistband. This without a doubt was the greatest boon to the male since the invention of the razor.

Ladies and gentlemen, Mr. Harry Burns.

—Sylvester McGovern

ADDITIONAL MATERIAL

Ladies and gentlemen, tonight I am going to present to you, Mr. Harry Allen, one of our community's outstanding clothing merchants. Harry is considered by the members of the clothing industry as one of the best salesmen in the business. If a fellow goes into Harry's store, he's coming out with a suit. That is a certainty. Last week Mrs. Jones dropped into purchase a suit of clothes that would shroud her deceased husband who was to be buried the next day. Harry not only sold Mrs. Jones the suit, but he sold her an extra pair of pants as well.

Ladies and gentlemen, Mr. Harry Allen.

—Baxter Walker

INTRODUCING AN INSTRUCTOR ON CONVERSATION

Professor **(name),** instructor of English in **(name of school or college)** is here to give us some valuable hints on how to successfully carry on an interesting conversation. Isn't it a fact that many well-educated people become bores as soon as they start to talk? Speaking correctly is an art that can be developed to the point where the listener is truly entranced even though the subject may be mediocre.

All nationalities carry on conversations, but some of the conversations are not carried far enough. They should be carried to the dump and thrown in. They say that many men have acquired a huge vocabulary by marrying it. A word to the would-be wise interrupts a monologue. This same would-be wise is usually a man of few words but keeps them mighty busy. Some women are rarely beaten in an argument. Still it would scarcely be right to say that in a battle of tongues she holds her own, for a woman, generally speaking, is generally speaking. The average woman's vocabulary is about five hundred words. That's a small inventory, but think of the turnover.

Watching a three-ring circus is like listening to some people talk. I know of a woman who scratched herself with a phonograph needle and died of lockjaw. A certain man called his doctor, and said, "Doctor, my wife just dislocated her jaw. If you're out this way in the next week or so you might drop in and see her."

I remember the first girl I ever went with. I couldn't hug her because she talked my arm off. A man went to his doctor, and said, "I have a habit of talking to myself all the time." The doctor said, "Oh, that's nothing to worry about." "Perhaps not," said the man, "but I'm such a big bore." One small boy said to another small boy, "My mother can talk on just about any subject." The other boy said, "That's nothing. My mother can talk without a subject." I'd better stop before I get the habit. Ladies and gentlemen, Professor **(name.)**

—Richard Drummond

INTRODUCING A TRACK STAR

Ladies and gentlemen, tonight we are fortunate in having as our speaker one of the outstanding college track stars in this part of the country—a man who has brought home many a trophy for Paynesville U, and a man whom the citizens of Paynesville are mighty happy to call their own. I feel that you will all agree with me when I say that Jack Little is one of the fastest men who ever toed the mark for a hundred-yard dash. His record proves it.

As is quite well known by all of us here in Paynesville, our track team journeyed down to Des Moines last spring for the Drake relays. Most of the credit for the team's splendid victory in that Corn Belt contest must go to Jack Little. However, on that trip Jack's speed was actually challenged, not on the cinder path, but in the hotel lobby. The team had just arrived in town and was congregating around the hotel lobby, waiting for an assignment of rooms, when a sort of mascot-type of a fellow with the Johnstown College crowd came up to Jack and said: "Are you Jack Little?"

"That's what they call me," answered Jack.

"Well," said the fellow, who was a little squirt, "I've heard that you're fast."

"Not so fast," Jack replied modestly.

"If you think you're fast," said the little squirt, needling Jack, "wait until you go up against Pete Owens. You're going to get a good look at his heels."

"Is that so?" said Jack, adding, "Just how fast is this fellow Pete Owens?"

The little squirt put his fingers in the armpits of his sweater-shirt, looked up at Jack and said: "This man Owens is so fast that when he turns his light out at night, which is twenty feet from his bed, he's under the covers before the room is dark!"

Ladies and gentlemen, Jack Little.   —Warren Holm

INTRODUCING A SHOE SALESMAN (Traveling)

It is with profound enthusiasm that I bring to this gathering a man who travels the country representing his firm selling shoes. Jack Snow is known in all parts of the United States for his energetic efforts in spreading the word about the latest styles in footwear.

Jack is an accommodating fellow, too. All of his customers like him, for when Jack arrives in town, he takes off his coat and rolls up his sleeves and helps his dealers make sales. And many a sale Jack makes, as Jack is an authority on styles. He can tell at a glance just what type of a shoe a customer should select.

During Jack's last trip to Summerville, he stayed longer than usual, assisting the clerks in Brown's Shoe Mart, fitting out the town's best ladies in the town's best shoes. One afternoon he was called by a clerk to help close a sale with a fussy woman who was having difficulty in making a selection.

"What is the matter, my dear lady?" inquired Jack in his usual courteous manner.

"Those shoes pinch me," answered the lady. "They're too pointed. I have a feeling that my big toe and my little toe are being welded together."

"That is just the effect you want," said Jack. "The long, slender shoe is the style this season."

"Is that so?" said the lady.

"Certainly," answered Jack. "Why, down in New York all you see on Fifth avenue is the long pump. At first glance you would imagine that the women were walking along on skates. The shoes are that slender."

"Gracious," said the lady.

"And do you know, madam," continued Jack, "that this new slenderized pump is doing wonders for women. It is giving them a new gait. They just seem to skim along on air with practically no hip movement."

"Heavenly days!" exclaimed the lady, "I wish that I could adopt these new styles, but I can't."

"You can't?" said Jack. "How's that?"

The woman pondered the thought for a moment, and then looked at Jack and quietly replied: "I've got last season's feet."

Ladies and gentlemen, Mr. Jack Snow.

—Horace Alton

INTRODUCING A RAILROAD EXECUTIVE

I have the honor tonight to introduce to you a railroad executive. John Sommers has represented his line in this community for a number of years, and during this service he has come face to face with many humorous incidents. People are everlastingly beefing at a railroad, and John has been the butt of many a beef. But John has taken it all good-naturedly.

One day a friend of John's called on him to solicit a job for a relative who had just come over from Europe.

"I want you to give my nephew a job on your line," said the friend.

"But," said John, perplexed at the request, "your nephew can't speak English. I can't put him to work for the road."

"Certainly you can," said the friend. "You can give him a job as a traincaller."

Then upon another occasion John was traveling on one of the company's trains, when he noticed a discussion going on between a fat lady and the conductor. Hurrying over to the lady's seat, John said to the conductor: "What's the matter here?"

"Matter!" said the conductor. "This lady insists that she is getting off at Powell Junction. I told her a half a dozen times that we have no station at Powell Junction; that it burned down six months ago."

"Well," said John to the lady, "did you hear that?"

"I certainly did," the lady replied. "For the past ten minutes I have been trying to tell that conductor that it'll be rebuilt by the time this train gets there."

Ladies and gentlemen, John Sommers.

—Larry O'Keefe

INTRODUCING A NEWSPAPER REPORTER

I was enthusiastic when I heard that I was to announce the presence of Billy Williams, as I have always considered Billy to be one of the best reporters in this part of the country. And I might add that as a result of his long service as a reporter, Billy has many an interesting yarn to spin. I know that we are going to hear some of them tonight.

Of course there was a time when Billy was a cub. That was a good many years ago. Now a cub is just about the greenest fellow around a newspaper office, with the exception of perhaps the office boy. Like all cub reporters Billy faced a succession of mistakes: misspelled words in the obituary column, or worse yet, reporting the death of the wrong man; the transposition of names under photographs and various other costly errors that gave an editor gray hair.

One day Billy was assigned to cover an elaborate dinner given in honor of a visiting international dignitary. All of the important citizens of the town were in attendance, as well as a bevy of the best-looking young ladies in the social register. Billy wrote up a pompous story, faithfully reporting the dignitary's speech, and which he appended with a flourish of color, such as a description of the room decorations, the lacey gowns of the ladies present and a brief comment on the menu. Billy filed his story and considered that he had composed a masterpiece.

When a copy of the first edition reached the desk of Managing Editor Patrick O'Flarrity, a roar of cyclonic proportions came out of that corner of the room.

"Williams!" screamed the managing editor. "Come over here!"

Billy hurried over to the boss's desk and when he arrived, he noticed that O'Flarrity had the paper opened to the page his dignitary's dinner story appeared.

"What do you mean by this?" yelled O'Flarrity in a rage, pounding his fist on the first edition.

"What do I mean by what?" said Billy.

"This!" cried O'Flarrity, who read: "Among the gorgeous ladies was Jonathan Peter Higgenbingham." "Don't you know that Higgenbingham's no lady, you dunce! And old man Higgenbingham's one of our biggest stockholders, too!"

"It can't be helped," said Billy, the factual reporter. "That's where he was!"

Ladies and gentlemen, Mr. Billy Williams.

—Larry O'Keefe

INTRODUCING AN OPTOMETRIST

Ladies and gentlemen, our principal speaker tonight comes from the worthy profession of optometry—the science of correcting the sight. The blessings that this profession have brought to mankind are profound, and in this respect our next speaker, Joe Cannon, is fulfilling a worthy service here in Oakdale. Many of you know Joe personally, as you often drop in at his store on Main street, so an eulogy on Joe at this time would be superfluous.

One day last summer Mrs. Tottleworth accompanied by son Chester visited Joe's store with the idea in mind of having little Chester's eyes examined. Chester was one of those unruly, spoiled little brats who threw a fuss at the slightest provocation. As Joe was leading the little urchin into the dark room, Chester kicked Joe in the shins and at the same time let out a howl that could be heard in the next block. It was with considerable difficulty that Joe obtained the eye examination, but at last it was finally accomplished.

"That will be ten dollars," said Joe to Mrs. Tottleworth.

"Ten dollars!" exclaimed the pompous lady, tilting up her chin and giving Joe one of those "I declare" looks.

"Yes, Madam, ten dollars," Joe repeated.

"Well!" said Mrs. Tottleworth. "I thought your price for an eye examination was only three dollars!"

"It is," Joe replied, "but this young brat of yours scared away three other young customers."

Ladies and gentlemen, Joe Cannon.   —Larry O'Keefe

INTRODUCING A TAX CONSULTANT

My friends, before I introduce our next speaker—who, by the way, is a very interesting and entertaining talker—I'd like to make a few remarks about Spring. To many of us the early days of Spring are among the most beautiful of the year. That's the time of year when we're happy with anticipation, waiting for the flowers to bud and blossom, the grass to shoot up, green and fresh, the leaves on the trees to come forth, and the withered shrubs to spring to new life. We're glad to be alive, and then suddenly comes that ominous warning: "Get it in, brother! It's the last day to file your income tax return." And then everything seems dismal and gloomy and the heck with the grass and the green leaves and we sweat and slave over figures and receipts and donations and short term gains until finally a ray of intelligence hits us and we go to see a man who straightens everything out for us and gives our poor, tired minds a chance to rest until the following year.

The tax expert is certainly a Godsend to many of us in our hours of mathematical despair. If most of us would see a tax expert shortly after the first of the year, maybe we wouldn't be so cranky around the fifteenth of April, now that the kindly internal revenue department has given us a month's respite to suffer and chew aspirin in.

Well, anyway, our next speaker is a tax consultant. He has very graciously consented to give us a talk. Whether he intends to give us any expert advice or not, I don't know, but his talk should be most enlightening.

In order to qualify as a tax expert a man must possess several talents and a lot of ability. He's got to have a mind like a Treasury Department lawyer's, a General Motor's C.P.A., and a U. S. Supreme Court Justice combined. We expect him to tell us what we can get away with—legally, of course. He's got to know how to add Line 6, Item B, to Line 1, Section 3A, and subtract it from the total in Section 9g, sub-division 114— and make it come out right.

He's got to know whether we're liable to go to jail if we don't declare that twenty-five dollar bond we won in a raffle at the Elk's picnic. Which reminds me that last year I thought I'd be very clever and figure out my return myself. I get that feeling every year. It usually lasts about a week or ten days before I become exhausted and go to the man who can really attend to it. Well, for about a week or so I struggled and figured—and each time I finished I found I had a different result.

Perhaps some of you can appreciate that. Of course, I was frequently interrupted by my wife trying to help me. Finally, I had to become quite severe with her. I explained to her in no uncertain tones that she didn't know the first thing in the world about arithmetic. I told her that her arithmetic was simply a confused jumble of figures and that she was only confusing me. She just smiled and walked away. Women annoy me at times.

However, I finally went to my tax man and after an hour or so he had it made out for me. I owed the Government four hundred and twelve dollars and twelve cents. I went home and said to my wife: "My tax consultant is a wonder. It only took him an hour and all I had to pay him was twenty-five dollars. What do you think I owe?"

She said: "Four hundred and twelve dollars and twelve cents." I said: "What? How did you know?" She said: "Oh, I figured it all out in my head." I said: "What?" She said: "It was simple. The Jones, our next door neighbors, have the same income that we have, and the same expenses. They had to pay four hundred and twelve dollars and twelve cents, so I knew ours would be the same."

I didn't mind her making a lucky guess—but still it annoyed me. It's the principle of the thing. Anyhow, in spite of her fantastic reasoning, I'm still going to consult my tax man when the time comes around—unless our speaker tonight drops a few hints that will enable me to fill out my return myself.

He should be able to, ladies and gentlemen. He's been successfully advising people on their tax problems for a long time. His reputation for efficiency is warranted by his past success in relieving the tax headaches of those of us who do not possess his accomplishments and understanding of the complicated and sometimes weird forms Uncle Sam requires us to fill out.

My friends, I find a great deal of pleasure in presenting to you a man really worthy to be called an expert tax consultant —a man who stands out among the leaders of his profession, Mr. —————. Thank you.   —Earl Jay Gilbert

INTRODUCING A SPEAKER ON EVOLUTION

Reverend (name) of the (name) Church is our guest speaker this evening, and I believe he will have something to say about evolution. Darwin said that man came from monkeys. Ha! That didn't take evolution. Men make monkeys of themselves.

And another argument against evolution is found in radio and television programs. According to them we are about where we started. And then, too, if we accept the Darwin theory we won't have anyone to blame for raising Cain.

One of the biggest objections to evolution is that it is too slow for this age. If there is anything to evolution, we sometimes doubt whether man's ascent from the monkey has started yet. There is one thing certain — teaching evolution in the schools won't make people accept it. Spelling is taught in schools too.

There may be some instances of evolution being in effect. A lawyer asked a witness in an assault and battery case, "What did you have at the first tavern you stopped?" "Four glasses of beer." "What next?" "Two glasses of whiskey." "Next?" "One glass of brandy." "Next?" "A fight." If there is such a thing as evolution you can blame it on the women. They're the ones that make monkeys out of men. And now, friends, Reverend (name).   —Arthur L. Kaser

INTRODUCING A DEPARTMENT STORE BUYER

The task of supervising a department in one of our big stores is not an easy one. It requires constantly keeping abreast of the times, so that suitable merchandise will be always on hand for the fickle woman purchaser when she arrives to rummage through the stock. A woman purchaser is at her best a rummager and hard to please, as John Anderson, our next speaker, will tell you, no doubt, when he steps up to the speaker's table.

The color is not right, the size is wrong, the design hideous and the pattern abominable. That is the common daily comment that John gets from his woman customers. One day about a month ago, a stout and finicky lady stopped at John's department for a search. For one continuous hour she fingered through the merchandise, holding this up to the light and draping that across her knees for an inspection. Then she would throw the stuff back on the table and move to another, where within a few moments that counter would also be in shambles. Throughout this entire procedure, there was no apparent inclination on the part of the lady to actually make a purchase.

All of the time the lady was messing things up in John's department, he stood by watching her and hoping that some miracle would take place and that the woman would break down and buy. When it was obvious that nothing of that sort would happen, John walked up to her and quietly said, "My dear madam, are you shopping?"

"Shopping!" exclaimed the lady. "Of course, I'm shopping. What do you think I'm doing?"

John hesitated for a moment and then casually said: "I thought perhaps you were taking inventory."

Ladies and gentlemen, John Anderson.

—Baxter Walker

INTRODUCING A DOCTOR

Friends, good evening. There's a reason for my saying "Good Evening" because you're going to hear a good talk by a good doctor and after you've heard it you all ought to feel good. If you don't, it's nice to know there's a doctor in the house.

Speaking of doctors, once I had a terrific earache. It got so bad I finally went to see a doctor. He was one of those brisk, fast-talking doctors and after he got my name and address he said, "What business are you in?" I said, "The construction business."

He said, "Fine, fine. Earache, huh? Uh-huh, uh-huh. Let me look in your ear with this instrument. Well, well. Now the other ear. Well, well. Very peculiar. Now strip to the waist." Then he started pounding my chest, my back and every place he could reach, and listening with his stethescope. Then he said, "Sit down. Take it easy. Just relax. Don't be alarmed. How long have you had this condition? Three weeks, huh? You should have come to see me before. But don't be nervous. I've had two cases like this before. One of them got well. I think maybe I can pull you through."

I was beginning to get anxious. I said, "What's the matter with me, Doc?" "Oh," he said, "Just a little case of otomyces (O-TO-MI-CEZ) which will probably develop into an acute cenosis (SE-NO-SIS) unless deterioration sets in." I started biting my nails. I said "Listen, Doc—" but he kept right on going. "Nothing to worry about. We might be able to save you. I'll call in Dr. Brown from Chicago and Dr. Miller from New York to assist me in preparing a detailed prognosis—a little expensive, but they're excellent specialists in their fields—they seldom make mistakes. In making his diagnosis Doctor Brown is guided by his studies in the science of numerology, while Doctor Miller swears by the Lucky Gypsy Dream Book. Then we'll have Dr. Smith of the State Veterinary College do the operating."

I said, "Listen, Doc—" But he kept right on talking—"Nothing to worry about—Dr. Smith is an excellent man—he certainly knows how to handle a knife—he hasn't had a fatality in several weeks. Of course, he doesn't believe much in anaesthetics—now, don't worry—you'll probably only be in the hospital about three months—then a six-month sea voyage with a doctor and two trained nurses in constant attendance in case of a serious relapse—if you're not on your feet by that time we'll try to think of something else—nothing to be alarmed about—just go home and make out your will."

I said, "Hey, Doc—listen—where am I going to get the dough for all this?" The doc says, "You're in the construction business, aren't you?" I said, "Sure—I get forty dollars a week digging sewers."

The doc looked at me, then he said, "Oh." Just "Oh." Then he sat down and said, "Go to a drugstore and get two aspirins, a bar of soap and go home and wash the dirt out of your ears. Two dollars, please." Sounds like a funny kind of a doctor, doesn't it? Well, ladies and gentlemen, here's the strange part of it. I went home and did what he said and, by gosh—it cured my earache! After all, that's what I wanted.

Now, ladies and gentlemen, the doctor who is going to address you tonight is not the doctor who cured my earache—but I guess most of you know he's good, too. Friends, it is with a great deal of pleasure that I present to you that well-known and well-liked disciple of Aesculapius, Dr. ——— ——— .

—Earl Jay Gilbert

INTRODUCING A STATE LEGISLATOR

Tonight we are going to learn something of that great science of making laws, as we have with us an outstanding member of our state legislature—Senator John Fulbright. Senator Fulbright has served in the state legislature for a great number of years, and he has served our state well, as is evidenced by the number of times that he has been re-elected to office.

Those who seek passage of legislation in our state always seek the support of Senator Fulbright, as such support over in our state house is almost tantamount to passage of a bill.

Perhaps one of the reasons why Senator Fulbright is honored and respected so highly on the floor of our Senate is the diligent manner in which he prepares his arguments. Some legislators rush in totally unprepared and as a result the bill they are trying to put over fails miserably. But not so with Senator Fulbright. Every word that he says on the senate floor has been carefully considered for its worth before it is uttered. Every speech that he delivers has been carefully written and rehearsed. And it should be pointed out that Senator Fulbright overlooks no opportunity to rehearse a speech, as is indicated by this incident.

Some time ago Senator and Mrs. Fulbright were traveling on a train, on their way to an important gathering, where the Senator was to deliver the principal oration. During the course of the train ride, which took several hours, the Senator spent the time rehearsing his talk, while Mrs. Fulbright passed away the hours reading a magazine. In a low monotone, resembling the buzzing of a bee, the Senator mumbled over the lines of his speech loud enough to be distinguished over the roar of the car wheels. When a passage of great importance was reached, he gesticulated by pounding his fist on his knees or pointing his index finger at the woman's hat in the seat in front of him. Mrs. Fulbright kept reading her magazine.

After an hour of this procedure, a lady across the aisle, who had been watching the Senator, leaned over and said to Mrs. Fulbright:

"You have my deepest sympathy, my dear lady; I have one just like that at home."

Ladies and gentlemen, the honorable John Fulbright, a distinguished member of our state legislature.

—Fuller Marlow

INTRODUCING A TEACHER

Our speaker of the evening, ladies and gentlemen, comes from one of the grandest professions in the world. I won't take much of his time but I would like to give you a few interesting details about his background. As a teacher he has had many experiences.

There was the time he had a class on nature study. He was getting along quite well with the birds, the bees and the children. He asked one small boy what a canary could do that a man could not do. The answer came quickly: Live on bird seed.

He asked another bright pupil in the same class where an elephant could be found. The lad reasoned that an elephant was such a big animal that there was little chance of it getting lost.

From one of the parents he got quite a headache. That was when he failed to pass a certain son in history class. The parent thought it was quite unfair to ask little Johnny a lot of questions about things that happened before the lad was born. Our hero went back to Biblical times to try for a certain illustration. He asked a certain lad what happened to Lot's wife. The lad answered that she was turned into a pillar of salt. Correct. The teacher wanted to know what Lot did next. The boy informed him that he reached for a stalk of celery now that he had the salt for it.

Despite all this, ladies and gentlemen, I proudly present the speaker of the evening, Mr. —————.

—Louis J. Huber

INTRODUCING AN ARTIST

They wanted someone to introduce the speaker of the evening, and so I've been asked if I wouldn't mind going before this audience. No, of course I wouldn't mind going before this audience, I said. I'd only mind if I saw the audience going before me. (That's a joke, heh, heh!)

They tell me the speaker-to-be is an artist. Well, I can't say I'm particularly prepared for this subject. An artist is someone who usually paints a lot of nude women, isn't he? That's rather a ticklish subject. Especially if they have their clothes off.

But it does sound like it might be an interesting thing to do, and maybe to talk about. Hm!

When I was a boy we used to talk a lot of what we'd like to do when we grew up—much of it in a kidding way. Like, "I'd like to be a trackwalker for an airplane company." "I'd like to be the announcer who calls out the stations on a trans-Atlantic liner."

I don't remember that we ever spoke of growing up and becoming artists and drawing nude women. Probably not. Boys under sixteen aren't much interested in women. Mostly, I guess they're interested in being boy scouts. It's only when they're past sixteen that they change, and become girl scouts. (That's a joke, heh heh!)

So I'm kind of unprepared. I haven't had much experience on this subject. Anyway, I haven't kept any notes on it—one doesn't usually keep notes on a subject of that kind, does one? Though it does sound like it might prove interesting reading.

So I'm a little unprepared, and you'll have to bear with me. (That's spelled B-E-A-R, by the way.)

About the only artist I knew personally was rather an eccentric character. When a lady sat for a painting for him, this fellow would leave her face blank. Then suddenly he'd press a compact into her hand, with rouge and lipstick, and say to her: "You carry on! You can do that part much better than I can, I'm sure!" He figured she had had more experience.

About the nearest I can make any claim to association with the artist world is that I had a brother who became interested in this business, for a while. He started first, as a draftsman. Just a junior draftsman; he was one of the under drawers. (That's a joke, heh, heh!) Later, he quit and went to New York, to study art. And you know, in just a little while, we heard **he was selling everything.** First he sold his car, then his overcoat, then finally his art equipment. That was that.

As far as Dad was concerned, Dad said he could do all the drawing he wanted, as long as he didn't draw on him.

As for brother, the real fact of the matter was that he had been spending most of his time drawing corks.

But enough of this fol-de-la-roll—let's get on to the real business of the evening. Allow me to introduce to you the speaker, —————.

—George A. Posner

————————

INTRODUCING A SPEAKER ON THE Y. W. C. A.

"A candle throws a tiny beam,
But still its light has guiding power;
If you follow its small gleam
You'll near your goal, hour by hour."

Man turns toward the light as a flower turns toward the sun. This is true in every realm—physical, mental, spiritual— that the light guides us.

Tonight, we honor an organization that has been a guiding light because its originators followed a light within. I refer to the Young Women's Christian Association. In its early days, that guiding light was like a little candle shining in the night. I am going to ask Miss ————— to tell us about those early beginnings—the days when Christian women were trying to aid their sisters by prayer and thoughtful help.

—Helen Ramsey

INTRODUCING A POLITICIAN

I have the honor of introducing a political figure this evening. Now what is a politician? There have been many definitions. Someone has said: "A politician is a man who divides his time between running for office, and running for cover."

Anyway, it seems he is always running! And it's quite logical. He's not so dumb—not to be a moving target!

Someone else has said he is just like a contortionist. He is able in some uncanny manner to keep one ear to the ground while straddling the fence. He claims he hears his country calling, and that he is answering the call—but some claim he is a ventriloquist. He is there to pour the oil when our country is passing through troubled waters, and there are some who say that the oil he pours is banana oil. And the reason many of them are sent to Washington is that their fellow citizens have decided it would be safer to get them out of town, and that's the only way they could do it.

This may be a lot of talk, of course. There are two sides to every question. That's why we have two political parties, because there are two sides—the outside and the inside.

The gentleman I am about to introduce has been a politician for a very long time. In fact, from the day of his birth, when he indicated emphatically to the world it was time for a change. And he was a born fighter, too. They say when the doctor slapped him, he struck back. Of course, I don't know how true that is. Anyway, that was in Prohibition days, and he hadn't definitely formed an opinion, I guess. They say half the time he was a Wet and half the time he was a Dry.

Of course, all this is in fun. It is my pleasure to introduce Mr. —————.

—George A. Posner

ADDITIONAL MATERIAL

At a tempestuous political gathering a big stick of wood was hurled at the speaker. Luckily the aim was a miss and it fell with a thump on the platform.

He picked it up, and with unusual presence of mind, said: "Good heavens, one of our opponents has lost his head!"

A political friend after his defeat in an election, swore he would never again address a gathering.

But one day he was approached by a woman who sought to have him speak at the Ladies Protective Society.

"I can't," he explained firmly. "I have burned my bridges behind me."

The woman looked slightly surprised, but came to the rescue nobly.

"Oh, in that case," said she, "I'll lend you a pair of my husband's."

A lot of men who think they are political timber are merely wooden-headed.

At a political rally the emcee announced the speaker in the following fashion:

"In Ireland they have a quaint superstition. They say that just when a man is born a little fairy comes down from Heaven to kiss him. If she kisses him on the forehead he will grow up to become a great philosopher, or scientist, or poet. If she kisses him on the cheek he will be a good-looking man and probably become a great actor. If she kisses him on the mouth he will be a great orator, or singer. On the foot, an athlete, or a dancer. I won't say where the fairy kissed our next speaker, but he grew up to be a great chairman."

My wife and I see alike in politics. You know they say politics makes strange bedfellows, but they soon get accustomed to the same bunk.

According to a returned voyager . . . An anti-Communist, condemned to the firing squad, was asked what he wanted before he died. He replied: "I would like to be a member of the party."

"Well," said the commander, "that is strange indeed. Why did you finally come to take such a splendid attitude?"

"Oh," was the indifferent rejoinder, "I just thought it would be pleasant to know that when you shot me there would be one Communist less!"

Someone once asked a newspaper editor: "What's a Mug-wump?"

The newspaper editor replied: "A Mugwump is a political bird who strides a fence with his head on one side and his wump on the other."

You know, Jimmy Walker, the debonair ex-Mayor of New York, was a clever and witty statesman, among his other accomplishments. He once said, "All politicians have three hats —one they wear, one they throw in the ring, and one they talk through!"

Jimmy also said: "I never like to sit at a banquet table with Congressmen." When asked why, he replied: "It takes them so long to pass anything!"

That brings to mind the experience of another friend, a politician. Maybe you might classify this under the head of diplomacy. That's something a politician is supposed to know something about.

Well, this politician was making an address during the Prohibition era, and someone in the audience shouted:

"I demand to know, sir, are you a Wet?"

The politician paused for just a bare batting of an eye. Then he answered firmly, "I am . . ."

There were loud cheers from the Wets.

He continued: ". . . Not . . ."

Then there were loud cheers from the Drys.

Whereupon he ended: . . . "Going to tell you."

You know the politicians are agreed that "you can't fool all the people all the time" . . . once every four years is enough!

The governor of California was on a trip from San Francisco to Los Angeles. By mistake he had taken a seat in a coach in which were a large group of "mental cases" who were being transferred from an insane asylum to an outdoor farm in the south part of the state.

The conductor was checking them up and counting them when he came to the governor. "Six—seven—eight—," then he stopped, seeming to notice that the governor looked somewhat different.

"Who are you, sir?"

"I'm the Governor of California."

"Nine, ten, eleven . . ."

The politicians say the way to better politics is "take the money out of it."

And, believe me, they're doing it—taking all they can lay their hands on.

—George A. Posner

INTRODUCING A HUNTER

Ladies and gentlemen. Among the many pleasant tasks that goes with this job of being chairman is the introduction of our principal speaker. So I'll get right down to the job.

Our guest, ladies and gentlemen, is well known as a Nimrod, a hunter who never misses. For example: On his very first trip he went deer hunting. He came back with a beautiful redhead. Just a case of bad spelling.

His most successful trip into big game country happened just a short time ago. He looked for lions and didn't meet one. He went bear hunting and didn't shoot the first one he saw. He wanted one to match the gloves he had bought for his wife. He went tiger hunting and met one. The tiger was so close that he could feel his breath down his neck. Drama! Excitement! A tiger breathing down his neck! What did he do? He merely turned up his coat collar and kept on running through the jungle.

Such a hero is our speaker. Despite all I've said I present him to you with a great feeling of having an honor bestowed on me. I give you Mr. —————.   —Louis J. Huber

INTRODUCING AN AUTHORITY ON HEALTH

This is the most sanitary country in the world. It should be with so many countries cleaning us all the time. We have with us this evening an authority on sanitation who is speaking under the sponsorship of the Health Department.

Some time ago I was among several to be selected to look into the sanitary conditions of our community. At the first place I stopped I asked, "Have you taken any precaution to prevent spread of contagion in your family?" "Absolutely," was the reply. "We bought a sanitary cup and we all drink from it." During my rounds I dropped into a small restaurant for lunch. The waiter laid an unclean knife beside my plate. I called the waiter and said, "This knife isn't clean." He said, "Oh, it must be. The last thing I cut with it was a bar of soap."

A twelve-year-old boy sat down on the stool next to me. His hands were very dirty. I said to him, "Don't you wash your hands before you eat?" He just shook his head. I said, "Your face is clean, but how did you get your hands so dirty?" He said, "From washing my face."

I began talking to him about sanitary care. I told him that after I wash my face I always look in the mirror to see if it is clean. He said he didn't. He just looked at the towel. There was a cat sitting in a cushioned chair washing its face. I said to the boy, "Did you ever notice how clean a cat is?" He said cats weren't so clean, but I insisted cats were clean. I said that cats are usually washing their faces with their paws. The boy said it was just the opposite. He said cats washed their feet and wiped them on their faces.

Later that day I was talking to a man who was washing his car. I said to him, "You certainly keep your car nice and clean." He shook his head and said, "It's an even deal—it keeps me clean, too." A certain woman became rather frantic when, after scrubbing the little boy's face for fifteen minutes, she couldn't get through the black on his face. Finally she blurted, "Raymond Simpson, didn't I tell you never to blacken your face again? Here I've been scrubbing for fifteen minutes and it won't come off." The little boy struggled free and sputtered, "I isn't yoh Raymond. I's de janitor's li'l Clem."

Friends, I'm to introduce our speaker, **(name of health speaker.)**
                                             —Arthur L. Kaser

---

INTRODUCING A CATTLE RAISER

Our speaker for this evening, ladies and gentlemen, is a man who got his start as a simple country boy. He was born and raised on a farm. From the few stories that we have been able to gather about him it is quite easy to see why he is no longer a fellow farmer.

One of his experiences, so we have been told, had to do with a race horse that he had raised from a colt. He was trying to sell the steed. He got on it and began the ride around a large pasture. Every ten steps the horse would stop. When the would-be buyer asked our man about this he explained that the horse was partly deaf and that he stopped to hear if the rider had yelled "whoa" at him.

Our speaker also had some mighty interesting neighbors. There was the time he found a small hand mirror. He showed it to the man who lived on the next farm. The man was quite happy when he looked at it. He thought he had been presented with a picture of his father. At another time our friend came to the city to buy a saddle. The clerk asked whether he wanted a Western or an English saddle. He explained that a Western saddle has a horn. Our hero decided to take one without a horn because he was not going to use it in heavy traffic.

So I present him to you, ladies and gentlemen, no longer the simple country boy but a city slicker with a message you will all want to hear. Mr. ——————.
                                             —Louis J. Huber

INTRODUCING A MINISTER

The guest speaker, whom I shall present shortly, is a minister.

There are two types of people who can tell you of better places to be in than where you are——preachers and real estate agents. Not to mention my wife, of course. The places **she** can tell me to go! But that's outside of bounds, as the Army would say—our guest will doubtlessly speak of a better place.

You know, ever since I was a kid, I wanted to be a minister. I envied them; and I guess I still do. They—they're so different. They've got **privileges.** Imagine you or I going around places with our collars on backward. We'd probably end up by being hailed into the clink, as drunk or disorderly. Anyway, we'd be looked on askance—very much askance.

I remember how, as a kid, I used to stare round-eyed and envious at the minister shouting about "hell" and "damnation" and things like that for which my mother would have scrubbed my mouth with soap and water if I even dared mention them.

I remember the day a Presbyterian minister moved into our neighborhood. A number of us small boys were standing on a corner when he came walking by. They wear an outfit that is somewhat similar to that which a Catholic priest wears, you know.

Some of the kids said respectfully: "Good morning, Father."

After the minister had passed, one of the boys turned to the rest of us and said disdainfully: "What's the matter with you guys? He's no father; he has three sons."

As the saying goes, God moves in mysterious ways His wonders to perform.

I remember one Sunday when—either accidentally or on purpose—some pages in a religious concordance were stuck together. And the minister was reading from it to the congregation. As he turned the page he had been in the middle of a description of Noah's wife. Then he continued, on the new page, as follows: (it was a description of the ark) "A prodigious scow; her length 300 cubits; breadth 50 cubits; and height 30 cubits; wooden throughout of the like of gopher wood; and lined within and without with pitch."

And how the minister closed the book and after a pause, said: "Yeah, man was 'fearfully and wonderfully made,' in those days."

And then I remember how I came to church one morning, and looked at the bulletin board, and saw that the sermon scheduled for the adults was entitled: "Ye Are the Children of the Devil." While the subject for the Sunday School was titled: "Little Children, Obey Your Parents."

Ah, those were the days, in the small town we lived in. Revival meetings, traveling gospel leaders, all that. One event that sticks in my memory is the time a convert jumped up in the midst of one of these meetings, filled with a great zeal, and eager to give his everything in service for the cause. And the way he shouted devoutly: "I am willing and ready to do anything the Lord asks of me—so long, of course, as it's honorable."

And this one they tell, but it's hearsay and I'm not vouching for it, about an old colored person who got up in the midst of a furor of revival shouting, and shouted above the crowd: "Bredren and sister, I fo' one wishes to testify. You and I knows I ain't been what I oughter been. I'se robbed hen roosts and stole hawgs, an' tole lies, an' got drunk an' slashed folks wi' mah razor, an' shot craps and cussed and swore. But I thank de Lord deah's one thing I ain't nebber done. I ain't nebber lost mah religion."

Yeah, I don't know how true that one is. But the ministers, as sometimes is the case today, often had a struggle to make ends meet. I remember once there was a traveling show came to town, and the villain of the piece got seriously drunk and couldn't go on. Our minister offered to take the man's place. In doing his part in the show, I mean; not in the imbibing part, of course. So the manager of the play coached him for the part.

Now at one place a gun is fired, and the minister was told that he must clutch his heart and shout: "My God, I'm shot!"

"Oh, no, I won't use the Lord's name in vain," said the minister. "I'll say, 'My goodness, I'm shot'!"

"Heavens," pleaded the manager. "Who is going to believe you when you just murmur weakly, 'My goodness, I'm shot.' It isn't realistic! Won't you **please** say, 'My God, I'm shot'?"

But still the minister refused firmly and there was no swaying him.

Just before the curtain went up, the manager soaked a cherry in red ink, and put it in his gun ahead of a blank cartridge. And at the crucial moment he fired it at the minister who then clutched at his heart and murmured: "My goodness, I'm shot." Then suddenly he saw the red fluid on his shirt front! **"My God, I AM shot!"**

Well, this is all a little joshing, of course, as our esteemed guest will understand, and now I want to introduce him to you.

—George A. Posner

ADDITIONAL MATERIAL

A Sunday-school teacher, after conducting a lesson on the story of Jacob's ladder, concluded by saying: "Now is there anyone who would like to ask a question about the lesson?"

Little Susie looked puzzled for a moment, then raised her hand.

"A question, Susie?" asked the teacher.

"I would like to know," said Susie, "if the angels had wings, why did they have to climb up the ladder?"

The teacher thought for a few moments, and then looking around the class asked: "Is there any little boy or girl who would like to answer Susie's question?"

After a sermon, as the minister stood at the door of the church, greeting his parishioners, an old lady came up to him and asked: "Why do you always address your congregation as 'Brethren,' and never mention a woman in your sermons."

"But, madam," answered he, "the one embraces the other."

"Oh, but Reverend, not in church!"

A lady was showing her little son a picture of martyrs in a den of lions and trying to make him feel what a terrible thing it was.

He seemed duly impressed.

"Ma!" he said all at once, "just look at that poor little lion away back there. He won't get any!"

"How was the collection this morning?" asked the Reverend.

"Not good, not bad," answered the chief usher. "There's one hundred and seventy-six dollars and 47 cents, five buttons, three bus tokens, a slug; and what's this here? It's a note from somebody saying: "I'm awfully sorry I can't give you the cash, Reverend, but if you will come to my home at 347 Andy Street some evening, I'd be glad to show you how to fix your gas meter so that it won't register."

While in the midst of a rather lengthy sermon the minister of a fashionable congregation was horrified to see a small boy assiduously pelting various parishioners with chestnuts.

The boy, noticing him hesitate, shouted: "You just go on with your sermon, mister. I'll keep them awake!"

In one little village, the weather was so inclement one winter morning that only one parishioner, an old farmer, showed up for the service.

The minister looked at him warmly, and then said: "Mr.

Jones, you're a farmer. Now if you went down to your pasture land with a wagonload of hay, and only one cow would come to the feeding, you would feed her, wouldn't you?"

"Of course," said the farmer.

So the minister smiled kindly at the farmer, went into the pulpit, and preached the entire sermon, lasting an hour and a half, for his solitary listener.

When he had finished he asked the farmer: "Well, what do you say?"

"Well," said the farmer, "I said that if I took a wagonload of hay to the pasture and only one cow showed up, I'd feed her; but I didn't mean I'd give her the entire load of hay."

I asked my little son, Johnny, "Were you in church today?"

"Oh, yes," he answered.

"What was the subject of the sermon?"

"It was 'Don't you worry. You'll get the quilt'."

"My heavens, what's that?" both my wife and I puzzled. Then we thought a while, and she smiled, "Oh, I think I know. He means, 'Fear ye not. The Comforter cometh'."

A celebrated white preacher had been engaged to address the congregation of a little colored church and was being introduced by a very nervous colored pastor.

"Sistern and bredren," he began, "it affords me de extremist pleasuh to introduce de speaker of de evenin'. I wants to explain, dat while his skin ain't de same color as de odders heah, I assures you his heart is as black as any ob yourn."

Little four-year-old Johnny, being told to pray for his absent father, for his small brother who was ill, and the servant who had sprained her ankle, did so. But to his mother's astonishment he concluded as follows: "And now, God, please take good care of yourself, for if anything happens to you we will certainly be up against it for fair."   —George A. Posner

INTRODUCING AN ARTIST

When we invited our artist friend to speak here this evening he said he would be over as soon as he brushed up a little. I think what he meant was that he had to work out a little in the gym. Most artists are pugilists. They do all their work on the canvas.

He had just finished a painting of a little boy in a bathtub, and as he was leaving he noticed that the bathtub was leaking, so he had to spend some time to paint in a plumber to fix the leak.

I saw some of this artist's futuristic paintings. I asked him who posed for them and he said he always had to look around for a model with the hiccups. He painted my wife—I mean he painted a picture of my wife and it was so lifelike I said, "Yes, dear," every time I passed it.

That reminds me of one time I visited an uncle of mine. I saw he had a new painting in his study. I said, "Uncle, is that an old master?" He said, "No, that's the old missus."

Just once I tried my hand at painting. I painted something for the Art Institute in Chicago. It read: "Don't touch. Fresh paint."

I dropped over to our artist friend's house recently and saw he had done a new picture. It was a horse. I told him the horse was excellent, but where was the wagon? He said the horse would draw the wagon. As I turned to go I saw just about the crudest thing ever. I said to him, "I suppose this is one of those hideous caricatures you call modern art." He said, "No, that's just a mirror."

With that I'd better fade out after I introduce our speaker. Ladies and gentlemen, Mr. (name).

—Arthur L. Kaser

INTRODUCING AN AUTOMOBILE DEALER

Our speaker tonight is one of the best known automobile dealers in the city of Pottsville. Yes, you all know Bill Jones. You know what a fine fellow he is, and you all know that you get a square deal when you buy a car from Bill. But Bill is a rugged competitor, as some of the other automobile dealers in this locality know only too well. A fellow has to get up pretty early in the morning to get the best of Bill.

A number of years ago, at the early stage of Bill's career as an automobile dealer, there was a bitter feud going on between Bill and a competitive car dealer down the street. The feud had been progressing for a long time, and it became so severe that the two men practically refused to speak with each other when they met on the street. Throughout the course of this feud, Bill thought up every possible ingenious idea to demonstrate the better qualities of his car over what Bill called the inferior standards of the competitor's automobile.

One day Bill hatched up a scheme. He went to his competitor and said, "Jack, you've been doing a lot of bragging around town about that clunk of yours, and I'm going to prove to you that when I call your car a clunk, it is a clunk. I challenge you to a race at the county fair grounds!"

"You thought I was going to flinch, didn't you?" answered Jack. "I'll call your bluff, and take you up! Then we'll see which one of us sells a clunk!"

The details of the race were arranged, and Bill sought out an expert driver—a fellow by the name of Pat who said that he had driven at the Indianapolis Speedway. Jack did likewise, and he got a driver from some other famous speedway.

On the day of the race feeling was running high, and the whole town turned out at the county fair grounds to witness the spectacle. The two cars lined up and the crowd thundered an ovation that could be heard as far as the pumping station at the other end of the county. Just before the starter was ready to drop the red flag, Bill hurried up to his driver and said, "See here, Pat, there's an extra fifty in it for you if you win this race." "Think nothing of it," said Pat. "The race is as good as won right now."

So away they went, round and round the track, throwing up clouds of dust—the engines roaring like a tornado coming out of the southwest. First Bill's car was in the lead, then Jack's, and then Bill's and then Jack's, and the crowd cheered from the bottom of their lungs. Soon the cars were coming down the home stretch, nip and tuck. It looked like a tie—only one hundred yards to the finish line.

Then something terrible happened! There was a crash! The cars locked wheels and spun round and round, coming to rest with a horrible bang at the fence. Then there was another tragic moment. Both drivers bounced up in the air, and then suddenly plunged to earth.

"One's getting up!" yelled Bill, looking at the wreck with his field glasses. "It's Pat! My Pat!" screamed Bill. "He's getting back in the car! He's finishing the race! By the devil, if Pat isn't finishing the race! I've won! I've won! I've won! My Pat! My Pat!," yelled Bill, dancing with glee as Pat snailed the wreck victoriously over the finish line.

Jack walked over and examined the car. Then he walked over to Bill and said: "It's your Pat, all right! But it's my car!"

Ladies and gentlemen, Mr. Bill Jones.

—James Bolden

INTRODUCING A BABY SPECIALIST

After I was told by the chairman of the arrangements committee that I was to introduce a baby specialist, I made an attempt to find out just what is a baby specialist. So, I talked to my Uncle John, who is an old timer around these parts.

"Uncle John," I said, "I am going to introduce Dr. Walter Watters tomorrow night at the meeting. He's a baby specialist. What do you know about a baby specialist?"

"A baby specialist," said Uncle John, drawing on his pipe, "is some kind of a new fangled expert that I know nothing about. Years ago when a new kid was born in this neighborhood, Mrs. Flannigan took care of it. We could always tell when one of those events was to happen by the way Mrs. Flannigan hurried up the street, her feet flying and her hands busy rolling up her sleeves."

"There must have been a lot of excitement in those days?" I asked.

"Plenty," he replied, "and all of the neighbors got in on it. Take Riley's place next door; they had one every year. Well, the minute Mrs. Flannigan got in the house, we heard her yell at Mr. Riley: 'Keep that water boiling, you good-for-nothing, lazy bulk of a man. If ye were mine, I'd scald the very freckles off that ugly puss of yours.' Then everything would be quiet for about an hour or so, and we all waited. Soon we heard a kid cry. Then we heard Mrs. Flannigan slap the kid's bottom; and then the kid cried some more; after which Mrs. Flannigan threw the kid into Mrs. Riley's clothes basket and rushed home to put the stew on for old man Flannigan who hadn't worked since Mrs. Flannigan took up midwifing."

"But these baby specialists are scientific men," I said.

"Scientific?" questioned Uncle John.

"Well, they have a lot of new formulas and stuff like that," I said.

"I'll tell you something, my lad, nowadays when you take your kid down to Dr. Watters' office, Doc will take one look at the kid and say, 'That child's got silicalitis. I'll give him a couple of shots of silicasilicae.' In Mrs. Flannigan's day, when a kid got silicalitis, we merely placed him in a gravel pit, and told the kid to eat. After the kid had chewed up about a pound of sand, we said to him, 'How do you feel?' And when he said, 'Fine,' we knew that was the end of the silicalities."

"I wonder why Dr. Watters took up specializing in babies and kids?" I asked.

"There's always business," said Uncle John, adding, "See those kids kicking up that rumpus in Jones' backyard. Within ten minutes one of 'em will be heading for Doc Watters' office."

Sure enough, within three minutes I heard an awful howl. Then Mrs. Jones came running out of the back door, grabbed little Willie, set him in her car, and started in high gear straight down the street in the direction of Dr. Watters' office.

"There's one of the reasons why Doc is doing this specializing," said Uncle John, pointing with the stem of his pipe at a small boy, who, after a short run, was standing up by the alley, shamefully watching the proceedings.

"Who's that?" I asked.

"That," said Uncle John between puffs on his pipe, "is the kid who threw the rock."

Ladies and gentlemen, Dr. Walter Watters.

—Sylvester McGovern

INTRODUCING A GROCER (SUPERMARKET MANAGER)

There was a time when the life of a groceryman was a hard one, indeed. He sold pickles out of a barrel, butter out of a tub and sugar out of a gunny sack. He spilled most of his profit on the floor, packaging the stuff; and the rest of the profit, if any, was swallowed up in a maze of charge accounts. Such was the life of Al White, our next speaker this evening.

In the early days of Al's career in the grocery business, he worked for the love of it. Al liked the smell of grinding coffee, the tangy odor of cheese, which he sliced off with a big knife, the tantalizing smell of vinegar blended with kerosene, and the general all-around scent found only in an old-time grocery store.

Then one day the grocery-store smell disappeared. The pickles became bottled, the kerosene vanished and the cheese became wrapped in cellophane. "This is a sad state of affairs," said Al to himself as he opened his store one morning. "I don't like the smell of it. The zest and tang is gone." Then Al walked over to a shelf, picked out a bottle of vinegar, and looking at it became imbued with a touch of nostalgia. Said Al remorsefully, "What I wouldn't give to be able once again to fill a jug of vinegar from the spigot and let the cutting aroma linger around the edge of my mustache."

Then Al reflected: "The romance of this business is gone. I can't work for the love of it anymore. If I'm going to stay in it, I've got to make some money out of it," and he then changed the name of his store to a supermarket.

"The general idea," said Al to his clerks, "is to pack that stuff on the shelves and let the people help themselves. I'll stand up here by the cash register and take in the currency."

"How are people going to haul the stuff?" asked a clerk.

"Now if you're not a bright one," said Al to the clerk, adding "Who are our customers?"

"Everybody," answered the clerk.

"Everybody nothing," said Al. "Women!" he added. "Now what is a woman doing most of the time?"

"I don't know," answered the clerk.

"You don't know," said Al. "Why, she's wheeling a baby buggy, of course. Haven't you seen them coming in here year after year, pushing a new baby with the same old buggy?"

"I don't know," said the clerk.

"Well, I know," said Al. "We'll order some baby buggies. Just plain ones, no fancy trimmings like wicker and that sort of stuff. Then we'll have the women here all day long wheeling those baby buggies up and down the store, filling 'em up with provisions."

"That sounds like a good idea," said the clerk.

"The greatest idea since the invention of the coffee grinder," Al replied.

Then Al said to the clerk, "Have you sold the delivery trucks? I'm going to replace them with a Cadillac. And don't forget the sign, 'We Close on Wednesday Afternoon.' In the old days we had a picnic once a year on Wednesday; now we'll have a picnic every Wednesday."

As Al strolled over to the cash register, he remarked rather casually: "I'm not working for the love of it any more."

Ladies and gentlemen, Mr. Al White.

—Anthony C. Gregory

INTRODUCING A BABY SPECIALIST

Last week Bill Brown, the chairman of your arrangements committee, called me up and asked if I would preside at the next meeting. I said that I would if there were going to be any speakers that would be worth while introducing. "You will be introducing a baby specialist," said Bill. "A baby specialist!" I exclaimed, adding, "You mean a sitter?" "Heavens, no!" said Bill, "a doctor—the eminent Dr. Cecil Bridges."

"Well," said I, rather disappointed, " I hoped it would have been a sitter. There are so many things going on in this new profession of baby sitting, that there would be nothing to it to work up a good introduction. Why, my grandmother has taken it up," I continued. "And my three aunts have followed suit. The stories they tell. I heard that one baby sitter down in Iowa killed a kid because it bawled too much."

"You're on the wrong track," interrupted Bill. "Dr. Cecil Bridges is a pediatrician, an obstetrician, and a half a dozen other things that I can't pronounce."

"Are you sure he never was a baby sitter?" I asked.

"I don't know," said Bill. "Why don't you call him up and ask him?"

"I just got a hunch," I said.

"Well, play your hunch," said Bill, and he hung up.

I couldn't get it out of my mind that at one time Dr. Cecil Bridges was a baby sitter. How could a fellow spend a lifetime with kids unless he became case-hardened to them when he was very young? This thought was associated with my own kids and those three nephews of mine who splintered my baby grand piano into kindling wood. Perhaps once upon a time Doc Bridges was a baby sitter. That's where he might have got his start. "I think I'll call him up," I said to myself.

So I called up Dr. Bridges' office and a nurse answered the telephone. "I would like to talk to Dr. Bridges," I said.

"Dr. Bridges is engaged at the moment, extracting a telephone from the esophagus of little Willie Kinkey, who swallowed it last night," the nurse said.

"How long will that take?" I asked.

"Quite some time," she answered. "You'd better call back," the nurse continued. "There is a long waiting list. Little Jack Thimble has a severe gash on his right bottom where the neighbor boy bit him. Little Pettie Cubbear swallowed a pint of his father's linseed oil. I'm getting the stomach pump ready now. Then there's three other boys here with black eyes, and some of them quite black. And there's another boy with a nasty bump on his head. He got that when he dashed his head against the kitchen wall because his mother wouldn't give him his fourth lollypop. This is a busy day for the doctor. I think that you had better call back tomorrow."

"Perhaps you can answer my question," I said to the nurse.

"What is your question?" she asked.

"Was Dr. Bridges ever a baby sitter?"

"Don't get fresh!" she exclaimed, and hung up.

So I never did find out whether or not Dr. Cecil Bridges had been sometime in the remote past a baby sitter. Perhaps we will find out now. Ladies and gentlemen, Dr. Cecil Bridges.

—Sylvester McGovern

INTRODUCING A SPORTSMAN OR WHERE THE SPEAKER WANTS TO USE SOMEONE IN THE AUDIENCE AS THE BUTT OF HIS JOKE

Among Joe Black's many talents is that of a huntsman—a unique huntsman, who perhaps holds a record for the snaring of a bear—a record that is unrivaled in the hunting annals of this state.

It all happened about a year ago when four members of our club invited Joe to go bear hunting. All four of us had made several previous forays into the woods in chase of the bear, but this was Joe's first mission.

We arrived at the cabin, which was deep in the woods, before dawn, and proceeded to unload our gear. Judging from the paraphernalia Joe unpacked, he had bought out a sporting goods store—a brand new jacket and trousers, new squeaky boots, a red-crowned hunting cap and a shiny new Remington rifle. We donned our old, battle-worn hunting garments and Joe decked out in his new outdoor ensemble. We caught him peeking at himself in a cracked mirror that hung on the wall of the cabin. Evidently he was satisfied that he was properly attired to enter the hunt.

"We'll have breakfast first," said I, unwrapping some choice pieces of bacon and placing them on the skillet to fry.

"Breakfast!" exclaimed Joe. "I thought we were going to hunt bear."

"We are," all of us said, "after we have had breakfast."

"Not me!" yelled Joe. "I'm going to get my bear right now! Breakfast! Bah! You fellows are a bunch of sissies!"

With that remark Joe rushed out of the door and lumbered through the snow-clad forest hot after the bear. We watched Joe disappear into the woods and then we sat down and enjoyed our breakfast, as the odor of the frying bacon was delightfully tickling our nostrils.

Now if there's anything a bear likes better than wild blueberries, it's bacon; and a bear can smell cooking bacon a long way off. We continued with our breakfast, laughing and joking about Joe and his hunting uniform and contemplating on his prospects of getting a bear.

Just as we were finishing our second cup of coffee, we heard a terrible wail coming from the woods. Then we heard a crash of thickets and the breaking of branches. We all rushed out of the cabin door just as a most horrible scream screeched through the trees, and there we saw Joe, a big black bear right on Joe's heels. Both man and beast were flying through space like a rocket, with the bear seeming to gain on Joe with every stride. It was difficult to determine who was yelping the loudest, Joe or the bear. Just as they reached the proximity of the cabin door, Joe's new hunting boots hit a patch of ice, tossing his body into a jack-knife dive, which was followed by an abrupt thump on the icy pathway with a swift skid down the incline toward the cabin door. At the moment of Joe's take-off, his new Remington rifle flew skyward and disappeared among the pine boughs. And the bear slid, too, right over Joe's prone body, through the cabin door in pursuit of the bacon.

But Joe was on his feet in a flash. Quickly he reached out and slammed shut the cabin door, imprisoning the bear inside.

Brushing off the slush from his now battle-stained hunting suit, Joe looked up at us and in a panting voice yelled triumphantly: "There's your bear! Hold the door and I'll go get you another one!"   —Sylvester H. McGovern

INTRODUCING A SALESMANAGER

It is not often that a chairman has an opportunity of introducing a speaker so successful in the business world as Harry W. White. Harry W. White is not only a good speaker, a fine gentleman and a leader in this community, but he is one of the outstanding salesmanagers in this section of the country. His record in his present position is so phenomenal that his methods of training salesmen have been adopted by some of the largest organizations in the nation.

Before placing a young man on the sales staff of his company, Harry insists that the fellow meet certain qualifications, which I might say are numerous and exacting. In this respect there is one attribute that Harry demands as paramount, and that is ingenuity. If an applicant does not have it, there is no place for him on Harry's selling team.

But how to detect ingenuity in a human being? That's a very difficult thing to do. At first Harry tried several tests, all of which failed. Then he called in a crew of efficiency experts, and all Harry got out of that was a bill for a large fee. So one night while reclining in bed meditating on the problems that his company had to face this year and the next, he thought up a plan.

Bright and early the next morning, Harry rushed into the president's office and yelled out excitedly, "I've got a plan for sorting out the clever fellows from the blockheads."

"What kind of a plan is it, Harry?" asked the prexy, without looking up from a perusal of his golf score card.

"I can't tell you now," Harry said. "But come down to the Hotel Astor tonight and you will see. I'll have twenty applicants for dinner."

So that night the president and Harry hurried down to the hotel dining room where twenty young men were seated at a table. The arms of each man were strapped to a board, effecting a straight arm, with absolutely no possibility of bending an elbow. Before the twenty men stood twenty thick, juicy steaks, all untouched.

"What kind of an inquisition is this?" asked the president, disturbed by the sight before him.

"This is no inquisition," answered Harry. This is an ingenuity test. Some fellows got it, some haven't."

"Why, this is preposterous!" the president exclaimed.

"Not at all," said Harry. "If one of those fellows finds out how to eat that steak, he's got ingenuity; and with that kind of ingenuity he'd surmount obstacles in the field like a greyhound takes the hurdles."

"It looks cruel to me," said the prexy.

"Just a minute," yelled Harry excitedly. "Look at those two fellows over at the end of the table. They're beginning to eat!"

"By George, they are!" exclaimed the president, adding, as he craned his neck in the direction of the two masticating jaws, "But how in the devil are they doing it?"

A bright smile appeared on Harry's face, and he looked at the bewildered head of the firm and said victoriously: "They're feeding each other!"

Ladies and gentlemen, Mr. Harry W. White.

—James Bolden

INTRODUCING A HUNTER OR EXTENSIVE TRAVELER

I know that we are going to hear some excellent hunting stories this evening from George Bear, for when it comes to the chase, George is the champion in this neck of the woods. George's hunting fame has reached such proportions that he is being emulated by all of those who want to succeed in the greatest of all outdoor sports.

But like all men who acquire distinction in any field, there are always jealous rivals who attempt to make sport of one's success. Just such a thing happened to George a few years ago.

One day a strange advertisement appeared in the classified section of our local paper, under the heading of male help wanted. It has never been determined who put the ad in the paper, and if the culprit should be discovered, it is a certainty that his neck would be severely wrung, should George once get his hands around it. The advertisement announced that George Bear, a hunter of local distinction, was planning on launching a safari in pursuit of big game in the wilds of Africa, and that as a necessary adjunct to the trip, the services of an aid was required.

The aid would have to meet certain qualifications. He must be able to speak several different languages, including the tribal languages found in the densest of the African jungles. He must have a complete mastery of firearms, and at least a superficial knowledge of medicine and cuisine. In fact, the fellow would have to be a factotum with the ability to do most anything. Persons meeting those standards were urged to contact George Bear immediately, day or night, as the expedition was geared for an early departure.

At a back table in Sandy's Bar, Jake Willoughby, itinerant roustabout, sat drinking whiskey. Jake Willoughby had been at the table all day, having arrived in town on an early morning bus. Before Jake was an open newspaper, his thumb pressing down on George's ad. After gulping each successive drink the itinerant would re-read the ad and concentrate on the possibilities of joining in such a far-flung and exciting adventure. This repetitious procedure kept up all evening, until one p.m., when Sandy shooed out his customers and locked up.

Jake Willoughby staggered out into the cool night air, and meandered up the avenue in the direction of George Bear's home. How he got there is not explainable, as he seemed to be traveling by instinct. But he got there, where he weaved up the front walk, stepped up on the porch and rang the doorbell.

Upon hearing the bell, George jumped out of bed, full of concern at receiving a call at such a late hour.

"Who's there?" George cried out as he stood in the doorway attired in pajamas, his hair disheveled from sleep.

"It's me!" said Jake. "Are you the fellow who put the ad in the paper for a man to go to A-f-rica?"

"What about it?" exclaimed George, his anger rising by degrees.

"Well," said Jake, swaying and tottering like a pine tree in a heavy blow, "I was just walking by (hic) so I dropped in to shay I can't be going with you."

Ladies and gentlemen, Mr. George Bear.

—Dale Erwin

INTRODUCING A WILD ANIMAL HUNTER

Mr. (name) has recently returned to this country from (perhaps Africa) where he hunted wild animals with a movie camera. He is here with us this evening to show these interesting movies and tell of his experiences in the jungles of that country.

The wildest animal I ever saw was a dog with rheumatism and fleas. Our speaker tells me that if you meet a wild lion and wish to pacify it try stroking its nose with a wet sponge. You can obtain the same result in this country by throwing a lighted match into your gas tank.

I used to have an uncle who told me of his experiences while he was a wild animal doctor with a circus.

> Yes, my uncle treated the lions,
> But not the way you'd expect.
> He didn't treat them with medicines,
> He treated them with utmost respect.
> One day he tried something different,
> He thought the lion was dyin'.
> He looked down its throat—
> From the tombstone I quote:
> "Now here Dr. Jones is a-lyin'."

Now back to our sort of harmless animals. Not long ago my small niece and nephew were visiting in the country. One day little Debby came running to the house. "Mommy," she cried, "quick. Herby wants the mouth wash. He's ketched the cutest little black and white animal, but he thinks it's got halitosis." Which reminds me, that the skunk is the most high-hat of all animals. He's unapproachable.

By the way, do you know what is worse than a giraffe with a sore throat? A Ubanga with chapped lips. A giraffe will get a sore throat if it gets its feet wet, but not until a week later. One time I saw a kangaroo in a circus crying. I said to one of the men at the cages, "Why is the kangaroo crying?" He said, "Her little son ran away and left her holding the bag." I asked the man, "Do you happen to be a lion tamer?" He said, "Do I look like I'm that crazy? All I do is comb their manes and brush their teeth." He was a very little man which prompted me to remark, "You're such a little man to be in with those big lions." He said that was the secret of his safety. The lions were waiting for him to grow bigger. Ladies and gentlemen, allow me to present our guest speaker, **(name).**

—Richard Drummond

INTRODUCING THE PRESIDENT AT A BUSINESS MEETING OF A MANUFACTURING COMPANY

Gentlemen, this is probably one of the most important meetings this company has ever held—and a serious one, too. It requires the attention of every member of this staff. Its import reminds me of the story of a great storm at sea where the good ship Paducah was floundering in the waves. So severe was the storm that the captain asked all members of the crew to kneel down and pray for Divine assistance.

Pat Clancy immediately dropped to his knees, while Ole Larson stood passively by. "Father in Heaven," prayed Pat fervently, "send down your Only Begotten Son and calm these mighty waves."

The captain, noting Ole's nonparticipation in the heavenly beseechment, rushed over to Ole and said, "See here, Ole, we need all hands on this praying job. Get down on your knees and give Pat some help."

Ole knelt down on the sea-splashed deck, and while the ship was creaking and groaning in every fibre, he folded his hands and prayed. "Oh, Heavenly Father," supplicated Ole, "I heard this Irishman asking you to send down your Son to help us. But this is no kid's yob. By yimmine no, this is no kid's yob, Father. You'd better come yourself."

(Pause for laughs)

So we called in the Boss. Gentlemen, Mr. Jonathan Green, president of the Green Brass and Bearings Company.

—Sylvester H. McGovern

INTRODUCING A FUND RAISER

My friends, we've got a little treat for you tonight. We're going to hear from a man who wants to separate us from a little money. Now, this is not as bad as it may sound. This money will go to help the community and whatever helps the community helps all of us. I'm not going to mention the fact that whatever donations we make can be knocked off our income tax, but still there's a thought there.

We all know what the (Red Cross, Associated Charities, Community Fund) means. We're familiar with the aid and relief that is immediately forthcoming from this wonderful organization in times of emergency to those in distress and want. This necessary aid requires money—getting this money requires organization — the organization requires leaders — which, in turn, brings me to our next speaker—who has unselfishly devoted his time to raising funds solely to help others.

While we in this country are noted for our quick response to appeals for aid, it takes this particular type of good citizen to bring these appeals to our attention. My friend, the corner newsboy, says: "Raisin' dough's a tough racket. It takes a good guy to do it."

I have a friend who is usually in the front of any drive for charitable or humanitarian purposes in his community. I ran into his ten-year-old son recently, who showed me a newspaper picture of his father. I commented favorably on the picture and the boy said excitedly: "But look, Dad's got his hands in his own pockets!" I admitted that it was a rather unusual sight, and the boy said: "I'll tell you something confidential. Dad even puts some of his own cash in these deals!"

So if you see our next speaker put his hands in his own pockets, you can almost safely wager that he is figuring how much he himself can contribute to his own worthy cause, and my friends, when you hear him, I'm sure you will agree with me that he has, indeed, a cause most worthy of being brought to your attention. Ladies and gentlemen, Mr. ——————.

—Earl Jay Gilbert

INTRODUCING A GOLFER

They say there isn't much difference between gulf and golf. Gulf is a waste of water, and golf is a waste of time. We don't agree with that. Golf is not only a pleasant recreation, it's a health builder. Many doctors advise inactive men to do something strenuous like digging in Mother Earth, so these men play golf.

Of course, some people object to playing golf on Sunday, but the majority say it is no sin to play golf on Sunday, adding that the way some play the game is a crime. As I said, golf is a wonderful thing for those whose work keeps them inactive. A good cure is to hire a young boy to cut the grass so the man can play golf and obtain needed exercise.

There is one thing certain—you can't keep a good golfer down—town. It takes much practice to become a good golfer. Practice makes perfect—addicts of the game. May I give some advice? To keep from topping the ball turn it upside down.

I play a very poor game. If it weren't for the clubs I use, one wouldn't know whether I was playing baseball or croquet. One time I asked my caddy why he kept looking at his watch all the time. He said it wasn't a watch, it was a compass. I asked the caddy to answer me frankly. What did he think of my game? He said it was all right, but he preferred golf.

A man approached me and said, "Pardon, but would you care if I played through? I just heard that my wife has been taken seriously ill." You bump into those things? My wife, for instance, has threatened to leave me if I don't give up golf. That's really tough. I'll miss her.

I understand there is a new dictionary of golf terms just out. If it's complete, I don't see how it will pass the censors. Here's a good joke: I says to my partner, "I don't trust our caddy. I'm afraid he'll swipe my new golf ball." My partner says, "I wouldn't putt it past him." Remember, no matter how you slice it, it's still a golf ball. And now, some wonderful golfing advice from one who knows, **(name).**

—Richard Drummond

INTRODUCING AN AUTHOR

Ladies and gentlemen, this is an occasion that many of us have been waiting for. Tonight we're going to have the pleasure of listening to a talk by a well-known and popular author. I believe that we're all familiar with his writings. I think we all agree that he is one of the most brilliant of the modern writers. I suppose in reading his books most of us have been curious as to what the writer himself is like. To those of you who have been looking forward to meeting him with pleasurable anticipation, I can assure you that you will not be disappointed when you hear him.

We all have a tendency to admire and respect success in most forms—with perhaps a touch of envy reserved for successful writers—probably because most of us have had, at one time or another, a desire to do some creative writing ourselves. You know how it is—you get an idea that you know would make a whale of a story. It may be taken from some personal experience, or something that you've read or heard or seen will suggest an entirely new thought. Anyhow, you get an idea for a story. So you mull it around in your mind for a while, then decide to write it, which should be a very easy task. All you've got to do is sit down and put your idea on paper. Simple, isn't it? It would be silly not to write it, when with just a little effort, you can become famous and wealthy and astound your friends.

So the next morning, bright and early, you get some clean sheets of paper and some writing utensils, pull a comfortable chair up to the table, sit down and light a cigarette. You look at your pencils to make sure they're all sharpened, look at the clean sheet of paper and prepare to start what is unquestionably going to be a tremendous contribution to literature. You feel a little glow of pride. Perhaps Shakespeare and Hemingway and other well-known writers started the same way. You have a warm, brotherly feeling of kinship with them.

You also have a sort of patronizing feeling of superiority toward people who can't write. Poor souls! Well, you look at the paper again. Now what kind of a story would your idea be best suited for? You decide it would make a great detective story. Fine! Now how do you start a detective story? With a title, of course. Suddenly it hits you. So you put down in strong, firm characters—WHY WOMEN SIN — A MYSTERY. Now you've really got a start. Great! But wait—you've left out something important. So you write, again in large, firm characters, your name—WILLIAM KIPLING JONES. You lean back and admire it. By George, that looks great! You've got a wonderful start. Now you can concentrate on the story. Just one little word after another. Let's see—what are the best words to start with? Let's see, now. Hmm. Peculiar that you can't seem to think of anything appropriate. Better relax a little. The words will come later. You light another cigarette, examine your pencils again to make sure they're still sharp and begin to wonder how you'll spend your royalties. You can't decide whether to get a Cadillac or one of those new Buicks. Both good cars. Either one would be swell for a successful author. Maybe you'd better get them both. Suddenly it dawns upon you that it's lunch time. You'd better eat and finish the story after lunch. And that's all, brother. Another masterpiece is lost to the world of literature. That's about as far as most of us get.

Reminds me of the reporter who was preparing an article on Mark Twain. He took a trip down the Mississippi River hunting for anecdotes and information concerning the famous humorist. At a little river landing he ran across an old timer who had lived there for years. The reporter asked if he had known Mark Twain. The old man snorted. "Mark Twain—phooy!" he said. "Course I knowed him. Can't see why folks make so much fuss about him. He didn't amount to nothin'." "But," said the reporter, "Look at the stories he wrote." "Stories bah!" growled the old timer. "I knowed more stories than he ever knowed. Only difference is he writ 'em down."

That's the difference between many of us and regular authors. Like our speaker, they writ 'em down. Now, the gentleman who is going to address us tonight has firmly established himself as a top ranking writer because, first, he has something to say; second, he knows how to say it; and third, he writes in a style that is universally appealing—all of which goes to explain why his books are so widely read and why he has deservedly gained fame as an author.

At the risk of embarrassing him, I'm going to say that I think there's more than a little touch of genius in his writings. I also want to say that someday when I can find time, I'm going to read one of his books myself—that is, if I can get hold of one before my wife beats me to it and annoys me by telling me all about it before I get a chance to look at it. Now, ladies and gentlemen, I really take great pleasure in presenting to you, Mr. ——————.

—Earl Jay Gilbert

INTRODUCING A GOLFER

Tonight's guest speaker, ladies and gentlemen, is a man who has cut a wide swath in the golfing world. I will tell you only a few of the intimate details about him and leave the more public stories in his capable hands.

When he first started as a golfer he was told to tee the ball. He replied that he did tee it and he didn't want any more baby talk or he'd quit right then and there. That first game had other instances that are worth repeating. Someone asked him his score and our man told him he had a fifty-two. Everyone thought that was very good until they learned he was talking about the first hole only.

Another incident in that first game was when he was told to step up and drive. He stood there and waited for someone to hand him the ignition key. But he cleared matters when they told him to address the ball. He just said, "Hello, there."

And with that I give him his opportunity to say "hello, there," to you. I give you that short-driving but long-putting golfer, Mr. ——————.   —Louis J. Huber

INTRODUCING A FURRIER

Tonight I am going to introduce to you a man who sets the fur styles for the ladies in this community—Harry Menkin, president of Menkin's Furs, a man who is known all over this territory for the scientific way in which he drapes the feminine form in the tanned coverings of the wild beast.

Harry is a very patient man. Out of necessity he must be so, as his life is wrapped up in women. Women who complain and women who grumble are a part of his daily existence. But as the result of years of experience in handling milady, he sends them all away from his store, happy and contented as a Carnation cow, sleek and chic in a new fur coat, the cynosure of all eyes, including the husband when he gets the bill.

It is not unusual for a man in Harry's occupation to come in contact with some strange notions from the feminine sex. No doubt he will tell you about some of them when he comes before this microphone. However, I have one that I am going to tell myself.

During the last war a very good customer of Harry's came in the store and wanted to see an exclusive fur that was a scarce article during those strenuous times. She pleaded with Harry. She coaxed Harry. She just must have a coat of that fur.

"My dear Mrs. Throttelberry," said Harry very suavely, "It is impossible for me to procure the fur that you desire."

"Nothing is impossible," Mrs. Throttelberry replied, tilting her chin.

"But," said Harry, "there is a war on. The fur that you want can't get by the blockade."

Harry's reference to the war seemed to mellow the good Mrs. Throttelberry who said, "Oh, yes. The war." Then with a look of sublime patriotism she turned to Harry and said softly, "Mr. Menkin, I have two sons in this dreadful war. If I would have known twenty years ago that this horrible thing was coming, I would have furnished more."

Ladies and gentlemen, Mr. Harry Menkin.

—Gus Strauss

INTRODUCING A TIRE DISTRIBUTOR OR DEALER

Up until last night we were not sure that Harry Olds would be able to be here this evening. He has been so busy this last month running around the territory introducing that new tubeless tire that his factory has just brought out on the market. From what Harry says the new tubeless tire is a wonder. No punctures, no blowouts, no trouble. Just riding ease that the automobile never before has seen.

Harry's new tubeless tire has been the cause of a lot of social activity in our town of late. Last week Harry threw a big blowout at the Acorn Hotel for his dealers. At that time, Harry made a speech, which I heard was a good one. I presume that we will hear the same speech this evening. Then during the week-end a gala gala affair, in full dress, I understand, was held at Harry's home, with a visiting delegation of the top brass from Akron.

Among the guests attending the week-end convivial function at Harry's home was a third vice president from the factory by the name of MacPherson, a man of Scotch ancestry, whose capacity for absorbing spirits is boundless, when it is free. Harry told a story or two and then everyone laughed. Then MacPherson got up from his chair and proceeded to make the rounds, shaking hands and bidding each guest good night.

This alarmed Harry, who rushed over to MacPherson and excitedly said, "Why, Mac, you're not going to leave so soon."

MacPherson looked at Harry with a twinkle in his eyes and quietly said, "Nay, I'm not going yet. But I'm saying goodnight to ye while I know ye."

Ladies and gentlemen, Mr. Harry Olds.

—Jack Hurley, Jr.

INTRODUCING AN AMBASSADOR (British) OR DIPLOMAT

It is not often that a chairman has the distinction of introducing to his audience such a celebrated person as Sir John Clipps, the British ambassador to our country. The fine friendly relations that have existed so long between our nation and the British Empire have been assisted by the persevering and diligent efforts of Sir John, who has come to know the American way of life. Through that knowledge he has been able to communicate a better understanding between his people and ours, thereby avoiding some of those bitter difficulties that often arise between nations . . . some to a point of disaster.

Sir John has been with us so long that he is thoroughly acquainted with our idioms, with our slang, and with our hustle and bustle in our business world. However, there was a time when Sir John, fresh from London, was amazed at the way we Americans do things. He was astounded at the rapidity with which our manufacturing plants could produce goods. He was amazed at our high pressure methods of selling and merchandising. He was electrified at the ability of the American to make money . . . at his business acumen, and he discovered that that ability permeated throughout our entire strata, from the newsboy to the bank president. This American business acumen begins early in life, as Sir John learned one day when he bought a newspaper.

Walking up to a newsstand in Washington, Sir John said to the boy, "A copy of the Star, please."

The boy quickly gave him a copy of the paper and returned two cents from the five-cent piece Sir John extended in his hand. (That was when a newspaper cost only three cents.)

Sir John looked at the two pennies for a moment and then said to the boy, "My dear lad, is that all a newspaper costs in America? Why, back home the price is double."

The lad squinted from beneath the visor of his cap and then quickly replied: "If it'll make you feel at home, you can pay me double." Ladies and gentlemen, Sir John Clipps.

—Alexander Collins

INTRODUCING AN ARMY OFFICER

Tonight we have in our presence a man who has brought fame to the city of Centerville—a man whose exploits on the field of battle have been of the most heroic nature—a man who has served his country well.

It is a great honor for me to be able to say a few words about Captain Bert Walker before I introduce him to you as our next speaker. Captain Walker grew up here in Centerville. He is a product of our Main street, and along with millions of other boys from Main streets and the farms all over America, he took his position in the front line during the last great war. What he did there is common knowledge to all of us here in Centerville, as his name was constantly in the news dispatches.

When the war was over, he, like many other war heroes, was in constant demand as a public speaker as he had many interesting experiences to relate. This popularity brought an invitation to Captain Walker to many a state function, where dignitaries from our government and from those of foreign governments gathered to dine and exchange messages of good will.

On one occasion Captain Walker attended a dinner in Washington of the most elaborate proportions. Ambassadors, envoys, high ranking military officers and statesmen from many lands were among the invited guests. Captain Walker sat next to a dignified Chinese envoy. (That of course was when China was our ally.) Several times during the course of the dinner Captain Walker attempted to start a conversation with the little Chinaman, but to no avail. The Chinaman was one of those pompous little Orientals of a reticent nature, who busied himself with that tantalizing dinner. Every time Captain Walker would lead with an invitation to chat, the Chinese envoy would merely nod his head and continue with the task of scooping up his soup.

Never having been in China, (Bert's exploits were all in the European sector) Captain Walker was puzzled by the reticence of the Oriental mind. Noting that the little Chinaman was enjoying his soup immensely, Captain Walker turned once again to him and said, "Likee soup?" Still there was no response, the Chinaman continuing to eat his soup.

After the dinner was over, the chairman began to call upon the speakers, and imagine Bert's chagrin when the little Chinese envoy arose to his feet and gave a most interesting talk in the purest of English.

At the conclusion of the speech, the small fellow from the Orient sat down amidst a thunderous applause and then turned to Bert, whose face was red as a beet. With a broad smile, the Oriental said, "Likee speech?"

Ladies and gentlemen, Captain Bert Walker.

—Alexander Collins

INTRODUCING A SPEAKER ON COMMUNISM

We are quite fortunate at this time to have with us a guest speaker who is an authority on the cloak and dagger tactics of the Red agents in this country. It is like some insidious disease that gets into the system undetected. And what do the Reds claim they are doing? The Reds claim they aim at justice. Sure, they aim at justice and shoot it down if they can.

Some of their attempts are fatally successful. The Communists complain that theirs is a system of relief. They relieve everybody they can of all they have. They are trying to promote more trade relations. It would have more trade relations if it had less be-trayed relations. In its bid for more recognition Soviet's only hope is that it will not be recognized for what it is. In Russia all talking is left to the propagandists. The big boys are men of few words. After glancing through a Russian dictionary it's easy to understand why. I studied some Russian in school but when I started to recite I was sent home. They thought I had hay fever. Green cherries become red, and then soon become rotten. People who are green enough to become red will end up the same way. Ladies and gentlemen, permit me to introduce a real American, (name).

—Arthur L. Kaser

INTRODUCING AN AUTOMOBILE SALESMAN

The honor is mine this evening, and it is a rare honor, indeed, to stand up here and bring to this audience a man of chivalry—a direct descendant of Sir Walter Raleigh himself.

Contrary to common belief, chivalry is not dead. There are still a few chivalrous men living. Among these heroes is Bill Doyle, who is gallant by avocation and an automobile salesman by vocation. When Bill is not about selling Cadillac cars, he's out practicing chivalry. Strange as it may seem, Bill is one of the few men in this town who still tips his hat to a lady. True there are some psuedo-chivalrous men who stand up from a night club table when a lady comes or goes. But that is strictly a physical movement. A fellow who sits at a night club table for two or three hours is always glad to be able to stand up and stretch his legs. The leaving of the lady from the table is merely an excuse.

But with Bill, he is different. He is strictly one hundred per cent chivalrous. When making an exit through a door, he permits the lady to pass first. When entering an elevator with ladies present, off goes his hat. Some persons who call themselves gallant doff their lids in a hotel elevator, but not in an office building elevator. This kind of a Knight-Errant takes off his hat because he wants some good-looking girl to notice his neat hair comb, or if he's bald because he desires to impress some girl that he is a man of distinction and has a sufficient bankroll to take up a good-sized check at a night club. If this is not the case, then why don't these so-called chivalrous gentlemen take off their hats in an office building elevator?

Just last week Bill performed a chivalrous act that hasn't been equalled since Don Quixote sallied forth on his horse, Roziante, to ask for the hand of the fair Dulcinea. On the day this act of gallantry took place, it was raining pitchforks. Water was swishing down the streets, overflowing the gutters and flooding the sidewalks. Bill was driving leisurely down Main street. When he came to the intersection of Fourth, two charming maidens, with skirts lifted high, were standing at the street corner in distress. Before them stood a pool of water, two feet deep. And in order to reach the other side they would be forced to wade through the water and get their little tootsie wootsie's wet. It was a lamentable situation, that of the pretty little things with the nicely shaped calves and the dainty feet standing at the edge of the puddle in complete frustration.

At this precise moment, Bill arrived at the scene with his Cadillac. Did he pull up to the curb and say, "Girls, hop in, I'll drive you across the street?" Of course he didn't. Such an act would be very unchivalrous—common—just an ordinary pick-up that happens every day. But Bill did something different. He wheeled his Cadillac to the curb, opened both back doors, and then motioning to the two young things, he said very calmly, "Ladies, pass through the back door of the car and out the other back door to dry land beyond."

Ladies and gentlemen, Bill Doyle. —Alexander Collins

ADDITIONAL MATERIAL

Our next speaker on the program, Bill Doyle, the automobile man, in some respects is old-fashioned. He still wears a pocket watch. In Bill's daily routine he sometimes meets up with some pretty tough customers. One day last week a character who did not measure up to respectability came to Bill's showroom and asked for a demonstration. Bill looked the fellow over, and for a moment doubted the advisability of taking a chance. However, sales were slow that day and Bill decided to show the prospect how agile the new model took the curves and hills.

"Drive down this road," said the prospect with a mean look in his eye," and take a run at that hill."

Bill was suspicious of the man as he drove along the lonely road. Suddenly Bill reached for his watch. It was missing. Whipping a revolver out of his pocket, which fortunately he happened to be carrying, Bill stuck the gun into the ribs of the prospect and yelled out: "Hand over my watch!" which the fellow did and Bill kicked him out of the car.

That evening Bill's wife said, "Your forgot your watch this morning." Ladies and gentlemen, Mr. Bill Doyle.

—Alexander Collins

INTRODUCING A PACKING HOUSE EXECUTIVE

We have with us tonight an executive of the Walters Packing Company, an institution that grew up with Boulder Center. Here to speak for Walters is our good friend, Clarence Wilson—the man who is responsible for gaining nation-wide recognition for his firm and an outstanding reputation for himself.

Through Clarence's tireless efforts and excellent business acumen, Walters products are used by people in every state in the union, and of course, the name of our little city, imprinted upon every Walters label, is also a by-word throughout the land. I feel that I can say without fear of contradiction, that if it were not for our great industry, the Walters Packing Company, the town of Boulder Center would be unknown across the state line.

We, the citizens of Boulder Junction, owe Clarence Wilson a debt of sincere gratitude for what he has done for us. Many of Boulder Center's families gain their livelihood from Walters, where they are the best paid and the best treated workers in the entire state. Clarence has been personally responsible for the excellent working conditions at Walters, and his employees are continually singing his praise. In fact, it might be said that there are times when Clarence is too generous, which is indicated by the following anecdote.

Last year Clarence was so delighted with an unexpected increase in sales that he decided to buy each salesman on the staff a new suit of clothes, and he issued an order to that effect. The boys rushed down to their tailors and selected a suit of their choice, sending the bills to Clarence's attention, which were later paid by the company. Most of the fellows picked out suits in the $65 to $75 class. However, one salesman went a great deal higher. When Clarence received the invoice for this man's suit, he almost fell out of his chair. The amount was $150.

Clarence was shocked. For a considerable length of time, he fumbled with the invoice, weighing in his mind the character who picked out the high-priced suit. Finally, he called in his chief accountant and tersely said: "Bill, pay this invoice. I have packed a great many hogs in my day but this is the first time I've dressed one."

Ladies and gentlemen, Mr. Clarence Wilson.

—Charles Pearson

INTRODUCING A HUMORIST

Humor is what makes the world go round. Some humor makes the world go round with a headache. Good humor is a great builder-upper. Humor is as old as history, and like history, repeats itself. If Adam came back to earth today the only thing he would recognize would be the jokes.

It is often said that women lack the sense of humor. Right there is where I disagree. Women have a sense of humor. The more you humor them the better they like it. A good deal of humor comes from the fact that so many people take themselves seriously.

And jokes—there are all kinds of jokes: practical, petrified, and those you have to listen to on television.

You are already acquainted with our speaker of the evening, or you have heard considerably about him as a humorist. I believe he is the same one who was making a hurried trip south and stopped at a small filling station in the Kentucky hills. He said to the attendant, "Covered a heap of miles today. Before I left the highway I sure ate up the pavement." The attendant had never heard the term, and asked, "How could you eat up the pavement?" Our friend said, "I found a fork in the road." If he didn't say it, he'll shoot me.

Some humor is best when it is not intended to be funny, like the little boy who was kneeling at his bedside. He said to his mother, "Mom, do you suppose it will be all right if I put in a commercial about a new bicycle?" And then the one from the little girl who said, "I thank you from my bottom to my heart." And now, ladies and gentlemen, our speaker whose diet consists mostly of humor, Mr. **(name.)**

—Richard Drummond

INTRODUCING A WORLD TRAVELER

Ladies and gentlemen, our guest tonight is a man who has really been around. He's a world traveler, famous for his journeys to other lands and his lectures about them. He's one man who knows where he's been and how to talk so interestingly about his experiences that you can almost imagine you accompanied him.

Now, before we meet him I'd like to say a few words about the broadening influence of travel. In order to properly appreciate our own culture and manner of life and high standard of living we have to know about other countries and understand their different customs and their various standards of living. We can best understand that by visiting those countries personally or learning about them by reading or listening to someone who has visited them and can describe them clearly, in a fashion that makes us visualize them.

I remember when I was much younger I met a man who had travelled extensively. I was curious about his experiences, and fascinated about his visits to other countries, so I questioned him. I asked him what England was like. He said: "Peculiar people. Talk as though they had a mouthful of mashed potatoes. No baseball results on radio. Stupid. Rotten climate. Rotten coffee. Didn't stay long."

I said: "What about France?" He said: "Mostly foreigners. Think they were all trying to work some kind of confidence game. Too polite. They also sell postcards. Got out of there in a hurry." I said: "Italy?" He said: "More foreigners. Couldn't speak English. Couldn't find a Texas chili parlor in the whole country."

I said: "Were you in Greece?" He said: "Oh, yes. The whole place was filled with a lot of ruined old buildings. Instead of tearing them down and putting up modern office and apartment buildings they just let them stand there and occupy valuable space. Backward people." I asked about Japan. He said: "Funny people. Men wear women's kimonas and walk around bowing and hissing. Terrible breakfasts. No Post Toasties. Nothing but rice. They give you two drumsticks to eat with. Silly idea. Almost starved. Glad to get out of there."

I said: "I understand you're going to take another foreign trip soon." "Yes," he said. "Yes, I am. Going to Newark (any rival city) next month on a Moose (Elk's, Lion's, etc.) convention. Newark. Quaint place. In the process of becoming civilized. Some of the natives speak a fairly intelligible English. Post Toasties. In some places Grape Nuts, if you care to wait while they send out for them. Coffee not bad, considering."

That's one kind of traveler. He can take a trip around the world and come back knowing less than when he started. He closes his eyes and ears and despises everything that is new or strange to him. He has nothing but contempt for anything that is not familiar to him. But the real travellers are those who not only have the gift of seeing and absorbing what they see, and adapting themselves to strange customs and conditions, but also have the ability to give realistic descriptions of what they have seen and encountered.

Our next speaker is one of those men. He is justly famed for his journeys to far-away places and his vivid descriptions of those journeys. While hearing him relate some of his experiences is not quite the same as making those trips ourselves, it is the next thing to it. I'm sure you will agree with me when you hear him. Ladies and gentlemen, our speaker, Mr. ———————.

—Paul Weston

INTRODUCING A SYMPHONY ORCHESTRA CONDUCTOR

It is with pleasure that I now introduce the next speaker on this evening's program. There is only one regret that I have. I wish that we were going to hear his music tonight instead of his voice. It is not necessary for me to say that Frederick Glause is one of the world's renowned symphony orchestra conductors and composers. That is a matter of musical history. The music of his famed orchestra has brought happiness to thousands upon thousands of musical hearts, and his compositions are played the world over.

Music like the spoken word is seldom entirely original. This bar or that bar sometimes appears in several compositions and there is often a similarity of theme even among the works of the great masters.

Last year Frederick Glause was conducting a concert in Chicago, where his orchestra played for the first time his newly written symphony in nine movements. The hall was packed to capacity with a responsive audience.

As Conductor Glause lifted his baton, a hush fell over the crowd. Then the sweet strains of fifty violins vibrated throughout the auditorium. When the symphony was brought to a conclusion with a flourish of trumpets and pounding of tympani, punctuated here and there with the tones of the oboe, the audience rose in a body and applauded most enthusiastically. Frederick Glause's new symphony was a success, and was verified the next morning by the critics' reviews.

But to get back to the conclusion of the symphony. Just as Conductor Glause made his last bow, a stranger who was backstage rushed in from a wing and approached Frederick Glause.

"Do you know," he said, "that in your fourth movement there is a similarity of theme with the fourth movement of Wagner's Tannhauser?"

Conductor Glause stepped down from the podium, pointed his baton at the stranger and said irritably, "Any darn fool knows that." Ladies and gentlemen, Frederick Glause.

—Dwight Wilcox

INTRODUCING A BEAUTY EXPERT

How many girls here are beautiful? Hold it! Don't open your compact and admire your face in its tiny mirror. You can't tell a thing unless you look into a full length mirror. And that tells only part of it. Real beauty does not come from the face alone. How is your posture? How is your personality? Do you make and keep friends? Are you broadminded? Sincere? Modest? So many things go to make beauty.

Our speaker this evening is going to give some beauty hints that might surprise you. An expert has made this statement: that not one woman in a hundred can pass a beauty test, and apparently as a result of that situation, not one in a hundred can pass a beauty parlor.

Did you ever see a woman walk out of a beauty parlor who didn't look like she believed it? Beauticians say nothing is less attractive than an elderly woman with bleached or hennaed hair. Only the young dye good, it seems. My wife hasn't spoken to me for three days. I asked her the other day where she had been. She said she had just come from the beauty parlor. I said it was too bad it was closed.

It is rather unfortunate that we don't have beauty experts going around advising men on how to look better. Men **are** a sorry lot, aren't they? They go into a barber shop, get a haircut, and then go window-shopping. Heh! Window shopping! They are looking at their reflections in the windows. They don't know whether they're looking at a nylon display or used washing machines.

I was in a barber shop the other day when a man rushed in and said to the barber, "I want a shampoo and a wave. While you're doing it I'll run down the street and get some lunch." As he rushed out he tossed a toupee to the barber. I got into the chair. "Your hair needs cutting badly." "You're wrong," I said. "It needs cutting nicely. You cut it badly the last time." When he had finished cutting my hair he dropped a very hot towel on my neck and when I complained he said, "You don't expect me to scald my hands, do you?"

—Richard Drummond

INTRODUCING A BOY SCOUT EXECUTIVE

My friends, tonight we are going to have the pleasure of listening to a man who is a leader in a wonderful organization—the Boy Scouts of America. We all know what the organization is. We're familiar with the training the organization gives its youthful members in self-reliance, in courage, in patriotism, and many other virtues that help to make good citizens. By the way, I'd like to make the comment that no cases of juvenile delinquency are found among boys who have taken and lived up to the Boy Scout oath.

For the benefit of those who may not be familiar with the oath, I'll repeat it: "On my honor I will do my best to my God and my country and to obey the scout law; to help other people at all times; to keep myself physically strong, mentally awake, and morally straight."

My friends, that oath is simple in phrase, but powerful in effect, and when we realize that there are over two million Boy Scouts in the United States alone, without trying to estimate the number in perhaps forty other countries, we can realize the tremendous power for good, and decency, and right living they possess.

The leaders of this organization the executives, the scoutmasters and others must necessarily be men of high ideals and unselfish motives—men of understanding, with ability to inspire their youthful followers with the desire and the will to carry out their Scout oath, with all that it implies.

I'm reminded of the unworldly professor, a man who had spent most of his life in classrooms. In other words his knowledge of life was somewhat restricted. He had a twelve-year-old son, who spent much of his time reading comics, watching whodunit shows on television, frequently playing hookey from school, staying out late at night and generally not behaving himself as his father thought he should. The father became worried and finally managed to enroll the boy in the

Scouts hoping that he would quickly get over his foolishness and settle down to his studies.

A couple of days after the boy enrolled the professor called him into his study and said: "Son, now you're a Boy Scout and you're reaching an age when we should discuss some of the facts of life." The boy said: "Okay, Dad, what do you want to know?" The naive professor blinked and said: "A boy of your age—what do you know about life?" The boy started to enlighten his father, who listened in amazement for a few minutes then stopped him. "Son," he said, "if you learned all that in only two days as a Scout, I'm going to join up and get an education myself!" The boy said: "You won't have to, Dad. I'll keep you informed as I go along."

However, to prevent anyone from thinking that this is intended as a reflection on the Boy Scouts, I can state that the knowledge the boy imparted to his father was not acquired during his scout training. The boy had picked it up previously, as boys sometimes do. Those things come under the general heading of street corner misinformation, which the scout leaders try to dispel.

Our speaker is one of the leaders I mentioned, a man who is noted for his splendid work in the organization, helping to direct the training of these boys of today, the adults of tomorrow, who will take our places in the future. We need have no worry about what type of men they will make as long as we have men like our speaker, who can inculcate our youth with their own high principles and strength of character.

This gentleman, our speaker, needs no further eulogies. His work in and for the Boy Scouts of America speaks for itself. Ladies and gentlemen, I present Mr. ——————.

—D. W. Curtis

INTRODUCING A BUILDING AND LOAN EXECUTIVE

The Building and Loan Association is a comparatively new form of banking which apparently has a well-worthwhile service to offer the public, judging from the way these associations have skyrocketed during the past two decades. Now we're going to hear from a Building and Loan executive, John Albins.

When the chairman of the arrangements committee said to me a few days ago, "You are going to introduce John Albins, president of the Cloverleaf Home Building and Loan Association," I said, "Fine!" There is no better fellow in Sauk Junction than John Albins, and I know something about John that he doesn't know I know. That makes it very inviting."

One warm summer morning a shabbily dressed fellow walked into the Cloverleaf Home Building and Loan offices and approached John, who was sitting at his desk, calculating what he would have for lunch.

"Mr. Albins," said the fellow, "I want to contract a loan from this institution in the amount of one dollar and a half."

"You want to do what?" said John, startled.

"I want to make a loan for a $1.50," the man repeated.

"My good man," said John, "Cloverleaf doesn't make loans of such small amounts. We loan on mortgages on homes and buildings—one thousand, two thousand, ten thousands. Why, a loan of one dollar and a half is merely a touch."

Then John turned away from the fellow and fell to chatting with a group of other executives who were also getting ready to go to lunch.

The ragged character stood idly by. No one paid any more attention to him. He just lingered on, listening to the executives chatter with John. Suddenly the court house clock chimed out twelve strokes. The fellow looked up at John with pleading eyes and cried out in a loud whine that could be heard throughout the bank: "There she goes! It's lunch time for everybody, but it's just 12 o'clock for me!"

Ladies and gentlemen, Mr. John Albins.

—Harold Jacobi

INTRODUCING A GERMAN INDUSTRIALIST

Tonight I have the honor of introducing to you a distinguished man of commerce from Germany, Hans Schmidt. For a number of years before the outbreak of the last war and since its termination Mr. Schmidt has been making regular trips to America, furthering our interest in his goods.

Like all manufacturing concerns in his country, Mr. Schmidt's firm turns out precision merchandise that only the skill and exactness of his countrymen can produce. As a result, his goods are in great demand over here, and he is warmly welcomed by American merchants.

One thing that Mr. Schmidt misses while visiting the United States is good old German beer. It is his one great enjoyment back in his home country to spend an evening in the tavern, holding a foamy stein and joining in a community songfest that is a daily event over there.

Mr. Schmidt is a strong advocate of moderation, and he is continually preaching to that effect, especially to his young son, who like all German boys, usually goes with his father to the tavern to drink beer and take part in the songs.

One evening while sitting in a tavern, accompanied by his young son, he moralized on the danger of excessive partaking of beer. "You must always drink your beer very moderately," said Hans to his young son, Fritz. "One glass, two glasses, three glasses, no more. Otherwise you become intoxicated."

"But Father," said young Fritz, "how does one know when he is intoxicated?"

"It is very simple," said Hans, wiping the foam from his lips. "See those two fellows sitting way over in the end of the tavern. Well, if you should look in that direction and suddenly see four men, then you know that you are intoxicated."

Young Fritz fixed his eyes upon the table in the corner of the room, and then quickly exclaimed, "But Father, there is only one man sitting at the table."

Ladies and gentlemen, Mr. Hans Schmidt.

—Charles Marvin

INTRODUCING A SMALL MANUFACTURER

The man who is going to address you in a few moments is one of the celebrated manufacturers in this section of the state. True, his plant is not the largest concern in Spruceville, but it is one of the best. The Ezee Manufacturing Company, of which John Blake, our next speaker, is the president, is large enough to command national respect for its fine product, and yet it is small enough to permit John to supervise its functions personally.

John watches over all of the operations of his plant. He can call each of his employees by his first name. He not only has charge of all marketing and selling, but he directs production as well. In view of all this John is a busy man and his presence is required in many different places at the same time. He is likely to be called to the plant, where his personal attention is needed to adjust some machine that is not performing properly.

There are times, too, when John visits the plant, unannounced. One day John hatched up an idea. It wasn't a new idea, as the custom was in practice in many larger plants, but it was a new idea for the Ezee Manufacturing Company. The idea simply consisted of putting up a box at a convenient place in the plant and calling for suggestions from the employees about bettering the efficiency of the organization.

It was with great delight that late one Friday afternoon, the first week-end of the plan, John removed a stack of papers from the suggestion box and hurried back to his office to study them. As he glanced over the papers, carefully reading each suggestion, a smile broke over John's face. "A great crowd, I've got out there," he said to himself.

John continued to thumb through the papers. Each suggestion seemed to be of considerable value to the company.

Finally, when John picked up and read the last suggestion in the box, a deep frown suffused his face. Wrinkling up his brows and puckering up his lips he mournfully read the unsigned message: "Take the rubber heels off your shoes."

Ladies and gentlemen, Mr. John Blake.

—Alexander Collins

INTRODUCING A RADIO STATION OR
TELEVISION STATION MANAGER

We are honored this evening by the presence of Bill Howard, manager of television station KXXX, who as our next speaker, is going to tell us about what goes on behind the scenes in a television station.

The duties of a television station manager are quite varied. He is responsible for the type of programming his station gives to the public, and in this respect is subject to much criticism by the viewing public, who are always hard to please. He must satisfy the owners by showing a profit, which of course is based upon the sales of advertising, which he directs. In other words, Bill Howard leads a busy life, holding together his temperamental personnel, pleasing the stockholders and the public at the same time. That sometimes is an impossible situation.

Consequently, he must watch his operations with an eagle eye, and when something is said or shown over the air that has the appearance of an erronious nature, he must rectify the situation immediately. Last winter a fellow by the name of Joe Woods conducted daily newscasts over Bill's station. Joe was a cub reporter and new at the business. One day, while Bill was sitting in his office monitoring his programming, he heard Joe make a statement that didn't sound plausible.

Calling the young newscaster into his office, Bill said to him, "See here, Joe, on the whole I am pretty well satisfied with your newscasts, but occasionally you become inaccurate. You know that accuracy is the background of every good newscaster. Now why did you make such an outlandish statement as the one I just heard you give over the air: 'The speaker looked down upon two thousand nine hundred and ninety-nine eyes?' You should know that you can't arrive at an odd figure when counting eyes."

The newscaster pondered over the question a moment and then with a big smile looked down at Bill and quickly said: "There was a one-eyed man in the audience."

Ladies and gentlemen, Bill Howard.   —Roger Hart

INTRODUCING AN ART DEALER

Bluffville boasts of one of the best art stores in this section of the state, which is a tribute to the citizens of Bluffville, as it indicates that our people are of an artistic nature and purchase and enjoy fine things.

Much credit in this respect must go to Pete Olson, proprietor of Olson's Art store on Main street, for Pete, by stocking only quality artistic reproductions in his store, has educated our citizens to appreciate the works of good art.

You can find a copy of the world's celebrated artists at Pete's store—a Rembrandt, a Van Gough. You can find paintings in oil, paintings in water color, exquisite and delightful little statues and vases. In fact, if it's an artistic ornament for the home worth talking about, it will be in Pete's store.

Pete constantly is on the lookout for the latest creations. A short time ago he ordered out a new modern painting—one of those cubist things with elongated lines, odd-looking circles and block-type heads, which only an exponent of modern art can understand or appreciate. Pete suddenly was called out of town and during his absence this sensational painting arrived by express. It was promptly hung on the wall by Joe Smith, one of Pete's clerks.

After Pete had completed his business out of the city, he hurried home and rushed to his store, anxious to inspect the new modern painting. When he got his first look at the extreme daubs of color that was hanging on the wall, Pete's heart sank in dismay. Turning to his clerk, he yelled, "Joe, come over here!" And adding as the clerk arrived in proximity of the painting, "What in the hell do you mean by hanging this modern upside down?"

Demonstrating a gesture of silence, the clerk put his finger to his lips and whispered, "Shh, I just sold it the way it is to that lady standing over there."

Ladies and gentlemen, Mr. Peter Olson.

—Roger Hart

INTRODUCING A COMEDIAN

Tonight I have the pleasure of introducing a famous comedian of radio, stage and television—Berton Meryl. I have decided that in making this introduction I am not going to tangle with a man of Berton's experience at wit, as it is quite certain that something horrible would happen to me once he got to this microphone. But I am going to tell one on him—one that I know he won't tell himself.

About a year ago Berton Meryl's health was impaired. He had been working strenuously day and night on his television shows, and the strain on his constitution was heavy. He was almost at the breaking point. He began to feel listless. He was losing his pep, and in a sense he became melancholy—which is a bad thing for a comedian. I am sure you all will agree to that.

One day after rehearsal he felt so down in the dumps that he decided to call on a physician. He was promptly ushered into the doctor's private office, where he unfolded his troubles to Dr. Henri Strauss, a renowned nerve specialist. After he had related his case, without jokes (Sometimes one wonders if a comedian can talk sense at all), the good doctor analyzed the case. Then Dr. Strauss sat back in his swivel chair, filled up his pipe and thoughtfully said:

"My dear man, it is quite apparent that your work brings you in contact with the gloomy things in life. All of your business associates must be melancholy people, and it is certain that your friends are no better. You have been living a very morbid existence, young man. What you need is laughs, laughs! And more laughs! Get that funny bone of yours working! Cast off those silly fits of despondency! Yes, young man, all you need is laughs. There's nothing else wrong with you. Go home and turn on your television set and laugh with Berton Meryl."

Berton staggered out of the office door and just as he was about to ring the elevator bell, he suddenly said, "My God! I am Berton Meryl." Ladies and gentlemen, Berton Meryl.

—Alexander Collins

INTRODUCING A FARMER

The speaker I will have the pleasure of introducing to you today is a farmer. You know, my father was a farmer, too; a gentleman farmer, he called himself.

Do you know what a gentleman farmer is? According to some he is supposed to be a farmer who raises nothing but his hat. Or very little besides that. Except maybe prices. And every once in a while the **roof**—about parity, whatever that is. But let's not go into that now. Most of it, of course, is largely talk. The gentleman farmer is a worthwhile member of our economy, quite worthwhile.

Oh, the farmers these days are independent, conscious of their high position, better off financially than they ever were. I was visiting one gentleman farmer the other day and I said: "Mighty spry-looking bunch of Plymouth Rock hens you got there." He used to have Rhode Island Reds, but he got rid of those when the Senator McCarthy ruckus started—about Communist infiltration, and all that.

But I asked him: "Those hens laying many eggs these days?" He drew himself up straight, this gentleman farmer, looked at me haughtily and said: "Maybe. But in my position, you know, they don't have to."

No, I couldn't imagine them laying eggs in his position.

Reminds me of the neighbor who phoned me he was so sunburned he couldn't stand up or sit down, and my wife heard it and said: "If he tells the truth, he lies."

I was going to ask my farmer friend if it was true what Bob Hope broadcast—that it was so windy down on the farm in his section last fall that one hen laid the same egg four times. But, like the hen, I let it go.

Yes, they're settin' pretty. The farmers, the hens—both. I told him so. "You fellows are certainly getting a lot more for your farm produce than you used to," said I. "You'll have to admit that."

"That's right," he agreed. "But you know we used to just raise crops. Today we have to know the botanical name for what we're raising, the entomological name of the bug that eats it, and the chemical name of what kills it—and dern it, somebody has to pay!" He may have something there.

I insisted: "But you still must admit that things are a lot better for you than they were a number of years ago. Nowadays you can at least afford to buy your wife decent clothes."

"Yeah," said he. "Now I can afford to buy my wife decent clothes. But she won't wear them; she wants to wear the kind the other women are wearing!"

That sounded like more truth than poultry. And anyway, I could see I wasn't getting anywhere, so I went on to his neighbor's place.

When I asked that farmer how things were at his farm, he said after a minute or two of reflection: "Well, the sody pop and hot dog stand biz has fell off a little. So has the fillin' station, but they're gonna hold 'Othello' over fer another week in my barn."

Yeah, things are different than they were on my father's farm in California when I was a kid. A spade was a spade, and **a rake was a rake,** and not some character in summer stock out in your barn.

My father had a farmhouse that contained twenty rooms and a path. Not a bathroom in the place. He wanted to be one of the filthy rich. He added so many wings to the place, in the winter it started to fly south. Or maybe it was such a windy country. I remember asking Dad: "What are all those smoke-stacks sticking out all over the land?" And he answered: "Those aren't smoke-stacks, son; they're wells that were turned inside out!"

The rooms in the house looked small to me, but my dad said that was just because the mice were so big.

The milking of the cows was my job from the time I was six years old, just after I was weaned. But it wasn't hard; the cows were so cooperative. All I had to do was hold on tight, while the cow jumped up and down.

We had one farmhand who was so lazy he just clamped

on to one of the cow's, er, faucets, and waited for an earthquake to come along and do the work.

I remember one day I was milking when a big wind storm came up—a sudden twister—and first thing I knew I was left holding the bag. I was sure a surprised little **squirt**.

As far as laziness goes, though, you couldn't beat the villagers. In the winter all they did was sit on the east side of the railroad depot, and follow the sun around to the west; and in the summer squat on the west side and follow the shade around to the east.

But the work of a real farmer is never done. He works from early sunrise to long after sundown. Such a farmer is our speaker today. I am pleased to present to you, Mr. ———.

—George A. Posner

INTRODUCING A HORSEMAN

Ladies and gentlemen, tonight's speaker is a man who has distinguished himself as an equestrian.

Many of you know of his activities. Many of you know of his work in the horse world. You know he is an expert rider. You know he knows all about our four-footed friends. But did you ever hear about the time he rode in one of our most famous races? It was a thrilling finish. He wasn't much of a favorite but the horse was one. The race started. He led at the quarter pole and he led at the half. At the three-quarter pole he was second. They neared the finish. He moved up on the leader. He passed the leader. He won! And here is the surprising part of the whole story. His horse finished second. No one had told him that he had to be on the horse to win the race. He had given himself every handicap. He had even carried the saddle in that race.

Right now I am going to put him in the saddle, ladies and gentlemen. I give you the only man who ever beat his own horse, Mr. ————.

—Louis J. Huber

INTRODUCING A RAILROAD EXECUTIVE

My friends, our next speaker is a railroad executive. He is one of that vast brotherhood who proudly bears the appellation of railroad man. That term has a deep significance for all railroad workers, from switch tender to railroad president. To many it conjures up mental visions of those early railroad Empire builders who developed our first great railway systems and laid a foundation for the growth, the progress and the general welfare and prosperity of this nation.

I was told a story recently of an incident in the life of James J. Hill, whom we remember as one of the earlier giants of the industry, when he was building the Great Northern Railroad from Lake Superior to Puget Sound, a project that cost many millions.

It seems, according to the story, that there was quite a ceremony during the laying of the last piece of steel track. Mr. Hill, surrounded by various dignitaries and lesser lights, was all prepared to make a speech regarding the historic event when his attention was attracted by a shiny object lying on the ground. He reached down and picked up a new railroad spike. He looked at it, frowned indignantly, and sent for his construction foreman, Mike O'Grady.

"Mr. O'Grady," he said, "I just picked up this brand new spike lying here on the ground. Can you explain why you are so careless with railroad property?" O'Grady looked at the spike. "God bless you, Mr. Hill," he said in a voice choked with emotion. "I've had six men looking for that spike for the last four days!" You don't have to believe that one. Seriously, Hill, Harriman and a number of others, were all men of great vision who had the courage and the will to make those visions come true.

And the railroad executives of today, like our next speaker, closely approach the traditions and examples set for them by their predecessors in being men of vision and foresight—men who are alert and forceful and capable, always striving to improve their services to the public. They are men who always know what they are doing and why. Which reminds me of a story.

Early one morning a passenger on a train which had stopped for an hour or so at a small junction got off to stretch his legs. He noticed an old man with a lantern and a hammer, who went up to the front wheels of the first car, held up his lantern and leaned over with his ear close to the wheel and then tapped the wheel with his hammer, and listened. The old man moved down to the next wheel and repeated the process of tapping the wheels and listening. The passenger followed him down the full length of the train and finally he said to the old man: "You're very industrious this morning." The old man said: "Yes, sir, I been doin' this for a long time. Every mornin' I get up at four-thirty and I'm on the job at five with my lantern and my hammer. Ain't missed a mornin' for the last thirty-two years!" "Well," said the passenger, "you're to be highly commended. But tell me, why do you tap those wheels with that hammer?" "I'll be darned if I know," said the old man.

Well, I suppose at times we've all encountered people like that old man, who never quite seem to know what they're doing or why. But, my friends, you'll never find those characters among railroad men.

Now there are approximately six hundred and fifty railroads operating in the United States and about two hundred and twenty thousand miles of road bed, not including trackage. On some roads there are double tracks, triple tracks, quadruple tracks, and even more. The total track mileage runs into very high figures. Every day on these tracks hundreds of trains have to be operated on strict schedules, which help to give us the finest railroad systems in the world.

It necessarily follows that the men chosen to run these huge transportation arteries must be men of exceptionally high caliber, fully aware of their terrific responsibilities and fully capable of handling them.

Our speaker tonight is an outstanding example of leadership in this group. There's a well-substantiated rumor flying around that he got his present job as (——————) because he deserves it. And you can be sure of one thing, no matter what official title he might bear, you'll find that he is always proud to be known, first, last and always—as a railroad man. Ladies and gentlemen, Mr. ————— (General Manager, President, etc.) of the ————— Railroad System.

—James Leeson

INTRODUCING A BOSS

It is my great pleasure, ladies and gentlemen, to introduce to this gathering a man who is in a class by himself. Our speaker is a boss. What a small word that conjures up such frightful thoughts! Too many of us think of a boss as an ogre.

Just the other morning one of his employees came in late. Our man suggested in plain words, that the late-comer should have been there at eight o'clock. The employee asked: "What happened? Did I miss something?"

Our man had quite a little trouble with a certain employee. The fellow was guilty of fibbing, telling small lies. Something had to be done about it. The boss asked the employee what happened to people who told lies. The employee knew the answer. Eventually they would be advanced to the boss' position.

He is quite efficient in his own office and thereby sets a good example for the employees. He enters in the morning and says, "Good morning, Joe," to the first employee. Three syllables, not counting the name. From then on he just says "ditto."

We're just joking. The boss we have with us is well-loved by all his employees. And we feel sure you will feel the same way about him. I give you Mr. —————.

—Louis J. Huber

INTRODUCING A SUPREME COURT JUSTICE

It is a rare occasion, indeed, when this organization is so honored by the presence of such a distinguished man as Justice of the Supreme Court, Wendell W. Wooters. Justice Wooters is a busy man sitting on the bench with his associates pondering over the intricate matters of law. No doubt it is quite an encroachment upon his time to come here and talk with us this evening.

I know that you feel as pleased as I do in having him with us tonight. So I am not going to become involved in a long description of Justice Wooter's professional life, but am going to tell one little anecdote before I call him up to the microphone.

One day last spring after the supreme court had recessed, Justice Wooters felt that he needed a constitutional walk through one of our parks. The day was bright and sunny and the atmosphere brisk—just what the justice needed to counteract a long and dreary winter of sitting on the bench. So the Justice, attired in his new salt-and-pepper spring suit, meandered along the paths of the park, passing blooming lilacs, leafing elms and acres of fresh green grass. It was a heavenly day —a day when it was good to be alive. As he strolled on, his mind completely free from the tedious concentration on the statutes, he came to a park bench, which was standing under a shady oak. This tempted the justice to sit down for a short rest.

Now this was an ordinary green park bench, not a legal bench behind which the justice had spent the winter months. Before it a garden of flowers bloomed in profusion. The green grass of spring rolled away over a gentle knoll that was crested with birches. The scene was relaxing, and the justice took advantage of this situation.

As soon as Justice Wooters had seated himself comfortably on the bench he noticed a small boy stretched out on the grass. His attention was drawn to the boy's eyes which seemed to be glued upon him. This prompted Justice Wooters to call out to the boy, "Sonny, why aren't you up and about, frolicking around in this spring sunshine, instead of reclining on the grass like an invalid? A boy your age should have more pep. You should get up and play."

"I don't want to get up and play," said the boy.

"You don't want to get up and play!" exclaimed the Justice. "Have you any reason?"

The boy continued to focus his eyes on Justice Wooters and the park bench and then piped out, "Yes, I'm waiting for you to get up. They just painted that bench you're sitting on."

Ladies and gentlemen, The honorable Wendell W. Wooters, justice of our Supreme Court.   —Horton Smith

---

INTRODUCING A STOCK BROKER

Gentlemen, tonight we have with us a man of the financial world, Mr. Willis Wilkinson, president of the famous firm of Wilkinson and Wilkinson. I am going to refrain from becoming involved in the intricacies of the stock broker's business as that is a specialized profession in itself—that of protecting the investments of thousands of sellers and purchasers of stock on the exchange. Mr. Wilkinson, I am sure will do that very ably when he comes to the microphone. But I am going to tell you about an anecdote that happened at Mr. Wilkinson's office some time last year.

A colored messenger boy rushed into the offices of Wilkinson and Wilkinson, all out of breath. Brushing aside the receptionist, he hurried to the door of Mr. Wilkinson's office, and was about to make an entry, when the receptionist jumped up from her desk and rushed over to the colored fellow.

"See here," she said, "you can't go in there. That's Mr. Wilkinson's private office."

The colored boy let out a big smile, displaying two rows of perfect white teeth. Then in a slow drawl he said: "That's all right for me to go in there. You see I'm the coon of Kuhn, Loeb & Company."

Ladies and gentlemen, Mr. Willis Wilkinson.

—Bradley Huston

INTRODUCING A BAKER

One of the businesses to branch out in the past quarter of a century is the baking business—the fellow who replaced Grandma's toiling at the kitchen stove. For a great number of years now the modern housewife has been running to the bake shop where she can get Grandma's quality products without getting scorched over the oven.

Our principal speaker this evening is a baker—a man who bakes the best bread, cookies and cakes in Orchard Center. Many of you have met Joe Martin before, if not at his bake shop on Main Street, perhaps at some civic gathering around town, as Joe is a civic-minded businessman, and rarely misses a meeting. I don't know what Joe is going to talk to you about tonight, but I am certain that he is not going to relate the story which I am about to tell.

A baker, like a florist, meets people on days of ceremony— birthdays, weddings and anniversaries, as that is the time that something special in the way of a cake is desired. Incidentally, Joe specializes in fancy cakes—those five-layer affairs with fluffy frosting and the script icing.

One day a fellow came into Joe's shop and ordered a very special cake, giving Joe definite instructions as to how he wanted it styled.

"Just write out the word, 'Love' in fancy letters on the top," said the fellow. "A baby pink will do," he added. Then the fellow went away and said that he would return the next day for his cake.

At the time agreed upon the man appeared at Joe's shop and asked for his cake. "There it is," said Joe, proudly displaying the cake on the palm of his hand.

The fellow examined the cake with the eyes of a gourmet, then in an indignant tone of voice cried out, "What's this?"

"What's what?" said Joe, alarmed.

"This!" exclaimed the man, pointing to the word, "Love," neatly streamlined in pink on a background of white icing.

"What's wrong with that?" asked Joe.

"What's wrong with that?" exclaimed the man. "Can't

you see the word 'Love' is spelled wrong? It should begin with a small 'l'."

"That's a minor matter," said Joe in an apologetic tone.

"Minor, be damned," said the fellow. "I want that changed to a small 'l.' I'll be back tonight to pick it up."

That evening the fellow returned and Joe again brought out the cake. "That's more like it," said the fellow, critically examining it.

"I am glad to hear that," said Joe. "I'll pack it for you right away."

"Never mind," said the man, "I'll eat it right here."

Ladies and gentlemen, Mr. Joe Martin.

—Alexander Collins

INTRODUCING A POLICEMAN

It is our great pleasure tonight, ladies and gentlemen, to hear from a man who is an arm of the law. That, as you know, means that he is a policeman. In that capacity he has had many experiences and I would like to tell you about a few of them.

Duty is his first word. He never fails to pinch a ripe peach. By the time he gets around again it will have what looks like a bad spot and it ends its days between his teeth.

You've all heard the story of the policeman who found a dead horse on Kuscioski Street. He dragged it around to Smith Street because he didn't know how to spell the long word. Our man had to drag his horse even further—to B Street. Because he didn't know how to spell Smith either.

As a jail keeper he has also had his moments. He wanted to be good to the prisoners and offered to let them have a daily exercise. After he lost three prisoners he realized that the ones who chose pole vaulting had a slight edge on the other boys.

Seriously, we have our jokes about the law, but we don't really feel that way. They all do a job that entails many unpleasant angles. We admire them for it. Just as we admire the man who is with us tonight, Mr. —————.

—Louis J. Huber

INTRODUCING A GENERAL CONTRACTOR

Tonight we are going to hear from a man who has been in the general contracting business for a number of years. A man who came up from the ranks, and started his business as a hod carrier, but who now has reached the top of his profession as a builder of bridges and skyscrapers. It is going to be a pleasure to listen to Harry Bellows, for the building business is a fascinating one, full of romance and excitement. It is quite certain that Harry has some good ones up his sleeve that he will pull out and spill tonight.

It is generally believed that a general contractor is a rough, uncouth, knock-em-down sort of an individual who chews tobacco and expectorates with a violence. He is reported to have a vocabulary of profane words unequalled by none, and a voice that can carry from one end of a tunnel to the other, no matter as to the length. He originally got that way, it is said, from driving mules. Of course, right now I am not referring to Harry specifically, but to contractors in general.

A contractor's employees are pretty tough customers as a rule, and it takes a rugged man to handle them. Then on the other hand many of them are lazy and require constant prodding and supervision. One day last summer Harry assigned two of his laziest workers to a job of cutting down some trees on a site where Harry was starting a new project. About the middle of the afternoon, Harry, questioning in his mind the amount of progress these two colored fellows were making, jumped into his car and drove out to the location.

As Harry pulled up on a side road and approached the building site, a funeral procession was proceeding down the highway, headed by a brass band dirging out a requiem. Consequently, Harry arrived unnoticed by George Washington Brown and Abraham Lincoln Jones, who were slouched against a tree. George Washington Brown was facing the road in view of the passing funeral procession. Abraham Lincoln Jones was on the opposite side of the tree. Gum-shoe like, Harry walked slowly over to within ear-shot of the drowsy conversation that was being exchanged under the tree.

"Whut's dat noise I hear out dere?" said Abraham Lincoln Jones.

"Dat am a fune'l going by," George Washington Brown replied.

"Am it a big one?" asked Abraham Lincoln Jones.

"It am de biggest I eber seen," said George Washington Brown. "Brass band, people with banners. Must be a hundred cars rollin' down dat highway."

Abraham Lincoln Jones was silent for a moment, and then between yawns said: "I sure do wish I was facin' round the other way. . . . I'd mighty like to see dat dere fune'l."

Ladies and gentlemen, Mr. Harry Bellows.

—Paul Dickson

INTRODUCING A NURSE

Ladies and gentlemen, it is my great pleasure to introduce to you a member of a proud profession. As a follower in the footsteps of Florence Nightingale, she has chosen for herself a great career of nursing.

I can hear you asking: What is a nurse? And even if I didn't hear you I'd be giving the same answer. Yes, what is a nurse? A nurse is a lady in white who gives you nothing but black looks and green pills.

And what else? A nurse is a vision who is giving while she is taking. Giving a withering glance while she is taking your temperature. A nurse is an angel of mercy but you wouldn't call her that when she is making a pin cushion out of you with her hypodermic.

Our speaker of the evening has many traits that make her successful in her career. If a man has a pulse that is too slow, she simply holds his hand and immediately the pulse count increases. If a man's pulse is too fast, she also knows what to do. What? Why, she calls a doctor, of course.

And now I would like to call her. A member of the profession that makes it easier when you are sick, and happier when you are well. May I present to you, Miss —————?

—Louis J. Huber

INTRODUCING A SECRETARY OF THE
BETTER BUSINESS BUREAU

Tonight I am going to introduce to you a man who represents an organization that protects the public against the swindler and the sharp-practice artist. He is the local secretary of the Better Business Bureau, which is doing a splendid job in our community. Some of you might have an opportunity to get first-hand information on the excellent service that John Carney offers down at his headquarters in the Ironsides building.

The Better Business Bureau is a nation-wide concern, with offices in the principal cities of the country. It is constantly on the lookout for the faker and the shady operator, of which unfortunately there are too many floating around these days. The Better Business Bureau's files are bulging with information of these fast operators, and once a swindler puts over a scheme and someone is fleeced out of his hard-earned cash, the Better Business Bureau notifies all of its offices immediately. Complete details are given on the modus operandi of the scheme, together with a minute description of the perpetrators. As a result, a community is put on guard before the glib-tongued boys arrive in town.

Sometimes people call in the support of the Better Business Bureau when it is too late—when the horse has been stolen from the barn. An example of this took place right here in our town about a year ago. A certain lady in our city, very gullible and susceptible to fast talk, and not too heavily endowed with brain matter, was fleeced out of her life's savings by one of these villains. After her cash had vanished into the slippery hands of the confidence man, she went to John and told all.

After she had completed her confession, John said to her, "Mrs. Jones, didn't you know about the Better Business Bureau?"

"Yes, I knew about it," replied Mrs. Jones sheepishly.

"Well, for heaven's sake," said John, "why didn't you come and see us before you fell for that scheme?"

The lady looked up at the ceiling and then quietly said, "I was afraid that you wouldn't let me go through with it." Ladies and gentlemen, Mr. John Carney.

—Hal Huntington

INTRODUCING A HUMORIST

I've discovered that it's not only bad form but sometimes bad luck to attempt to be funny when you introduce a humorist because he's pretty sure to top you with his opening remarks.

So I'll tell a little story about a friend of mine, a salesman, who went on a selling trip to London many years ago. He invited a prospective customer, a British merchant, to luncheon at a swank London hotel. As he described it to me, the dining room was dimly lighted, the diners spoke in whispers, the waiters didn't walk—they glided over the deep carpet. He said it was like being in church.

Anyway, when they were seated he told a funny story to his prospect, then he laughed heartily at his own joke. He followed this with another story and again laughed uproariously at his own joke. He looked up at his prospect and the Britisher was regarding him with a peculiar expression. He looked around the dining room and the other diners were craning their necks and staring at him in horror.

He said to the merchant: "What's the matter? Why are all these people looking at me like that?" The Britisher said: "You **laughed—aloud!**" My friend was astounded! He didn't know what to make of it, so he called the head waiter over and said: "How long have you been working here?" "About thirty years," said the head waiter, "man and boy." "Well," said my friend, "did anybody ever laugh in here before?" "Oh, yes, sir," said the waiter. "We've had several complaints."

And I believe I can assure you that, before our speaker is through, we will have quite a number of similar complaints here. May I present our talented speaker, Mr. —————?

—Paul Weston

INTRODUCING A MOVING AND STORAGE EXECUTIVE

With the coming of good highways and the improved motor truck a new industry sprang up in this land—the moving and storage business. Today the moving and storage business is a phenomenal one. When a family decides to move from Boston to Los Angeles, a moving van is called in and within a few days the household effects are transplanted into a new home.

However, it is not as simple as that, as Bill Owens, our next speaker, will tell you when he comes before the microphone in a few minutes. Much patience is required, especially in packing, as valuable furniture, expensive dishes and costly pieces of art have to be handled and packed with great care. That is where the specialist comes in, and Bill prides himself upon his ability in that respect.

There is nothing that Bill enjoys more than to supervise the packing of valuable articles. He has made a profound study of it, and as a result he has devised many new innovations for transplanting these delicate works of art. If necessary, Bill will go out on the job himself and direct the work.

Last summer a finicky woman engaged the services of Bill's company to move her household goods. She possessed many valuable antiques and was fearful that Bill's crew might cause some damage in handling. To satisfy her whims, Bill agreed to come out himself and help with the load.

When Bill arrived on the scene, the lady pointed out an old grandfather's clock of rare origin. "This clock," said the woman, "has been in our family for five generations. I want it carried out of this house without a scratch."

"My dear lady," said Bill, "I have handled six generation clocks without a scratch. This instrument will be packed away without a nick, and if I might say, without losing a tick."

Bill picked up the tall clock and proceeded down the walk with it, the pendulum swinging loosely and the bottom of the clock pounding with each forward step on Bill's shins.

When he reached the main sidewalk, a gentleman filled with strong water was passing by on his way home. The inebriated man, upon seeing Bill struggling down the sidewalk with the big clock, took off his hat and viewed the sight with astonishment. Then he called out to Bill . . . "Shay, fellow, why don't you get a watch?"

Ladies and gentlemen, Mr. Bill Owens.

—William Crawford

INTRODUCING A MUSICIAN

Tonight's speaker, ladies and gentlemen, is a man who knows his notes. He also notes his nose. This is a simple job because of its size.

He started his musical career at an early age. When he was two he played on the linoleum. One year later he played under it. His mother, sensing his talent, had swept him there.

Actually, he is a man of notes. He respects them to the extent that he never plays them. Nor does he ever pay them even when they are due. There was a time he played an organ. He had to give that up when his monkey died.

This talent did not come to him naturally. He cultivated it. He's been asked to plow it under but so far he has refused. He plays the piano like Fritz Kreisler. Since Mr. Kreisler is a violinist you can see what I mean.

I'm just kidding. Our speaker does play the violin like Kreisler. Exactly like him; he uses both hands. There was a time when he played second bass in a symphony orchestra. To this day he doesn't know why they shifted him to right field.

Despite all this our man has been successful in his field and we are proud and privileged to have him with us tonight. I proudly present to you, Mr. ——————.

—Louis J. Huber

INTRODUCING A FRENCH WINE MERCHANT

The next introduction on the speaking agenda is going to be very difficult for me to make, indeed, for I am going to introduce to you a French wine merchant. I know nothing of French and less about wine. I am not sure that I can pronounce Monsieur Pierre Jacques' name correctly.

But to do justice to such a renowned international figure as Monsieur Jacques, I felt that it was my responsibility to do a little research on a wine merchant. Consequently, I went over to the Historical Reference Library and called upon Miss Bessie Catts, who has tended the shelves over in that institution for the past fifty years. It was quite certain that Miss Catts would have little personal knowledge about wine. But she knew where to find it—on the book shelves.

"Miss Catts," I said upon entering the library, "I want to look up a little information on the subject of wine."

"Wine," exclaimed Miss Catts, reaching for a book. "Why, the tenth dynasty of Nebuchadnezzar fell to ruins on account of that beverage. It's almost as treacherous in that respect as a kiss. Those two things have been the downfall . . ."

"I don't want to go that far back," I said, interrupting Miss Catts' dissertation. "I want something more current. I want to find out something about a modern wine merchant."

"My dear man," said Miss Catts, "there is nothing modern about a wine merchant."

"Nothing modern about a wine merchant!" I repeated.

"Absolutely nothing," said Miss Catts. "It says right here on page 232 of 'The Fruits of the Grape' that one generation plants the vine, the next generation ferments the wine and the third generation sells it."

"Then Monsieur Jacques is selling his grandfather's wine," I said.

"He certainly is," said Miss Catts.

That's about all that I could get out of Miss Catts, which wasn't very much. So I hurried out of the library and while walking down the street I bumped into a friend of mine.

"Jack," said the friend, "I hear you are going to introduce Monsieur Jacques at the meeting tomorrow night."

"That's right," I said.

"Well," said the friend, "I'll tell you a good one about that fellow Jacques."

"Tell it quick!" I exclaimed. "Heaven knows I need something."

"It was like this," said the friend. "Monsieur Jacques had a young fellow on his staff who had the misgiving of consuming more of Monsieur Jacques' product than he sold. A short time ago this fellow made a sales trip to America and was not heard from for a period of three weeks. Monsieur Jacques became alarmed and hopped a plane in Paris. Immediately upon arriving at Idlewilde airport, he hurried to the last known address of the missing salesman, which was a rooming house. Monsieur Jacques knocked furiously on the door but received no response. After several minutes of more knocking, a window in the second story flew open and a woman stuck out her head.

"Is this where Monsieur La Bissoniere lives?" Monsieur Jacques called out to the woman.

"Yes," she replied. "Carry him in."

Ladies and gentlemen, Monsieur Pierre Jacques.

—Frank Colton

INTRODUCING A COMMISSIONER OF AGRICULTURE OR COUNTY AGENT

The duties of a Commissioner of Agriculture cover a wide field. He is responsible to the people of the state for the enforcement of laws pertaining to agriculture, dairy and food, which are numerous, indeed. He is in charge of a weed eradication program which is vital to the healthy growth of our crops. He supervises the distribution of food against adulteration, contamination and short weight or measure. In short he has a tremendous responsibility in safeguarding the health and welfare of our people.

Such is the life of Henry B. Bosworth, our Commissioner of Agriculture. In addition to the long hours at his desk where the work seems to everlastingly pile up, the Commissioner must make numerous trips through the farm belt, getting first hand information on current situations. Last summer there was a disastrous grasshopper plague in our northern tier of counties. The pests were eating everything in sight, and valuable crops were disappearing with the rapidity of a snow ball in August. This problem required an on-the-scene investigation by the Commissioner, who promptly motored to the locality of the pestilence and rented a furnished home for the duration of his stay.

One day as he was returning from a check of nearby fields, he saw a wagon load of hay overturned in a ditch. A young farm boy was feverishly working with a pitchfork, removing the hay from the upside down wagon. Walking over to him, the Commissioner said: "Young fellow, that's a pretty big job for a little fellow like you . . . and on a hot day too. Come on up to my house, it's just on the top of the hill, and I'll fix you a nice chocolate ice cream sundae."

"I can't," said the farm lad as he continued to pitch hay. "My paw won't like it," he added.

"The hay will wait," said the Commissioner. "You're all tired out from that work. Come on up!"

After more coaxing the lad stuck the pitchfork in the hay and followed the Commissioner up to the crest of the hill, where they entered the house and soon each was enjoying a plate of ice cream smothered with chocolate sauce.

While the boy was eating the ice cream, he twitched in his chair, half arising from the seat as his little mouth gulped down the frosty confection.

"I've gotta hurry. Paw won't like it," said the youngster nervously.

"Don't rush, my lad," said the Commissioner, "The hay will wait. I'll get a second helping."

"Can't," said the boy. "Paw won't like it."

"By the way," said the Commissioner, "Where is your father? I didn't notice him as I came by the upset wagon."

The lad, who by this time had arisen from his chair, leaned over and lapped up the remainder of the chocolate sauce from the dish. Then with an upturned face smeared with brown coloring, he looked up at the Commissioner and said, "He's under the hay."

Ladies and gentlemen, the honorable Henry B. Bosworth, our Commissioner of Agriculture.

—Ray Hensrud

INTRODUCING AN ATOMIC SCIENTIST

The changes that have taken place in our way of life during the past fifty years are astounding—almost frightening. There are persons in the audience who remember the horse and buggy, the kerosene lamp and the horse drawn street car. One by one they have seen these antiquated adjuncts to our physical existence replaced by a new discovery of science that brought with it an alleviation upon the strain of living.

The horse and buggy has been discarded for the automobile and the airplane, the kerosene lamp for the electric bulb and the horse-drawn street car for the trolley. One by one new inventions have appeared—the telephone, the radio and television, all the product of the hard working scientists who labored for years in the laboratory, seeking out these great mysteries.

There seems to be no end to the discoveries that come from the brain of man. Just when we were of the opinion that we had reached the stage of fulfillment, the greatest scientific discovery of all has been unfolded before our eyes. Most of us here this evening can recall our high school days when we struggled in the physics class tinkering with the "static" jar. We also remember the talk in those days about splitting the atom—one of the unfathomable natural secrets that had not been solved. Scientists were attempting to split the atom, which to most of us meant something like splitting a piece of wood, so little did we know about the science of physics.

Of all the sciences physics is probably a greater mystery to the layman than any other. It is submerged in a maze of mathematical formulas that are beyond the comprehension of the average intellect, as Dr. Walter B. Wittman, our next speaker, can explain to you. Dr. Wittman is one of our notable physicists. He was a leading figure in the discovery of the atom bomb, and along with other scientists he is now still laboring for the perfection of atomic power that some day will dwarf the scientific developments of the past.

But I have reached the end of my knowledge of physics. In this respect I am something like the two fellows who were talking about the greatest physicist of them all—the renowned Albert Einstein.

"Einstein," said one fellow to the other. "Who's he?"

"Einstein's the guy that discovered the fourth dimension," the first fellow replied.

"Fourth dimension?" asked the second fellow. "What's that?"

The first fellow thought the matter over a few moments and then replied: "Well, there's length, breadth and thickness, that's three. The fourth is time."

Which reminds me, it's time to introduce to you the distinguished Dr. Walter B. Wittman. Dr. Wittman.

—Raymond Steele

ADDITIONAL MATERIAL

Just recently I learned that there are many kinds of doctors. It appears that when a fellow gets through with four or five years of college, he gets a couple of degrees. Then if he wants to stick around for a couple of more years, he gets another degree called a doctor's. In this respect he can become a doctor of almost anything he chooses. Some of these fellows are called a doctor of philosophy.

Usually when we think of a doctor, we think in terms of medicine, dentistry or perhaps a clergyman—a fellow who can save a limb, a tooth or a soul.

Last week I called up the home of our speaker of the evening and said to the colored maid who answered the phone and who apparently was new to the household, "Is Dr. Walter B. Wittman at home?"

It was apparent also that the maid had been pestered with medical calls, as she replied, "The doctah's in all right, but before you go further, the doctah's one who can do nothin' for you." Ladies and gentlemen, **Dr. Wittman.**

—Raymond Steele

INTRODUCING A LAUNDRY AND
DRY CLEANING EXECUTIVE

Tonight I am going to introduce to you one of our most prominent launderers and dry cleaners, Mr. Jake Strauss. Jake is the fellow who has taken the drudgery away from the housewife. He, personally, has replaced the old-time wash tub and board, the clothes lines and pins, and the ironing board and iron in the homes of Pine Center. That is quite a replacement.

Jake got into the laundry business as a result of a series of information. One day a number of years ago Old Man Jones, our local carpenter, went to Johnathan Blake, who opened our first clothing store, and said, "Johnathan, something is going on in this town. Everybody wants bigger closets."

"Is that so?" said Johnathan.

"It certainly is," said Old Man Jones, adding, "What does that mean?"

Johnathan reflected for a minute, pulled on his whiskers, and then said, "It must mean that folks are planning on buying more clothes. When I opened my store there was only one suit and one dress plus a few kids' overalls hanging in the closet. I'm going to get ready for an expansion."

The next day the clothing store man was walking down the street where he met Jake Strauss. "Jake," he said, "do you know that something is going on in this town? People are building larger closets. That means that a clothing expansion is going to take place."

"Is that so?" Jake replied, and then he walked on in deep meditation. "A clothing expansion," he said to himself. "Who's going to wash and clean all of those clothes? Why me, of course!" And Jake went into the laundry and dry cleaning business, prepared to meet the 100-shirt and 100-dress era that was on the way.

Jake is a frugal man, and through his frugality he has built one of the finest laundry and dry cleaning plants in this section of the state, which has been piling up a profit for him year after year. Jake will never lose his frugality. One day last week Jake ran out of postage stamps. Hailing Lester Wann, a local handy man who was passing by, he said, "Lester, here's three cents. Run down to the post office and fetch me a stamp."

Lester took the three cents and hurried on his way. When he returned with the stamp stuck to his thumb, Jake said, "Just a minute, Lester. I think I have a dime in my pocket." Then Jake fumbled around in his trouser pockets, but he couldn't locate the dime.

Lester watched the proceedings for a few seconds, and when it appeared that no success was being made in the search, he said to Jake: "Mr. Strauss, look again. Look hard! If you had a dime you got it!"

Ladies and gentlemen, Jake Strauss.　　—Dale Curtis

ADDITIONAL MATERIAL

Our next speaker on this evening's program, Mr. Jake Strauss, one of the community's outstanding launderers, has many problems to meet during a day's business. It is a difficult task to please the public all of the time, and there is no business in which a customer beefs more than the laundry business. There is always something wrong with the finished product. Either the shirts have shrunk, the buttons are missing or the spots weren't removed.

Last week a fellow came into Jake's office in a huff and said to Jake, "Just take a look at this!"

Jake held the material up to the light and examined it. He carefuly folded the material, felt of its edges, smoothed it down on the counter and then casually remarked to the man: "I can't see anything wrong with this lace."

"Lace!" said the man. "That was a sheet!"

Ladies and gentlemen, Mr. Jake Strauss.

—Dale Curtis

INTRODUCING A FARM BUREAU OR
FARMERS UNION MAN

When I was told that I was going to introduce Joe Evans of the Farm Bureau at our dinner tonight, I figured that I had better check up a little bit on Joe, so that I would have the proper information at hand to usher him up to the speaker's table with suitable ceremony.

I have known of Joe's fine work with the Farm Bureau for a long time, and I have some personal knowledge about Joe's strenuous battles for the betterment of agriculture. We all know that Joe has been a champion of the farmer. His efforts before the state legislature and the national congress have been relentless, with the result that many improvements for agriculture are now recorded as laws of the land.

But I wanted to know if Joe ever was a farmer. He has been in Bureau work for so long that I wanted to make certain that Joe had at some time or other been a real down-to-earth dirt farmer. Well, I found out that he had been a farmer, and I believe a good one at that. But best of all, by mere chance I ran across an anecdote about Joe that has been repeated a thousand times by the folks up in his home county.

It appears that back in the early days when Joe was farming a piece of land in the northern part of our state, the facts behind this anecdote took place. That was the day of poor roads—before the days of farm-to-market roads that Joe so ably helped to make possible by his work in the Bureau. The road, if it could be called a road, traversed the countryside from Joe's farm to town, and it was nothing but a mudhole when it rained, and a dust bowl when it was dry. On his way to market his products Joe was forced to travel this road. There was no other way, and each day as he lumbered along over its curves and its hills, he would generally become stuck in the mud, especially at one point just before a rise, where the mud was always the ooziest.

When this daily occasion came about, Joe would get off

his truck and unload, after which the old machine would grunt and groan, spin and tremble and finally jerk itself out of the slime. Then Joe would reload and proceed on his way.

One day Joe was driving to town with an empty load, and as he slid down the hill and splashed into the mudhole, which was exceptionally muddy that day, the truck settled down in the slime to the level of the hubcaps. Joe raced the engine. He threw it into forward gear. He threw it into reverse gear, but with no results. The truck just stood there tossing out two spouts of black ooze with every spin of the wheels.

Joe took off his hat, wiped the beads of perspiration from his forehead, and then remarked to himself: "Darn it, stuck in the mud and nothing to unload!"

(Pause)

Well, that's about my position at this moment. I'm stuck in the mud with nothing more to unload. Ladies and gentlemen, Mr. Joe Evans.   —Hal Huntington

ADDITIONAL MATERIAL

Our next speaker, Joe Evans, often goes out of his regular line of duty while carrying on the work of the Farm Bureau.

One day last summer he was visiting a farmer in the southern part of the state, and after talking over farm problems for several minutes, the farmer remarked that he had a mule that would not move under any circumstances.

"I've got just the thing," said Joe. "It's the latest invention of the Bureau. Where is the mule?"

The farmer brought up the mule and Joe gave the animal a shot. The result was stupendous. The mule switched its tail, tossed its head and went down the road like a gunshot. "How much does that stuff cost?" asked the farmer. "A quarter," said Joe.

Then the farmer quickly said, "Give me a half a dollar's worth so I can catch the mule." Ladies and gentlemen, Mr. Joe Evans.   —Hal Huntington

INTRODUCING A GENERAL

Before I introduce the next speaker I want to thank the arrangements committee for their good judgment in making such an excellent selection for this evening. It is not often that a chairman of my humble standing has the opportunity of introducing a General of the United States Army. Most of my experiences have been confined to bragging about the merchants on Main street, which I must admit has been a difficult task, as the field for the choice of notable deeds is very limited. The best I could get was a good golf score or some sensational hunting exploits where the rabbit was peppered by four blasts of the gun. Otherwise, I would have to compress my remarks about how Joe Brown stacks his shoes or Bill Whalen runs his garage.

But tonight we have something different—General John J. Fields of the United States Army—a man who has fought his country's battles in many foreign lands—a man gallant on the field of battle and brave on the speaker's platform. What more could a chairman ask for?

General Fields' experiences and exploits are so numerous that it would be impossible to even superficially cover the ground in my short introduction. Consequently, I am going to limit my portion of this procedure with an anecdote involving the General during the last war.

The battle in France was raging furiously. Shells were bursting everywhere. The sky was raining bombs. General Fields hastened over a hill on his way to a command post, where he planned to get some first-hand information on the progress that was being made by our troops, as well as to issue some fresh orders for an advance. Just as he walked over the crest of the hill he came face to face with a colored GI, who was sprinting a marathon at a hundred-yard-dash clip, in the opposite direction. The colored soldier's legs were shuttling like dancing electrons. His white eyeballs were protruding like two golf balls. In other words, that colored fellow was flying through space.

Startled at the sight of the fleeing GI, General Fields called a sharp, "Halt!"

When the colored soldier abruptly terminated his forward motion, the General exclaimed, "What do you mean by running away from the front lines?"

The soldier, panting with a shortness of breath, said: "Boss, I ain't running from dese lines. Mah legs have just decided to take me some place else and I'se just obligin' thass all."

"Well, turn around and go back to your company," exclaimed the General.

"Who is you to be givin' those o'ders?" the colored soldier said. "You ain't no lieutenant."

"I'm the General in charge of the division," General Fields said very emphatically. "Now get back to your company before I have you court-martialed for deserting your post."

The colored soldier make a hesitating about-face and with faltering steps began to walk back toward the front line. After he had taken a few paces, he craned his neck at General Fields and softly mumbled, "I sure must have run a long way to git back to where dese generals is."

Ladies and gentlemen, General John J. Fields.

—Leslie Kirk

ADDITIONAL MATERIAL

During the last war our next speaker, General John J. Fields, was attending a social affair with his troops.

It was a festival of some proportions. The boys were having a good time.

"Do you know that old duck of a general standing over there?" said a sergeant to a pretty young lady, at the same time pointing to General Fields. "He's the meanest sour puss I've ever seen."

"Do you know who I am?" asked the girl. "I'm his daughter."

"Do you know who I am?" asked the sergeant.

"No," said the girl.

"Thank heavens!" said the sergeant.

Ladies and gentlemen, General Fields.   —Leslie Kirk

THE WHITE LIGHT

We have all held a glass prism so that a white light shining through has shown all of the colors of the rainbow. The colors we saw were only the qualities of the primal white light.

If we think of my very good friend and your versatile speaker for the moment as the white light and hold a prism or crystal up to him, we see him in many different settings.

First, we see him leaving high school at the end of the second year and working for eight years as a clerk, salesman, and cashier. Then we see him working his way through the University of Wisconsin, an adult special student, and by carrying extra work finishing the last two years of high school and the regular college course in four years. It was during this picture of his varied life that I first knew Al Haake. College boys all have their heroes, and Al was one of mine. While he was a senior, he was earning money by preaching in a small country church. He was president of the YMCA and editor of the college daily.

Al Haake was awarded many honors at Wisconsin, being elected a member of Phi Beta Kappa and of the forensic honorary Delta Sigma Ro. He was awarded a "W" for his debate work on the platform at Wisconsin.

The next picture shows him teaching economics at Wisconsin for eight years. During the second of those years he was my teacher in a class in "Money and Banking" where we struggled with the quantity and anti-quantity theories of money. He was a good teacher.

Then our speaker this noon earned his Ph.D. at Wisconsin. He studied under such famous teachers as Richard T. Ely, John R. Commons, E. A. Ross, and William A. Scott.

The next picture shows him as head of the Economics Staff at Rutgers University.

Then follow many business pictures in which he was a prominent member of the MacManus, Inc., Advertising Agency, Director of Research and Assistant to the President of the

Simmons Company, Managing Director of the National Wholesale Furniture Association, business speaker for the National Association of Manufacturers, and radio broadcaster.

Just as all of the colors of the spectrum were made by the one white light, so all of these pictures have been made by my good friend and pal, Al Haake, who is celebrating a birthday today. Happy birthday, Al, and may you have many more of them.

Introduction of Dr. Alfred P. Haake at the Sales Managers Conference in Minneapolis, Minnesota, by Harry A. Bullis, now Chairman of the Board of General Mills, Inc.

FAREWELL TO A DISTRICT MANAGER

Tomorrow noon after forty-three years with the F. W. Woolworth Company this young man will be unharnessed and put to pasture.

His company has rather an interesting arrangement with their district managers. Every sixth nickle that comes in goes to the district manager. Then they retire them early so they can count up how much they have and by the time they have finished counting it, they are eighty and can relax and enjoy the money.

Actually Alex could have retired three years ago, but Barbara Hutton has been rather expensive to maintain and she had first grab at the cash register, but now that she is safely bedded down again, Alex thought he had better get out.

When you call him Alex you are really calling him Alex for short. For the record we really should give you his full name which is: Alexander, Herman, Ludwig, Johannes, Karl, Franz, Wolfgang von Goethe, Gallenkamp. This really averages out okay since his father's name was plain George.

Best of luck to you, Alex. May we hear from you?

—Evald C. Bank, President,
Minneapolis Rotary Club

SECTION THREE

BRIGHT BITS FOR CHAIRMEN

In this section you will find a varied assortment of useable material for chairmen — brief introductions, appropriate short stories, and anecdotes. Although many are designed for specific situations, no attempt has been made to classify them. However, in many instances the sub-title will indicate the appropriate situation in which the bit may be used.

EVERLASTING

(To be used as a warning to the speaker not
to exceed the time limit.)

The pompous toastmaster introduced the equally pompous speaker of the evening. The man started with elaborate words and phrases. The introduction was long and boring.

The speaker took his turn. He also went on with long and unnecessary words. Then he started on another topic.

"As most of you know," he told them. "I am a graduate of Yale. To you it is just the name of a college but to me it means everything. Each letter has a separate and distinct meaning. The first letter is Y and that takes me back to my Youth. It takes me back to my carefree days."

And so far into the evening. Came the letter A and the letter L and — after two hours of this — the little but last E.

"To me," he waxed. "This letter stands for Everlasting. And now what does the word YALE mean to you?" he asked his audience.

"To me it means," answered a loud voice, "that I'm glad you didn't go to Pennsylvania or we'd be here for the next two days."

—Louis J. Huber

IT'S ALL A FAKE

This zany story may be used when the chairman is to introduce a magician, a humorist, an entertainer, an actor, or someone connected with the radio or theatrical profession.

A man entered a booking agent's office and said he had a vaudeville act which he thought was pretty good.

"Let's see it," offered the theatrical agent.

So the fellow pulled a toy piano out of one pocket and set it up on a table. Then he took a mouse out of another pocket, and set it on a little piano stool in front of the toy piano.

The little mouse began playing the catchiest music—ragtime, boogie-woogie, ballads. His technique was simply out of this world.

"Why, that's wonderful!" enthused the agent. "That act would make a big hit. How about a thousand a week?"

"Oh, that isn't all there is to it," said the gent. "Look." And he took a little canary out of another pocket, set it up on the edge of the piano. The little mouse than began playing classic pieces of opera. And the canary accompanied him in exquisite harmony!

When they had finished the agent's enthusiasm knew no bounds. "The act's a knockout," said he. "Would you take $5,000 a week?"

But then the gentleman grew strangely silent, hesitated, then hung his head. Finally he uttered: "I am sorry, mister, but I have to confess to you the act is really a fake."

"A fake?" gasped the agent.

"Yes, the canary doesn't really sing. You see, the mouse is a ventriloquist."   —George A. Posner

---

DON'T PUBLISH, PLEASE

This story may be effective if used when introducing a bishop, a minister, or a church dignitary.

On his arrival in a large city, a certain prominent bishop made a speech at a banquet in which he told a number of amusing anecdotes which had occurred during his travels. As he expected to repeat his speech next day at another gathering, he asked the reporters not to mention the jokes in any accounts they might turn in to their newspapers.

A cub reporter who wrote up the event ended his piece with the following: "The bishop told a number of stories that cannot be published."   —George A. Posner

---

SOME STAYED HOME

This is an effective story to use when the attendance at the meeting has fallen below expectations.

Frank Nye, brother of the well-known humorist Bill Nye, once innocently made a political speech in a town whose citizens were almost solidly on the opposite side of the fence. The audience joyously hissed and booed throughout the address. Afterward the auditorium janitor undertook to comfort the shaken campaigner. "Never mind, Mr. Nye," the old Irishman said. "This bunch is nothing but the ragtag and bobtail of the town. Everyone with any sense stayed at home."

—The Christian Science Monitor

I am merely the toastmaster—the punk that sets off the fireworks.   —Gene Buck

---

SOFT SOAP

"A politician," said Bob Hope, "is merely a person who borrows your pot to cook your goose in; and as such he shakes your hand before election, and you afterward. His greatest asset is his lieability—and his chief product is soft soap which, as you know, is 99 percent lye."   —George A. Posner

SIN NO MORE

This story may be used when introducing a minister. It may be revised to fit the speaker and the occasion.

A minister came out of his church in New York to find he had been given a parking ticket. He went to traffic court and waited in the crowd until at last his name was called. The judge asked if he had anything to say. He answered, "Yes." And as an expectant hush settled over the courtroom he added: "Blessed are the merciful for they shall obtain mercy."

The walls reverberated with delighted laughter. When order was restored the judge spoke: "All the circumstances considered, I give you a suspended sentence. Now I will say something to you I have long wanted to say to a clergyman." There was another hush. "Go thou and sin no more."

—Roscoe Brown Fisher

BRILLIANT BY CONTRAST

Clarence Budington Kelland was acting as master of ceremonies at a huge dinner party. The speakers' table was distressingly populous. Mr. Kelland got up, a slip of paper in his hand.

"Gentlemen," he began, "the obvious duty of a toastmaster is to be so infernally dull that the succeeding speakers will appear brilliant by contrast." The succeeding speakers began to chuckle heartily.

"I've looked over this list, however," added Kelland, "and I don't believe I can do it."

The speakers stopped chuckling and the diners bellowed.

—John Goldstrom

LEAVE THE MEETING ALIVE

To warn the speaker about a time limit.

In a town deep in the heart of Texas a visiting speaker had noticed, with slight concern, when he was introduced to his audience that some of the stalwart members carried holsters with guns. The fact made no impression upon him when he got to talking. He spoke forty minutes, fifty minutes, and continued beyond an hour. It was then, however, that the gun-toting members in the audience had a singular and frightening effect upon him; heretofore they had given him only passing concern. He noticed they had removed their guns from the holsters and were pointing the business ends of them in his general direction.

With his complacency somewhat disturbed, he stopped his speaking and turned to the chairman and asked if these men in the audience were "fixin'" to shoot him. The chairman said, "No, they're not fixin' to shoot you. They wouldn't be that discourteous. They're just fixin' to shoot the man who brought you here."

It is our policy in this club to close our meetings promptly at 1:30 and I warn you to watch our clock because I'd like to leave this meeting alive. —V. Spencer Goodreds

---

RESULTS

To be used as fill-in material when the audience might question the actions or procedure of the chairman.

I have often been asked why a chairman does this or that. It's like most other jobs. There are certain rules or regulations that govern the procedure. The results usually show how successfully these rules were adhered to.

Speaking of results, let's see what happened on Noah's Ark. One day Noah discovered a small leak in his boat, so he ordered the dog to stick his nose in the hole to stop the flow of water. The dog obeyed, but the hole grew bigger. Then Noah asked Mrs. Noah to place her big hands over the leak. She obeyed, but the hole grew bigger. As a last resort Noah himself sat on the hole.

My friends, what were the results? First, have you noticed today that a dog's nose is always cold? Also, a woman's hands are usually cold? And then, too, why does a man always stand with his back to a fire? —Arthur L. Kaser

HE DIDN'T REMEMBER

Our speaker here tonight has won quite a reputation because of his remarkable ability to remember names and faces. He tells me that he has cultivated this unique skill by developing a formula through association. I have been told on the side that it doesn't always work. I am reminded of the woman's absent-minded husband who was simply driving her frantic. She finally thought she had worked out a scheme which would help him to remember.

"Listen, Ernie," she said. "When you go downtown today I want you to deliver a message to Mr. McCormack. It's very important, so please don't forget it, dear. Remember the name. McCormack! It rhymes with 'stomach.' You know that big pot of yours—it's big enough for you to remember, for heaven's sake. If you'll remember the association—stomach, McCormack —I'm sure not even an absent-minded guy like you could go wrong."

Well, he came home late that night, and his wife asked: "Did you remember to deliver the message, dearest?"

"The message? The message? Oh, yes, darling. You know, I hunted all over town, but I simply couldn't find that fellow, Kelly."   —George A. Posner

---

FIVE MINUTES

Why should a speaker or a toastmaster consume fifteen minutes in making a five-minute speech? It seems Nat Goodwin, the famous actor, found the answer:

A stutterer once met the famous comedian, and asked, "Mr. G-G-Goodwin, c-c-can you g-g-give m-m-me f-f-fifteen m-m-minutes of y-y-your t-time?"

"Certainly," replied Mr. Goodwin. "What is it?"

"I want to have a f-f-five minutes' c-c-onversation w-w-with y-you."   —V. Spencer Goodreds

BEST OF ALL

The only introduction that I know that is beyond improvement is: "Ladies and Gentlemen . . . the President of the United States."

If you get him for a speaker, I'll be glad to come over and say those nine words.

—George Grim, News Commentator

INTRODUCING A BISHOP

A bishop of the Anglican Church had reached the occasion of his fiftieth wedding anniversary and the friends and clergy of his diocese had made the occasion a memorable event by giving him a golden wedding anniversary party. Among the guests attending was a very attractive young French girl, who was a little confused as to the purpose and meaning of the celebration, beyond knowing it had some vague connection with marriage.

Presently she came upon the bishop. He greeted her and expressed his delight at her presence at his golden wedding party. She then replied, "Oh, yes, thees golden wedding, I do not understand—what does thees mean?"

"Well, my dear young lady," said the bishop, "it simply means I have been living with the same lady for fifty years, and . . ." Before he could continue, she responded with an element of surprise.

"Ooh! I see! You have been leeving with thees same lady for feefty years, and now you are going to marry her."

—V. Spencer Goodreds

OLD STORIES

"Ladies and gentlemen: I shall not take your time tonight by boring you with the telling of old stories or 'chestnuts,' but I shall be very happy to introduce speakers who will."

—Joe Laurie, Jr.

NOT HELPING A BIT

A lady, after giving a census reporter all the necessary information regarding the family, such as names, ages, sex, was asked by the enumerator what the political faith of the family was.

She replied: "It is decidedly mixed. I am a Republican, my husband is a Democrat, the baby is Wet, the cow is Dry, and the dog is a Socialist."

"Why, Madam, why do you say your dog is a Socialist?"

"Because he does nothing but sit around all day and howl."

Our speaker today has a real message for us. We know that he has distinguished himself in his profession because of his intense devotion and application to duty. He's one man that hasn't had the time to "sit around all day and howl."

—Joseph W. Fordney

POOR TIMING

This story may be adapted to various situations by the chairman, especially when the speaker by coincidence is to speak on a subject that has just broken in the news.

Not too many years ago, a certain newscaster worked two jobs in a small eastern city. He spent his afternoons coaching the high school athletic teams and the early morning hours as a disc jockey and news announcer for the local radio station.

"Poor timing," he explains, "cost me my radio job. One morning I concluded the newscast by reading a story from the South telling how a pack of dogs broke loose from a dog catcher's wagon and raced crazily through the fields of a tobacco plantation.

"Course, there was nothing wrong with that report," he adds but then I followed it with a commercial that began quizzically: "Does your cigarette taste different lately?"

—Victorian Magazine

BRAINS IN YOUR STOMACH

A story, to be effective, either in an introduction or in a speech, must have application. I recall introducing a short man who was sensitive about his size. I told about the little judge who was running for re-election and a great big bruiser of a fellow was running against him. The big bruiser got up and turned toward the little judge on the platform saying, "You are such a little runt that I could swallow you up." The little judge got up and said: "If you did that, you would have more brains in your stomach than you have in your head!"
—Judge Luther W. Youngdahl, Washington, D. C.

LITTLE BULL

When I was president of the Odin Male Chorus, we had Oley Bull, a relative of the famous original Bull, as the piano soloist for the concert. After the concert, I introduced him to the assemblage at a buffet supper. He is a little fellow, but is packed full of dynamite when it comes to music, so when introducing him, I told the story of the three bulls seeking pasture.

The big bull came to a tremendous piece of pasture and took control there. The middle-sized bull came to a middle-sized piece of pasture and took control there. But the little bull just walked on and on and on—which only goes to show that a little bull goes a long, long way!
—Judge Luther W. Youngdahl, Washington, D. C.

WHILE ROME FIDDLED

To explain why a brief introduction is used

A well-known American author and lecturer who has an intense dislike of flowery introductions once had to sit through twenty-five minutes of commendation of his abilities and works by a chairman with the name of Rome. Finally, when the author-lecturer was called by the chairman to speak, he prefaced his remarks as follows:

"Ladies and gentlemen, I have just been burning while Rome fiddled."   —Julian L. Meltzer.

WHAT OTHERS ARE DOING

When introducing a speaker on business

In these days of extreme competition in all lines of business, we are indebted to our speaker who has consented to be here to tell us about trends in business in general and more specifically about recent developments in our own industry. I am reminded of the story about the rooster.

A large red rooster, who was the commander of his flock, found a hole under his own fence one afternoon, and strayed off into the adjoining barn lot. The neighboring lot happened to be an ostrich farm and while strolling around he chanced upon an ostrich egg. He didn't know what it was, but he pecked at it and found it would roll.

So he pecked again and again, and during the process rolled it down to the hole through which he had crawled, on through the hole and into his own barnyard. The hens gathered around to see what it was all about. Looking earnestly at his ladies the rooster said: "Girls, I haven't brought this here because I have any complaint to make, but in these days of competition I just wanted to show you what others are doing."

Our speaker tonight will tell us what others are doing.

—Wm. J. Woolley

LONG CREDIT

Our speaker today is the executive secretary of our local Credit Men's Association and is fully qualified to tell us what policies we should follow in extending credit to our customers.

I am reminded of the business man who in making his last will and testament for the distribution of his property turned to his lawyer and said: "There is just one other request that I wish to make. I want to name my pall bearers in my will." Whereupon he proceeded to name the six men.

"This," said the attorney, "is an odd request, and I am very much interested to know if these men are particular friends of yours?" The business man informed the attorney that they were not. In fact, he said that some of them were not even friendly. "Why, then, do you name them as pall bearers?"

The business man replied: "You see, it's like this. These men are all wholesalers, and have been carrying me all my life, and I want them to carry me to the end."

—Wm. J. Woolley

BRILLIANT FATHER
When introducing a minister

Three small boys were earnestly discussing the ability of their respective fathers. The son of a song writer said: "My father can come home in the evening and sit down and write a song, and take it downtown the next morning and sell it for twenty-five dollars."

"But my dad," eagerly spoke up the son of a short story writer, "can write a story in an evening and take it down the next morning and sell it for fifty dollars."

The preacher's son was puzzled for a moment, then he had an inspiration. "My father," he said, "gets up into the pulpit and talks half an hour. And it takes twelve men to carry the money up to him."

We have that third father here today as our speaker. He has endeared himself to all the people of the community and is one of our most successful preachers in this city. Of course we know that his church is always filled to capacity and in gratitude to his splendid messages, I have no doubt that it really takes twelve men to carry up the collection. —Rev. John Barlow

THE NERVOUS CHAIRMAN

Ladies and gentlemen, all of you know that it's a new experience for me to act as your chairman. At this moment I feel just like the college student who was to deliver a memorized oration. He started off with courage: "Washington is dead. Lincoln is dead." He got this far when everything went blank, he stopped, embarrassed of course, and said in a weak voice: "And I—I'm beginning to feel pretty sick myself!"

—Lawrence M. Brings

KEEP THE INTRODUCTION SHORT

I believe it is better for a chairman to curb his desire to talk a lot. Make the preliminaries short. It takes up a lot of time and nothing is gained.

A farmer entered a restaurant in a large city and asked: "What are the hours for meals here?" He was informed that breakfast was served from seven to eleven, dinner from eleven to three, and supper from three to eight. The customer looked puzzled. "But," he said, "I came here to see the town, not to eat all day long."   —Arthur L. Kaser

ONE CONSOLATION

When the chairman garbles his phrasing in an embarrassing manner

Pardon me for meaning what I didn't say—I mean for saying what I didn't say—Isn't it awful when you say something so beautiful and it comes out so rotten? But there is one consolation. It happens to everybody some time or another.

A very eminent American visited England. On his return to this country he was asked if he did any shooting while there. "Oh, yes," he replied. "I did quite a bit of shooting. It was great fun, too, when I shot at Lord Baddleton's country seat, but I missed it."   —Arthur L. Kaser

PROFANE SILENCE

When introducing a minister

The other day on one of our golf courses a distinguished clergyman who happens to be our speaker today was playing a closely-contested game of golf. He carefully teed up his ball and addressed it with the most approved grace; he raised his driver and hit the ball a tremendous clip, but instead of soaring into the azure it perversely went about twelve feet to the right and then buzzed around in a circle. The clergyman frowned, scowled, pursed up his mouth, and bit his lips, but said nothing, and a friend who stood by him said: "Doctor, that is the most profane silence I ever witnessed."

—Frederic A. Ward

HOW FAST CAN WE TRAVEL?

When the speaker is late in arriving

I apologize for putting pressure on everyone today to shorten the announcements because I wanted to be sure that we did not encroach on the speaker's allotted time. Now that I am ready to actually introduce the speaker, I find that he hasn't yet arrived. I am reminded of a personal observation that aptly illustrates how much this looks like a rehearsal.

Visiting a friend in the hospital, I saw a car scream into the hospital's emergency entrance, slam to a stop. An excited young man jumped out, took the steps three at a time, spun through the revolving door.

"What's the trouble, sir?" asked an anxious nurse.

"My wife's going to have a baby."

"Well, bring her in."

"Oh, the baby isn't due for another month. I'm just timing myself to see how fast we can get here!" —Airston T. Scott

---

OFF THE SUBJECT

When the subject before the meeting is getting off on a tangent

Gentlemen: It appears to me that we're getting way off the track. We started out with a simple little proposal. But what has happened? We have rambled off this way and that way, until we are a long way from our starting point.

In this connection we are like the camper who went out west. He drew his car alongside of a road, took out his coffee pot and pulled an egg out of a bag. Then he proceeded to prepare his dinner. But there was only a very small amount of wood on hand, just enough to boil the coffee. But how about the egg? There was no more fire and he had to fry the egg. So the ingenious camper set fire to the prairie grass, and then holding the frying pan over the blazing grass, he followed the fire, keeping the pan over the flames.

"A-ha," said the camper, "the egg is beginning to fry."

Then the camper looked around and discovered that he was a mile away from the coffee pot.—Harold Butterworth

THAT REMINDS ME!

When the chairman or the speaker reminds his audience to remember something important

Gentlemen: We are changing the date of our meetings from Tuesday to Thursday, beginning the first of the month. I hope that you will all bear that in mind. In order that you won't forget, try to associate Thursday with some important fact. For instance, our meetings are now held on Tuesday, and next week they will be held on Thursday. So take this as an example: Tuesday begins with a "T." Our new meeting day also begins with a "T." What is the only other day of the week beginning with a "T"? Thursday. Simple as that.

Or if that doesn't work, try to think of some other association like the fellow did who was listening to the radio. The newscaster was giving a graphic description of an earthquake in California. The newscaster shouted: "The walls rattled and crumbled. Furniture was smashed to smithereens. Dishes flew in all directions . . ."

"Good heavens!" exclaimed the man. "That reminds me, I forgot to mail my wife's letter."

—Dale Farnsworth.

BUSY CHAIRMAN

I have been the chairman at so many of these banquets and public functions lately that I feel that I should bow out of these duties. I am convinced that I must do so soon, particularly after the reception my wife gave me the other night at dinner.

After we were all seated at the table, she rapped for order and in her most gracious manner said: "Children, we have with us tonight a guest of whom we have all heard, even if we do not know him personally. He is a man who has a reputation for good humor at every luncheon club in the city. This evening we have the honor and pleasure of being numbered among the admirers of this entertaining man. It is with great pleasure that I present to you—your father!"

—James Nolan

POKEY TACTICS

When the chairman tries to speed up the meeting

We are certainly progressing with the business of this meeting in a very slow manner. At the rate we are going, we'll be here all night. John Thompson seems to think that we have nothing to do but talk about his issue. We have other matters on the agenda, and I wish that John would complete his so that we may proceed with the remainder of the program.

John's pokey tactics remind me of the fellow who went up in the country to buy a horse. He selected an old wreck of a nag with spavined legs, which was ready for the soap factory. Its ribs were caved in and its backbone swayed like a hammock. While the purchaser was practically pushing the nag up the street, a country rube called out: "Hey, Mister, what are you going to do with that horse?"

The fellow with the horse cupped his hands and yelled: "I'm going to race him."

The country wag put his hands on his hips and yelled back: "You'll beat him!"   —Anton C. Wade

MISUNDERSTANDING

When a speaker or chairman finds a misunderstanding about the date of a meeting

We are having considerable difficulty in getting over to our membership the time of our regular meeting. I called up Jack Brown and told him that our meeting was to be held on Monday. Jack missed the last meeting, because he said that he thought it was Tuesday.

Many others seem to be laboring under the same misunderstanding, which reminds me of a story about three Englishmen who were driving through a village in a convertible, the wind howling in their ears. Said one Englishman above the wind of the open car, "Is this Windbly?" "No, this is Thursday," said the second. "So am I," said the third, "Let's stop in and have one."   —Howard C. Wilford

LAID END TO END

According to the bureau of statistics, there were over three million persons who acted as chairmen last year. In fact, if the chairmen in this country were laid end to end— (pause) —it might be a good idea!   —Harold Gregory

SPEECH RECIPE FOR CHAIRMEN

Here's a good recipe to follow in a speech of introduction. Consult the speaker for his subject. Write down all his qualifications for discussing the subject. Learn his correct name. Bring to a boil in less than one minute.

—Harold Gregory

GETTING ACQUAINTED

The agreeable chore I have of introducing our speaker reminds me of the story of the boy and girl who met for the first time on Monday and were married the following day, Tuesday. The sudden wedding prompted someone to remark: "Well, that's one way of getting acquainted!" And here's another pleasant way of getting acquainted. Ladies and gentlemen, meet our speaker, Mr. —————. Mr. —————, meet the ladies and gentlemen.   —Leo McDonald

POSSIBLE RETALIATION

A well-known speaker once said that a toastmaster or chairman was a man who eats a meal he doesn't want so he can get up and tell a lot of stories he doesn't remember to people who have heard them before and then proceeds to introduce a man they all know. So, bearing that in mind as a warning against possible retaliation, I'll make my introduction as brief as possible. Ladies and gentlemen, our speaker, Mr. —————.

—Robert Kaercher

NEXT TIME I'LL SAY I'M A BANKER

This story may be used when introducing a teacher, educator, or professor.

Two summers ago I took an automobile trip through the New England states. But for one unfortunate occurrence, it was a happy and agreeable vacation. As I was driving down the highway, approaching a small village, I inadvertently ran through a red light. It was just my luck that a traffic cop was behind me, who promptly gave me a ticket which commanded me to make an appearance before the local judge.

I nervously went into the courtroom and stood up when my name was called.

"Ahem," said the judge, looking down at me over his spectacles. "What is your occupation?" he asked in the manner that all judges ask questions.

For a moment I thought the matter over, as I was a stranger in town and, of course, no one there would know my occupation. I was trying to think of some poorly paid profession which might prompt the judge to set the fine at a low figure, if not dismiss the case entirely. My mind rambled along until I mentally came to a schoolteacher—the poorest paid profession of all. Surely this judge won't soak a school teacher over a dollar for an offense like this. So I stood up to the court and cried out proudly, "I'm a schoolteacher."

The sound of the word "schoolteacher" seemed to have an electric effect upon the judge. He almost leaped out of his chair. His eyes lighted up like a neon sign. He was almost hilarious.

"My man," he said, "I have been waiting thirty years for this opportunity, but without success until you visited our fair city. I have been hoping and praying for all of these years that a schoolteacher would be hauled before my tribunal of justice. I have an old score that I have to settle."

Then with judicial dignity he issued the sentence. "Sit down there," he said, "and write 'I went through a red light' five hundred times."
　　　　　　　　　　　　　　　　　　　—Jack Cosgrove

SPEAKER ARRIVING LATE
When the speaker arrives late

I am happy to announce that our speaker has finally arrived and while his unavoidable tardiness has caused a little delay in the proceedings I'd like to take a couple of minutes more of your time to tell a little story.

A colored man who was driving a mule hitched to a small cart on a country road came to a crossroads where a white man was standing. "Whoa, mule," the colored man said. "'Scuse me, please suh, but kin you tell how far it is to Memphis?" "Fourteen miles," said the white man. "Yes, suh, thank you, suh," said the colored man. "Git up, mule."

He drove for a couple of hours and came to another crossroads where there was another white man standing. "Whoa, mule," he said. "'Scuse me, please suh, but kin you tell me how far it is to Memphis?" "Fourteen miles," said the white man. "Yes, suh, thank you, suh. Git up, mule."

He drove for several hours more and came to another crossroads, where still another white man was standing. "Whoa, mule. 'Scuse me, please suh, but kin you tell me how far it is to Memphis?" "Just fourteen miles from this corner," the white man told him. "Yes, suh, thank you, suh. Fourteen miles. Git up, mule. Well, at least we're holding our own!"

And I think our speaker should know that's what we've been doing while we were waiting for him—just trying to hold our own. Now that he's arrived I think we're all happy to know that now we're actually going to get some place. Ladies and gentlemen, our speaker, Mr. ——————.

—D. W. Curtis

LONG-WINDED SPEAKER

Ladies and gentlemen, the request to introduce the speaker who has just finished speaking came unexpectedly and caught me off guard. I usually have at least a two-hour introductory speech prepared beforehand, but this time I was unable to prepare anything. However, I am happy to note that our speaker more than made up for the brevity of my opening remarks.

—James Leeson

THE BEST YOU CAN

In introducing our speaker I'd really like to say something very brilliant—something you would appreciate and remember —but I find myself at a loss for words. Instead I'll tell you the story about the judge who had just sentenced a man to jail for twenty years.

The man said: "Judge, I'm a sick man. I'll never live through it. I can't do twenty years."

The judge said: "Don't let it get you down, son. Just do the best you can." So that's what I'm doing now—the best I can. My friends, allow me to present our speaker, Mr. ———.

—James Leeson

SOUVENIR

A novel treatment in making an introduction

(The chairman picks up a thick stack of papers.) Ladies and gentlemen, (Indicating the thick stack of papers.) I have here a few words which I have written as a sort of preface to my introduction of our next speaker. (Looks over the papers. Then clears his throat as though he were going to start reading from the papers.) Now to begin, I'm going to create something new in introductions. Tonight I'm simply going to introduce our speaker, and while I know you're going to be greatly disappointed, I'm not going to read this. (Indicates the stack of papers.) However, if any of you are interested in my prepared introduction, just drop me a letter enclosing postage at the rate of three cents an ounce and I'll be glad to send you a copy to glance at during your leisure or to keep as a souvenir. Ladies and gentlemen, our speaker, Mr. ————.

—Earl Jay Gilbert

DICTIONARY AND TWO ASPIRINS

Ladies and gentlemen, as I understand it our next speaker is going to give us a dissertation on a very deep and complicated subject. Usually, when contingencies of this sort arise I first introduce the speaker and then give each listener a dictionary and two aspirin tablets. However, as this gentleman is thoroughly familiar with his subject and has promised not to use words that are over six syllables, I am going to omit the dictionary and the aspirins.   —Leo McDonald

---

FIRST TALKING MACHINE

Explanation for giving a short introduction

We've all been bored by chairmen who never seem to know when to stop when making an introduction. So instead of indulging in any lengthy oratory regarding our next speaker I'm going to relate an anecdote about a long-winded chairman who introduced Thomas Edison at a gathering many years ago.

After making many references to Mr. Edison as the inventor of the first talking machine, the chairman finally quit and sat down. The famous inventor said, in acknowledging the introduction: "Mr. Chairman, while I deeply appreciate your flattering remarks, I feel that I should call your attention to an error in your statements. I did not invent the first talking machine. God invented that. The machine I invented is the first one that can be easily shut off." So you may consider me shut off, while we listen to the gentleman who is going to address us. Ladies and gentlemen, let me present Mr. ————.
                                    —Robert Kaercher

SOMETHING ORIGINAL

In deference to our next speaker it has been suggested that in my introductory remarks I say something original. I've wracked my brain but I cannot seem to think of anything original, so I'm going to shift the responsibility to our speaker's shoulders and let him have the opportunity of saying something original. I'm sure he will welcome and appreciate the challenge. Mr. ————, you're on your own.
                                    —Paul Weston

WHEN THE SPEAKER ARRIVES LATE

Ladies and gentlemen, our speaker has arrived. I am reminded of the story of the farmer who was working on a hot day in a distant field when his hired man rushed up to him and said excitedly: "Mr. Jones, your wife has just died!"

The farmer ran home and found his wife lying on the floor, but it seems she had only had a fainting spell, so after she recovered consciousness he went back to work.

Shortly after his hired man rushed up again. "Mr. Jones, your wife has just died!" The farmer hastened back home again, and found she had had another fainting spell.

After she recovered consciousness he trudged back to work, only to be interrupted again by the hired man with the same news. He rushed back home again, but this time he found she was really dead. "Well," said the farmer, "this is more like it!"

And now that our speaker has finally arrived, I'll repeat the farmer's comment—which I know you'll all heartily endorse—this is more like it! Ladies and gentlemen, our speaker, Mr. ——————.   —D. W. Curtis

---

BROTHER, WHERE ARE MY CLOTHES?

The job of being a chairman at public meetings sometimes becomes embarrassing. Several years ago I received an invitation to act as toastmaster at a nudist colony dinner. Now that was a strange request, and for some time I deliberated on whether or not I should accept the offer. I had acted as chairman of ladies' club meetings, GAR conventions and for other varied groups in the past. So I decided I would make the complete cycle and I agreed to emcee the nudist dinner. In fact, I looked forward to it once I had made up my mind.

Throughout the whole week, I tried to visualize myself up at the speaker's table, introducing Miss Greenleaf, without the leaf, a crowd of Adam and Eve's. And, of course, I would have to accept the custom of the cult and appear as they did. All week long I practiced in the bathroom before the mirror, making bows, gesticulating and wiping the cigar ashes off my bare chest.

On the evening of the dinner I felt that I was in proper form to officiate at the ceremonies. So I hastened out to the camp and was ushered into a waiting room where I was informed that when a buzzer flashed, it would be the signal for me to make an entry to the banquet hall.

I quickly undressed and eagerly awaited the call. Soon it came—a long buzz. I rushed through the door out of breath and into the brilliantly lighted dining room. Imagine my horrification when I, standing on the podium attired only in my birthday clothes, discovered that the guests, each and every one assembled were attired in "soup and fish" or swishing gowns!

—Kenneth Seaman

TOO LAZY TO STOP

Last month I was acting as chairman of a meeting over in one of our adjoining states. It was quite a large meeting, and the audience was receptive. Among others on the speaking program was a United States senator from one of the western states.

When it came time to introduce this man, I calculated that his prominence in world affairs required that I spend a little more time on him than usual. So I went to great efforts to point out to the audience the noble character of the man. It appears that I lapsed into some sort of coma, as I was told afterwards that I talked on for an hour, much to the embarrassment of the senator who was squeaming in his chair and throwing me looks with ulterior meanings.

Somehow or other I finally came to the conclusion of my introduction. The Senator jumped up from his chair, walked over to the rostrum and as he passed me, he said to me under his breath, "The trouble with you is that when you start, you're too darn lazy to stop."

—Robert Walgreen

DIRTY LINEN

One day last summer I was freshening up in the wash room of the Athletic Club, preparatory to going up to the twelfth floor, where I was going to act as a master of ceremonies for a Red Cross dinner.

I noticed that the towel with which I was wiping my hands did not appear to be clean. So I called George, the attendant.

"George," I said, "What is the matter with this towel? It looks dirty."

George took the towel and examined it closely. "I can't see anything wrong with it, Mr. Jones. Looks perfectly clean to me," said George.

"But it smells like fish," I exclaimed.

George flopped his whisk broom back and forth in his hands and began to dust off the back of my coat. He then quietly remarked, "Perhaps you have been using it previously."

—William Hurley

MELTING POINT

Last month I was acting as chairman at a meeting in the southern part of the state. We had at that time a speaker who I considered one of the finest orators in this section of the country. At times he is a regular Daniel Webster, and then upon other occasions, he delivers a very smooth, unemotional lecture.

At this particular meeting he was wound up. He soared off into the clouds and then swooped down upon his listeners with the fury of a thunderbolt. He pitched his voice to such a voluminous roar that at times the microphone cracked, and he emphasized every pertinent point with a menacing gesture. All in all, his speech was terrific. He electrified his audience.

When he had retaken his seat along side of me, I leaned over to him and said, "You sure were on fire tonight."

The speaker wiped the perspiration from his forehead and chin, looked over to me and said: "I had need of fire tonight, for I had icebergs around me to melt."

—Earle Howard

THREE SMACKS

So that I would be in good shape for the dinner tonight, where my wits would be taxed introducing all this evening's illustrious speakers, this afternoon I took a Turkish bath and a rub.

It was while I was steaming away in the bath, the perspiration flowing off me like the Dixie dew, I worked out my introductions. But that is not the point that I am driving at. After I had finished my bath, a huge bulk of a man with hands as big as hams pounded away on my muscles, twisted my legs and arms, cracked my neck and kneaded my stomach. I got up from the table feeling as fit as a race horse. As I started to walk away, this giant of a man let go with his mammoth hand on my bottom—three resounding smacks that stung like the bite of a bee and resounded throughout the bath chamber like the cracking of a rifle.

"See here, man!" I exclaimed. "What's the idea?"

"Think nothing of it," replied the Herculean individual. "Our bell is out of order and those three smacks are the signal to the outer office to send in the next patient."

—Harry Schultz

STEALING THUNDER

The list of humorous speakers on this evening's program brings back to my memory an event of some time ago that brought me some embarrassment. I was acting as toastmaster of a celebrated dinner at that time, and the principal speaker on the agenda was a famous humorist—a man known for his wit.

In making my introduction of the speaker, I dwelt for some length on his particular type of humor. I became so intrigued with the subject that I talked longer than usual. And I realized afterwards that I was encroaching upon his time—and his subject.

When I had finally concluded the introduction with elaborate phrases and praises, the speaker stood up to the microphone. I saw at once that he was indignant.

In a loud voice full of rancor he said: "I had planned to give a lecture to this audience on the topic of 'Wit and Humor' which has been thoroughly covered by the chairman in his introduction. Consequently, there is no further need of talking about 'Wit and Humor.' I will therefore confine my speech to the very interesting subject of 'How to Raise Wheat.'"

—Charles Foley

THE RESULT OF LONG-WINDED SPEECHES

A few years ago I was acting as chairman at a gathering of this nature. During the course of the meeting, which was well attended, it was decided to take up a cash subscription for a children's room in our local hospital. I was appointed to lead the speaking, pleading for donations, which would be deposited in a basket that was to be passed through the audience.

I worked myself up to a feverish pitch. Dramatically, I pointed out the dire straits of our little children. I rose to great heights of oratory, dwelling upon the wonderful benefits that would come to the little ones through the generosity of my listeners. I begged. I pleaded. I talked for an hour. And when I had completed this excellent speech, the basket was passed.

At the conclusion of the meeting, I walked down the street with my friend, Bill Jones. As we were stepping along the sidewalk at a good clip, on the way to pick up our cars, Bill said to me, "That was a long-winded speech you made tonight, Jim."

"Long-winded, did you say?" I said with surprise.

"Exceedingly long-winded," said Bill. "When you first started to talk I had in mind placing $25 in the basket. After you had spoken for half an hour, I mentally reduced my donation to $10. When you continued to ramble on for three-quarters of an hour, I decided that $1 would be enough."

"Well," I said, "How much did you put in?"

Bill looked at me and smiled . . . one of those devilish smiles . . . and quietly said: "Jim, you talked me completely out of it. After listening to you for an hour, my sympathy for the movement had completely vanished. So I reached in and took out a quarter."

—Gus Strauss

FOR A CHAIRMAN WITH A MUSTACHE

Most people can wear a mustache and nobody pays any attention to it. However, it is just the contrary with me. My mustache is constantly being referred to as a "soup-strainer," a "hairbrush," and other uncomplimentary comparisons.

Some years ago I was a chairman at a Chinese Tong dinner. It was a most elaborate affair, consisting of at least forty courses. A prominent Chinaman from the old country who was a frequent visitor to the United States sat at my right. During the course of the dinner, we conversed with each other about various subjects. Finally, the question of pigtails came up and I said to the Chinese businessman: "I am glad to hear that the practice of wearing pigtails on the part of the Chinese is beginning to become dissipated. That's a silly custom, that of wearing pigtails," I added.

"Not so silly," replied the Chinaman, between spoonfuls of soup which he was scooping up with great relish.

"It looks silly to me," I said.

The Chinaman put down his spoon, pushed his empty soup bowl over to one side of the table and pointing to my mustache said, "Why do you wear that silly mustache?"

"Well," I said trying to think up a reason. "I've got a monstrous mouth."

The Chinaman pulled over his cup of tea and just before he sipped the brew remarked tersely, "I should think so, judging from your remarks."   —Earle Howard

---

FOR A TALL CHAIRMAN

People are continuously cracking wise about my height. As I passed through the door of this hall this evening, a bystander cried out, "Duck." However, I try to take advantage of my height whenever possible. Last week, I and the president of the concern with which I am employed took a business trip together. As we boarded the plane at the airport, each of us carried a briefcase; our regular baggage, of course, having been checked at the ticket counter.

We walked into the plane and approached the front part of the ship. There we selected two agreeable seats, and prepared ourselves for a comfortable trip. Before we had strapped on our safety belts, the president of the company (whose name was John) made several attempts to put his briefcase in the package shelf that girds the inside of the plane. Being a short man, he had difficulty reaching up to it. I immediately came to his assistance, saying: "Let me put your case up there, John; I am higher than you."

The president of the firm looked up at me with a frown and said emphatically, "Jim . . . you are longer."

—Earle Howard

ABSENT-MINDED

I have been acting as chairman at so many meetings of this kind that I am becoming absent-minded. I suppose that it is brought about by the deep concentration that is required in arranging the agenda night after night, and the brain-searching work that one is obliged to do, thinking up something to say about all the speakers.

Of late my absent-mindedness is becoming acute. One night last week I arrived home from a meeting quite late. All of the way home I was thinking about what I should have said and didn't say, and about the various boners that I had made in connection with the introductions.

I walked up to my own front door and searched in my pockets for the key. Not being able to find it, I knocked on the door. An upstairs window flew open and my maid stuck out her head. "Mr. Jones is not at home this evening," she said.

"Very well," I answered meekly, and as I turned away, I yelled up to my own maid, "Tell him that I will call another time."

—Rex Murphy

FOR A BIG CHAIRMAN

People have accused me, on account of my huge proportions, of bluffing my way through a meeting. I tried those tactics once and they failed. Last month at a gathering in the northern part of the state, over which I presided, I was obliged to introduce a speaker of diminutive size. I thought that I would try a new stunt on this half-pint. And he was a half-pint . . . he weighed three pounds less than a straw hat. So I said, "Ladies and gentlemen, the next speaker on the program is so small physically that I could swallow him and I'd never know I ate a thing."

This brought the house down. The little fellow got up—we had to stand him on a chair so that he could see the audience—and said, "If the chairman has any idea about swallowing me, it might be a good thing for the chairman, for in that case he'd have more brains in his belly than he's got in his head."

—Earle Howard

DUST 'EM OFF

At a meeting over which I presided several years ago, a vigorous debate developed over a very minor matter. Feeling was running high and the membership was about equally divided. I personally had taken a definite stand on one side of the question.

For over an hour we debated the subject. Speaker after speaker took the rostrum and filled the air with oratory. Finally, I called upon my ace in the hole—Charley Johnson, by far the best talker in the room. After I had given Charley the floor, I went over to him and whispered in his ear, "Give 'em hell, Charley!"

Charley turned around to me and said quietly, "Why use dynamite when insect powder will do?" —George Dixon

NO CHOICE

A short time ago I was the chairman of a meeting in which a heated debate took place on the subject of atheism. I don't know just how it all started, but one fellow, who said that he was an atheist got to his feet and started a harangue on the topic. Others joined him, but the majority attempted to hoot him down. For some time pandemonium held sway and it was with great difficulty that I was able to hold any control whatsoever over the group.

While all of the excitement was in progress, I noticed that a fellow sitting at one of the front tables had not said a word. Turning to him I inquired, "Are you an atheist or a Deist?"

"Neither," was the reply, "I'm a dentist."

—Howard Fulton

TRIED AND TRUSTED

Last winter I was sitting beside Mr. Julius Strong, the celebrated banker. Throughout the course of the dinner we carried on a conversation about various things. Feeling inclined to impress Mr. Strong about my knowledge of his banking staff, I said, just as I had completed munching an olive, "I know Mr. Brown of your banking house. I have always understood that he is a tried and trusted employee."

Banker Strong, suspended his spoonful of soup in mid-air, turned to me and tartly replied, "He was trusted, that is correct. He will be tried when we catch him."

—Gus Strauss

WIND

A fellow speaker of mine, who is quite popular as a master of ceremonies, came to me one day and showed me a copy of a speech that he was going to make before an important meeting. I took his manuscript and sat down in an easy chair, where I leisurely went over it, word for word. When I had concluded analyzing his proposed talk, my friend said to me, "Bill, what do you think of it?"

I handed him back his typewritten copy and frankly remarked, "Harry, I hate to say this, but it's all wind."

Harry looked strangely at me as he folded his speech and put it in his pocket, and then he softly said, "Bill, an automobile tire is filled with nothing but wind, but it makes a car run nice and smooth."

—William Brower

GOOD ADVICE

When a chairman tries to disentangle a mixed-up meeting

Gentlemen, we're all snarled-up. We started out in orderly procedure trying to get somewhere with the business of this meeting. We were attempting to adopt a simple resolution. But now what have we got? So many amendments have been presented, that at this time it is impossible to identify the original proposal introduced here tonight . . . which brings to my mind a story:

In some distant year ahead a series of atomic bombs exploded, completely wiping man from the face of the earth. Every tree, every twig, every blade of grass was gone. There was nothing left but desolation.

In a remote part of Africa, two monkeys emerged from a cave and looked around perplexedly at the wasted earth. "Not a tree to swing from," the male monkey said to his mate.

"Nothing," answered the mate.

"Well," said the male monkey in deep thought, "there's nothing to do but start all over again."

(Pause)

I feel that is good advice. Let's start all over again.

—Hugh Lincoln.

SATISFACTORY REPLACEMENT

When a substitute speaker is secured

Ladies and gentlemen, due to unforeseen and unavoidable circumstances the gentleman who was to address us tonight has been forced to make a last-minute cancellation, but fortunately we have been able to secure the services of another excellent speaker, whose talk I'm sure you will find interesting, entertaining and enjoyable.

This situation reminds me of a little story. A colored man walked into the County Clerk's office in a small Southern community and asked for a marriage license. The clerk said: "Where's the girl you're going to marry?" The colored man said: "Just look out the window. She's sittin' there in that wagon."

The clerk looked out and saw a colored woman in a wagon surrounded by eight or ten children of assorted sizes. "Whose children are they?" he asked. "They're ours," said the colored man. The clerk said: "It took you a long time to get here, didn't it?" "Yes, suh," said the Negro. "The road was pretty rough."

And my friends, the road has been pretty rough for us also, telephoning, sending telegrams, scurrying around trying to find a satisfactory replacement for the gentleman who was to speak originally. But I know you'll find our replacement a more than satisfactory substitute and I really take great pleasure in introducing Mr. —————————.   —D. W. Curtis

GLAD TO SEE YOU

Whenever I'm called upon to introduce a person of prominence I'm reminded of the story about the Governor of a certain state who for years had used the same speech, with little variation, whenever he was called upon to make an address.

It seems he was called upon to talk to the inmates of the state penitentiary. Facing the assembled convicts the Governor cleared his throat and began his talk with: "Fellow citizens . . ." He was interrupted by a roar of laughter from the prison audience. The Governor started again: "I mean, fellow convicts . . ." The laughter was really uproarious this time. The Governor started again: "What I really mean to say is—I'm glad to see so many of you here." That tore it.

The Governor made a hasty exit, to probably the greatest applause and yells of laughter he had ever received in his career. It probably cured him of making the same set speech whenever he addressed a gathering, but I can assure you that the gentleman who is now going to address you always prepares a new speech for every occasion and I know you'll enjoy hearing him. My friends, may I present our speaker, Mr. —————————?   —Robert Kaercher

GODSPEED

When the speaker has been delayed

My friends, as you know, our speaker has been delayed. But we have a pleasant surprise for you. We are going to have another excellent speaker fill in until the gentleman arrives. He's a man you all know and like. You'll enjoy listening to our surprise speaker.

Talking about surprises, reminds me of the Sister of Charity who was walking down the street when a man stopped her and handed her a one-hundred-dollar bill, and asked her to give it to the first impoverished person she met. She said she'd be glad to, and continued on her way.

A block or so farther she passed a man standing in a doorway. He was ragged and dishevelled. He badly needed a shave and haircut, his shirt was soiled and torn, his toes stuck out from his worn-out shoes. She sized him up for a moment, then handed him the hundred-dollar bill and said: "Godspeed, my friend." He took the bill and said: "Thank you, Sister."

The next day she was walking down the same street and the same grimy individual stepped out of his doorway and handed her a roll of bills. "Here, Sister," he said. "Eleven hundred bucks. Godspeed won and paid ten to one."

We'll take it for granted that the good Sister was considerably surprised, but that's nothing compared to the big surprise our substitute speaker is going to get when I call upon him. He doesn't even know yet that he's going to be called upon!

However, knowing how quickly the gentleman responds to an emergency, I'm sure he'll forgive this sudden request and help us out. I now call upon a man who knows he will have our sincere gratitude and appreciation by taking over from here. My friends, I present Mr. —————.

—D. W. Curtis

KNOWING EVERYTHING

Here's a little story to start with. A man was walking down the street with his seven-year-old grandson and they passed a colored woman. The little boy, who had never seen a colored woman before, said: "Grandfather, look at that woman—her face is all dirty." "No, Willie," said the grandfather, "that's her natural color. Black." "Is she black all over?" asked the boy. "Yes, Willie," the old man replied, "She's black all over." "Gee, Grandfather," said the boy, "You know **everything,** don't you?"

Now, while I'm not like the boy's grandfather—I don't know everything—but I do know that we are now going to hear an excellent address well worth listening to. Ladies and gentlemen, may I introduce our speaker, Mr. ——————?

—Robert Kaercher

KEEP IT CLEAN

Suggested for a little fun at a businessmen's informal gathering

I know you'll be glad to learn that we're now going to hear from a man, who, at a moment's notice, will talk to us on any subject mentioned in this list. (Reads from list: the popcorn industry in Liberia, the political situation in Portugal, how to make Scotch whiskey from spinach, or any other ridiculous fancies.) Now if you gentlemen will call out your choice from this list, I'll have our speaker address you on the subject. (After the subject is chosen.) Fine. Now for our speaker. I'm going to call upon the gentleman to give us a fast five-minute discourse on (Subject.) Mr. —————— (Selects the most timid and retiring man in the group.) up and at 'em—and keep it clean!

—James Leeson

FALSE HOPES

I had the pleasure of acting as master of ceremonies at an important wedding one day last summer. My old friend, Bill Owens, was the lucky bridegroom. Bill is a nephew of old man Todd and sole heir to the old man's large fortune. But old man Todd was a tight old fellow, and very few of the old man's handouts came Bill's way.

But to get back to the wedding. It was a gala gala affair, conducted in the height of fashion, with a huge dinner afterwards, and, of course, the customary run of speeches. That is where I came in, presiding at the speaker's table.

After half a dozen of Bill's friends had taken the floor and extended congratulations and compliments, I called on old man Todd. But as the old man's talk is not a part of this story, I will skip over it. Before the old man took to his feet, I had been chatting with him.

"Mr. Todd," I said, "Bill's a fine fellow."

"He certainly is," said the old man.

"He's got a beautiful wife," I added.

"Very pretty," said the old man.

When I had warmed the old man up this far I said, "Mr. Todd, you ought to do something exceptional in the way of a wedding gift for this very fine couple, especially when one considers that Bill is your nephew and only heir."

Old man Todd stroked his whiskers, and then with the devil in his eyes, leaned over and whispered in my ear, "I'm going to. As soon as this confounded dinner is over, I'm going to fake being awfully sick."   —Jack Cosgrove

---

AUDIENCE LEFT BEFORE SPEAKER

One of the trying problems of being a chairman at a public gathering is that of handling a young speaker who is making his first appearance before an audience. Usually this young fellow is scared to death. For a whole week he has rehearsed his speech in the bathroom, and during the time of his rehearsals he knows the entire speech word for word. But when he gets up to the speaker's table, ah, that is a different matter. Usually he becomes tongue-tied. His memory is a blank. He stutters, hems and haws and then sits down. It is the duty of the chairman to smooth the way for such a young fellow so that he will get off to some kind of a flying start.

I had just such an experience at my last meeting. A young man sat down for dinner at the head table. He was introduced to me as Jack Brown, who was scheduled to make the principal address of the evening. During the course of the dinner I watched Jack intensely. He was so nervous that he couldn't hold a spoonful of soup. He cut his steak with trembling hands, and his salad was splattered all over the table cloth, with traces of it on his cuffs.

After the dinner had been completed, I turned over to him and said, "Jack, do you know what it is to go before an audience?"

"No," said the lad meekly, "I spoke before an audience once, but most of it went before I did."   —Adolph Hintz

---

TRANSLATOR

At one time, I had the pleasure of introducing two distinguished speakers at a Scandinavian dinner. One of the speakers spoke in English, the other in Swedish.

Neither man was acquainted with the other. The fellow who delivered his talk in English got to the rostrum first, and gave a lengthy discourse on a very interesting subject. When he had concluded and regained his seat, there was little or no applause. Then the Swedish fellow mounted the platform, after a suitable introduction by myself, and flew into a momentous piece of oratory, gesticulating the pertinent points and otherwise conducting himself like a seasoned elocutionist. When he finished the applause was deafening.

Perplexed, the English speaker turned to me and said, "What in the world was that Swedish fellow talking about that he should get such an ovation?"

"He was translating your speech into Swedish," I said with a smile.   —Earle Burr

THE TABLE'S TURNED

There are times when a chairman faces an obstreperous audience, particularly if the meeting is of a political nature. I had one such experience in the southern part of the state last fall. My audience got out of hand, not only when the speakers were performing, but also while I was making the introductions.

As I was rambling along with an introduction of a speaker, naming his good points and throwing in a humorous phrase here and there, a fellow in the rear of the hall let out a big howl. When the first resounding screech echoed throughout the room, I ignored it and continued with my introduction. But after the second shriek and the third one disturbed the atmosphere, I lost my patience.

"Gentlemen," I said, "It seems that this audience is packed with fools. Wouldn't it be better to hear one at a time?"

Again a voice rang out from the back of the room: "All right. Get on with your speech."   —Anthony C. Gregory

---

BY THEIR SPEECH YE SHALL KNOW THEM

A fellow who acts as chairman of a public meeting sooner or later falls into some very strange assignments. Some few years ago I fell into mine. At that time I was invited to preside over an atheist gathering, although I did not know it was such, as the organization had a high sounding name. I found out later (had I known before I would not have accepted) that this club had a cardinal rule that no minister of the gospel would be permitted at its functions.

It was late in the fall and I had just selected a fine black topcoat and black hat to match. Ordinarily I prefer something a little brighter in the way of headgear, but the black hat seemed to fit into the ensemble, giving me the aspect of a man, should I say, of intelligence.

I was a little late in arriving at the meeting and when I approached the hall, I was surprised to see that the door was closed with a man on guard.

As I reached the door and had placed my hand on the knob, the guard rushed over to me quickly and eyeing me from head to toe, (no doubt taking me to be a gentleman of the cloth) yelled out, "You can't go in there!"

"The hell I can't," I exclaimed.

"My mistake," apologized the guard. "Walk right in."

—Jack Cosgrove

BREAKS UP MEETING

There are times at meetings of this nature when the speaking program runs on and on. Sometimes a few speakers are interjected into the regular schedule thereby lengthening the list. I presided at just such a meeting last summer. The speakers were numerous and each speaker was exceptionally lengthy. The audience was becoming bored, and I myself had just about become exhausted. If it were not physical exhaustion, at least it was mental. I had completely run out of phrases, and when it came time for the last speaker on the agenda, I didn't know what to say about him.

I groped around for something appropriate but I couldn't think of a thing that I hadn't used before. I was absolutely stumped. But I had to say something, so I merely uttered, "Mr. Jones will give his name and address."

Mr. Jones stood up and said, "I live at 555 Park Avenue. I wish you all good night."

—Gus Strauss

WHEN HE TALKS BEST

A tramp once went into the house of a very pious and hospitable old lady, and asked for something to eat. A square meal was kindly set before him, which he proceeded to attack without ceremony. "Don't you say something before you begin to eat?" expostulated the old lady, who believed in saying grace before a meal. "Me and **(Give the name of the speaker),**" replied the tramp, "always talks best after we've et."

—George A. Marden

BAD BLOOD

At a dinner that was held in the southern part of the state last summer I had the privilege to introduce two celebrated speakers. One was a noted humorist and the other a prominent lawyer.

Apparently there was some bad blood between the two speakers, and they knew each other well. I gave the humorist a suitable send-off, after which he amused the crowd for over an hour, laughing at his own jokes. All in all it was a witty and entertaining speech.

Then I introduced the lawyer, who walked to the podium as the humorist returned to his seat which was in earshot from the speaker's main stand.

As the lawyer stood before the microphone with each of his hands encompassed by the pockets of his jacket, he leaned over to the humorist and whispered sarcastically, "Isn't it unusual for a humorist to laugh at his own jokes?"

For a moment there was fire in the humorist's eyes and I detected that each bore some ancient grudge against the other. Then the humorist looked up at the lawyer and whispered back, "Isn't it unusual for a lawyer to have his hands in his own pockets?"   —Earle Hughes

---

MY ENEMY STEPS ASIDE

There is a prominent speaker in this community who at one time was a very good friend of mine. In fact we were the best of friends, until we had a falling out. The breach was so bitter that we remained enemies for several years. When we passed each other on the street, there was no recognition whatsoever on the part of either of us.

Last winter I accepted an assignment as chairman at a certain gathering. Lo and behold, was I embarrassed to learn that my enemy was on the speaking program. Well, there was nothing else to do but keep up my appearances. So when the time came for him to speak, I gave him the best introduction possible. He arose from his chair, bowed graciously to me and delivered what I must admit a very fine talk.

After the meeting had been concluded and the social festivities began, I walked out into the outer hall, and who should I meet face to face coming out of a narrow passageway but my bitter and relentless adversary. There was room for only one person to pass at a time.

I stood my ground, fire leaping from my eyes. With clenched fists and venom in my voice, I said, "I never step aside for scoundrels."

Said my enemy, stepping out of my way, "I always do!"

—Jack Cosgrove

A BAD OMEN

A couple of years ago I was invited to take over the chairmanship of a meeting in a small Illinois town, down in the coal mining region, where audiences are not exactly known for their chivalry. I was to introduce a well-known temperance lecturer who was making a circuit of the country, holding meetings for which he collected a fee.

I arrived in town about noon on the day of the meeting, and having nothing of importance to do, I walked about town, surveying what few interesting sights were on hand. With a view to finding out just what kind of interest there was on the part of the townspeople for the event, I dropped into the general store. There I found a shriveled-up native filling a jug from a molasses barrel.

"Howdy there," I said, walking up to him. "Anything important going on in this town today?"

"Well," answered the fellow, looking up from his task, "I 'spect there's goin' to be a lecture. I've been selling eggs all day."

—Earle Hughes

SILENCE
A story to help silence a heckler

The problem of handling a heckler is somewhat embarrassing, especially if the meeting is of a political or controversial nature, and opposing sides are on hand to upset orderly procedure. Fortunately for a chairman, the heckling generally takes place while the speaker is in action. Most audiences, even unruly ones, will usually permit the chairman to make the introduction without interruption.

There are many ways of subduing a heckler, but the most efficient method that I have seen took place at a political meeting in one of our southern counties last fall. The speaker, a candidate for the senate, was in fine fettle that evening. He soared away on the wings of an eagle to great oratorical heights. Right in the midst of his eloquence, a boisterous and uncouth fellow in the back of the hall yelled out some uncomplimentary remarks. When the fellow persisted, much to the annoyance of both the audience and the speaker, the candidate for the senate took off his glasses, walked up to the front of the stage and looking the heckler straight in the eye, called out: "Sir, we want nothing from you but silence, and very little of that!"
                                                —Earle Hughes

POPCORN AND GRAPES

Of all my engagements in which I acted as chairman, the most humorous incident took place at a meeting held last year in the city of Swanville. The audience consisted for the most part of young people—boys and girls of college age—and the principal speaker was a celebrated senator from the west coast.

Just outside the entrance to the hall was a popcorn vending machine, and apparently most everyone in attendance purchased a bag of the confection before entering the hall.

I noticed that while I was introducing the senator the staccato clicks were quite numerous, and interferred with my train of thought. But I completed my introduction, hoping that by the time the senator took the stand, a little more courtesy would be extended by the audience.

However, it was quite to the contrary. The munching and

crunching droned throughout the auditorium, punctuating, and at times completely blotting out whole phrases of the senator's stirring talk about "The Growth of the Citrus Industry in California." Finally the noise became exasperating. The senator stopped abruptly in the middle of a sentence, took off his glasses, folded up his paper and said to the audience:

"My dear friends, when I first began my oral delivery this evening, I was aware that some noise-making refreshments were in the possession of some members of the audience. I was hoping that the supply would quickly become exhausted. And in this respect I was confident, until I perceived that some sort of relay team was in operation, shuttling fresh bags into the hall from that confounded vending machine outside. Consequently, I have given up hope. Now, I am a sensitive man and the grating of teeth upon an object like a piece of popcorn, especially when the center corn is cracked, is, to say the least, a wear and tear upon my nervous system. It is impossible for me to do justice to "The Growth of the Citrus Industry in California," when my audience is constantly munching on Iowa popcorn. If I should ever have the pleasure of appearing before this audience again, I hope that you will substitute some less noisier means of refreshment, say—a soft, delicious and soundproof California grape."   —Sylvester McGovern

---

WHERE AM I?

The confusion of the past few minutes threw me off the track. I have to retrace my steps and get my bearings before introducing the next speaker. This reminds me of the story about two Irishmen.

Says Pat to Mike, "What would you rather be in, an explosion or a collision?"

"Sure and I'd say a collision," replied Mike.

"And why?" says Pat.

"Because," says Mike, "In a collision there ye are, but in an explosion, where are ye?"

That's my problem right now, where are ye?
                    —Earle Hughes

SHORT REPLY

One time I presided over a political meeting. It was one of those old-fashioned political affairs in which the charges flew thick and fast. Speaker after speaker took the floor, hurling slurs at an opponent.

The principal speaker was the most vituberant of all. For over an hour he stood before the microphone, unmercifully flaying his opponent, who sat at the table awaiting his turn to reply. When the man had completed his tirade, wiped the perspiration from his brow, uncurled his sneering lips and sat down, I introduced his adversary.

This fellow was a mild sort of a man, quite gentlemanly and quite scholarly. He walked slowly up to the microphone, cleared his throat and said in a well modulated voice: "Ladies and gentlemen, I do not feel that it is necessary to reply to my opponent's outlandish charges, as he is inebriated by the exuberance of his own verbosity."   —Baxter Walker

---

POSITIVE PROOF

Many times while I am acting as chairman at gatherings of this sort, the meeting is thrown open to a question and answer session. At such times the nature of the discussion becomes quite divergent and usually gets way off the track of its original purpose.

I recall one meeting up in Pine county, where after the speeches had been completed, the audience was invited to ask questions about the topic of the evening. As usual the topic was soon lost in the melee, and all sorts of queries were tossed at the speaker.

One fellow got up and said, "Mr. Speaker, who has the most power, a bishop or a judge?"

"Well, I don't believe that I know," said the speaker, "other than a bishop can say you be damned and a judge can say you be hanged."

"The judge, by all means," said a second fellow jumping to his feet. "When a judge says you're to be hanged, boy, you hang."   —Arthur Barry

ON TOO LONG
To use to warn a speaker about a time limit

One of the most embarrassing situations that a chairman is forced to undergo is that of controlling the long-winded speaker—the fellow who gets up to the microphone and never seems to want to give it up. When such an occasion arises, somehow or other the audience seems to blame the chairman. However, unless a time limit had been placed beforehand on each speaker, it would be quite discourteous for a chairman to interrupt.

I was presiding at a meeting up in the northern part of the state last fall, where I encountered just such a situation. I introduced a fellow who was some kind of a statistician. I thought that he would never finish his speech. When he finally sat down, I introduced the next speaker, who took care of the obligation for me.

The speaker who followed the long-winded one stood before the microphone and said: "In case you don't know who you were listening to just ahead of me, he is the famous Chinese statesman in disguise—On Too Long!"

—Bill Smaldwin

NO PROOF

A few years back I accepted an assignment to act as chairman for an important political meeting. It was during the height of a very bitter election campaign, and public feeling was running high, with considerable bitterness on both sides.

The principal speaker scheduled at this meeting was a notorious political figure, whose reputation was not of a salutary nature. I had never met the man before, but, of course, I knew of him and the nature of his character. As I walked up to the speaker's table, the politician was already seated on a chair, browsing over some papers that he had in his hand. The president of the club introduced me, at which time I said, meaning no malice, "I've heard a great deal about you."

The political boss looked me over with searching eyes and then suavely remarked, "Most likely, but you can't prove it."

—Earle Hughes

AUDIENCE VANISHES

Last January I was presiding at a meeting up in Stearns county. It was a long drawn-out affair, with a variety of speakers, all long-winded. The seventh and last speaker on the program was the longest winded of all. On and on he rambled, until his audience began to leave the hall, one by one.

Finally, there was only one man besides the speaker and myself left in the room and he was the custodian. But this did not deter the speaker. He continued to soar to the seventh heaven, piling clause upon clause, and phrase upon phrase. After an hour of this procedure, the only remaining man in the room—the custodian—tip-toed up to the rostrum and handed me a note.

I quietly unfolded it and with a chuckle read the following message: "When you are through talking, will you kindly turn off the lights, lock the door and put the key under the mat?"

—Earle Hughes

TOOTH HURTY ME

A few weeks ago I was the chairman at a community meeting on the East side. The audience consisted of local business men. On my right at the speaker's table was Dr. Wright, the dentist, and on my left was Woung Wen, proprietor of a Chinese restaurant. Each man was to make a speech on behalf of a local drive for funds.

As we were completing our dinner, Woung Wen said to me, "Will you ask Doc Wright what time he fixee my tooth tomorrow?"

I turned to the dentist at my left and said, "Doc, Woung Wen wants to know what time you can fix his tooth tomorrow."

"Tell him that two-thirty will be all right," said the dentist.

I passed the information on my right to Woung Wen. After a few seconds of hesitation, the Chinese whispered perplexingly into my ear, "Tella Doctah, tooth hurty me all right, but what time he fixee?"

—Bob Smerale

CANCELS ENGAGEMENT

I looked forward to the honor of introducing to you tonight the famed economist, Dr. Harold S. Doakes. Mr. Doakes, I am certain, would have given a splendid talk had he been able to attend. When the illustrious gentleman did not arrive on the morning train from Chicago, I became alarmed, so I called him long distance for an explanation.

He apologized profusely and said that he was unable to come to Swanville as he met up with a heart-rending situation at the Union Station, just as he was about to board the train. It appears that an elderly woman, in dire distress, was trying to secure sleeping accommodations on the train, for the purpose of going to a son who was dangerously ill. The train was sold out so Dr. Doakes obligingly gave up his ticket. The good doctor concluded his telephone conversation with me by saying, "I sent you a telegram giving the details."

This afternoon I received the wire which reads, "Regret will not be able to keep speaking engagement. Gave berth to an elderly lady last night."   —Bill Powell

---

SPEAKING FOR POSTERITY

During my engagements as a chairman I have met many long-winded speakers. In this connection I remember an incident that took place in the little town of Pumkinville. It was quite a gathering for the size of the community, and up to a point the audience was responsive.

I introduced the speaker who was billed as an authority on monetary systems, and it was quite evident that he was tracing the monetary system back to the days of the Babylonian emperors, and after consuming an hour and a half he had not yet reached the era of the French Republic. By this time there was a lot of twitching of chairs going on in the audience. It was becoming tiresome.

At one point the speaker yelled vibrantly, "I am speaking for posterity!"

Suddenly a voice cried out from the back of the hall, "If you don't hurry, it'll catch you."   —Gus Strauss

ABSTRACT PANTS

A few weeks ago I was the chairman at a Parents and Teachers meeting. The affair was well attended and it was one of those gatherings in which the children performed for the parents, showing not only their adeptness at recitations and dramatic skits but practical demonstrations of classroom activity as well.

It was so arranged that I was to introduce each of the teachers in the school, who in turn would call upon the pupils for a public showing.

Miss Evelyn McCarthy was perhaps the prettiest teacher there and it was with great delight that I introduced her to the audience.

"What do you plan to have your pupils do?" I said to Miss McCarthy pleasantly.

"I will ask one of them to compose a sentence using certain words," she said. Then she turned to her group of pupils and said, "Boys and girls, for this demonstration to your parents, I am going to ask one of you to make up a sentence with the words concrete and abstract. You all know that during the week I have been explaining to you that concrete is something that you can see, while abstract is something that you can't see. Do you all understand that?"

"Yes, teacher," chorused a group of children.

Then turning to a lad who was large for his age and also evidently quite worldly, Miss McCarthy said, "Johnny Moynihan, stand up and recite a sentence with the words concrete and abstract."

Young Moynihan jumped to his feet, while the parents watched eagerly, and then slowly mumbled, looking directly at the lovely Miss McCarthy, "My pants are concrete, yours are abstract."   —Arthur Barry

BRAINS VS. BRAWN

Last summer I was acting as chairman at a meeting of a sportsmen's club. It was a bazaar affair, where gadgets of various kinds, donated by the local merchants, were being auctioned off, the funds from which were to be used for a new clubhouse. Among the equipment on hand to go to the highest bidder were wheelbarrows, golf clubs, garden hose and other kinds of accessories for the home.

As most every member present was some sort of an athlete, I trained my theme of introductions along that line; and from time to time would relate some of my own accomplishments in the field of sports, perhaps forgetting myself and running to the bragging point.

When the speakers had concluded, the audience arose from the chairs and wandered about the hall, offering bids on the various items on display. As I was walking about, chatting with this group and that group, a young fellow came up to me and said: "Mr. Chairman, I paid particular attention to some of those athletic records that you smashed from the speaker's platform. How about a practical demonstration?"

"What kind of a practical demonstration?" I asked perplexingly.

"Well," said the fellow, who was a half-pint and evidently a wag, "I'll bet you five dollars (the money to go to the benefit fund) that I can wheel something in a wheelbarrow from here to the end of the hall that you can't wheel back."

"Anything that you can wheel up to the end of the hall with those puny arms of yours, I can carry back on the palm of my hand," I said. "The bet's on!"

The half-pint took hold of the wheelbarrow's handles with his little hands, and with a deep belly-laugh victoriously said to me, "Get in!" — Gus Strauss

MISTAKEN IDENTITY

Just before the meeting began this evening, I was sitting over in the corner of the room, looking over my notes and sort of making plans for the speaking agenda. A very attractive young lady walked by me several times, and each time she looked at me with an air of familiarity. This was quite distracting, as I was trying to concentrate on my introductions— on what I was going to say about that speaker and this speaker. Just as I would have formulated what I thought an excellent approach for the introduction of a speaker, I was disturbed by the fleeting odor of a provocative perfume swishing by. My eyes would immediately leave my papers to see a beautiful face and two inviting eyes that glittered with a sign of recognition.

This procedure kept up for several minutes and each time the charming girl passed by I was completely distracted. Finally, she stopped abruptly in front of my chair, leaned over close to me and then she quickly pulled away, exclaiming excitedly: "Oh! I thought you were the father of one of my children!"

That slayed me. I was terribly taken back, and my conscience began to rattle like the shaking of a trolley car. Those little red devils with pitch forks began to prick my brain unmercifully. "Father of my child!" No! It couldn't be!

After the girl had left I rushed over to Jack Brown of the arrangements committee. "Jack," I said, "who is that girl in the red hat sitting over in the corner of the hall?"

"Pretty little thing, isn't she?" Jack replied.

"Very pretty," I said. "She made an attempt to compromise me. She said that for a moment she thought that I was the father of one of her children!"

Jack threw his program schedule into the air and let out a big howl. Then he clapped his hands together, slapped his knees and laughed like I have never seen a man laugh before.

"This is a good one," he screamed. "Ho! Ho! Ho!"

"I see nothing funny about getting a paternity charge from a stranger in a public hall," I said indignantly.

"Paternity charge!" screamed Jack again, rolling with laughter. Then he wiped the laughing tears from his eyes and said: "I'll tell you who that young lady is—she's Miss Amelia Young, the first-grade teacher at the Blake school!"

—Arthur Barry

WHEN A SPEAKER JUMPS THE GUN

Some time ago I acted as chairman at a political meeting. I was introducing a candidate for public office. The hall was packed and the crowd was in a gay mood. As I rambled along with my introduction, dwelling upon the good points of the speaker, a voice from the back of the hall cried out, "I wouldn't vote for that guy if he were the Angel Gabriel."

Before I could say another word, the speaker jumped to his feet and yelled back at the heckler, "And if I were the Angel Gabriel, you wouldn't be in my constituency."

That ended the heckler and it also ended my introduction. The speaker continued on with his speech.   —Earle Burr

HE MIGHT NOT COME BACK

Last summer I was acting as master of ceremonies at the city of Swanville. It was a terribly warm evening and after the dinner had been completed and we had heard from two speakers, I decided that I would hold a short intermission so the audience could stretch their legs and step out into the cooler air before we continued with the speaking agenda.

I stood up and said, "Ladies and gentlemen, before I introduce the next speaker there will be a short recess."

I had no sooner uttered the words than a voice from the end of the room called out, "Who is the next speaker?"

I looked at the fellow who was sticking his head around a vase of roses and said, "My dear sir, I am withholding that information until you get back."   —Sylvester McGovern

METHOD OF MEASUREMENT

In my early days of acting as a chairman at meetings, I made many a blunder, some of which bounced back at me, much to my embarrassment. At one particular gathering I was to introduce a very famous man from the state of Wisconsin. I had never seen this gentleman, and somehow or other I had a feeling that he was a big man, physically. But when I met him for the first time at the speaker's table, I immediately realized that my impression was decidedly erronious. The speaker was a little man, probably not weighing more than one hundred and twenty pounds.

Being a novice in the matter of making introductions, I seized upon this discovery as my theme. "Ladies and gentlemen," I said, "I had heard so much about the next speaker that I felt I knew him personally. But somehow or other I had the wrong impression of him. I thought that I was going to have the opportunity this evening of introducing to you a big man, but now upon meeting him I find that he is very small, indeed."

With that faux pas I announced him.

The gentleman got to his feet, and I could tell by the expression on his face that he was not exactly pleased with the send-off I gave him.

Clearing his throat and with a stern look he said: "I am sorry to learn that your chairman is disappointed in my size. This is no doubt due to the methods you have in this state of measuring a man. In Wisconsin we measure a man from his chin up, but here you evidently measure him from his chin down."   —Dale Irwin

---

SOCK ON THE PEG

Last month when I was acting as chairman at a meeting of this sort, I had the privilege of introducing to my audience a very dear friend of mine who lost a leg in the last war. As a result of that unfortunate occurrence he now wears an artificial limb.

I made sort of a consoling talk in my introduction, referring to his handicap. I said something like this to my audience: "Jack can't play baseball. He can't participate in any kind of a sport that requires leg action. He made a great sacrifice for his country. Uncle Sam certainly owes him a living."

But Jack is a philosophical fellow. He stood up with an air of confidence. First greeting the audience with a big smile, he then turned to me and said, "The chairman is very sympathetic, for which I want to thank him. But there are some things that I can do with my artificial leg that the chairman can't do with his leg of flesh and blood."

There was a short pause, and then I cried out from my chair, "For instance, what?"

Jack let out a devilish laugh and then suddenly said, "Hold up my sock with a thumb tack!"   —Hillery Williams

LOST INTEREST

Before I present our next speaker I'd like to tell a little story about the minister who encountered a young couple wheeling a baby carriage down the street. He looked down at the baby and said: "My, what a healthy-looking baby. Boy or girl?"

"Boy," said the father.

"How old is he?" asked the minister.

"Oh, about six months," said the father.

"Your youngest?" asked the minister.

"Yes, sir," answered the father.

"What is his name?" the minister asked.

"Well, we ain't named him yet," said the father. "We kinda lost interest in him."

And that's why some people bore us. They don't know how to express themselves and we lose interest in them. But I think I can promise you that you won't be bored or lose interest in the gentleman who is now going to address us. He can really hold the attention of an audience. Here he is, ladies and gentlemen, Mr. —————.

—Leo McDonald

WRONG LEG

Last fall I was worried about my health as my blood pressure was running quite high. Like persons with ailments of that nature, I did considerable worrying over the matter. In fact, I developed a phobia on the subject, always fearing the worst.

Just at the time when I was at the height of my fear, I received an invitation to preside at an important dinner. For several days I debated whether or not to accept the assignment. But the dinner was so extremely important and the guests who would attend so renowned, that I decided I would take a chance.

I was seated at the speaker's table on the left side of a charming young lady and I must confess that in my mental state I was unable to appreciate her loveliness. The speaking program proceeded smoothly and I was able to introduce the speakers one by one. The last speaker was a long-winded fellow, who rambled on for an hour, quoting figures and facts, which were of no consequence to me, as my mind was on my own health.

After the speaker had completed his talk and the applause was resounding around the hall, I suddenly lurched back in my chair vivid with apprehension.

Alarmed at this sudden and unusual act, the beautiful girl at my left leaned over and said to me, "What is the matter, Mr. Brown, are you ill?"

"It finally has struck me," I cried out in panic. "My left side is paralyzed."

"Are you certain?" said the pretty girl holding my hand.

"Quite certain," I muttered. "I have been pinching my leg," I added feebly, "there is absolutely no feeling there."

The lovely young girl blushed profusely, firmly squeezed

my hand and then laughingly said, "Mr. Brown, you have nothing to fear. It was my leg you were pinching!"

—Horton Smith

NO LOSS FOR WORDS

My friends, I'd like to relate an incident concerning a well-known speaker who is noted for his ability never to be at a loss for words.

It seems he was practically kidnapped by gangsters one night in a certain mid-western city and driven to a banquet given in honor of a big-shot racketeer. The speaker was told to make a speech eulogizing the guest of honor. He tried to find out something about the big-shot's background and career to fit into his speech, but was told the only things they could tell about him would probably land them all in jail—to just go ahead and talk.

So he got up and said: "Gentlemen, we're here tonight to honor one of the most important men in this community—a man who is noted for many wonderful things. Who discovered the Mississippi River? Who built the first steamship? Who invented electricity? Who laid the Atlantic cable? Now, our guest of honor tonight did not do any of these things—but if he had been around at the time he certainly would have done them, because that's the kind of man he is. So let's give him three rousing cheers!" Needless to say his speech met with tremendous applause—most of which came from the head racketeer himself.

Now, my friends, our speaker did not do any of these things, either. But if he had been around at the time I'm sure he would have tried to do them, anyway. However, he has a long list of other successful accomplishments which most of us are familiar with—not the least of which is his ability to speak convincingly and entertainingly. I take a great deal of pleasure in presenting our distinguished speaker, Mr. —————.

—Leo McDonald

CHANCE TO GET IN A WORD

Our speaker from California (or Florida) reminds me of a story about the man who died out there whom nobody seemed to know. The funeral was held. A minister read a few passages from the Bible, and offered a prayer, and then he asked if there was anyone present who knew the deceased and wanted to make a few remarks. No one arose for a moment, but finally a lank, long-haired fellow stood up in the back part of the audience, and said: "If no one wants to occupy the time in speaking about the deceased, I would like to make a few remarks about our wonderful state of California."   —E. S. Lacey

---

GETTING A LOAN

When introducing a banker

Our speaker today is a banker, but I assure you he's not at all like the obstinate banker who refused to renew a customer's note. Times were bad, and the bank was entitled to its money he was told. The borrower moved wearily to the door. Over his shoulder he said: "Well, I never knew before that you had a glass eye."

"Come back," said the banker. "How did you know I have a glass eye? I had an accident years ago and the glass imitation was so well done that no one has ever detected it before."

"Well," said the borrower, "I thought one of your eyes had a gleam of human kindness and I knew that it couldn't be natural."   —Walter Lichtenstein

---

WHY WOMEN ARE ANGELS

When ladies are special guests

It's a real pleasure to welcome the ladies as our special guests tonight. Of course we men think of our honored guests as little angels. You know, always up in the air, always harping on something, and never having a darn thing to wear.
          —Lawrence M. Brings

PERFECT FIT

In the task of introducing our speaker tonight I am reminded of the politician who went to an important political banquet in a state of complete self-satisfaction over the fact that he had been chosen as chief speaker on such a momentous occasion. You can imagine his feelings when just as his meal was being served, he discovered he had forgotten his upper plate. What a predicament! Without his teeth he knew he could neither eat nor speak.

In complete panic, he turned to the emcee seated next to him and asked: "What'll I do? How soon do I go on? Do I have time to run home for my teeth?"

"Teeth?" asked the emcee. "Why not let me loan you a plate?"

He delved into his pocket and came out with a beautiful set. "Try these on for size."

Well, they didn't fit. But the helpful emcee came up with another pair. And still another. Finally there was a plate which fitted perfectly.

The politician enjoyed his dinner, and then delivered the speech of his career. After receiving the congratulations of his colleagues, he turned to the emcee and gratefully said: "I don't know how I can ever thank you. And what a lucky coincidence that you happen to be a dentist!"

"Dentist?" snorted the emcee. "Why, I'm not a dentist. I'm an undertaker!"   —George A. Posner

---

BRING THE CHECK

"Now I suppose they'll all get up and spout a while," remarked one banquet diner to the man next to him. "Did you ever hear a really good after-dinner speech?"

"Just once. A friend of mine said: 'Waiter, bring me the check.'"   —V. Spencer Goodreds

LET ME INTRODUCE

Ladies and gentlemen: Every once in a while there is born into this world a man marked by his Maker to tread the higher places in this world; one to whom has been given qualities of mind and soul and body which destine him to become a leader of men; to whom they learn to hearken, to learn from; and finally to love and to cherish. But enough about me, let me introduce the speaker . . .   —George A. Posner

---

THE SAGE

Ladies and gentlemen: You've been giving your attention to turkey stuffed with sage. Now do you mind giving your attention to a sage stuffed with turkey?

—George A. Posner

WON'T BE LATE

This situation reminds me of the little boy next door who was playing marbles with some other boys down the street when my wife was passing and saw him. Knowing it was well after the usual dinner hour, she said to him: "You'd better rush home, Jimmy, or you'll be late for dinner."

"Oh, no, I won't be late," he answered. "I've got the meat."

So maybe we can say, our speaker won't be late for the lecture—he has the speech with him!

—George A. Posner

BETTER MOUSETRAP

An introduction of John Mason Brown, Author, Dramatic Critic and the Associate Editor of the Saturday Review of Literature.

Being New Englanders, for the most part, we are all familiar with the traditional "make a better mousetrap" ideal, which we also know is credited to another New Englander, the Concord poet and philosopher, Emerson.

"If a man can write a better book, preach a better sermon, or make a better mousetrap than his neighbor, though he build his house in the woods, the world will make a beaten path to his door."

All of us like the better things of life. One of the better things in our lives the past few years has been the repeated fine talks by John Mason Brown. Because of them we have beaten a figurative path to his door. He undoubtedly preaches the proverbial better sermon, and makes the better mousetrap. Tonight, we are all attention as he engages in these activities. Mr. Brown. —V. Spencer Goodreds

ANTICIPATION

I know you're all waiting more or less patiently to hear our speaker, so I'll make this introduction short. I've heard it said that anticipation, waiting for something to happen, is greater than realization, but I think our speaker will help disprove that theory tonight. He has spent much time and thought and study in his research on his chosen subject. He is thoroughly familiar with it. His reputation and his experience qualify him as one of the foremost experts in his field. I know that no one will disagree with me when I state that we are very fortunate in having this opportunity of hearing the gentleman who is now going to address us. Ladies and gentlemen, may I introduce our guest speaker, Mr. —————?

—Leo McDonald

GOOD ADVICE

One Sunday last summer, I volunteered to give a short talk to a Sunday school class. It was quite a large class of young boys and girls dressed up in their Sunday best.

I stood up before my youthful audience not knowing what I was going to say. After a few seconds of standing there on the platform, which provoked a few giggles and twitters from the youngsters, I said: "What would you do if you were going to talk to such a fine crowd of bright youngsters like yourselves and had nothing to say?"

For a moment all was still. Then a little fellow over on one side of the room piped up: "Just keep quiet."

—Walter Coleman

INCREASE YOUR KNOWLEDGE

It's always a pleasure to find a speaker who not only knows his subject but knows how to talk about it. Some people have knowledge but don't know how to express themselves, which makes me think of a gathering of scientists which was held in a small city recently.

Along about two or three in the morning, several scientists, who had taken rooms in a small, obscure hotel, became involved in a very deep and learned argument, so two of them went down to the desk and asked the night clerk if he had an Encyclopedia Brittanica.

The clerk said: "What?"

"Have you got an encyclopedia?" the scientist repeated.

"No, I ain't," said the night clerk. "What do you guys want to know?"

Now, I don't know what you really want to know, but I can promise you that if you listen attentively to our speaker your knowledge will be greatly increased by the time he is through—and you don't need an encyclopedia to understand him, either. Ladies and gentlemen, our speaker, Mr. —————.

—Leo McDonald

THE ONE STORY

Suggested for informal club luncheons

I've been asked to say a few words about this bird that's going to speak next. We've all known him for a long time but there isn't much to say about him—except that he's got one story he likes to tell. We've all heard it many times—and we'll probably have the treat of hearing it again in the next few minutes, God forbid.

Seriously, I'll admit he tells it well, but why shouldn't he after so many repetitions? However, his real claim to distinction lies in the fact that he possesses an incomplete set of varicose veins—one of several treasured mementos of a mis-spent life.

Well, anyway, it's your turn, Bill Smith. Get up and speak your piece. We hope you stick to the point, but even if you don't, Bill, we love you just the same.   —Leo McDonald

---

WRONG NUMBER

Before I perform the pleasant chore of introducing our next speaker I want to tell you a short story concerning an absent-minded Professor who was awakened at about four one morning by his phone ringing.

He picked up the receiver and said: "Hello" and the voice at the other end said: "Is this three three three three?"

"No," said the Professor, "this is thirty-three thirty-three."

"Wrong number," said the caller. "Sorry to have disturbed you."

"That's quite all right," said the Professor, "I had to get up anyway to answer the phone."

Well, I hate to disturb our speaker, he looks so comfortable, but it begins to look as if he has to get up now and let us have the pleasure of listening to him. So my friends, I'll present our speaker, Mr. ——————.   —Leo McDonald

GREAT PRIVILEGES

Suggested for an introduction to a speaker who is going to talk on some controversial subject

Before proceeding with my introduction I'd like to tell you a story I just heard. It seems an American G. I. met a Russian soldier in Europe. The Russian said: "What is this democracy you Americans are always talking about? Give me an example."

"Well," said the G. I., "I can fly from here to Paris. I can fly from Paris to Washington, and in Washington I can walk down Pennsylvania Avenue to the White House. I can go in and ask to see President Eisenhower. I can say to the President: 'President Eisenhower, you're a louse.' And I won't be shot."

The Russian said: "Why, we've got the same thing. I can fly from here to Moscow. I can go in the Kremlin and see Malenkov. I can say to him, 'Comrade Malenkov, President Eisenhower is a louse,' and I won't be shot either!"

And that little story carries a world of meaning. Of course, we all know that it has nothing to do with our speaker. I'm quite sure he has no such deplorable thoughts about our esteemed President. But the story illustrates one of the many great privileges we enjoy in this blessed country of ours—the right to openly express our opinions and the recognition of others to have the same privilege. And now we're going to have the privilege of hearing an address from our eminent guest. Ladies and gentlemen, Mr. —————. The floor is yours, sir.

—Earl Jay Gilbert

GET OUT THE BEST WAY

I believe it's customary, when making an introduction to a speaker, to relate a humorous story. Having no story of my own I'll borrow one from the late Walter Kelly, the Virginia Judge of vaudeville fame. Impersonating a colored man he said:

I was busy shinin' up the gas station this mornin' 'bout nine o'clock when a little colored boy named Willie Jones come runnin' up and says "Mister Southall," he says, "Mister South-all, a wildcat's just busted in through your kitchen window—and your wife's in the house there, all alone!" "Well, Willie," I says, "Willie, if that wildcat ain't got no more sense than to bust in my house when my wife's there, all alone—**let him git out the best way he kin!**"

Now, my reason for telling that story is that sometimes a speaker's mind will go blank, and he'll forget part of his speech. Please don't misunderstand me, I'm not wishing any bad luck to our speaker. I'm with him, heart and soul, but if it should so happen that he is in a forgetful mood tonight, all I can do for him is to let him **git out of it the best way he kin!**

I'll add that I would be greatly surprised if such a horrible catastrophe should occur to our talented guest, whom you are now going to meet. My friends, our speaker, Mr. —————.

—Earl Jay Gilbert

RISE AND SHINE

Suggested for informal club luncheons

My friends, this is a funny world. Fred Brown is going to give us a talk. This guy is something of a mystery to me. He can't sing, he can't dance, he can't tell stories—but in spite of that he persists in doing all those things!

Personally, I think he's got the gall of a door-to-door book salesman. In years he is supposed to be in his thirties (forties, fifties), but I've been doing a little research work and I've discovered an interesting fact. From what I've learned, this gentleman could have been one of the greatest men in this country today, but unfortunately he got up during a cabinet meeting and insulted Lincoln.

I'm glad to see though, that he has a sense of shame about that fact being made public. If you'll look closely you'll notice he's blushing. However, to give credit where credit is due, it must be stated in all fairness that the guy can really talk. So rise and shine, Fred, while we relax in the reflected glow of your genial personality.   —Earl Jay Gilbert

REGULAR GUY

Folks, have you ever noticed how many toastmasters or chairmen when they introduce a speaker, will start out by saying: "I am going to introduce a man **who** . . ." and then proceed to build up their speaker by using a lot of adjectives like distinguished, great, honored, popular, remarkable, notable, celebrated, renowned, far-famed, foremost, pre-eminent, and so forth—whatever they can dig out of the dictionary.

Well, all I'm going to say about our speaker is that, to use a common expression, he's a regular guy with a host of friends in all walks of life. I'm proud to be known as one of them. He came up through life the hard way. His well-merited success is due to his own efforts. And last, but not least, he's an entertaining speaker whom you're going to enjoy listening to. My friends, our speaker, Mr. ——————.

—Leo McDonald

WRONG WORDS

Once in a while a chairman will make a mistake that gets him in hot water. Sometimes thoughts come to him instantaneously and he will use them without thinking about the consequences. This has happened to me on several occasions.

Last winter I had the privilege of acting in the capacity of chairman at an important civic dinner given in honor of a visiting statesman of celebrated proportions. This man was a public figure whose name was known throughout the world, and the very fact that he was a person of such prominence made me, in a sense, shaky.

Throughout the course of the dinner, he sat at my side, and chatted with me on various topics. I tried to carry on the conversation in the best manner possible, but my nervousness was quite pronounced. As the dinner progressed to the point of completion, I became exceedingly excited and I was anxious to get my short introduction over with. The visiting celebrity seemed to be in no hurry whatsoever. Leisurely he sipped his coffee and puffed on his expensive cigar, while I smoked cigarette after cigarette, trying to attain a state of serenity.

When it looked as if the speaker would continue to drink his coffee until the small hours of the morning, I decided upon a plan of action. And that is where I made my blunder. Not thinking of what I was doing, I turned to him and said, "Should we let the guests enjoy themselves a little while longer, or should we have your speech now?"

—Ken Seaman

DOESN'T LIKE MUSIC

Tonight we're going to have the refreshing treat of hearing an address by a man whose talks are always enlivening and stimulating. He speaks with the certainty and conviction that go with his knowledge and his experience in public speaking.

I am reminded of a story. Toscanini, the famous symphony leader, had engaged a new second violinist. At the first rehearsal the new man glared at the music before him on the rack and savagely attacked his violin with vicious strokes of his bow, glowering and making terrible faces. Toscanini stopped the rehearsal and said: "What's the matter? Don't you like this orchestra?"

"Sure, I like it," said the man.

"Perhaps you don't like me?" asked Toscanini.

"Sure, I like you fine," the violinist answered.

"Then," asked the maestro, "why do you make those horrible contortions—those terrible faces when you play?"

"I don't like **moosic**!" the fellow said.

Now, I don't know whether our speaker likes "moosic" or not, but I do know he enjoys talking to an audience on a subject he's thoroughly acquainted with. Audiences enjoy listening to him. He delivers his addresses clearly, concisely and entertainingly, and my friends, no one can ask for more in a speaker. Ladies and gentlemen, permit me to introduce our speaker, Mr. —————.

—Earl Jay Gilbert

OFF THE BEAM

The chairman differs from the speaker

There are so many ways—far too many ways, alas—for getting yourself misquoted, or misinterpreted. in our amazing English language, especially in these super amazing days of be-bop slang.

There was a certain enterprising coal dealer who adopted for his slogan the following motto which he had printed on all his stationery: "It's a Black business, but we treat you White."

A customer, on getting his bill for a supply of coal, returned the following sarcastic note with his check: "A Black business but you treat us White, eh? You should change that motto to read: 'It's a Dirty business, but we Clean you good'."

There are ways, and ways, and WAYS of getting "off the beam" in the gentle art of transferring thought by means of the spoken word; and of course the absent-minded speaker is the one who has the most to contend with. I'll tell you about one.

No, it isn't the one who lectured on forgetfulness and smoked halfway through his cigar band while doing so. Or the one who shaved the cat and then kicked himself in the face. Or the one who dictated to his dog, and then tried to give his stenographer a bath. Or who kissed a stamp, then licked his wife and put her in a corner.

Although those are all pretty good, though old, I want to tell you about the fellow who had a talk to make on a patriotic subject. He had spent a lot of time and trouble in preparing it. His weakness, however, was in remembering names, and so, as an added precaution against forgetfulness when he came to the club on the evening designated for the address, he carried on a slip in his inside coat pocket the names of the three great presidents he was going to mention.

The address went off very nicely; and in conclusion he shouted:

"And finally, my friends, we must never forget the War of the Revolution; that great crisis, the Civil War; and that stupendous eruption, the World War; and the three great patriots who brought us through it all . . ."

Here he hesitated, stuttered, and glanced covertly toward his inside coat pocket, where the reminder snugly rested, and shouted:

"Those three great patriots—Hart, Shaffner and Marx!"

About the cutest example of the misreading of a prepared manuscript, I think, occurred in the office of a publisher who puts out lurid detective stories.

An author came tearing into the place, in quite a lather, shouting to the editor: "Look here! My story has been completely spoiled by careless proofreading! Here, at the conclusion, where the judge looks down at the detective and asks, 'Are you Pendleton King?' what does the printer make him say? Listen! 'The great detective, snatching off his false beard, replied: '1 A.M.'"

"That certainly leaves the reader in the dark," the waggish editor answered.   —George A. Posner

---

MISINTERPRETATION

The chairman differs from the speaker

It is so easy to misinterpret a spoken remark. Bear with me.

For instance, some of the neighbors overheard a remark made to me by my wife as I opened the door to her this morning.

So this neighbor said to another: "She must have been to the zoo, because I heard her mention 'a trained deer'."

The other neighbor said, "Oh, no. They must be planning a trip because she asked him: 'Did you find out about the train, dear?'"

So they talked it over with another neighbor who it seems had also heard it; and this neighbor said: "Not at all. They were discussing music. She had just come from a concert, because she said, 'A trained ear,' very distinctly."

So when they met at the woman's club, they asked my wife to settle the disagreement.

My wife laughed: "Well, that's certainly funny. You are poor guessers, all of you. The fact is, I had been in the country overnight, and I was asking my husband if it rained here last evening."

A washerwoman applied to a man for work, and he gave her a note to a friend of his who ran a hotel. The note read:

"Dear Mr. Smith: This woman wants washing."

The answer came back: "Dear Mr. Barger: I dare say she does, but I don't fancy the job."

Yes, there are ways, and ways, of interpreting a phrase; and you may get an interpretation far different than what you ever intended.   —George A. Posner

STRANGE REACTION

The chairman differs from the speaker

They say the Good Lord purposely made women beautiful but dumb. Beautiful so that the men would love them; dumb so that they would love us men. In the case of a lot of us **men,** though, it seems he not only left out making us beautiful, but he also gave most of us more than our share of dumbness. Kind of a bum break!

Right now I'll **hasten** to say, I'm speaking just for myself. Because I don't quite get the point our speaker was driving at. I believe that what he said could have more than one interpretation. Perhaps he will do us the courtesy of going into it just a little more so that we don't, by some mischance, get the wrong deduction.

You never know just how people are going to take things. For instance: Some of my relatives read so much about the bad effects of drinking—and it worried them so, reading about all those bad effects coming from drinking—that they decided to give up—READING!

Not to mention the big to-do about the evils of smoking which Readers Digest and other magazines, as well as newspapers, related recently. Lecturers went around the country filling big auditoriums full of people listening to all the evils done by the (quote) filthy weed. (unquote) And a lot of those people seemed so impressed they went right home and set fire to their cigars! And by way of further punishment, CLAMPED THEM IN THEIR TEETH!

And that is why I say again, you can't always tell just how people are going to react to what you tell them.

Now, seriously, what I'd like elucidated further is ————.

—George A. Posner

LITTLE THINGS

The chairman differs from the speaker

Sometimes it is the case of a detail—a quite small detail—left out in the story which makes a whale of a difference in the listeners' interpretation of it.

For instance, there was quite a good deal of excitement on a street car which had stopped at a corner to pick up passengers when the shrill voice of a female was heard shouting: "Just a minute, motorman, I haven't got my clothes on!" The passengers all began stretching their necks! And what they found out eventually was that a Negro woman hadn't got her basket of laundry aboard.

———

Then there is the classic—perhaps you have heard it—of the cute kindergarten teacher who took such a great interest in her little pupils, and often took the trouble to meet the parents of her little charges? She, on entering a street car, saw a gentleman who looked most familiar, and said to him: "Why, how do you **do**, Mr. Brown!" in a very sweet and affable manner. And when this fellow she had addressed didn't even seem to know her, but looked dazed, she realized her mistake, and said: "Oh, I beg your pardon—I thought you were the father of one of my children!"

Well, you can picture the effect of this upon the rest of the passengers; and perhaps understand why the young lady left the car at the next stop.

Yes, as a popular son has it: "Little things mean a lot!" In more ways than one, maybe.

So perhaps our speaker has inadvertently omitted a little detail or two which might have helped us clarify the picture.

—George A. Posner

WRONG INTERPRETATION

The chairman differs from the speaker

It is so easy to misinterpret or misunderstand what a person may say or write. It's truly remarkable how people will blunder into the wrong interpretation, too.

During the late war, a news correspondent was unexpectedly called to the French front and had no time to tell his wife before he left. So he thought it would do just as well to wire her after he had crossed the channel.

He had a dreadful, stormy passage across the channel. He was frightfully seasick, and on top of that he had to give up his berth to an old lady, the mother of a general.

So he finally got across and sent a wire. And this is what his wife read: "Rather upset. Dreadful passage. Gave birth to an old lady on leaving Dover."

Yes, a mistinterpretation can be really serious.

In that same war, we have this story of a recruit sentry, evidently a green one, calling out to an officer: "Halt, who goes there?"

And the officer answered: "Friend."

So the recruit sentry repeats: "Halt, who goes there!"

And the officer answers: "I said, 'Friend' once. I don't believe you know the regulations."

"Yes, I do!" answered the recruit. "I'm supposed to say 'Halt' three times, then fire!"

They haven't told me how that particular story ended, but I expect there must have been some action by that officer immediately.   —George A. Posner

CIRCUMSTANCES ALTER CASES

When the Chairman thinks the Speaker hasn't been explicit
enough, or too hasty in his reasoning

As Sgt. Friday would say: "We want the facts, sir, just the facts." But we do want all the facts if we are to get at the logical conclusion.

A short while after the burst of the hectic Florida boom in the 20's a certain businessman returned to New York, after a year's stay in that southern state.

His friends asked: "Well, how was business down there? How did you make out?"

"Oh, I came back with half a million," he replied.

"Go on, what are you telling us?" they chorused. "Everyone who's returned from there lately tells us how terrible business is, and how much money they lost. And you say you made half a million!"

"I didn't say I made half a million," returned the businessman. "I said I came back with half a million—I left New York with a million."

So you see, knowing all the facts, may put a different complexion on things.

―――――――

Circumstances make a big difference. Time, and places, and different situations make a whale of a difference.

At Christmas, in a certain barracks during the late war, everybody was celebrating, except one certain soldier who sat glumly in a corner.

"What's the matter, Bill? Why all the gloom?" a buddy inquired. "It's Christmas, pal; join in the fun!"

"Bah!" answered the other. "I don't care about Santa Claus is all I say! Twenty years ago I asked him for a soldier suit— and now I get it!"

―――――――

Inadequately stating a truth, or giving out what is a half truth, may be worse than a downright lie.

Aboard a trans-Atlantic liner, a sailor suddenly shouted: "Man overboard!" There was great excitement, and as soon as was possible, with a great grinding of the powerful engines, the ship was finally brought to a stop. And then a sailor came up to the captain, saluted and said: "I'm sorry, sir, I made a mistake when I said: "Man overboard!"

"Full speed ahead!" shouted the captain, and again there was great confusion and clangor, as the ship righted itself onto its course, and finally steamed on ahead.

"Thank God, all's well," said the captain. "And what are you waiting for there?" he asked the sailor. And the sailor said: "It wasn't a man overboard; it was a woman, sir."

Which reminds one, many an after-dinner speaker who rises to the occasion, stands too long.

Set down the facts; and when you've got the facts set down, set down!   —George A. Posner

------

HASTY ACTION

When the Chairman feels the Committee or Members are being too hasty in forming or acting upon a Resolution

Wait a minute! Suppose we take it a little easier. Suppose we consider this matter a little more; not be too hasty in acting upon it. There can be such a thing as working too fast, or without due consideration, you know.

Here's a little illustration I think rather appropos, and which you might mull over. Maybe you'll get a chuckle out of it.

The Chicago gangster, Al Capone, had a **gracious** way of sending a bouquet of fancy and expensive flowers to the home of any hoodlum he had "rubbed out," to grace the funeral.

The mobster had a favorite florist he kept so busy he had him on his regular payroll. Anyway, Capone insisted that these floral tributes must not only be of the most lavish sort, but they must be among the first to arrive at the victim's home.

The fact was that all this was in the form of an alibi for Capone, intended to show that the departed was indeed a very dear friend—to throw the police off the track.

This florist, in his desire to please, at one time slipped up—and the wreath arrived before the police had even identified the body!   —George A. Posner

WRONG CONCLUSION

*When the Chairman thinks that the Members
have been too hasty*

Let's try to consider all the angles in the case carefully and not be carried away by what may prove to be devious or false reasoning.

In court one day a lawyer pleaded a case for a client who had broken a jewelry store window with a brick, thrust an arm inside and taken a valuable watch.

Said this crafty lawyer to the judge: "Your Honor, I'll admit that my client here took a brick in his hand, and smashed the store window. And thrust in that arm and took out the watch. But it was the arm, and the arm only, which was the offender, and it certainly would not be justice to incarcerate in jail the entire person of my client! Would it?"

The surprised judge thought this over for a moment and then decided to fight fire with fire. He said:

"Oh, so it was the arm of the man alone that was the offender? Very well then, we shall incarcerate the arm of the man in jail for five years. He can accompany it or not, as he wishes!"

Then what was the surprise of the entire courtroom when the prisoner calmly unscrewed his artificial arm, and walked out.

One may jump to a hasty and ill-advised conclusion, because he was biased in the first place—looking at the facts through the colored glasses of prejudice.

A mother said to her daughter: "How can you say that that young man doesn't love you? With my own eyes, I saw him cry over your hand when you cut your finger."

"Sure," said the daughter. "That was just to get salt in the wound."

There was a certain cute movie star who wanted a quick divorce from her husband, and her lawyer suggested Mexico.

"But I don't speak Mexican," she protested.

"That's all right," he told her. "It's all mostly a matter of form anyway. They won't ask you much. Whatever they say and whenever there's a pause, just say, 'Si, si,' and you'll get by."

So to Mexico they went; to a small village, and the beautiful movie star created a sensation. The town turned out en masse at the courtroom when the case was tried. True to her instructions, the darling smiled prettily whenever there was a pause or anyone in authority looked at her as if expecting a reply, and answered, "Si, si." And every time she did so there would be a thunderous burst of applause from the delighted people.

And so here, finally, was the judge addressing her, and there were new wild bursts of cheers every time she said, "Si, si." Her lawyer was frantically motioning to her and shaking his head, but she paid no attention, since it seemed the people loved it.

Finally it was all over. The lawyer came over to the star. "You idiot!" he began.

"What's the matter? I'm divorced, am I not?" asked the star.

"Divorced, heck! You just married the mayor!"

—George A. Posner

BALONEY

Gentlemen, I'd like to tell you of a little incident that happened to me in northern Michigan on a trout fishing trip. For several days I'd been trying to land a monster trout—the biggest trout I ever saw. I tried every type of fly and bait I could think of, but he'd just swim over, sniff at the bait disdainfully, sort of shrug his shoulders and swim back to his hangout under a big rock.

Finally in desperation I stuck a little piece of baloney sausage from my lunch on the hook and tossed it in—and boy! Did he go for it! He was so eager to get that baloney that he snapped off every hook I had—five of them. I stood there, wondering what to do, when that trout came swimming up to the bank carrying one of my hooks in his mouth and carefully placed it on the sand.

Gentlemen, I watched while that fish made five trips. He brought back every one of those hooks and laid them out in a neat row on the bank. Then he looked up at me coyly, wagged his tail, and dived back under his rock and peeked out at me pleadingly, actually begging me to put more baloney on the hooks. But I was all out of it.

Now, my friends, I understand our next speaker possesses a sharp, lively wit, and is quite an entertaining talker. He has had some unusual experiences, and if he'll be kind enough to recount some of them to us I know we'll find them of absorbing interest. But I'll really take my hat off to him if he can top the peculiar incident I've just related without once using the word "baloney," so I'm going to give him a chance right now. My friends, allow me to present our speaker, Mr. ——————.

—D. W. Curtis

BE EXPLICIT

The Speaker thinks the Chairman hasn't been very explicit

I believe a public speaker, a lawyer, a doctor, or anyone who has any relations with the public, ought to have these two words tacked up above his desk, and thoroughly memorized: "Be explicit."

Yes, don't beat around the bush. Put it straightforwardly, thoroughly, and succinctly; as the courts put it, in short: "The truth, the whole truth, and nothing but the truth!"

A certain lawyer had as his client a gentleman in his declining years, who got about in a wheel chair. And one day this lawyer learned that his old client had inherited a fortune of two million dollars. He said: "I'd better break the news gently to the old coot, or he's liable to drop dead with heart failure. Watch how diplomatically I'll do it."

So a meeting was arranged; and when old Jones was wheeled into the office, the lawyer, after making him comfortable with a lot of pillows draped strategically about, said softly:

"Mr. Jones, what would you say if I told you you had inherited a couple of million dollars?"

"Say?" cackled Jones. "Why, you danged fool. You know what I think of you!—I'd say 'Half of it goes to you.'"

The lawyer dropped dead. —George A. Posner

NOT SPEAKING

As this is more or less a family night affair, our speakers will no doubt dwell on the domestic problems confronting most families.

Pat O'Leary was opening an envelope when his friend, Dennis, came along. "Letter?" inquired Dennis. "Yep," said Pat. " 'Tis a letter from me wife." He pulled a sheet of paper from the envelope. Dennis gazed at the paper and blinked his eyes. "A letter from your wife, did ye say? They ain't no writin' at all on it." "I know," said Pat. "Me and the missus ain't speakin'." —Arthur L. Kaser

IT'S HOW YOU SAY IT

When the Chairman considers the Speaker
was taking things too literally

There's such a thing as taking things too literally. We aren't arguing the motives, the honesty or conscientiousness involved. But there still are faults in the conclusion you have arrived at. At least, it seems so to me.

The late Al Jolson's favorite story was that of a man named Gereerta Pasgudnick, who lived on Sixth Avenue. He sent his valet to buy a pair of slacks at a store down the street.

"Remember," said he. "That fellow is practically a thief. Whatever he asks, you offer him half."

So the valet went down to the store designated, and asked to see a pair of slacks.

"Now here's one that's very nice," said the clerk, "at a special price of only twelve dollars."

"Twelve dollars? I'll give you six," said the valet.

"I'll ask the boss," responded the clerk, and went to the back of the store. After a discussion there, he returned.

"The boss said you could have them for eight dollars."

"I'll give you four," said the valet.

"Let me go back and see the boss again," said the clerk.

Again he went to the back of the store, and said to the boss: "When I asked for twelve dollars, he offered me six; and now when I told him he could have them for eight dollars, he wants them for four."

Choking sounds came out of the boss's throat, and finally he calms down a little and says: "The cheapskate! . . . Well, O.K. Go back and tell him he can have them for six."

So the clerk came back and said: "The boss will let you have them for six dollars, mister."

"I'll give you three," said the valet.

Now when the clerk returned to the boss with this latest offer, that worthy gentleman lost all control of his feelings. He fumed. He tore his hair. He jumped up and down. It seemed he was going to have an apoplectic stroke.

"Take those pants," he said, when he had calmed down enough so that he could speak. "Take those pants back to that cheapskate and tell him he can have them for NOTHING! Only," said he, "tell him to take them, and get the heck out of my store!"

The clerk returned and said: "The boss says you can have these pants for nothing . . ."

"I must have two pair," said the valet.

Yes, the way you phrase a thing can make all the difference in the world. So, gentlemen, we must be careful and circumspect.

For instance, if you tell a woman: "When I look at your face, darling, time stands still!" that means one thing. But put it, "Your face is enough to stop a clock," and you have something else again!

When you tell a woman she is a vision, it's one thing; but telling her she is a sight, is something else again, too!

And on the other hand, ladies, when you tell a man he looks like one of the gods of ancient time, it's one thing; but if you say to him: "God, you look ancient," it's quite another!

—George A. Posner

UP TO HIS NECK

The chairman may use the following to advantage if he has pulled a "boner"

I feel like the little boy Junior was so excited about. Junior came racing into the yard yelling to Mommy.

"Mommy, you know Alan Lander's neck?"

"Do I know what?"

"Do you know Alan Lander's neck?"

"I know Alan Landers," said mother, "so I suppose I know his neck. Why?"

" 'Cause," said Junior, "he just fell in the creek up to it!"

—Arthur L. Kaser

BEST OF INTENTIONS

*When the Chairman thinks the Members have been
too hasty in acting*

Yes, one can make a blunder, even with the best of intentions, because there may be an angle he has overlooked, or been unaware of, which may make a lot of difference.

There was a young man who went into a florist shop, bought two dozen beautiful red roses, told the man to wrap them up, and wrote a card to go with it, sealed in an envelope. The card read: "Darling, on your birthday, I am sending you 24 roses, one for each year of your lovely life. Love, George."

The florist, in sending off this gift to the young lady, thought to himself: "This young fellow has been quite a good customer of mine. I'll throw in an extra dozen!"

The florist acted before studying all the angles.

Oh, of course there is such a thing as self-assurance, optimism—I won't say conceit—but one can go overboard in the spirit of carefree nonchalance.

A young soldier who was stationed in Korea, came to his commanding officer and said: "I'd like a furlough so I can go and see my wife in the States. She is going to have a baby."

"Oh, is that so?" inquired the officer. "And when do you expect this happy event to occur?"

Said the soldier: "Nine months after I arrive there."

The classic example of nonchalance which comes to mind at present was a flat broke gent who walked into a swank restaurant and ordered oysters, with the assurance he would find a pearl inside one of them, to pay for the meal.

—George A. Posner

ROAR LIKE A LION

Before our speaker appears on the scene, I'd like to relate a little incident about a white man who lived near the Mississippi River. It seems that one blisteringly hot day he had to go about three miles up the river on business. On the river bank near the spot where his rowboat was tied, he saw a colored man named Sam lying in the shade of a bush.

He said to the Negro: "Boy, can you row?"

Sam languidly replied: "Naw, suh."

The white man said: "Well, I need some ballast anyway—jump in the back of the boat."

Sam crawled in and promptly fell asleep. The white man rowed the three miles up the river in the blazing sun, transacted his business and started home. About half way back he stopped to rest. He was soaking wet and he ached all over. He looked at his blistered hands, sighed deeply, and reached for the oars.

Sam raised up in the back of the boat and drawled: "Boss, don't you want me to get up there and paddle for awhile?"

"I thought you said you couldn't row!" exclaimed the white man.

"Oh," said Sam, "You meant row a **boat**! I thought you meant ro' like a **lion**!"

Now, I don't know whether our speaker tonight is going to "ro' like a lion," or coo like a dove. But, judging from his excellent reputation as a speaker, whatever he does or however he does it, I think we'll all be glad we had the privilege of listening to him. May I present our speaker, Mr. ——————.

—Earl Jay Gilbert

GREEN CHAIRMAN

The first time I held the position of chairman I was certainly green about it. I hardly knew which end of the gavel to hold in my hand. I said to a friend of mine, "Confidentially, Rod, just what are the duties of a chairman?" Just as confidentially he told me, "A chairman is approximately the equivalent of parsley on a platter of fish."   —Arthur L. Kaser

SLING SHOTS

Before I present our speaker, I want to tell you a tale concerning a small-town selectman who liked to make long, rambling speeches which never seemed to end—with the result most of his hearers usually fell asleep while he was talking.

He mentioned this fact to his family at dinner one night before he was to give a talk at the town hall and said he hoped his audience would stay awake at least until he was through talking.

That night as he started his discourse he was suddenly interrupted by several sharp yelps of pain coming from the gathering before him. He looked out and saw his eight-year-old son in the back of the auditorium with a sling shot and a handful of small pebbles.

"Keep right on talkin', Paw," shouted the youngster, "I'll keep 'em awake!"

Well, if our speaker's past record means anything I hardly think we'll need to use slingshots or any other artificial means of keeping awake while he's talking to us. The gentleman comes to us with the reputation of being an eloquent speaker, who knows the value of words and doesn't waste them, and I think we're all anxious to hear him. Ladies and gentlemen, our speaker, Mr. ——————.   —Leo McDonald

HE KNOWS WHEN TO STOP

It may seem to some of you that this is a simple and agreeable job—to introduce a prominent and well-liked person like our speaker. I admit that it's agreeable, but sometimes it's rather difficult to know just what to say without going overboard.

We know that the gentleman is unquestionably entitled to considerable praise for his achievements. But if his accomplishments are dwelt on a little too long or too much, you destroy the effect you want to convey. And if you don't dwell on them long enough, you feel that you're not doing justice to the speaker.

So I'm just going to say that we know him as a man whose opinions are worth hearing and knowing. He is able to express himself clearly and intelligently—and he possesses an exceptional gift—a gift that everyone who desires to become a public speaker should have—he knows when to stop talking. Ladies and gentlemen, I take great pleasure in introducing our speaker, Mr. —————.   —D. W. Curtis

DEAD FOR FOUR DAYS

Where the speaker is to dwell on things military

The Army was holding maneuvers in a southern state. A lady drove her car to a bridge that spanned the river at this point and was halted by a sentry. He spoke pleasantly but firmly. "You can't cross the bridge, lady. It has just been blown up." The lady surveyed the untouched bridge, and then looked at the sentry, puzzled. She got out of her car to get a closer look. She saw another soldier approaching. "Officer," she inquired, "can you give me a logical reason why I cannot cross this bridge?" "Lady," said the soldier, "I can't give you a logical reason for anything. I've been dead for four days."

—Arthur L. Kaser

BEAUTIFUL TURNOUT

Just before introducing the speaker at an Optimist Club

We will never be able to get rid of all the pessimists. They will be popping up for evermore.

McDoogle was unable to attend the funeral of the ward boss Dugan. The following day Casey was telling McDoogle about the affair. "I'm tellin' you, McDoogle, there never was a funeral like it. 'Twas even better than that Mardi Growl thing they have in New Orleans. There be mountains of flowers. Just about everybody in the ward was there. Such a beautiful turnout you never did see. Then when everything was a-goin' at the highest Tim Finnegan got run over by a truck and cast a gloom over the whole proceedin's."

—Arthur L. Kaser

HEARD THE FIRST TIME

Those who are hard of hearing or who have a friend or relative with the affliction should be very much interested in what Dr. (name) has to say to you this evening on the modern methods of combating this problem. Deafness is nothing to take lightly. Any affliction of the senses can be serious. However, there are times when some humor creeps in.

Two civil engineers were invited to attend a council meeting in Wellington where a new water project would be under discussion. The engineers had forgotten to take along their road map, consequently they were unable to pin point their destination. They saw an old fellow sitting beneath an apple tree, and the driver hailed him. "Which way to Wellington?" The old fellow cupped his ear. "Heh?" The questioner spoke much louder. "Which way to Wellington?" The elderly man shook his head. "Can't ye talk a mite louder?" The driver yelled at the top of his voice, "Which way to Wellington?" The old man shook his head again. "Don't want one. Ain't got no place to keep it."

The engineers gave up in despair and drove on. After driving for about four miles they saw a sun-bonneted lady weeding her flowers by the front fence. The driver of the car stepped out and approached the gate, but before he could say a word the old lady pointed down the road, and said, "Turn left at the next crossroads and go six miles. That's Wellington. I heard you the first time."   —Arthur L. Kaser

---

COMMERCIAL FROM HEAVEN

Our speaker for this evening, as you are aware, is the much-beloved Reverend (name) who has a wonderful message for you.

One Sunday morning a little girl came home from Sunday School clutching a small pamphlet. Her daddy asked her what she had in her hand. "Oh," said the little girl, "it's a commercial from Heaven."   —Arthur L. Kaser

LIVE BUTTERFLY

Before I introduce our renowned artist I would like to tell you of an amusing experience he had a number of years ago. He had some of his early paintings on display in an exhibit. Two learned-looking men were critically surveying one of his paintings. One said to the other, "This painting should never have been hung here. One can readily see that it has been done by an amateur, and not a good one, at that. It lacks technique and understanding. For instance, he has attempted to paint a butterfly on that flower. What a daub it is. It is really disgusting. Butterfly! Piffle! It looks more like he had accidentally dropped his brush on the canvas."

At this point the butterfly flew away.

—Arthur L. Kaser

DEAD SILENCE

I've been carrying a certain story around for a long time awaiting an appropriate time to tell it. The time has come, for in a minute I am going to introduce a well-known man of the clergy.

A famous bishop, who was very fond of children, set out one evening to attend a party given "by children for children."

"Don't announce me," he said to the servant at the door.

Leaving his coat and hat downstairs, he quietly opened the drawing room door, having been assured of the presence of company by the buzzing of voices inside. Dropping on his hands and knees, he entered, trying to neigh like a horse and bleat like a goat. His performance was received in dead silence, and, looking up, he found himself in the company of people in formal dress, awaiting the summons to an eight o'clock dinner. The children's party was next door.

—Arthur L. Kaser

TIME LIMIT

An introduction to use when it is imperative that a time limit be placed on the speakers.

Gentlemen, before we start here's a short story to illustrate a point. A man whose watch had stopped was trying to find out the time. He said: "There isn't a man in this town who knows the right time. I've stopped six different men in the last fifteen minutes and asked each of them for the correct time—and every one of them gave me a different answer!"

He'd overlooked an obvious fact—time flies on. Now we all know about our important ruling that each speaker has been allotted a time limit of —— minutes for his talk. It would be decidedly unfair to our other speakers to allow anybody to exceed that limit, and I can assure you that your chairman does not want the unpleasant duty of having to stop anyone because he is running over that limit. So please remember, gentlemen, minutes—and tempus fugit! I now call upon our first speaker, Mr. ——————.

—D. W. Curtis

TEETH WILL BE PROVIDED

I am happy to present to you this evening a well-known local minister. But first a little story told to me by an evangelist. It was the night of the revival meeting. The evangelist was going strong. His subject was eternal damnation. With all the eloquence at his command he urged the congregation to flee from the wrath to come.

"Oh, my friends," he exclaimed, "on that last day, that last dread day, there will be weeping, and wailing, and gnashing of teeth!"

An elderly lady stood up and said tremulously, "I ain't got any teeth."

"Sister," shouted the evangelist, "teeth will be provided."

—Arthur L. Kaser

HOLLERS GOOD

A friend told me that recently he and his wife went to hear a public address by a well-known man. After it was over my friend asked his wife what she thought of the lecturer. She said: "At first I thought he was simply **marvelous**—but he talked me out of it."

Now we've all had that same boring experience. But I believe I can promise you that you won't be bored tonight when you hear our speaker. In introducing him I naturally hesitate to use the words "simply marvelous," but I will say that I think you'll find him an excellent speaker.

I'll digress for a moment and mention a certain highly publicized motion picture knock-about comedian who saw the late John Barrymore in Hamlet. When he was asked how he liked Barrymore, he said: "The guy hollers out good!" So, ladies and gentlemen, I take pleasure in introducing our speaker—a man who hollers out good! Mr. —————.

—Leo McDonald

TERRIFIC IDEA

My friends, I know you're waiting, more or less patiently, for our speaker, and I want to make my introduction as short as possible and still do justice to the gentleman. But there's so much to tell you about him that if I should give him the introduction he really should have, I wouldn't be able to confine myself to a few short phrases.

I find myself in the position of the Hollywood producer who said to his associates: "I woke up last night with a marvelous, terrific idea—but it was lousy."

Well, my ideas about introducing the gentleman have not been exactly marvelous—or even terrific. So I'll content myself by saying that I think you'll find him unusually interesting and an exceptionally good speaker. I'll now give him the opportunity of proving to you that sometimes I can be right. My friends, Mr. —————.

—Earl Jay Gilbert

STICKS TO WATER

The following could be used at a WCTU, or other temperance meeting:

A high-ranking military officer was recently approached by a group of well-meaning ladies who protested the use of champagne to christen ships. The officer said, "Ladies, you have the wrong idea about champagne for the christening of a ship. Instead of opposing it, you should encourage its use." The ladies gasped. The man continued, "Just remember that after the first taste of wine, a ship takes to water and sticks to it ever after."   —Arthur L. Kaser

HIT ME AGAIN

A few years ago I was selected to introduce the speakers. As one speaker was going strong, waving his arms and shouting, I noticed the man next to me had fallen asleep. The speaker waxed louder and louder. Then the sleeping man began to snore, and he snored louder and louder. It was causing quite some commotion. I picked up my gavel to rap for order. Somehow I accidentally hit the sleeping man on the head. Looking up sleepily, he said, "Hit me again. I can still hear him."

—Arthur L. Kaser

MIXTURE

I understand the man you are about to hear is very much against the mixing of church and state. I think the same as he. which brings to mind this riddle: What is the difference between a preacher and a politician?

A preacher makes up his bed and lies in it. A politician makes up his bunk and lies out of it.   —Arthur L. Kaser

SOME THINGS ARE IMPOSSIBLE

Gentlemen, I consider myself highly flattered in being chosen to introduce our guest speaker—a man whose indomitable will has made him overpower and conquer many obstacles that have whipped other men of less courage.

His entire career makes me think of the sign in the Sykorsky Airplane plant which reads: "According to recognized aero-technical tests, the bumblebee cannot fly because of the shape and weight of his body in relation to the total wing area. The bumblebee doesn't know this—so he goes ahead and flies anyway."

Our speaker has never fully realized that some things are impossible to do. So he, too, has gone right ahead and done them anyway. His achievements are too well-known for me to dilate on them, so I'll just say that I'm proud of the privilege I have in presenting to you, Mr. —————.

—D. W. Curtis

LOOK INTO YOUR FACES

This evening I want to introduce our speaker who is a dentist. Once before I introduced a speaker who was a dentist. He began his speech with, "I am glad to look into your faces again."

—Arthur L. Kaser

REQUEST FOR CONTRIBUTIONS

The publishers of this volume contemplate that "Clever Introductions for Chairmen" will be so well accepted that there will soon be a demand for a companion volume.

In anticipation of the publication of a second volume, the publishers invite the readers and users of this book to submit original introductions for possible inclusion. Payment will be made for accepted introductions and appropriate stories for chairmen with the understanding that such material becomes the exclusive property of the publishers. Rejected material will be returned promptly.

LAWRENCE M. BRINGS
T. S. DENISON & COMPANY
315 Fifth Ave. South
Minneapolis 15, Minnesota